SOURCES FOR FRAMEWORKS OF WORLD HISTORY

SOURCES FOR FRAMEWORKS OF WORLD HISTORY

VOLUME TWO: SINCE 1350

Lynne Miles-Morillo

WABASH COLLEGE

Stephen Morillo

WABASH COLLEGE

NEW YORK   OXFORD
OXFORD UNIVERSITY PRESS

Oxford University Press is a department of the University of Oxford.
It furthers the University's objective of excellence in research,
scholarship, and education by publishing worldwide.

Oxford   New York
Auckland   Cape Town   Dar es Salaam   Hong Kong   Karachi
Kuala Lumpur   Madrid   Melbourne   Mexico City   Nairobi
New Delhi   Shanghai   Taipei   Toronto

With offices in
Argentina   Austria   Brazil   Chile   Czech Republic   France   Greece
Guatemala   Hungary   Italy   Japan Poland   Portugal   Singapore
South Korea   Switzerland   Thailand   Turkey   Ukraine   Vietnam

Copyright © 2014 by Oxford University Press

Published by Oxford University Press
198 Madison Avenue, New York, New York 10016
http://www.oup.com

Oxford is a registered trademark of Oxford University Press

CIP data is on file at the Library of Congress
ISBN: 978-0-19-933228-1

Printing number: 9 8 7 6 5 4 3 2 1

To students everywhere who are *doing* history.
(And a debt of gratitude to our patient progeny, who lived
with this project for many moons indeed.)

CONTENTS

INTRODUCTION

This is a book of primary sources designed to accompany *Frameworks of World History*. Primary sources are the basic working material for working historians, including student historians. Historical sources are pieces of the past that have come down to us today and that allow us to reconstruct, at least partially, a model of the time and place of their origin. They are the evidence that historians use to construct hypotheses of the past. But sources do not really speak for themselves: historians must interpret them, and historical interpretation involves many possible steps. Two sources can corroborate each other, if they agree, assuming that they are truly independent sources (i.e., that one is not a copy of the other or that both are copies of a lost original). Interpreting any source requires an explanatory model of the world to guide that interpretation. The *Frameworks* model of networks, hierarchies, and cultural frames and screens is one such model, and the text makes the model explicit so that you can examine it, determine whether you agree with it, and use it to interpret the evidence in this book. You can also invert the use of the evidence and the model by using the evidence to test and refine the *Frameworks* model. That's how science works—including historical interpretation.

Let's help you get into this process by exploring two questions. First, what is a *primary* source? Second, how do you go about interpreting a primary source?

WHAT IS A PRIMARY SOURCE?

Historians generally talk about two kinds of sources, *primary* sources and *secondary* sources. "Primary" and "secondary" do *not* refer to the importance of a given source, either in general or for the purposes of a particular historical investigation. **In the most basic terms, *primary sources* are sources *from the time, place, and people under investigation.*** Thus, Abbot Guibert of Nogent's autobiography, which he wrote himself during his life in the early 1100s (to be utterly clear to the point of silliness), is a fine primary source for Guibert's life and even for the events he reports on and the people he tells us about. We can even consider him a primary source for aspects of the First Crusade, even though he did not witness it personally, because the information he gives us come from the time of the First Crusade. When his reports are secondhand, however, we must be skeptical of the reliability of his information more than we are of his personal narrative, and other sources, ideally eyewitnesses, should corroborate any such information in his story. (We are skeptical of the reliability of his personal narrative as well, but one person's own biases about his or her own life are easier to assess than the biases of any secondhand information.)

This definition of a *primary source* is idealized, of course. Things are not always simple or straightforward. Sometimes we accept certain accounts as primary sources because they are as close to the time period as we can get. Our sources for the life of Alexander the Great include only a handful of truly primary sources: a brief inscription that mentions him in passing, a handful of coins he issued, and the archaeological remains of his activities, including cities and, in one spectacular case, a coastline that he altered. (He built a causeway out into the Mediterranean during his siege of the island city of Tyre in 332 BCE. It remained after the siege, silted up, and the island is now a peninsula.) But the major narratives we have of his life and campaigns are Roman, they date from several hundred years after Alexander's time, and they do not show a particularly good understanding of his time. They refer to and sometimes even incorporate bits and summaries of narratives written during Alexander's time. We still accept these Roman sources as "primary sources" for Alexander's life because they are the closest we can get.

What we've just said about sources for Alexander also demonstrates that primary sources need not be written sources. *Anything* from the time and place we are studying can be a primary source: works of art, archaeological finds, scientific data about the natural world (the natural world being, after all, an aspect of a time and place), and so forth. Even written evidence comes in many forms beyond self-conscious narratives. Government documents, fictional writing, daily newspapers, and mundane bits of writing such as grocery lists or restaurant menus—all of these can be primary sources.

Primary can of course still have its ordinary, non-history–specific meaning of "chief" or "main": "The primary source for my paper on Abraham Lincoln is the movie *Abraham Lincoln: Vampire Hunter.*" *Primary* here indicates that the film was the main source of information you consulted. However, this would not a *primary* source in terms of types of historical sources (nor would using primarily that source be a very good idea).

What then is a *secondary source,* if so many things can count as primary sources? *Secondary sources* are sources that discuss the topic, the time, place, and people under study, but on the basis of primary sources or of other second-hand accounts. Thus, if you were writing a paper about Alexander the Great, any biography of him written by a current day historian (indeed, any biography written after the Roman accounts that we characterized above as "just about almost primary") would be a secondary source, no matter how useful, informative, or well-written a secondary source. And of course, like primary sources, not all secondary sources are created equal. A scholarly biography of Alexander might be a *good* secondary source; a medieval epic poem about Alexander consisting mostly of legends or a movie such as Oliver Stone's 2004 *Alexander*? Not so much. To introduce a further complication, however: what if your research topic were on "the historical reception of Alexander the Great from medieval times to the present", in which you examine what people at different times and places thought of Alexander, whether what they thought were true or not? In that case, both that legend-encrusted medieval epic and today's Hollywood dreck would be excellent primary sources. And what if your research topic is something going on today (or close enough to be called "contemporary history"—topics involving people who are still alive)? In that case you gain the possibility of oral interviews, news footage, and so forth, as primary sources. But another historian's synthesis of such information, even though it is from the time of the topic, has already become a secondary source. Journalism, sometimes called "the first draft of history," lies in an interesting gray zone here.

Confused? Let's sum up. *Primary sources* are sources whose information about a topic comes, as closely as possible, from the time, place, and participants in the topic. For most purposes, that will work for you. But this definition says nothing about the *quality* of the information a source offers. To evaluate that, we need to say a few things about how to read and evaluate a primary source.

HOW TO READ A PRIMARY SOURCE

There are, as we have noted, many different kinds of primary sources. The interpretation of some primary sources, such as the archaeological remnants of buildings and, even more, ancient bones and other natural substances, requires at least some specialized knowledge. We will focus here on the most common kinds of sources selected for inclusion in this book, written documents. The principles for reading these works for many visual sources as well, especially ones such as paintings or drawings that tell a story.

Reading a source is like interrogating a witness in a trial. Reading a source productively—so that its story gets you closer to understanding "what happened"—requires answering two fundamental questions. First, how reliable is the source, that is, does its story give us a reasonably accurate representation of the reality it describes? Second, what information can we derive from the source? These questions of assessment and interpretation are tied together.

Assessing the reliability of a source that purports to tell a factual story involves answering the same questions you would ask of a living witness. Who is the witness? In other words, who wrote or compiled the source? Sometimes we can't answer this question precisely, as with a routine government document (author: nameless bureaucrat) or an oral epic poem (author: many people in a culture). But we can get a sense of what kind of person or persons created the source.

When and where did the author create the source? Were they close, temporally and chronologically, to the events the source describes? Generally, the closer the better.

Finally, what can we know about why the author wrote the document? What audience did the author intend to address and for what reason? How do these factors shape the story the author tells? What you are trying to figure out with such questions is what the author's *perspective* is and whether the author has a *bias*. As the "Issues in Doing World History" box in Chapter 27 of *Frameworks* says about historians, everyone has a *perspective* that comes from where that person exists in time, place, social position, and so forth. The world will look different to an elite male author than to even a privileged woman, to any peasant, to a slave, or to a member of an ethnic or religious minority. That an author has a perspective does not mean the source is unreliable. Perspective is inevitable: a historian has to account for what a source author's perspective allows him or her to see well, and what conversely that perspective might obscure. An author with a *bias*, on the other hand, is intentionally telling a distorted story, such as an author writing a very partisan account from within a heated political battle.

Once you have done a rough assessment of the reliability of the source, you can begin to extract information from your witness. (These two steps often occur at the same time, of course, because evidence from within the source can tell you about the source's reliability.) What can the source tell us?

One basic division among sources is between those that purport to tell a factual story and those that are overtly fictional. In some ways, fictional sources are easier to deal with (including sources that purport to tell a true story but obviously do not), because you can stop worrying about the "truth" of the story. Instead, if the story comes from the time and place you are studying and is reasonably representative of its time (and yes, that's another hard question), you can generally get two sorts of information fairly easily. First, what was "normal" at the time in terms of everyday life? This is the social history question. You see this by ignoring the main story and looking at the background details, the ones that are there because that's what the author assumed was normal about the world without thinking much about it. Suppose, for example, you read the following passage in a murder mystery.

Investigator: Where were you on Thursday evening last week between 7 and 10?

Suspect: I was home watching *The Simpsons* on TV.

What do we know? We know nothing about what the suspect might actually have been doing. Maybe he was at home, maybe he was out committing the heinous murder at the heart of the plot. He's an unreliable witness. But his very unreliability means that he will want his story about what he was doing to sound plausible. Thus, we know about the people in this society at this time that they had an easily observed system of timekeeping, that they had TVs, that watching TV was a normal activity, that *The Simpsons* was probably a well-known show, and that living in a private home was probably normal. So we know quite a bit.

The other thing we can learn from fictional sources is even more obvious. What did the society believe? This is the cultural history question. From our brief passage above we can infer something about beliefs regarding privacy, for example. But even more, if we step back and observe that the passage came from a best-selling mystery novel, we can infer that mysteries were a form of popular entertainment. You can then interpret the whole story for at least some of the beliefs, concerns, and outlooks of the culture from which the story came.

You can ask these same questions about nonfiction sources. But you can also ask further questions about the particular events the source narrates. What happened? Who wanted what to happen to whom? Why? When it comes to such factual questions, there are ways to assess how reliable this particular information is. The two main ways are to test the source against physical reality and against what other sources say. The physical reality test is especially good at evaluating the often unreliable numbers in older sources: Herodotus claims that the Persian king Xerxes marched a million men across a pontoon bridge on his way to invading Greece. Not possible. Testing against other sources can mean using not just individual sources, but what other similar sources say in general. This is what the *Frameworks* model is: a generalization based on many primary sources. So test a source against the model. Does what it describes fit the model? If so, that suggests a reliable source. If it doesn't, perhaps the source is unreliable, or perhaps the model needs some modification. Your call.

Let's finish this with a brief example of extracting information from a source. These are a well known pair of judgments from *The Code of Hammurabi*:

> 196. If a man put out the eye of another man, his eye shall be put out.
> 199. If he put out the eye of a man's slave, or break the bone of a man's slave, he shall pay one-half of its value.

This is the famous "eye for an eye" judgment and a less well-known but similar clause. What do they tell us? The easy answers are that the Babylonians dealt with crime by means of physical punishment, and that their society had slaves, and that the punishment for a crime varied with the status of the victim. In other words, this was a society with class divisions. Other pieces of the Code confirm and extend those conclusions, which fit the general patterns of early state-level complex societies.

What else can we learn? Well, we know that the "code" looks on close reading more like a set of judgments or precedents than a set of laws, so we can safely assume that the crimes mentioned not only happened, but probably happened frequently enough that is was worth the king's while to advertise the punishment. They were carved into a massive pillar set in the middle of Hammurabi's city. We can therefore infer that at least some people in the society could read. Those who couldn't, we can guess, might have been impressed by the size and complexity of the pillar. The Code therefore served to display royal power—again, a common theme for early states (and later ones, too).

There is even more to learn from these passages (see Chapter 3 of *Frameworks* for what this passage says about limiting vengeance, for example). The sources collected here, in other words, are rich in information about many of the people and places of the past. Dig in and enjoy doing history.

SOURCES FOR FRAMEWORKS OF WORLD HISTORY

CHAPTER 14

Innovation and Tradition: 1350 to 1550

INTRODUCTION

In this chapter we continue to look at reactions to the fourteenth century crises brought about by the Mongols and the bubonic plague pandemic, examining the crisis in western Europe. Two sources show two of this period of crisis that reveal important developments in European societies. The period of crisis was followed by reconstruction of the Eurasian trade network and its expansion to encompass the Americas. We see these developments through two Chinese accounts and two European accounts of oceanic voyages. Finally, the combination of crisis and expanded network flows produced a culture of innovation in western Europe that is represented in our final source.

14.1:   Western Europe in Crisis

14.1a: *Statute of Laborers* (1351)

Parliament, representing the interests of elite landowners, passed the Statute of Laborers in 1351 to reinforce the Ordinance of Laborers of 1349, which had been issued by King Edward III. Both responded to concerns about labor shortages caused by the plague, which hit in late 1348. Commoners (working folk, including peasant serfs) were demanding (and receiving) much higher wages than they had been accustomed to receive before the plague. This law specified acceptable wages. The repetition of the wage restriction in 1349 and 1351 indicates the failure of the measures, ignored by workers and employers alike. Wages, in both real and nominal terms, shot up in the decades after the plague. This result—that labor shortage should lead to higher wages—seems natural to us: supply and demand rule. But it is the exact opposite of the result we should expect from Agrarian hierarchies, in which labor shortages led to lower labor freedom, which is in fact what the Statute aimed to achieve. Its failure is therefore deeply significant.

Whereas lately it was ordained by our lord king and by the assent of the prelates, earls, barons and others of his council, against the malice of servants who were idle and not willing to serve after the pestilence without excessive wages, that such manner of servants, men as well as women, should be bound to serve, receiving the customary salary and wages in the places where they are bound to serve in the twentieth year of the reign of the king that now is [that is, in 1347 before the plague], or five or six years before, and that the same servants refusing to serve in such a manner should be punished by

1

imprisonment of their bodies, as is more plainly contained in the said statute. Whereupon commissions were made to diverse people in every county to enquire and punish all those who offend against the same. And now for as much as it is given to the king to understand in the present parliament by the petition of the commons that the servants having no regard to the ordinance but to their ease and singular covetousness, do withdraw themselves from serving great men and others, unless they have livery and wages double or treble of what they were wont to take in the twentieth year and earlier, to the great damage of the great men and impoverishment of all the commonality; whereof the commonality prays remedy. Wherefore in the parliament by the assent of the prelates, earls, barons, and those of the commonality assembled there, in order to refrain the malice of the servants, there are ordained and established the underwritten articles.

Item that carters, ploughmen drivers of ploughs, shepherds, swineherds, day men, and all other servants shall take the liveries and wages accustomed in the twentieth year or four years before so that in the countryside where the wheat was wont to be given they shall take for the bushel 10 d [enarius, or pence], or wheat at the will of the giver until it be otherwise ordained. And that they be hired to serve by a whole year, or by other usual terms, and not by the day; and that none pay at haymaking time more than a penny a day; and a mower of meadows for the acre 5 d, or 5 d by the day; and reapers of corn in the first week of August 2 d, and the second 3 d and so on until the end of August and less in the country where less was wont to be given, without meat or drink, or other courtesy to be demanded, given, or taken; and that all workmen bring their tools openly in their hands to the merchant towns, and they shall be hired there in a common place and not privately.

Item that none take for the threshing of a quarter of wheat or rye over 2½ d and the quarter of barley, beans, peas and oats 1½ d, if so much were wont to be given. And in the country where it is usual to reap by certain sheaves and to thresh by certain bushels they shall take no more nor in other manner than was wont the said twenty year and before, and that the same servants be sworn two times a year before lords, stewards, bailiffs and constables of every town to observe and perform these ordinances; and that none of them go out of the town where he lives in the winter to serve the summer if he may serve in the same town, taking as before is said. . . . [T]hose who refuse to make such oath, or to not perform as they were sworn to do or have taken upon them shall be put in the stocks by the said lords, stewards, bailiffs and constables of the towns for three days or more or sent to the next gaol, there to remain until they satisfy themselves. And that stocks be made in every town for such occasion, between now and the feast of Pentecost.

Item that carpenters masons and tilers and other workmen of houses shall not take by the day further work except in the manner as they were wont to do. . . . And those who carry by land or by water shall take no more for such carriage to be made than they were wont to do in the said twentieth year and four years before.

Item that cordwainers and shoemakers shall not sell boots or shoes nor any other thing touching their craft, in any other manner than they were wont to do in the said twentieth year.

Item that goldsmiths, saddlers, horsesmiths spurriers, tanners, corriers, tawers of leather, tailors and other workmen, artificers and labourers, and all other servants not here specified, shall be sworn before the justices, and do use their crafts and offices in this manner as they were wont to do the said twentieth year, and in the time before, without refusing the same because of this ordinance, and if any of the said servants, labourers, workmen or artificers, after such oath made, come against this ordinance, he shall be punished by fine and ransom and imprisonment after the discretion of the justices.

Item that the stewards, bailiffs and constables of the said towns be sworn before the same justices to enquire diligently by all the good ways they may, of all them that come against this ordinance and to certify the same justices of their names at all times, when they shall come into the country to make their sessions, so that the same justices upon the certificate of the said stewards, bailiffs, and constables, of the names of the rebels shall cause their bodies to be attached before the justices, to answer of such contempts so that they make fine and ransom to the king in case they be attainted [convicted], and moreover to be commanded to prison there to remain until they have found surety to serve and take and do their work and to sell things vendible in the manner aforesaid. And in case that any of them come against his oath and be thereof attainted, he shall have imprisonment of forty days, and if he is convicted another time, he shall be imprisoned for a quarter of a year so that every time he offends and is convicted he shall have double pain. . . .

Item that the justices make their sessions in all English counties at least four times each year, . . . and also at all times that shall be necessary, according to the discretion of the justices, and those who speak in the presence of the justices or do other things in their absence or presence in encouragement or maintenance of the servants, labourers or craftsmen against this ordinance, shall be grievously punished by the discretion of the justices. And if any of the servants, labourers or artificers flee from one county to another, because of this ordinance, then the sheriffs of the counties where such fugitives shall be found shall cause them to be taken at the commandment of the said justices of the counties from where they flee, and bring them to the chief gaol of the shire there to abide until the next sessions of the justices. And that the sheriffs return the same commandments before the same justices at their next sessions. And that this ordinance be held and kept as well in the city of London as in other cities and boroughs, and other places throughout the land, within franchises as well as without.

From: The National Archives of the UK, "Second Statute of Labourers, 1351," Catalogue reference C 74/1, m. 18, online at http://www.nationalarchives.gov.uk/pathways/citizenship/citizen_subject/transcripts/stat_lab.htm, (transcription and translation of the document), http://www.nationalarchives.gov.uk/pathways/citizenship/citizen_subject/docs/statute_labourers .htm, (image of the original document and archival information).

QUESTIONS:

1. Agrarian hierarchies normally responded to labor shortages by restricting peasant freedom: that is, states and elites would meet potential labor shortages by locking in the available labor. What characteristics of the English peasant economy visible in this source might have made such a response difficult to enforce? (For example, what role do cities play in the distribution of agricultural labor?)
2. What cultural attitudes does the Statute express? How might those attitudes have contributed to the Statute's failure?

14.1b: *The Peasants' Revolt of 1381* (Jean Froissart, 1393)

This account of the great Peasants' Revolt that hit England thirty years after the passage of the Statute of Laborers comes from the *Chronicles* of Jean Froissart (1337–1410). Froissart spoke and wrote in French but had connections with the English royal court. He was not an eyewitness to the revolt, but his narrative gives us a clear picture of the attitudes of the elite towards the commoners. He wrote this section in the early 1390s. Froissart claims that "It was because of the abundance and prosperity in which the common people then lived that this rebellion broke out." Common workers after 1351 did enjoy higher wages and better diets than earlier generations had. The royal government, having failed to regulate wages in 1351, tried to exploit the new wealth of the peasantry in 1381 by instituting a Poll Tax—essentially a head tax, or an amount levied on each person in the kingdom. The tax was new and widely hated, and triggered the revolt (note that Froissart fails to mention it).

While these negotiations and discussions were going on [between John of Gaunt, Duke of Lancaster, and the Scots, with a view to renewing the truce between England and Scotland], there occurred in England great disasters and uprisings of the common people, on account of which the country was almost ruined beyond recovery. Never was any land or realm in such great danger as England at that time. It was because of the abundance and prosperity in which the common people then lived that this rebellion broke out, just as in earlier days the [French peasant revolt], by which the noble land of France suffered grave injury.

These terrible troubles originated in England from a strange circumstance and a trivial cause. That it may serve as a lesson to all good men and true, I will describe that circumstance and its effects as I was informed of them at the time.

It is the custom in England, as in several other countries, for the nobles to have strong powers over their men and to hold them in serfdom: that is, that by right and custom they have to till the lands of the gentry, reap the corn and bring it to the big house, put it in the barn, thresh and winnow it; mow the hay and carry it to the house, cut logs and bring them up, and all such forced tasks; all this the men must do by way of serfage to the masters. In England there is a much greater number than elsewhere of such men who are obliged to serve the prelates and the nobles. And in the counties of Kent, Essex, Sussex and Bedford in particular, there are more than in the whole of the rest of England.

These bad people in the counties just mentioned began to rebel because, they said, they were held too much in subjection, and when the world began there had been no serfs and could not be, unless they had rebelled against their lord, as Lucifer did against God; but they were not of that stature, being neither angels nor spirits, but men formed in the image of their masters, and they were treated as animals. This was a thing they could no longer endure, wishing rather to be all one and the same; and, if they worked for their masters, they wanted to have wages for it. In these machinations they had been greatly encouraged originally by a crack-brained priest of Kent called John Ball, who had been imprisoned several times for his reckless words by the Archbishop of Canterbury. This John Ball had the habit on Sundays after mass, when everyone was coming out of church, of going to the cloisters or the graveyard, assembling the people round him and preaching thus:

'Good people, things cannot go right in England and never will, until goods are held in common and there are no more villeins and gentlefolk, but we are all one and the same. In what way are those whom we call lords greater masters than ourselves? How have they deserved it? Why do they hold us in bondage? If we all spring from a single father and mother, Adam and Eve, how can they claim or prove that they are lords more than us, except by making us produce and grow the wealth which they spend? They are clad in velvet and camlet lined with squirrel and ermine, while we go dressed in coarse cloth. They have the wines, the spices and the good bread: we have the rye, the husks and the straw, and we drink water. They have shelter and ease in their fine manors, and we have hardship and toil, the wind and the rain in the fields. And from us must come, from our labor, the things which keep them in luxury. We are called serfs and beaten if we are slow in our service to them, yet we have no sovereign lord we can complain to, none to hear us and do us justice. Let us go to the King—he is young—and show him how we are oppressed, and tell him that we want things to be changed, or else we will change them ourselves. If we go in good earnest and all together, very many people who are called serfs and are held in subjection will follow us to get their freedom. And when the King sees and hears us, he will remedy the evil, either willingly or otherwise.'

These were the kind of things which John Ball usually preached in the villages on Sundays when the congregations came out from mass, and many of the common people agreed with him. Some, who were up to no good, said: 'He's right!' and out in the fields, or walking together from one village to another, or in their homes, they whispered and repeated among themselves: 'That's what John Ball says, and he's right.'

The Archbishop of Canterbury, being informed of all this, had John Ball arrested and put in prison, where he kept him for two or three months as a punishment. It would have been better if he had condemned him to life imprisonment on the first occasion, or had him put to death, than to do what he did; but he had great scruples about putting him to death and set him free; and when John Ball was out of prison, he went on with his intrigues as before. The things he was doing and saying came to the ears of the common people of London, who were envious of the nobles and the rich. These began saying that the country was badly governed and was being robbed of its wealth by those who called themselves noblemen. So these wicked men in London started to become disaffected and to rebel and they sent word to the people in the counties mentioned to come boldly to London with all their followers, when they would find the city open and the common people on their side. They could then so work on the King that there would be no more serfs in England.

These promises incited the people of Kent, Essex, Sussex, Bedford and the neighboring districts and they set off and went towards London. They were a full sixty thousand and their chief captain was one Wat Tyler. With him as his companions were Jack Straw and John Ball. These three were the leaders and Wat Tyler was the greatest of them. He was a tiler of roofs, and a wicked and nasty fellow he was.

[The crowd marches through Canterbury, sacking the palace of the Archbishop on the way, and makes its way to London, where they have several meetings with King Richard II, at the time only 16 years old, and some of his leading nobles. At one of these, in a field outside of London at Smithfield, the king with perhaps

sixty supporters, virtually surrounded by the rebel mob, entered into negotiations with Wat Tyler, who (according to this account) was acting belligerently and seemed to be trying to provoke a fight with the king's supporters.]

Just then the Lord Mayor of London arrived on horseback with a dozen others, all fully armed beneath their robes, and broke through the crowd. He saw how Tyler was behaving and said to him in the sort of language he understood: 'Fellow, how dare you say such things in the King's presence? You're getting above yourself.' The King lost his temper and said to the Mayor: 'Lay hands on him, Mayor.' Meanwhile Tyler was answering: 'I can say and do what I like. What's it to do with you?' 'So, you stinking boor,' said the Mayor, who had once been a King's Advocate, 'you talk like that in the presence of the King, my natural lord? I'll be hanged if you don't pay for it.'

With that he drew a great sword he was wearing and struck. He gave Tyler such a blow on the head that he laid him flat under his horse's feet. No sooner was he down than he was entirely surrounded, so as to hide him from the crowds who were there, who called themselves his men. One of the King's squires called John Standish dismounted and thrust his sword into Tyler's belly so that he died.

Those crowds of evil men soon realized that their leader was dead. They began to mutter: 'They've killed our captain. Come on, we'll slay the lot!' They drew themselves up in the square in a kind of battle-order, each holding before him the bow which he carried. Then the King did an extraordinarily rash thing, but it ended well. As soon as Tyler was dispatched, he left his men, saying: 'Stay here, no one is to follow me,' and went alone towards those half-crazed people, to whom he said: 'Sirs, what more do you want ? You have no other captain but me. I am your king, behave peaceably.' On hearing this, the majority of them were ashamed and began to break up. They were the peace-loving ones. But the bad ones did not disband; instead they formed up for battle and showed that they meant business. The King rode back to his men and asked what should be done next. He was advised to go on towards the country, since it was no use trying to run away. The Mayor said: 'That is the best thing for us to do, for I imagine that we shall soon receive reinforcements from London, from the loyal men on our side who are waiting armed in their houses with their friends.'

While all this was going on, a rumor spread through London that the King was being killed. Because of it, loyal men of all conditions left their houses armed and equipped and made for Smithfield and the fields nearby, where the King now was. Soon they were some seven or eight thousand strong. . . . The leaders conferred together, saying: 'What shall we do? There are our enemies who would gladly have killed us if they thought they had the advantage.' Sir Robert Knollys argued frankly that they should go and fight them and kill them all, but the King refused to agree, saying that he would not have that done. 'But,' said the King, 'I want to have my banners back. We will see how

they behave when we ask for them. In any case, by peaceful means or not, I want them back.' 'You're right,' said the Earl of Salisbury. So the three new knights were sent over to get them. They made signs to the villeins [commoners] not to shoot, since they had something to discuss. When they were near enough for their voices to be heard, they said: 'Now listen, the King commands you to give back his banners, and we hope that he will have mercy on you.' The banners were handed over at once and taken back to the King. Any of the villeins who had obtained royal letters [of emancipation from serfdom] were also ordered in the King's name to give them up, on pain of death. Some did so, but not all. The King had them taken and torn up in front of them. It may be said that as soon as the royal banners had been removed, those bad men became just a mob. Most of them threw down their bows and they broke formation and started back for London. Sir Robert Knollys was more than angry that they had not been attacked and all killed. But the King would not hear of it, saying that he would take full vengeance later, as he did.

From: Froissart, Jean, *Chronicles*, Geoffrey Brereton, ed. and transl., pp. 211–213, 226–228, © 1968 Penguin Books.

QUESTIONS:

1. What cultural screen images do the leaders of the peasant uprising project to their followers? What cultural frame values lie behind the actions of most of the rebels in the wake of their leader's death? Are the screen images and frame values in agreement?
2. What attitudes toward the rebels does Froissart himself express? How well do you think he understands the revolt?

CHINA AT SEA

14.2a: *Inscription of World Voyages* (Zheng He, c. 1433)

Between 1405 and 1431, the great Chinese admiral Zheng He led seven expedition of Treasure Fleets from China on behalf of the third Ming Emperor. The Yongle emperor's expeditions combined trade, diplomacy, and military display; and the lands they visited, from southeast Asia to India and beyond to Arabia and east Africa, sent items of trade and tribute back to China. But Ming policy changed after 1431: Yongle's successors sent out no more Treasure Fleets, focusing instead on the Mongol frontier. Officials burnt all of Sheng He's logs. All that remains to us is a long lost stone tablet, erected sometime before Zheng He's death in 1435, on which Zheng He had inscribed the following account of the great Treasure Fleet voyages.

A record of the miraculous answer [to prayers] to the goddess the Celestial Spouse [a Daoist diety revered by maritime travelers].

The Imperial Ming Dynasty unifying seas and continents, surpassing the three dynasties even goes beyond the Han and Tang dynasties. The countries beyond the horizon and from the ends of the earth have all become subjects and to the most western of the western or the most northern of the northern countries, however far they may be, the distance and the routes may be calculated. Thus the barbarians from beyond the seas, though their countries are truly distant . . . have come to audience bearing precious objects and presents.

The Emperor, approving of their loyalty and sincerity, has ordered us, Zheng He and others at the head of several tens of thousands of officers and flag-troops to ascend more than one hundred large ships to go and confer presents on them in order to make manifest the transforming power of the (imperial) virtue and to treat distant people with kindness. From the third year of Yongle [1405] till now we have seven times received the commission of ambassadors to countries of the western ocean. The barbarian countries which we have visited are Zhancheng [Vietnam], Zhaowa [Java, Indonesia], Sanfoqi [Sumatra, Indonesia], and Xianlo [Siam] crossing straight over to Xilanshan [Sri Lanka] in South India, Calicut, [India] and Kezhi [India], we have gone to the western regions of Hulumosi [Ormuz], Aden [Yemen], Mogadishu [Somalia], altogether more than thirty countries large and small. We have traversed more than one hundred thousand *li* [35,000 miles] of immense water spaces and have beheld in the ocean huge waves like mountains rising sky high, and we have set eyes on barbarian regions far away hidden in a blue transparency of light vapors, while our sails loftily unfurled like clouds day and night continued their course rapidly like that of a star, traversing those savage waves as if we were treading a public thoroughfare. Truly this was due to the majesty and the good fortune of the Imperial Court and moreover we owe it to the protecting virtue of the divine Celestial Spouse.

The power of the goddess having indeed been manifested in previous times has been abundantly revealed in the present generation. In the midst of the rushing waters it happened that, when there was a hurricane, suddenly there was a divine lantern shining in the mast, and as soon as this miraculous light appeared the danger was appeased, so that even in the danger of capsizing one felt reassured that there was no cause for fear. When we arrived in the distant countries we captured alive those of the native kings who were not respectful and exterminated those barbarian robbers who were engaged in piracy, so that consequently the sea route was cleansed and pacified and the natives put their trust in it. All this is due to the favors of the goddess.

It is not easy to enumerate completely all the cases where the goddess has answered [my prayers]. Previously in a memorial to the Court we have requested that her virtue be recognized . . . and a temple be built at Nanking on the bank of the river where regular sacrifices should be made forever. We have respectfully received an Imperial commemoration exalting her miraculous favors, which is the highest recompense and praise indeed. However, the miraculous power of the goddess resides wherever one goes. . . .

We have received the high favor of a gracious commission from our sacred Lord [the Yongle Emperor], we carry to the distant barbarians the benefits of respect and good faith [on their part]. Commanding the multitudes on the fleet and being responsible for a quantity of money and valuables in the face of the violence of the winds and the nights, our one fear is not to be able to succeed. How, then, dare we not to serve our dynasty with . . . all our loyalty and the gods with the utmost sincerity? How would it be possible not to realize what is the source of the tranquility of the fleet and the troops and the salvation on the voyage both going and returning? Therefore, we have inscribed the virtue of the [Celestial Spouse] on stone and have also recorded the years and months of the voyages to the barbarian countries . . . in order to leave the memory forever.

I. In the third year of Yongle [1405] commanding the fleet we went to Calicut [India] and other countries. At that time the pirate Chen Zuyi had gathered his followers in the country of Sanfoqi [island of Sumatra], where he plundered the native merchants. When he also advanced to resist our fleet, supernatural soldiers secretly came to the rescue so that after one beating of the drum he was annihilated. In the fifth year [1407] we returned.

II. In the fifth year of Yongle [1407] commanding the fleet we went to Zhaowa [Java], Calicut, Kezhi [India], and Xianle [Siam]. The kings of these countries all sent as tribute precious objects, precious birds and rare animals. In the seventh year [1409] we returned.

III. In the seventh year of Yongle [1409] commanding the fleet we went to the countries (visited) before and took our route by the country of Xilanshan [Sri Lanka]. Its king Alagakkonara was guilty of a gross lack of respect and plotted against the fleet. Owing to the manifest answer to prayer of the goddess, [the plot] was discovered and thereupon that king was captured alive. In the ninth year [1411] on our return the captured king was presented [to the throne as a prisoner]; subsequently he received the Imperial [forgiveness and] favor of returning to his own country.

IV. In the eleventh year of Yongle [1413] commanding the fleet we went to Hulumosi [Ormuz] and other countries. In the country of Samudra [northern tip of Sumatra] there was a false king [named Sekandar] who was marauding and invading his country. The [true] king [Zaynu-'l-Abidin] had sent an envoy to the Palace Gates in order to lodge a complaint. We went there with the official

troops under our command and exterminated some and arrested [other rebels], and owing to the silent aid of the goddess, we captured the false king alive. In the thirteenth year [1415] on our return he was presented [to the Emperor as a prisoner]. In that year the king of the country of Manlajia [Malacca, Malaysia] came in person with his wife and son to present tribute.

V. In the fifteenth year of Yongle [1417] commanding the fleet we visited the western regions. The country of Ormuz presented lions, leopards with gold spots and large western horses. The country of Aden [Yemen] presented [giraffes], as well as the long-horned [oryx]. The country of Mogadishu [Somalia] presented [zebras] as well as lions. The country of Brava [Somalia or Kenya] presented camels which run one thousand *li*, as well as camel-birds [ostriches]. The countries of Zhaowa [Java] and Calicut [India] presented animal *miligao* [hides]. They all vied in presenting the marvelous objects preserved in the mountains or hidden in the seas and the beautiful treasures buried in the sand or deposited on the shores. Some sent a maternal uncle of the king, others a paternal uncle or a younger brother of the king in order to present a letter of homage written on gold leaf as well as tribute.

VI. In the nineteenth year of Yongle [1421] commanding the fleet we escorted the ambassadors from Ormuz and the other countries who had been in attendance at the capital for a long time back to their countries. The kings of all these countries prepared even more tribute than previously.

VII. In the sixth year of [Yongle's successor, 1431] once more commanding the fleet we have left for the barbarian countries in order to read to them [an Imperial edict] and to confer presents.

We have anchored in this port awaiting a north wind to take the sea, and recalling how previously we have on several occasions received the benefits of the protection of the divine intelligence we have thus recorded an inscription in stone.

From: Filesi, Teobaldo, *China and Africa in the Middle Ages*, David Morison, transl. (London: Frank Cass, 1972), pp. 61–65.

QUESTIONS:

1. According to the inscription, what were the goals of voyages? Do these goals reflect greater influence of hierarchy values or network values? How?
2. After 1431, the Chinese abruptly stopped their overseas voyages. Based on Zheng He's account and the values that inform it, what might have happened if Chinese Treasure Fleets had continued their voyages for another seventy-five years and had then met Vasco da Gama's Portuguese fleets in the early 1500s?

14.2b: *Ma Huan, Overall Survey of the Ocean Shores* (1451)

Ma Huan (c. 1380–1460) was a Chinese Mulsim voyager and translator who accompanied Zheng He on three of the Treasure Fleet expeditions in 1413, 1421, and 1431. He began his *Overall Survey of the Ocean Shores* after the first voyage and expanded it after each subsequent voyage. He visited many countries, including the three whose descriptions are excerpted here—Calicut, Java, and Mecca—serving as a special envoy to the latter. His descriptions demonstrate his broad interests in foreign lands, as he writes about government, customs, religion, systems of criminal punishment, among other topics, in addition to providing notes about trade goods and the length of the maritime routes connecting the places he visited. His book therefore demonstrates the fact that networks always carried ideas along with material goods. He also represents and contributed to the growth of knowledge generated by network activity.

THE COUNTRY OF KU-LI [CALICUT]

In the fifth year of the Yongle [emperor; 1407] the court ordered the principal envoy the grand eunuch Zheng He and others to deliver an imperial mandate to the king of this country and to bestow on him a patent conferring a title of honour, and the grant of a silver seal, [also] to promote all the chiefs and award them hats and girdles of various grades.

[So Zheng He] went there in command of a large fleet of treasure-ships, and he erected a tablet with a pavilion over it and set up a stone which said 'Though the journey from this country to the Central Country [China] is more than a hundred thousand *li*, yet the people are very similar, happy and prosperous, with identical customs. We have here engraved a stone, a perpetual declaration for ten thousand ages.'

The king of the country is a [warrior caste] man; he is a firm believer in the Buddhist religion [actually, he was Hindu]; [and] he venerates the elephant and the ox.

. . . The king of the country and the people of the country all refrain from eating the flesh of the ox. The great chiefs are Muslim people; [and] they all refrain from eating the flesh of the pig. Formerly there was a king who made a sworn compact with the Muslim people, [saying] 'You do not eat the ox; I do not eat the pig; we will reciprocally respect the taboo'; [and this compact] has been honoured right down to the present day.

. . .

As to the pepper: the inhabitants of the mountainous countryside have established gardens, and it is extensively cultivated. When the period of the tenth moon arrives, the pepper ripens; [and] it is collected, dried in the sun, and sold. Of course, big pepper-collectors come and collect it, and take it up to the official storehouse to be stored; if there is a buyer, an official gives permission for the sale; the duty is calculated according to the amount [of the purchase price] and is paid in to the authorities. Each one *po-ho* of pepper is sold for two hundred gold coins.

The Che-ti mostly purchase all kinds of precious stones and pearls, and they manufacture coral beads and other such things.

Foreign ships from every place come there; and the king of the country also sends a chief and a writer and others to watch the sales; thereupon they collect the duty and pay it in to the authorities.

The wealthy people mostly cultivate coconut trees-sometimes a thousand trees, sometimes two thousand or three thousand; this constitutes their property.

THE COUNTRY OF CHAO-WA [JAVA]

As to the place where the king resides: the walls are made of bricks, and are more than three *chang* [about 31 feet] in height; in circumference they are something more than two hundred paces; [and] in the [walls] are set double gates, very well-kept and clean.

The houses are constructed in storeyed form, each being three or four *chang* in height; they lay a plank [flooring, over which] they spread matting [made of] fine rattans, or else patterned grass mats, on which the people sit cross-legged; [and] on the top of the houses they use boards of hard wood as tiles, splitting [the wood into] roofing [material].

The houses in which the people of the country live have thatch for their roofs. Every family has a store-room built of bricks in the ground; . . . [in this] they store the private belongings of the family; [and] upon this they live, sit and sleep.

The people of the country, both men and women, are all particular about their heads; if a man touches their head with his hand, or if there is a misunderstanding about money at a sale, or a battle of words when they are crazy with drunkenness, they at once pull out these knives and stab [each other]. He who is stronger prevails. When [one] man is stabbed to death, if the [other] man runs away and conceals himself for three days before emerging, then he does not forfeit his life; [but] if he is seized at the very moment [of the stabbing], he too is instantly stabbed to death.

The country has no [such] punishment as flogging; no [matter whether] the offence be great or small, they tie both [the offender's] hands behind his back with a fine rattan, and hustle him away for several paces, then they take a *pu-la-t'ou* and stab the offender once or twice in the small of the back or in the floating ribs, causing instant death. According to the local custom of the country no day [passes] without a man being put to death; [it is] very terrible.

Copper coins of the successive dynasties in the Central Country are in current use universally. . . .

The people of the country are very fond of the blue patterned porcelain-ware of the Central Country, also of such things as musk, gold-flecked hemp-silks, and beads. They buy these things in exchange for copper coins.

The king of the country constantly sends chiefs, who load foreign products into a ship, and present them as tribute to the Central Country.

THE COUNTRY OF THE 'HEAVENLY SQUARE' [MECCA]

They profess the Muslim religion. A holy man first expounded and spread the doctrine of . . . this country, and right down to the present day the people of the country all observe the regulations of the doctrine in their actions, not daring to commit the slightest transgression.

The people of this country are stalwart and fine-looking, and their limbs and faces are of a very dark purple colour.

The menfolk bind up their heads; they wear long garments; [and] on their feet they put leather shoes. The women all wear a covering over their heads, and you cannot see their faces.

They speak the A-la-pi [Arabic] language. The law of the country prohibits wine- drinking. The customs of the people are pacific and admirable. There are no poverty-stricken families. They all observe the precepts of their religion, and law-breakers are few. It is in truth a most happy country.

As to the marriage- and funeral-rites: they all conduct themselves in accordance with the regulations of their religion.

If you travel on from here for a journey of more than half a day, you reach the Heavenly Hall mosque, the foreign name for this Hall is K'ai-a-pai [Ka'ba]. . . . The Hall is built with layers of five-coloured stones; in shape it is square and flat-topped. Inside, there are pillars formed of five great beams of sinking incense wood, and a shelf made of yellow gold. Through out the interior of the Hall, the walls are all formed of clay mixed with rose water and ambergris, exhaling a perpetual fragrance. Over [the Hall] is a covering of black hemp-silk. They keep two black lions to guard the door.

Every year on the tenth day of the twelfth moon all the foreign Muslims—in extreme cases making a long journey of one or two years—come to worship inside the Hall.

From: Ma, Huan, Chengjun Feng, and J. V. G. Mills, *Ying-yai sheng-lan. 'The overall survey of the ocean's shores'* [1433], (Cambridge, England: Published for the Hakluyt Society at the University Press, 1970), excerpts from pp. 137–78.

QUESTIONS:

1. What do Ma Huan's observations tell us about the operation of maritime networks in the fifteenth century? What are the similarities and differences from maritime network operations of earlier centuries shown in Chapter 8?
2. Based on what he observes about each country, what is Ma Huan interested in? What does he find agreeable and what does he find peculiar about each place? That is, what do his observations reveal about his frame values and about Chinese frame values more generally?

EUROPE AT SEA

14.3a: *A Journal of the First Voyage* (Vasco da Gama, 1497–98)

Vasco da Gama (1460–1524) made two voyages to India, in 1497–98 and 1502–3. The success of these voyages, despite setbacks including conflicts with locals in both East Africa and Calicut described in this selection, connected western Europe to the lucrative maritime network of the Indian Ocean world. Indeed, da Gama himself launched Portugal on a path not just of participation in this network, but on a mission to establish Portuguese dominance through the exercise of military force at sea. As we noted earlier, the opportunity to pursue this mission arose from Ming China's withdrawal from active participation in the region. Da Gama's official logs of the journeys were lost, so this account is from an anonymous member of the fleet. Its details can be verified through other sources.

In the name of God. Amen. In the year 1497, King Dom Manuel . . . despatched four vessels to make discoveries and go in search of spices. Vasco da Gama was the captain of these vessels. . . .

1497. Mozambique. The people of this country are of ruddy complexion and well made. They are Muhammadans [Muslims], and their language is the same as that of the Moors [Arabic]. Their dresses are of fine linen or cotton stuffs, with variously colored stripes, and of rich and elaborate workmanship. They all wear robes with borders of silk embroidered in gold. They are merchants, and have transactions with white Moors [Arabs], four of whose vessels were at the time in port, laden with gold, silver, cloves, pepper, ginger, and silver rings, as also with quantities of pearls, jewels, and rubies, all of which are used by the people of this country. We understood them to say that all these things, with the exception of the gold, were brought thither by these Moors; and that further on to where we were going, they abounded, and that precious stones, pearls and spices were so plentiful that there was no need to purchase them as they could be collected in baskets. All this we learned through a sailor the Captain [Vasco da Gama] had with him, and who, having formerly been a prisoner among the Moors, understood their language.

In this place and island of Mozambique, there resided a chief who had the title of Sultan. He often came aboard our ships attended by some of his people. The Captain gave him many good things to eat, and made him a present of hats, shirts, corals and many other articles. He was, however, so proud that he treated all we gave him with contempt, and asked for scarlet cloth, of which we had none. . . .

One evening, as we left the ship for the mainland to obtain drinking water, we saw about twenty men on the beach. They were armed with spears, and forbade our landing. After the Captain heard this, he ordered three bombards [small cannon] to be fired upon them, so that we might land. Having effected our landing, these men fled into the bush, and we took as much water as we wanted. [The next day], a Moor rowed out to our ships, and told us that if we wanted more drinking water, that we should go for it, suggesting that we would encounter more trouble and be forced to turn back. The Captain no sooner heard this [threat] than he resolved to go, in order to show that we were able to do them harm if we desired it. We then armed our boats, placing bombards in their poops, and started for the shore. The Moors had constructed [a defensive wall] by lashing planks together . . . [but as we approached] they were at the time walking along the beach, armed with spears, knives, bows, and slingshots, with which they hurled stones at us. But our bombards soon made it so hot for them

that they fled behind their walls, but this turned out to their injury rather than their profit. During the three hours that we were occupied in this manner [bombarding the beach] we saw at least two men killed, one on the beach and the other behind the wall. When we were weary of this work we retired to our ships to dine. . . .

[Vasco da Gama sailed from Mozambique to Swahili city-state of Mombasa, a two week voyage]

On Saturday, we cast anchor off Mombasa, but did not enter the port. . . . In front of the city there lay numerous vessels, all dressed in flags. And we, anxious not to be outdone, also dressed our ships, and we actually surpassed their show. . . . We anchored here with much pleasure, for we confidently hoped that on the following day we might go on land and hear [Catholic] mass jointly with the Christians reported to live there in a neighborhood separate from that of the Moors. . . .

But those who had told us [about the Christians] had said it [to trap us], for it was not true. At midnight there approached us a *dhow* with about a hundred men, all armed with cutlasses and shields. When they came to the vessel of the Captain they attempted to board her, armed as they were, but this was not permitted, only four or five of the most distinguished men among them being allowed on board. They remained about a couple of hours, and it seemed to us that they paid us this visit merely to find out whether they might not capture one or the other of our vessels. . . .

These and other wicked tricks were practiced upon us by these dogs, but our Lord did not allow them to succeed, because they were unbelievers.

[The fleet then sailed across the Indian Ocean for 23 days, guided by a Muslim navigator, and came to Calicut, where Ma Huan also visited.].

After we were at anchor, four boats approached us from the land, and they asked of what nation we were. We told them, and they then pointed out Calicut to us. . . . The city of Calicut is inhabited by

Christians [actually Hindus]. They are of tawny complexion. Some of them have big beards and long hair, whilst others clip their hair short or shave the head, merely allowing a tuft to remain on the crown as a sign that they are Christians. They also wear moustaches. They pierce the ears and wear much gold in them. They go naked down to the waist, covering their lower extremities with very fine cotton stuffs. But it is only the most respectable who do this, for the others manage as best they are able. The women of this country, as a rule, are ugly and of small stature. They wear many jewels of gold round the neck, numerous bracelets on their arms, and rings set with precious stones on their toes. All these people are well-disposed and apparently of mild temper. At first sight they seem covetous and ignorant. . . .

When we arrived at Calicut the king was away. The Captain sent two men to him with a message, informing him that an ambassador had arrived from the King of Portugal with letters . . . [The king] sent word to the Captain bidding him welcome [and sent] a pilot . . . with orders to take us to [an anchorage] in front of the city of Calicut. We were told that the anchorage at the place to which we were to go was good . . . and that it was customary for the ships which came to this country to anchor there for the sake of safety. We ourselves did not feel comfortable . . . and we did not anchor as near the shore as the king's pilot desired. . . .

On the following morning . . . the Captain set out to speak to the king, and took with him thirteen men. We put on our best attire, put bombards [small cannon] in our boats, and took with us trumpets and many flags. On landing, the Captain was received by government officials, along with a crowd of many men, armed and unarmed. The reception was friendly, as if the people were pleased to see us, though at first appearances looked threatening, for they carried naked swords in their hands. A palanquin was provided for the captain, such as is used by men of distinction in that country. . . . When we arrived [at the king's palace], men of much distinction and great lords came out to meet the Captain, and joined those who were already in attendance upon him. . . .

The king was in a small court, reclining upon a couch covered with a cloth of green velvet, above which was a good mattress, and upon this again a sheet of cotton stuff, very white and fine, more so than any linen. . . . The Captain, on entering, saluted in the manner of the country: by putting the hands together, then raising them towards Heaven, as is done by Christians when addressing God, and immediately afterwards opening them and shutting fists quickly. . . .

And the Captain told him he was the ambassador of the King of Portugal, who was Lord of many countries and the possessor of great wealth of every description, exceeding that of any king of these parts; that for a period of sixty years his people had annually sent out vessels to make discoveries in the direction of India, as they knew that there were Christian kings there like themselves. This, he said, was the reason which induced them to order this country to be discovered, not because they sought for gold or silver, for of this they had such abundance that they needed not what was to be found in this country. . . . There reigned a king now whose name was Dom Manuel, who had ordered [Da Gama] to build three vessels, of which he had been appointed Captain, and who had ordered him not to return to Portugal until he should have discovered this King of the Christians, on pain of having his head cut off. That two letters had been entrusted to him to be presented in case he succeeded in discovering him . . . and, finally, he had been instructed to say by word of mouth that he [the King of Portugal] desired to be his friend and brother. . . .

[The next morning], the captain got ready the following gifts to be sent to the king: twelve pieces of [cotton cloth], four scarlet hoods, six hats, four strings of coral, a case containing six wash-hand basins, a case of sugar, two casks of oil, and two of honey. And as it is the custom not to send anything to the king without the knowledge of the Moor [his financial advisor], and other officials, the Captain informed them of his intention. They came, and when they saw the present they laughed at it, saying that it was not a thing to offer to a king, that the poorest merchant from Mecca, or any other part of India, gave more, and that if he wanted to make a present it should be in gold, as the king would not accept such things. When the Captain heard this he grew sad, and said that he had brought no gold, that, moreover, he was no merchant, but an ambassador; that he gave of that which he had, which was his own private gift and not the king's; that if the King of Portugal ordered him to return he would entrust him with far richer presents; and that if the king would not accept these things he would send them back to the ships. Upon this they [the government officials] declared that they would not forward his presents, nor consent to his forwarding them himself. When they had gone there came certain Moorish merchants, and they all mocked the presents which the Captain desired to be sent to the king.

From: A Journal of the First Voyage of Vasco da Gama, 1479–1499, E. Ravenstein, transl., Hakluyt Society Series 1, vol. 99 (London: The Hakluyt Society, 1898), pp. 22–68 passim.

QUESTIONS:

1. Characterize the observations and impressions are recorded in the journal. How does the Portuguese attitude towards the people they meet compare with the Chinese attitude found in the two previous sources?
2. Are Portuguese attitudes and observations shaped more by their motives and cultural frame values, or by actual experiences? What frame values do you see here and how do they affect Portuguese interactions? Are they closer to network or hierarchy values?

14.3b: *Letter Describing His First Voyage* (Christopher Columbus, 1493)

Christopher Columbus (1451–1506) was the son of a Genoese woolworker. He became a sailor, visiting locations in the Atlantic world as far flung as Iceland and the west coast of Africa. Determined to find a route across the Atlantic to the fabled riches of the Far East, he sought patronage from the monarchies of Portugal and Spain. After several initial rebuffs, he finally convinced King Ferdinand and Queen Isabella to fund an expedition. Between 1492 and 1504 he made four voyages across the ocean, exploring islands in what we now know is the Caribbean, not the outer regions of East Asia. Between his first and second voyages he wrote a letter to the king and queen describing his discoveries. That letter is excerpted here.

Since I know that you will be pleased at the great victory with which Our Lord has crowned my voyage, I write this to you, from which you will learn how in thirty-three days I passed from the Canary Islands to the Indies, with the fleet which the most illustrious king and queen, our sovereigns, gave to me. There I found very many islands, filled with people innumerable, and of them all I have taken possession for their Highnesses, by proclamation made and with the royal standard unfurled, and no opposition was offered to me.

To the first island which I found I gave the name "San Salvador," in remembrance of the blessed Savior, who had marvelously bestowed all this; the Indians call it "Guanahani." To the second island, I gave the name "Santa Maria de Concepcion" [Rum Cay] to the third, "Fernandina"; to the fourth, "Isabella" . . . and so each island received a new name from me.

When I came to Juana [Cuba], I followed its coast to the westward, and I found it to be so extensive that I thought that it must be the mainland, the province of Cathay [China]. And since there were neither towns nor villages on the seashore, but only small villages whose residents all fled immediately, I continued along the coast, thinking that I could not fail to find great cities and towns. . . .

Hispana [Hispaniola] is a marvel. The sierras and the mountains, the plains, the arable and pasture lands, are so lovely and so rich for planting and sowing, for breeding cattle of every kind, and for building towns and villages. The harbors of the sea here are such as cannot be believed to exist unless they have been seen, and so with the rivers, many and great, and of good water, the majority of which contain gold. In the trees, fruits and plants, there is a great difference from those of Juana [Cuba]. In this island, there are many spices and great mines of gold and of other metals.

The people of this island, and of all the other islands which I have found and of which I have information, all go naked, men and women, as their mothers bore them, although some of the women cover a single place with the leaf of a plant or with a net of cotton which they make for the purpose. They have no iron or steel or weapons, nor are they inclined to use them. This is not because they are not well built and of handsome stature, but because they are very timid. They have no other arms than spears made of reeds, to which they fix a small sharpened stick. They do not dare to make use of these weapons against us, for many times it has happened that I have sent ashore two or three men to some town to have speech with them, and countless people have come out to them, and as soon as they have seen my men approaching, they have fled, a father not even waiting for his son. This is not because we have done them any harm; on the contrary, at every place where I have been and have been able to have speech with them, I have given gifts to them, such as cloth and many other things, receiving nothing in exchange. But they remain by nature incurably timid.

It is true that, once they have been reassured and have lost their fear of us, they are so innocent and so generous with all that they possess, that no one would believe it who has not seen it. They refuse nothing that they possess if it be asked of them. On the contrary, they invite any one to share it and display as much love as if they would give their hearts. They are content with whatever trifle or gift that is given to them, whether it be of value or valueless. . . . I gave them a thousand handsome good things, which I had brought, in order that they might conceive affection for us and, more than that, might become Christians and be inclined to the love and service of your Highnesses and of the whole Spanish nation, and strive to aid us and to give us of the things which they have in abundance and which are necessary to us.

They do not hold any creed nor are they idolaters; they only believe that power and good are in the heavens. . . . This belief is not the result of ignorance, for they are actually of a very acute intelligence, they know how to navigate the seas, and it is amazing how good an account they give of everything. [Instead], this belief is because they have never seen people clothed or ships such as ours.

As soon as I arrived in the Indies, I took by force some natives at the first island that I found in order that they might give me information about these places. And so it was that they soon understood us, and we them, either by speech or signs, and they have been very helpful. I still have them with me, and they are always assured that I come from Heaven, despite all the discussions which they have had with me. They were the first to announce this wherever I went in the islands, and others went running from house to house, and to neighboring towns, crying loudly "Come! Come! See the men from Heaven!" So all, men and women alike, once their fear was set at rest, came out to welcome us, and they all brought something to eat and drink, which they gave with extraordinary affection and generosity.

In all the islands, they have very many canoes, which are like our rowboats, except they are not so broad, because they are made of a single log of wood. But a rowboat would not be able to keep up with them, since their speed is incredible. In these they navigate among all the islands, and carry their goods and conduct trade. In one of these canoes I have seen with seventy and eighty men, each one with his oar.

In all these islands, I saw no great diversity in the appearance of the people or in their manners and language. On the contrary, they all understand one another. . . . and if their Highnesses assent, this will [assist] their conversion to our holy faith of Christ, to which they are very ready and favorably inclined. . . .

In all these islands, it seems to me that each man is content with one wife, except the chiefs or kings who may have as many as twenty wives. It appears to me that the women work more than the men. I have not been able to learn if they hold private property, but it seemed to me that they all shared what they had, especially of eatable things. In these islands I have so far found no human monstrosities, as many expected . . . on the contrary, the whole population is very well formed. They are not black like the people in Guinea [West Africa], but their hair is flowing. . . .

And so I have found no monsters, nor have I heard of any, except on an island called Charis. . . . This island is inhabited by a people who are regarded in all the islands as very fierce, and they are cannibals who eat human flesh. They have many canoes with which they range through all the islands of India and pillage and take whatever they can. They are no more malformed than are the others, except that they have the custom of wearing their hair long like women, and they use bows and arrows. . . . They are ferocious towards these other people who are excessively cowardly, but I regard them as no more fearsome than the others. . . . I have also been told of another island, which they assure me is larger than Hispana, where the people have no hair. In this place there is reportedly incalculable amounts of gold. . . .

To conclude this report . . . their Highnesses can see that I can supply them as much gold as they may need if their Highnesses will continue to assist [my voyages]. Moreover, I will provide them spices and cotton, as much as their Highnesses shall command; and mastic and aloe, as much as they shall order to be shipped; and slaves, as many as they shall order to be shipped and who will be from the idolaters. I believe also that I have found rhubarb and cinnamon, and I shall find a thousand other things of value. . . .

Our thanksgiving must be directed the most to the eternal God, Our Lord, Who gives to all those who walk in His way triumph over things which appear to be impossible, and this was one such glorious example. For although men have talked or have written of these distant lands, all was conjectural and without evidence. . . . It is our Redeemer who has given the victory to our most illustrious king and queen, and to their renowned kingdom . . . and all Christendom ought to feel delight and make great feasts and give solemn thanks to our Lord and Savior Jesus Christ, with many solemn prayers for the great exaltation which they shall have in the turning of so many pagan peoples to our Holy Faith, and afterwards for the temporal benefits, because not only Spain but all Christendom will have hence refreshment and gain.

These deeds that have been accomplished are thus briefly recorded while aboard ship, off the Canary Islands, on the fifteenth of February, in the year one thousand four hundred and ninety-three. I remain, at your orders and your service.

The Admiral

From: Columbus, Christopher, *The Voyages of Christopher Columbus, Being the Journals of his First and Third, and the Letters Concerning his First and Last Voyages*, Cecil Jane, transl. and ed. (London: Argonaut Press, 1930), pp. 259–64.

QUESTIONS:

1. Characterize Columbus' observations. How do they compare to those of da Gama, Ma Huan, and Zheng He? What does he emphasize most? What evidence do you see in the text that Columbus is shaping his account for his audience and his own purposes?
2. Describe the screen image of the peoples of Caribbean that Columbus projects. Describe what you think the Caribbean peoples' screen image of Columbus might look like. What accounts for the differences?

FRAMING INNOVATION

14.4: *Giorgio Vasari: Lives of the Most Eminent Painters, Sculptors, and Architects* (1550)

Leonardo da Vinci (1452-1519): painter and sculptor of florence

Giorgio Vasari (1511–74) was an Italian painter, architect, writer, and historian. He was successful in his own right, more as an architect than a painter. He became best known, however, for his *Lives of the Most Eminent Painters, Sculptors, and Architects*, published in 1550 and dedicated to Grand Duke Cosimo I de' Medici, a major patron of Renaissance artists. The work celebrates the creative genius and competitive nature of great Italian (especially Florentine) artists; his biographies of artists established a lasting genre in art historical writing. He was the first author to use the term "Renaissance" in print, and in general he provides a fine example of the European Renaissance emphasis on innovation and individualism. This selection is his biography of Leonardo da Vinci, painter, inventor, and the quintessential "Renaissance Man."

THE GREATEST GIFTS are often seen, in the course of nature, rained by celestial influences on human creatures; and sometimes, in supernatural fashion, beauty, grace, and talent are united beyond measure in one single person, in a manner that to whatever such an one turns his attention, his every action is so divine, that, surpassing all other men, it makes itself clearly known as a thing bestowed by God (as it is), and not acquired by human art. This was seen by all mankind in Leonardo da Vinci, in whom, besides a beauty of body never sufficiently extolled, there was an infinite grace in all his actions; and so great was his genius, and such its growth, that to whatever difficulties he turned his mind, he solved them with ease. In him was great bodily strength, joined to dexterity, with a spirit and courage ever royal and magnanimous; and the fame of his name so increased, that not only in his lifetime was he held in esteem, but his reputation became even greater among posterity after his death.

Truly marvelous and celestial was Leonardo, the son of Ser Piero da Vinci; and in learning and in the rudiments of letters he would have made great proficience, if he had not been so variable and unstable, for he set himself to learn many things, and then, after having begun them, abandoned them. Thus, in arithmetic, during the few months that he studied it, he made so much progress, that, by continually suggesting doubts and difficulties to the master who was teaching him, he would very often bewilder him. He gave some little attention to music, and quickly resolved to learn to play the lyre, as one who had by nature a spirit most lofty and full of refinement: wherefore he sang divinely to that instrument, improvising upon it. Nevertheless, although he occupied himself with such a variety of things, he never ceased drawing and working in relief, pursuits which suited his fancy more than any other. Ser Piero, having observed this, and having considered the loftiness of his intellect, one day took some of his drawings and carried them to Andrea del Verrocchio, who was much his friend, and besought him straightly to tell him whether Leonardo, by devoting himself to drawing, would make any proficience.

Andrea was astonished to see the extraordinary beginnings of Leonardo, and urged Ser Piero that he should make him study it; wherefore he arranged with Leonardo that he should enter the workshop of Andrea, which Leonardo did with the greatest willingness in the world. And he practiced not one branch of art only, but all those in which drawing played a part; and having an intellect so divine and marvelous that he was also an excellent geometrician, he not only worked in sculpture, making in his youth, in clay, some heads of women that are smiling, of which plaster casts are still taken, and likewise some heads of boys which appeared to have issued from the hand of a master; but in architecture, also, he made many drawings both of groundplans and of other designs of buildings; and he was the first, although but a youth, who suggested the plan of reducing the river Arno to a navigable canal from Pisa to Florence. He made designs of flour mills, fulling mills, and engines, which might be driven by the force of water: and since he wished that his profession should be painting, he studied much in drawing after nature, and sometimes in making models of figures in clay, over which he would lay soft pieces of cloth dipped in clay, and then set himself patiently to draw them on a certain kind of very fine Rheims cloth, or prepared linen: and he executed them in black and white with the point of his brush, so that it was a marvel, as some of them by his hand, which I have in our book of drawings, still bear witness; besides

which, he drew on paper with such diligence and so well, that there is no one who has ever equaled him in perfection of finish; and I have one, a head drawn with the style in chiaroscuro, which is divine.

And there was infused in that brain such grace from God, and a power of expression in such sublime accord with the intellect and memory that served it, and he knew so well how to express his conceptions by draughtsmanship, that he vanquished with his discourse, and confuted with his reasoning, every valiant wit. And he was continually making models and designs to show men how to remove mountains with ease, and how to bore them in order to pass from one level to another; and by means of levers, windlasses, and screws, he showed the way to raise and draw great weights, together with methods for emptying harbors, and pumps for removing water from low places, things which his brain never ceased from devising; and of these ideas and labours many drawings may be seen, scattered abroad among our craftsmen; and I myself have seen not a few. He even went so far as to waste his time in drawing knots of cords, made according to an order, that from one end all the rest might follow till the other, so as to fill a round; and one of these is to be seen in stamp, most difficult and beautiful, and in the middle of it are these words, "Leonardus Vinci Accademia." And among these models and designs, there was one by which he often demonstrated to many ingenious citizens, who were then governing Florence, how he proposed to raise the Temple of S. Giovanni in Florence, and place steps under it, without damaging the building; and with such strong reasons did he urge this, that it appeared possible, although each man, after he had departed, would recognize for himself the impossibility of so vast an undertaking.

He was so pleasing in conversation, that he attracted to himself the hearts of men. And although he possessed, one might say, nothing, and worked little, he always kept servants and horses, in which latter he took much delight, and particularly in all other animals, which he managed with the greatest love and patience; and this he showed when often passing by the places where birds were sold, for, taking them with his own hand out of their cages, and having paid to those who sold them the price that was asked, he let them fly away into the air, restoring to them their lost liberty. For which reason nature was pleased so to favor him, that, wherever he turned his thought, brain, and mind, he displayed such divine power in his works, that, in giving them their perfection, no one was ever his peer in readiness, vivacity, excellence, beauty, and grace.

From: "Vasari's Life of Leonardo da Vinci," http://members.efn.org/~acd/vite/VasariLeo.html.

QUESTIONS:

1. What qualities about Leonardo does Vasari emphasize and admire most? That is, what stands out about this screen image of Leonardo? What do these qualities suggest about European (or at least Italian Renaissance) frame values?
2. Reread the source from a traditional Agrarian Era emphasis on tradition. What strikes you as odd here? How would you reemphasize tradition in the life of Leonardo?

CHAPTER 15

The Late Agrarian World I:
Networks of Exchange, 1500-1750

INTRODUCTION

The Late Agrarian Era was characterized and in large part created by network connections that became, in the wake of Columbus' voyages starting in 1492, increasingly global. The sources presented in this chapter show us aspects of the operations of that global network of exchange. Network flows were not just a matter of economic transactions, but of cultural exchanges and the growing tension between network values and hierarchy values around the world. These sources reflect that variety.

15.1: *The evils of cochineal* (Tlaxcalan cabildo, 1553)

This source is a record of one of the regular meetings of the cabildo, or local ruling body, of Tlaxcala (pronounced "tlash-KAH-lah"). The Tlaxcalans had been the chief enemies of the Aztecs and it was their alliance with the Spanish that brought down the Aztec Empire. The Tlaxcalans then found themselves incorporated into the new Spanish Empire. Tlaxcalan elites played a role in ruling the new empire through participation in the cabildo. But inclusion in the Spanish world and its global connections meant that the Tlaxcalan world inevitably changed despite the best efforts of Tlaxcalan elites to maintain continuity. Here, the cabildo debates the corrosive impact of vastly expanded network connections on traditional political, social, and gender relationships. The concern in this document is particularly the effects of the trade in cochineal (a red dye made from insects of the same name that live on cactus plants) on the Tlaxcala community.

In the loyal city of Tlaxcala on Friday, the third day of the month of March of the year 1553, there assembled in cabildo the magnificent lord Alonso de Galdós, Corregidor in the province of Tlaxcala for his majesty, with Miguel Cardenel, Spaniard, as interpreter; and it was in the presence of the very honorable lords don Domingo de Angulo, governor; and the alcades ordinaries don Diego de Paredes, Félix Mijía, Alonso Gómez, and don Diego de Guzmán; and of the four rulers, don Juan Maxixcatzin, don Julián Motolinia—don Juan Xicotencatl is sick;—it was in the presence of don Francissco de Mendoza; and the regidores don Julián de las Rosa, Buenaventura Oñate, Antonia del Pedroso, Antonio Téllez, Hernando Tececepotzin, don Juan de Paz, Baltasar Cortś, Pablo de Galicia, Pedro Díaz, and

Tadeo de Niza; not (done) before don Domingo de Silva, who is sick, and Lucas García, acting as judge in Coyoacan; it was done before us, Fabián Rodrígues, Diego de Soto, and Sancho de Rozas, notaries of the cabildo of Tlaxcala. They deliberated about how the cochineal cactus, from which cochineal comes, is being planted all over Tlaxcala. Everyone does nothing but take care of cochineal cactus; no long is care taken that maize and other edibles are planted. For food—maize, chilis, and beans—and other things that people need were once not expensive in Tlaxcala. It is because of this (neglect), the cabildo members considered, that all the foods are becoming expensive. The owners of cochineal cactus merely buy maize, chilis, etc., and are very occupied only with their cochineal, by which their money, cacao beans, and cloth are acquired. They no longer want to cultivate their fields, but idly neglect them. Because of this, now many fields are going to grass, and famine truly impends. Things are no longer as they were long ago, for the cochineal cactus is making people lazy. And it is excessive how sins are committed against our Lord God. These cochineal owners devote themselves to their cochineal on Sundays and holy days; no longer do they go to church to hear mass as the holy church commands us, but look only to getting their sustenance and their cacao, which makes them proud. And then later they buy pulque and then get drunk; all of the cochineal owners gather together. If they buy a turkey, they give it away for less than its price, and pulque, too; they lightly give away their money and cacao. Not remembering how our lord God mercifully granted them whatever wealth is theirs, they vainly squander it. And he who belonged to someone no longer respects whoever was his lord and master, because he is seen to have gold and cacao. That makes them proud and swells them up whereby it is fully evident that they esteem themselves only through wealth. And also the cochineal dealers, some of them noblemen, some commoners, and some women, line up here in the Tlaxcala

marketplace and there await the cochineal. When they are not collecting cochineal quickly, then they go to the various homes of the cochineal owners, entering the houses. And there many things happen; they make the women drunk there, and there some commit sins. They go entering the homes of anyone who has cochineal plants; they already know those from whom they customarily buy dye, and sometimes they also go on Sundays and holy days, whereby they miss attending mass and hearing the sermon, but go only wanting to get drunk. And these cochineal dealers act as if the women who gather dye have been made their relatives [literally, "mothers," i.e., a person who will do anything for one limitlessly out of obligation]. Some of the men hire themselves out to Spaniards to gather dye for them, and they give them money and cacao. And later they distribute the women to them, making them like their relatives; to some they assign seven or eight (women), or thereabouts, to gather dye for them. Because of this many improper things are done. And of those who hire themselves out, many are likewise ruined, because some act as slaves in the hands of the Spaniards. If it were not for cochineal, they would not become such. And both the cactus owners and the cochineal dealers so act that for little reason they begin to pair with each other [i.e., to be companions], or to take one another as co-godparents, or just feed one another, gathering and collecting together with their wives. They feed one another, however many of them there are; they give one another a great deal of food, and the chocolate they drink is very thick, with plenty of cacao in it. When they find the chocolate just a little watery, then it is not to their liking and they do not want to drink it. Some pour it on the ground, whereby whoever has given his very good cacao to someone is affronted, but they imagine themselves very grand because of it. And also then they buy pulque or Castilian wine; even though it is very expensive, they pay no heed, but give (the price) to the person selling it. And then they become entirely inebriated and senseless, together with their wives; they fall down one at a time where they care congregated, entirely drunk. Many sins are committed thee, and it all comes from cochineal. And both the cactus owners and the cochineal dealers, some of them, sleep on cotton mats, and their wives wear great skirts, and they have much money, cacao, and clothing. The wealth they have only makes them proud and swaggering. For before cochineal was known and everyone planted cochineal cactus, it was not this way. there were some people of whom it was clearly evident that they lived in knowledge of their humility, but just because of the cochineal now there is much drunkenness and swaggering; it is very clear that cochineal has been making people idle in the last eight or nine years. But in the old days there was a time of much care in cultivation and planting; everyone cultivated the soil and planted. Because of this, the cabildo members said it is necessary that the cochineal cactus decrease and not so much be planted, since it causes idleness. It is greatly urged that everyone cultivate and plant; let much maize, chilis, beans, and all edible plants be grown, because if our lord God should wish that famine come, and if there are in people's possession much money, cacao, and cloth, will those things be eaten? Will there be salvation through them? It cannot be. Money, cacao, and cloth do not fill one. But if people have much food, through it they will save themselves, since no one will (starve);

no one will die being wealthy. Therefore two or three times the lord viceroy who presides in Mexico City, don Luis de Velasco, has been told and it has been brought to his attention how the dye brings affliction, and he has been informed of all the harm done. And after that the lord viceroy gave orders in reply, ordering the lord Corregidor that in his presence there be consultation here in the cabildo to approve how many plantings of cochineal cactus are to be kept by each person; it is to be a definite number, and no longer will there be planting at whim. And in consulting, some of the cabildo members said that five plantings of cochineal cactus should be kept (by each person), and others said that fifteen should be kept. But when the discussion was complete, everyone approved keeping ten plantings of cactus, and the lord Corregidor also approved it. No one is to exceed (the number). And the women who gather dye in the marketplace are to gather dye no more. Nevertheless, it is first to be put before the lord viceroy; what he should order in reply will then be made public. Then in the cabildo were appointed those who will go to Mexico City to set before the lord viceroy what was discussed as said above. . . . It is by order of the cabildo that they will go to Mexico City. The most illustrious lord viceroy will decide how to reply; then it will be announced all over Tlaxcala in what manner cochineal cactus is to be kept.

From: Lockhart, James, Frances Berdan, and Arthur J.O. Anderson, *The Tlaxcalan Actas,* (U of Utah Press: Salt Lake City, 1986), pp. 79–84.

QUESTIONS:

1. The cabildo focuses on cochineal, but what are they really upset about? Why do they focus, for example, on the activities of women? And why are they critical of people showing off their cochineal-obtained wealth? How does this source show network activity threatening hierarchy?
2. How well do you think the cabildo understands the problem they are seeing? What measures do they propose to deal with the problem? How practical do those measures seem to you? How well equipped is this hierarchy to manage its network connections?

15.2:   *On Merchants* (Zhang Han, 1593)

Zhang Han (1511–1593) was a Ming Chinese merchant from a family that had entered commerce only a generation earlier. The family's success is representative of the opportunities the rich and expanding Chinese economy afforded to many people from a variety of backgrounds. Yet these very opportunities created the same potential threats to the stability of Chinese hierarchy that the Tlaxcalan cabildo faced in the same century. Zhang Han wrote the essays collected in *On Merchants*, which was published when he died in 1593, over the course of his career. In his writings he advised those following him on how to conduct business within the ethical framework of society, and they show us how cultural attitudes and mechanisms can defuse the potential subversiveness of network activity.

How important to people are wealth and profit! Human disposition is such that people pursue what is profitable to them, and with this profit in mind they will even face harm. They gallop in pursuit of it day and night, never satisfied with what they have, though it wears down their spirits and exhausts them physically. Profit is what people covet. Since all covet it, they rush after it like torrents pouring into a valley: they come and go without end, never resting day or night, never reaching the point at which the raging floods within them subside such that they finally come to rest. Thus it is written: "The people come in droves, and it's all for profit that they come; the people go in droves, and it's all for profit that they go." They use up all their energy chasing after the most negligible profits, and become forgetful of their diurnal exhaustion. How is this any different from thinking the hair's tip big and the mountains small? It isn't that the hair's tip is in fact big and the mountain in fact small; rather, they see only the hair's tip, and do not see the mountain. It is as though they were being led on by the nose and pushed from behind.

Thus it has come to be that the children of merchants may take pleasure in their food and clothing. Their ornamented stallions are harnessed into teams, their carriages stretch on one after the other like bolts of cloth across the land or like ripples across a river; flying dust falls from the sky and mud-caked sweat pours like rain. Crafty, clever men latch on to their wealth and power, flattering them and scurrying about at their disposal. The young women of Yan and the girls of Zhao play on string and reed instruments, perform on zithers, dangle long sleeves and trip about in pointed slippers, vying for beauty and currying favor.

The merchants boast that their knowledge and ability are sufficient to get them anything they want. They set their minds on monopolizing the operations of change in the natural world and scheme to exploit the natural transformations of man and animal. They shift with the times; when they offer their goods for sale, they control the prices. Tallying it all up, they do not let a hundredth part slip by. Yet they are unembarrassed by the pettiness of this knowledge and ability. Doesn't the saying, "Great knowledge is expansive, petty knowledge is finicky," describe this?

In ancient times the sage kings treated the primary sector as important and placed restrictions on the secondary sector; they valued agriculture and depreciated commerce. Hence the commercial taxes were double the agricultural taxes. From the time that Emperor Wu of the Han adopted Sang Hongyang's policies, setting up the Office of Price Adjustment and Transportation, monopolizing all commodities in the empire, and selling them when they were dear and buying them when they were cheap, merchants had no way to realize profits and the prices of goods remained stable. This was called the System of Equalization and Standards. He further decreed that merchants could not wear silk, ride in carriages, serve at court, or become officials. He increased their taxes and duties, and thereby disgraced them with misfortune. From this time on, those who pursued this profession saw their possessions exhausted because of this severity. On several occasions, when the Xiongnu barbarians encroached on the border, the supply of grain in the border regions for the great number of people stationed there for defense was not enough. Therefore, people were conscripted to transport grain. Those who made it to the border were bestowed with rank or else excused from former crimes. The merchant laws were relaxed, and they were ordered to help the country in a time of trouble. But as the merchants became increasingly wealthy, the state's resources became more and more inadequate. Therefore the emperor used Bu Shi and promulgated the String Cash Law, and used the Covert Slander Laws of Zhang Tang and Du Zhou to tax the people. Those who taxed most successfully became honored officials. Thereafter, most merchant families of middle fortunes went bankrupt and had their goods confiscated, with nothing left for themselves. Local traders were also in great difficulties.

At the beginning of the Tang dynasty, the Grain Tax-Corvee-Cloth Tax system was initiated; beyond these no other exactions were made. The legal structure became rather lax. With the setting up of the Ever Normal Granaries system, both officials and private individuals could accumulate goods, selling them off when they were dear and buying them up when they were cheap. Further, a palace market using courtiers was set up, where several hundred people were ordered to pretend that they were buying things. The government forced down the prices on merchants' goods, which was purchasing in name but confiscation in fact.

The Song dynasty forestalled the corrupt practices of the Tang. The Office of Miscellaneous Purchasing was established, engaging capital officials and eunuchs to run it jointly, lest there be incursions into the profits. When the state storehouses were sufficiently provided for, they were ordered to discontinue purchasing. Then there was "harmonious purchasing," by which the officials were ordered to extend state funds solely for the purpose of getting people to buy. When Wang Anshi took control of the government, he put the Green Sprouts and Equitable Transport laws into effect, that made funds available in the spring that were collected in the autumn. He concentrated entirely on enriching the state. The rich and powerful merchants were all suspicious and uneasy, watching this but not daring to act, and so the whole point of trading was gone. This is the danger in taking the primary sector as unimportant and the secondary as important, for they were unable to maintain the overemphasized secondary sector.

The Ming dynasty set up prohibitions concerning border markets. It has been more meticulous than previous dynasties. Transport is supervised by the Customs Houses under the jurisdiction of the Ministry of Revenue. Wood products are supervised by the Office of Produce Levies under the jurisdiction of the Ministry of Works. The salt taxation system has both Distribution Commissions and Distribution Superintendancies; as well, there are censors to review it. The administration of the tea tax is also handled in this way. The rest is controlled by the Ministry of Revenue. Thus the laws for exactions on merchants are precise and comprehensive.

. . .

I have had occasion to survey the general outline of profitable trade. Profits in the southeast are greatest in gauze (lo), Han damask (qi), tabby-weave silk (juan), and ramie, and the best place for these is the Suzhou region. My ancestors rose up by means of the loom, and now there are a great many from the region who have become extremely wealthy through textiles. Profits in the northwest are greatest in wool, serge, felt, and fur, and the best place for these is Shaanxi. A certain family surnamed Zhang has for many generations followed the occupation of sheep-rearing, and claims to have ten thousand head of sheep. The wealthiest people in the northwest are from Shaanxi; the wealthy are also numerous in Shandong, Henan, North Zhili, and Shanxi. Merchants who are after rich profits either go west into Sichuan or else south into Guangdong and Guangxi, making on pearls, glittering stones, and timber a profit sometimes fivefold, sometimes tenfold, sometimes even a hundredfold or more, quite beyond computation.

But the profits on salt and tea are greatest. Those who aren't big merchants cannot take on these trades. Yet the trading laws impose restrictions on tea in the northwest and on salt in the southeast. It is forbidden for tea to reach the barbarians in the northwest. Since most of it is produced in the southeast, this law has been observed for a long time. It is forbidden for salt to go beyond the regions where it is marketed, yet it is everywhere, so this law has been notoriously difficult to enforce. The profit from tea when provided to the people or sold to the state is ten or twenty percent. The profit from salt when provided to the people or sold to the state is seventy or eighty percent. Hence, "if the sources are great then wealth will be abundant, and if the sources are small then the wealth will be scarce. On one hand the state will be enriched and on the other the people will also be enriched; . . . the clever have a surplus and the stupid are lacking." This is the general pattern. Most of the wealthy from my home province of Zhejiang have built that wealth through salt, though a certain merchant surnamed Jia in Hangzhou created his wealth by selling tea, and after several gene- rations that wealth has not been exhausted. "The Book of Zhou says: 'If peasants do not go out to farm there will be a dearth of food. If artisans do not go out to work there will be a scarcity of objects. If merchants do not go out to barter there will be a cutting off of the three treasures. . . . These are the sources from which the people are clothed and fed.'"

As for the border markets in the northwest and the maritime markets in the southeast, we should compare their profits and losses, and their advantages and disadvantages, for the national economy and the livelihood of the people. This is not a black and white issue. Those who compute in favour of the state recognize the profits of the border markets but not those of the maritime markets. There is a major failure in their logic. The markets on the border began by dealing in silks adulterated with ramie, but today they deal in brocades. Horses are all that the tribal chieftains trade in return. I think that if China exchanges adulterated silk for broken horses, the profit is still on our side. They carry it off and no harm comes of it. Today however we sell our brocaded silk. Once they take the gold thread and go, they never return it. When the tribesmen get the silk worn in China for useless hacks, doesn't that go against common sense? The avarice of the tribal chieftains becomes harder to control, and their appetites are never satisfied. The country has now used up the reserves of the Ministry of Agriculture. Every year we give them over a million, yet still we are not spared their harsh demands. Suppose one day they go back on their treaties and charge over into our borderlands? Their ambitions are not hard to fathom. Who can control them? If we want to preserve peace for a hundred years, I can't believe that this is the way to do it.

In the southeast, the various foreigners gain profits from our Chinese goods, and China also gains profits from the foreigners' goods. Trading what we have for what we lack is China's intention in trade. Originally we called it "tribute," and thus China's stature received greater honour and the foreigners became more compliant. In fact, a lot goes out and little comes back. The payment of tribute doesn't amount to one-ten-thousandth of what is transacted in trade. Besides, their minds are set on getting their profit through trade, not through imperial gifts. Even if their tribute were greater and our gifts more meager, they would still want to trade. We should store this wealth with the people. Why shrink from doing so? You might say, "The foreigners frequently invade; the situation is such that we cannot do business with them." But you don't understand that the foreigners will not do without their profits from China, just as we cannot do without our profits from them. Prohibit this, keep them from contact, and how can you avoid their turning to piracy? I maintain that once the maritime markets are opened, the aggressors will cease of their own accord. They are certainly not as unfathomable as the northern barbarians. What is paid out through the border markets is entirely the precious reserves of the state or the wealth of the rich. What is traded in the maritime market is entirely goods produced among the people, of no consequence to the finances of the state. The border markets operate at a loss and no gain results, whereas the maritime markets could operate at a profit and no harm would ensue. Why don't the government planners think of this?

As for taxes on China's merchants, even though they do contribute to the government's revenue, they are exacted through too many channels. This must be stopped. At every point where a merchant passes a customs house or a ford, the officials there either insist on unloading the carts or docking the boats and checking through the sacks and crates, or just overestimate the value and collect excessive payment. What has passed the customs house or ford has already been taxed, yet the markets then tax it again. One piece of merchandise should be subject to one taxing. There are the institutionalized surtax and the regular tax. The merchants cannot bear the interference caused by the further demands of constables and the exactions of sub-officials. How can merchants who have to pay double what they should not feel heavily afflicted?

I held office as Bureau Secretary in the Ministry of Works in Nanjing, and was responsible for customs duties in upper and lower Longjiang. At the time I was working together with Associate Censor Fang Keyong. I said to him: "In ancient times, 'at the passes and in the markets outsiders were inspected but their goods were not taxed'. The taxation of merchants was not what the dynasties of the sage emperors thought fitting to impose. Whether it has been imposed or not has depended on individual officials. How can we let people say that in the present they lack benevolent government?" Fang agreed with me, and together we rescinded merchants' taxes by twenty percent. From this time on, merchants delighted in coming, their boats sculling in like spokes to a hub. The state tax revenue when compared with before actually increased by fifty percent. From this it can be seen that people's minds are moved by the government's benevolence.

From: Brook, Timothy, "The Merchant Network in 16th Century China," in *Journal of the Economic and Social History of the Orient* XXIV (May 1981), (Brill Academic Publishers: Leiden, 1981).

QUESTIONS:

1. Zhang Han is intimately familiar with the Chinese state's management of network flows. What lessons does he draw from the history of that management? In his view, what interests need to be balanced in setting management policy? What debates about network management can you extract from Zhang Han's presentation of the issues?
2. What frame values lie behind the debates that Zhang Han presents, that is, what does Zhang assume about the intersection of networks and hierarchies? How are his values similar to or different from the values of the Tlaxcalan cabildo?

15.3: *Compendium and Description of the West Indies* (Antonio Vasquez de Espinosa, 1629)

Antonio Vasquez de Espinosa (d. 1630) was a Spanish-born Carmelite friar who gave up an academic career to perform ministry work in Spanish America. He published a number of books based on his experiences among the indigenous peoples of Mexico and Peru, for whom he developed great sympathy. *Compendium and Description of the West Indies* is the best known, and the book was probably not fully finished when Espinosa died in 1630. He does not consider himself an historian, but he is a keen observer and commentator. In this excerpt, he describes the mining of mercury (used to extract silver from ore) and the operations of the great silver mine at Potosì in Peru, whose "mountain of silver" significantly affected global network flows during the hundred years from 1550 to 1650, when it was most productive.

This is how they extract the mercury. On the other side of the town there are structures where they grind up the mercury ore and then put it in jars with molds like sugar loaves on top of them, with many little holes, and others on top of them, flaring and plastered with mud, and a channel for it to drip into and pass into the jar or place where it is to fall. Then they roast the ore with a straw fire from the plant growing on the puna, like esparto grass, which they call ichu; that is the best sort of fire for the treatment of this ore. Under the onset of this fire it melts and the mercury goes up in vapor or exhalation until, passing through the holes in the first mold, it hits the body of the second, and there it coagulates, rests, and comes to stop where they have provided lodging for it; [but] if it does not strike any solid body while it is hot, it rises as vapor until it cools and coagulates and starts falling downward again. Those who carry out the reduction of this ore have to be very careful and test cautiously; they must wait till the jars are cold before uncovering them for otherwise they may easily get mercury poisoning and if they do, they are of no further use; their teeth fall out, and some die. After melting and extracting the mercury by fire, they put it in dressed sheepskins to keep it in His Majesty's storehouses, and from there they usually transport it on llamaback to the port of Chincha (which is 5 leagues N. of Pisco), where there is a vault and a Factor appointed by the Royal Council, and he has charge of it there; then they freight it on shipboard to the port of San Marcos de Arica, from which it is carried by herds of llamas and mules to Potosi. In the treatment of the silver they use up every year more than 6,000 quintals, plus 2,000 more derived from the ore dust, i.e., the silver and mercury which was lost and escaped from the first washing of the ore, made in

vats. The way they handle this is as follows: every year they burn over 300,000 quintals of this ore dust in ovens, which are made in Tarapaya and other places; out of it they get a large amount of very high- grade silver together with the mercury referred to; and since when I deal with the district of the Archdiocese of the Charcas, I shall tell what I know about the mines of Potosi and their processes, this statement must suffice with regard to quicksilver and the district of Huancavelica. The Viceroy appoints a Governor here for the administration of justice, to see that the complement of the mita of Indians coming to work in the mines, is full, and to supervise the smelting.

CONTINUING TO DESCRIBE THE MAGNIFICENCE OF THE POTOSI RANGE; AND OF THE INDIANS THERE UNDER FORCED LABOR (MITA) IN ITS OPERATIONS

According to His Majesty's warrant, the mine owners on this massive range have a right to the mita of 13,300 Indians in the working and exploitation of the mines, both those which have been discovered, those now discovered, and those which shall be discovered. It is the duty of the Corregidor of Potosi to have them rounded up and to see that they come in from all the provinces between Cuzco over the whole of El Collao and as far as the frontiers of Tarija and Tomina; this Potosi Corregidor has power and authority over all the Corregidors in those provinces mentioned; for if they do not fill the Indian mita allotment assigned each one of them in accordance with the capacity of their provinces as indicated to them, he can send them, and does, salaried inspectors to report upon it, and when the remissness is great or remarkable, he can suspend them, notifying the Viceroy of the fact.

These Indians are sent out every year under a captain whom they choose in each village or tribe, for him to take them and oversee them for the year each has to serve; every year they have a new election, for as some go out, others come in. This works out very badly, with great losses and gaps in the quotas of Indians, the villages being depopulated; and this gives rise to great extortions and abuses on the part of the inspectors toward the poor Indians, ruining them and thus depriving the caciques and chief Indians of their property and carrying them off in chains because they do not fill out the mita assignment, which they cannot do, for the reasons given and for others which I do not bring forward.

These 13,300 are divided up every 4 months into 3 mitas, each consisting of 4,433 Indians, to work in the mines on the range and in the 120 smelters in the Potosi and Tarapaya areas; it is a good league between the two. These mita Indians earn each day, or there is paid each one for his labor, 4 reals. Besides these there are others not under obligation, who are mingados or hire themselves out voluntarily: these each get from 12 to 16 reals, and some up to 24, according to their reputation of wielding the pick and knowing how to get the ore out. These mingados will be over 4,000 in number. They and the mita Indians go up every Monday morning to the locality of Guayna Potosi which is at the foot of the range; the Corregidor arrives with all the provincial captains or chiefs who have charge of the Indians assigned them, and he there checks off and reports to each mine and smelter owner the number of Indians assigned him for his mine or smelter; that keeps him busy till 1 p.m., by which time the Indians are already turned over to these mine and smelter owners.

After each has eaten his ration, they climb up the hill, each to his mine, and go in, staying there from that hour until Saturday evening without coming out of the mine; their wives bring them food, but they stay constantly underground, excavating and carrying out the ore from which they get the silver. They all have tallow candles, lighted day and night; that is the light they work with, for as they are underground, they have need of it all the time. The mere cost of these candles used in the mines on this range will amount every year to more than 300,000 pesos, even though tallow is cheap in that country, being abundant; but this is a very great expense, and it is almost incredible, how much is spent for candles in the operation of breaking down and getting out the ore.

These Indians have different functions in the handling of the silver ore; some break it up with bar or pick, and dig down in, following the vein in the mine; others bring it up; others up above keep separating the good and the poor in piles; others are occupied in taking it down from the range to the mills on herds of llamas; every day they bring up more than 8,000 of these native beasts of burden for this task. These teamsters who carry the metal do not belong to the mita, but are mingados—hired.

HOW THEY GRIND AND TREAT THE SILVER ORE

The mills to grind the ore are run by water, like water mills (acenas) or gristmills. . . . Most of the mills have two heads (of water?), with great heavy stone hammers which pound the ore, the ones rising and the others falling, just as in a fulling mill, until the ore, hard as flint though some of it is, has been reduced to meal. . . .

After grinding and sifting the ore they dump it into containers. . . . Then they put the mercury in, so that by this arrangement it may better embrace and combine with the silver, and shorten the process, and bring about a union of the mercury with the silver, having thrown salt in with it; they knead it twice a day with their feet, just as they do clay in the making of tile or brick, and they remix with mercury twice a day; then they put the containers on furnaces and start the fires underneath in small ovens, so that the heat may cause the mercury to amalgamate more quickly with the silver. . . .

At the moment which seems right to them, according to the ore and the treatment given it, the mercury having already absorbed the silver, they dump this ore into large tubs with water running into them. These have a device with paddles or wheels in continual motion inside the tubs, so that the ore dust is carried off by the running water, and the combined mercury and silver, being heavier, goes to the bottom and settles there in the tubs. The rest of the ore, which was not well washed in these tubs or other puddling operations, they finish refining, until the silver and mercury alone are left, without any dust. This lump, which is soft as dough, is put in a linen cloth and squeezed hard until they press out and separate all the mercury they can from the silver. Then they put the lumps of silver which have had the mercury squeezed out, into clay forms or pots shaped like sugar loaves, with an aperture at the end of the narrowest point, and set

them in ovens specially made for the purpose; when they start the fire, the mercury goes out through the hole as vapor or smoke, but nothing is lost, thanks to the preparation made.

After the fire has severed the mercury from his friend the silver, the cone (pifia) of pure silver comes out the size and shape of a loaf of very white sugar, for silver looks very white and spongy. Each cone is usually of 40 silver marks, slightly more or less; that is the ordinary product from one container; but if the grade and richness of the ore permit, they may get two cones, as happened at the beginning when the rich range was first exploited; the same is true of certain new mines; but ordinarily it is only one. They make up a bar by melting two together. The silver refined by the mercury process is so fine and white that it is always above the 2,380 grade; and to make it fit for use by the silversmiths, they reduce the grade to . . . the legal sterling standard, by addition of copper or other alloy.

From: http://archive.org/stream/smithsonianmisce1021942smit/smithsonianmisce1021942smit_djvu.txt.

QUESTIONS:

1. What are the conditions of labor for the workers in the mercury and silver mines according to Espinosa? Why are there abuses? Whose interests do the operations of the mines serve?
2. Do the operations of the Potosì mine represent hierarchies working for network interests, networks working for hierarchy interests, or some combination of both? Explain. Would the Tlaxcalan cabildo or Zhang Han approve of the operations?

COLONIZATION

15.4a: *A Discourse on Western Planting* (Richard Hakluyt, 1584)

Richard Hakluyt (1552/3–1616) wrote this tract to gather support from English investors for founding a colony in Virginia. At the same time, he also wanted to convince Queen Elizabeth that such an enterprise would benefit England socially and economically and that it would advance English causes on the international stage. Hakluyt was an ordained priest and served as ambassador to France and as Secretary of State to both Queeen Elizabeth I and King James I. His tireless campaign to promote the colonization of Virginia finally paid off in 1606, when King James granted the right to establish a colony to The Virginia Company (the collective identity of two joint stock companies, the London Company and the Plymouth Company). His writings about the Americas were widely circulated and provided literary material for William Shakespeare, among others. Ironically, he himself never sailed farther than the English Channel.

1. That this western discovery will be greatly for the enlargement of the gospel of Christ whereunto the princes of the reformed religion are chiefly bound among whom her Majesty is principal.

. . . Then it is necessary for the salvation of those poor people who have sat so long in darkness and in the shadow of death that preachers should be sent unto them: But by whom should these preachers be sent? By them no doubt who have taken upon them the protection and defense of the Christian faith: now the Kings and Queens of England have the name of defenders of the faith: By which title I think they are not only charged to maintain and patronize the faith of Christ, but also to enlarge and advance the same. . . . Now the means to send such as shall labor effectually in this business is by planting one or two colonies of our nation upon that firm [land], where they may remain in safety, and first learn the language of the people near adjoining (the gift of tongues being now taken away) and by little and little acquaint themselves with their manner and so with discretion and mildness distill into their purged minds the sweet and lively lines of the gospel. . . .

4. That this enterprise will be for the manifold employment of numbers of idle men, and for breeding of many sufficient and for utterance of the great quantity of the commodities of our Realm.

. . . Truth it is that through our long peace and seldom sickness (two singular blessings of almighty God) we are grown more populous than ever heretofore: So that now there are of every art and science so many, that they can hardly live one by another: nay rather they are ready to eat up one another; yea many thousands of idle persons are within this Realm, which having no way to be set on work be either mutinous and seek alteration in the state, or at least very burdensome to the common wealth, and often fall to pilfering and thieving and other lewdness, whereby all the prisons of the land are daily pestered and stuffed full of them, where either they pitifully pine away, or else at length are miserably hanged. . . . [T]hese petty thieves might be condemned for certain years in the western part, especially in Newfound Land in sawing and felling of timber for masts of ships and deal boards, in burning of the fires and pine trees to make pitch, tar, rosin, and soap ashes, in beating and working of hemp for cordage: and in the more southern parts in setting them to work in mines of gold, silver, copper, lead, and iron. . . . In sum this enterprise will minister matter for all sorts and states of men to work upon: namely all several kinds of artificers, husbandmen, seamen, merchants, soldiers, captains, physicians, lawyers, divines, cosmographers, hydrographers, astronomers, historiographers, yea old folks, lame persons, women, and young children by many means which hereby shall still be ministered unto them, shall be kept from idleness, and be made able by their own honest and easy labor to find themselves without surcharging others. . . .

5. That this voyage will be a great bridle to the Indies of the king of Spain and a mean that we may arrest at our pleasure for the space of ten weeks or three months every year one or two hundred sails of his subjects' ships at the fishing in Newfound Land.

11. That the Spaniards have exercised most outrageous and more than Turkish cruelties in all the West Indies, whereby they are everywhere there become most odious unto them who would join with us or any other most willingly to shake of their most intolerable yoke, and have begun to do it already in divers places where they were lords heretofore.

12. That the passage in this voyage is easy and short, that it cuts not near the trade of any other mighty princes, or near their countries, that it is to be performed at all times of the year, and needs but one kind of wind: that Ireland being full of good havens on the south and west side, is the nearest part of Europe to it, which by this trade shall be in more security, and the sooner drawn to more civility.

In this voyage we may see by the globe that we are not to pass the burnt zone nor to pass through the frozen seas, but in a temperate climate. . . . [I]t may be sailed in five or six weeks, whereby the merchant need to expect two or three years for one return, as in the voyage of Sir Frances Drake, of Fenton and William Hawkins, but may receive two returns every year in the self same ships. . . . [Hakluyt seriously underestimates the voyage time.]

14. That this action will be for the great increase maintenance and safety of our navy, and especially of great shipping which is the strength of our Realm, and for the support of all those occupations that depend upon the same.

. . . there is a great hope the Country being as big as all Europe and nothing in fruitfulness inferior to it, as I have proved before at large in the third chapter, that we shall have two fleets as big as those of the king of Spain to his West Indies employed twice in the year at the least, especially after our fortifying in the country, the certain place of our factory being there established, whereby it must needs come to pass that our navy shall be mightily increase and maintained: which will not only be a chief strength and surety in time of wars, as well to offend as defend, but will also by the maintainance of many masters, mariners, and seamen, whereby they their wives and children shall have their livings, and many cities, towns, villages, havens, and creeks near adjoining unto the seacoast, and the Queen's subjects, as brewers, bouchers, smiths, ropers, shipwrights, tailors, shoemakers, and other victuallers and handicrafts men inhabiting and dwelling near thereabouts shall also have by the same great part of their living. . . .

20. A Brief collection of certain reasons to induce her Majesty and the state to take in hand the western voyage and the planting there.

1. The soil yields and may be made to yield all the several commodities of Europe, and of all kingdoms, dominions, and territories that England trades with, that by trade of merchandise comes into this Realm.

2. The passage there and home is neither too long nor too short, but easy and to be made twice in the year.

3. The passage cuts not near the trade of any prince, nor near any of their countries or territories and is safe passage, and not easy to be annoyed by prince or potentate whatsoever.

4. The passage is to be performed at all times of the year. . . .

6. This enterprise may stay the Spanish king from flowing over all the face of that waste firm of America, if we seat and plant there in time. . . .

8. This new navy of mighty new strong ships so in trade to that Norumbega [Virginia] and to the coasts there, shall never be subject to arrest of any prince or potentate, as the navy of this Realm from time to time has been in the ports of the empire. . . .

10. No foreign commodity that comes into England comes without payment of custom once twice or thrice before it come into the Realm, . . . and by this course to Norumbega foreign princes' customs are avoided. . . .

12. By the great plenty of those regions the merchants and their factors shall lie there cheap, and shall return at pleasure without stay or restraint of foreign prince, . . . and so he shall be rich and not subject to many hazards, but shall be able to afford the commodities for cheap prices to all subjects of the Realm. . . .

16. We shall by planting there enlarge the glory of the Gospel and from England plant sincere religion, and provide a safe and a sure place to receive people from all parts of the world that are forced to flee for the truth of God's word.

17. If frontier wars there chance to arise, and if thereupon we shall fortify, it will occasion the training up of our youth in the discipline of war. . . .

18. The Spaniards govern in the Indies with all pride and tyranny, and like as when people of contrary nature at the sea enter into galleys, where men are tied as slaves, all yell and cry with once voice liberta, liberta, as desirous of liberty or freedom, so no doubt whensoever the Queen of England, a prince of such clemency, shall sit upon that firm of America, and shall be reported throughout all that tract to use the natural people there with all humanity, courtesy, and freedom, they will yield themselves to her government and revolt clean from the Spaniard. . . .

22. The fry [children] of the wandering beggars of England that grow up idly and hurtful and burdenous to this Realm, may there be unladen, better bred up. . . .

23. If England cry out and affirm that there is so many in all trades that one cannot live for another as in all places they do, this Norumbega (if it be thought so good) offers the remedy.

From: Quinn, David B., and Allison M. Quinn, eds., *Discourse of Western Planting,* (London: Hakluyt Society, 1993).

QUESTIONS:

1. What kinds of reasons does Hakluyt cite to persuade the Queen to invest in this enterprise? Does he emphasize economic, military, social, or religious reasons most heavily?
2. How does the attitude towards trade and the proposal for colonization by a partnership of state and private interests compare to the attitudes expressed by the Tlaxcalan cabildo or Zhang Han?

15.4b: *Letter to William Pitt the Elder* (Robert Clive, 1759)

Robert Clive (1725–1774) rose through the ranks of the British East India Company unit of the British Army to become Commander-in-Chief of India. Under his military and political leadership, the Company became the leading political power in the subcontinent, and British India became the cornerstone of a growing British Empire in South and East Asia. This letter to William Pitt the Elder, the prime minister of Britain at the time, dates from the early years of his leadership and lays out his plans and ambitions while asking for additional military investment by the State. Clive's career (he also served as a Member of Parliament) and this letter illustrate perfectly British participation in the global network, a peculiar but very successful partnership between state (hierarchy) and private investment (network mechanisms; the company was a joint stock company). That success was qualified, however: company rule in India created serious problems that led to administrative reforms of the company and to a decline in Clive's political reputation.

The close attention you bestow on the affairs of the British nation in general has induced me to trouble you with a few particulars relative to India, and to lay before you an exact account of the revenues of this country, the genuineness whereof you may depend upon, as it has been faithfully extracted from the Minister's books.

The great revolution that has been effected here by the success of the English arms, and the vast advantages gained to the Company [British East India Company] by a treaty concluded in consequence thereof, have, I observe, in some measure, engaged the public attention; but much more may yet in time be done, if the Company will exert themselves in the manner the importance of their present possessions and future prospects deserves. I have represented to them in the strongest terms the expediency of sending out and keeping up constantly such a force as will enable them to embrace the first opportunity of further aggrandizing themselves; and I dare pronounce, from a thorough knowledge of this country's government, and of the genius of the people, acquired by two years' application and experience, that such an opportunity will soon offer. The reigning Subah [provincial governor of the Mughal Empire], whom the [British] victory at Plassey invested with the sovereignty of these provinces, still, it is true, retains his attachment to us, and probably, while he has no other support, will continue to do so; but Muslims are so little influenced by gratitude, that should he ever think it his interest to break with us, the obligations he owes us would prove no restraint: and this is very evident from his having lately removed his Prime Minister, and cut off two or three principal officers, all attached to our interest, and who had a share in his elevation. Moreover, he is advanced in years; and his son is so cruel, worthless a young fellow, and so apparently an enemy to the English, that it will be almost unsafe trusting him with the succession. So small a body as two thousand Europeans will secure us against any apprehensions from either the one or the other; and, in case of their daring to be troublesome, enable the Company to take the sovereignty upon themselves.

There will be the less difficulty in bringing about such an event, as the natives themselves have no attachment whatever to particular princes; and as, under the present Government, they have no security for their lives or properties, they would rejoice in so happy an exchange as that of a mild for a despotic Government: and there is little room to doubt our easily obtaining the Mughal's grant in confirmation thereof, provided we agreed to pay him the stipulated allotment out of the revenues, viz. fifty lacs [i.e. 5 million rupees] annually. This has, of late years, been very ill-paid, owing to the distractions in the heart of the Mughal Empire, which have disabled that court from attending to their concerns in the distant provinces: and the Vizier has actually wrote [sic] to me, desiring I would engage the [Subah] to make the payments agreeable to the former usage. . . . That this would be agreeable to the Mughal can hardly be questioned, as it would be so much to his interest to have there countries under the dominion of a nation famed for their good faith, rather than in the hands of people who, a long experience has convinced him, never will pay him his proportion of the revenues, unless awed into it by the fear of the Imperial army marching to force them thereto.

But so large a sovereignty may possibly be an object too extensive for a mercantile Company; and it is to be feared they are not of themselves able, without the nation's assistance, to maintain so wide

a dominion. I have therefore presumed, Sir, to represent this matter to you, and submit it to your consideration, whether the execution of a design, that may hereafter be still carried to greater lengths, be worthy of the Government's taking it into hand. I flatter myself I have made it pretty clear to you, that there will be little or no difficulty in obtaining the absolute possession of these rich kingdoms; and that with the Mughal's own consent, on condition of paying him less than a fifth of the revenues thereof. Now I leave you to judge, whether an income yearly of upwards of two millions sterling, with the possession of three provinces abounding in the most valuable productions of nature and of art, be an object deserving the public attention; and whether it be worth the nation's while to take the proper measures to secure such an acquisition, an acquisition which, under the management of so able and disinterested a minister, would prove a source of immense wealth to the kingdom, and might in time be appropriated in part as a fund towards diminishing the heavy load of debt under which we at present labor. Add to these advantages the influence we shall thereby acquire over the several European nations engaged in the commerce here, which these could no longer carry on but through our indulgence, and under such limitations as we should think fit to prescribe. It is well worthy of consideration, that this project may be brought about without draining the mother country, as has been too much the case with our possessions in America. A small force from home will be sufficient, as we always make sure of any number we please of black [Indian] troops, who, being both much better paid and treated by us than by the country's powers, will very readily enter into our service. . . .

The greatest part of the troops belonging to this establishment are now employed in an expedition against the French in Deccan; and, by the accounts lately received from thence, I have great hopes we shall succeed in extirpating them from the province of Golconda [in central India], where they have reigned lords paramount so long, and from whence they have drawn their principal resources during the troubles upon the coast. . . .

May the zeal and the vigorous measures, projected from the services of the nation, which have so eminently distinguished your ministry, be crowned with all the success they deserve, is the most fervent wish of him who is, with the greatest respect,

Sir,

Your most devoted humble servant,

[Signed] Robert Clive

Calcutta,

7th January, 1759

From: John Malcolm, *The Life of Robert, Lord Clive* (London: John Murray, 1836), 2: pp. 119–25.

QUESTIONS:

1. What mechanisms of cooperation between the British state and the British East India Company does Clive reveal in this letter? How did Hakluyt's plan for colonizing Virginia foreshadow these mechanisms?
2. What would the Tlaxcalan cabildo, Zhang Han, or Espinosa make of Clive's letter and the institutional arrangements connecting the British state and the Company? Would they approve or disapprove? Would they even understand them? In other words, how do British frame values in 1760 differ from the frame values revealed by the other sources in this chapter?

The Late Agrarian World II: Hierarchies in a Global System, 1500–1750

INTRODUCTION

The networked Late Agrarian Era posed challenges to the rulers of hierarchies but also provided new resources for managing those problems. The selection of sources presented here show how different hierarchies faced their challenges, which ranged from managing the internal politics of vast Agrarian empires to dealing with rivalries and military conflict involving other hierarchies and the activities of the global network.

16.1:   *Memoirs* (Jahangir, 1605)

The third Mughal emperor, Nur-ad-Din Mohammad Salim (1569–1627), known by his imperial name Jahangir ("world-grasper"), ruled the Mughal Empire from 1605 until his death. He proved to be an able ruler, building on the strong foundations of his father Akbar's and grandfather Babur's reigns to maintain political stability and a thriving economy—he was probably the richest ruler in the world at the time. He was a patron of the arts, and he followed in the tradition of his father and grandfather by writing his memoirs as his reign progressed. They are known by the title *Jahangirnama,* like the *Baburnama* and the *Akbarnama.* He went beyond the recounting of political and military deeds that was the focus of his predecessors' memoirs, however, as he included thoughts about art, culture, and religion as well as personal reflections. This selection recounts the opening of his reign.

For a memorial of sundry events incidental to myself, I have undertaken to describe a small portion, in order that some traces thereof may be preserved on the records of time. On Thursday, then, the eighth of the latter month of Jummaudy, of the year of the Hidjera one thousand and fourteen [1605], at the metropolis of Agrah, and in the forenoon of the day, being then arrived at the age of thirty-eight, I became Emperor, and under auspices the most felicitous, took my seat on the throne of my wishes. Let it not produce a smile that I should have set my heart on the delusions of this world. Am I greater than Solomon, who placed his pillow upon the winds? As at the very instant that I seated myself on the throne the sun rose from the horizon, I accepted this as the omen of victory, and as indicating a reign of unvarying prosperity. Hence I assumed the titles of Jahangir Padshah, and Jahangir Shah: the world-subduing emperor; the world-subduing king. I ordained that the following legend should be stamped on the coinage of the empire: " Stricken at Agrah by that Khossrou, the safeguard of the world; the sovereign splendour of the faith, Jahangir, son of the imperial Akbar."

Having thus seated myself on the throne of my expectations and wishes, I caused also the imperial crown, which my father had caused to be made after the manner of that which was worn by the great kings of Persia, to be brought before me, and then, in the presence of the whole assembled Amirs, having placed it on my brows, as an omen auspicious to the stability and happiness of my reign, kept it there for the space of a full astronomical hour. On each of the twelve points of this crown was a single diamond . . . , the whole purchased by my father with the resources of his own government, not from any thing accruing to him by inheritance from his predecessors. At the point in the centre of the top part of the crown was a single pearl . . . ; and on different parts of the same were set altogether two hundred rubies. . . .

For forty days and forty nights I caused the nuggaurah, or great imperial state drum, to strike up, without ceasing, the strains of joy and triumph; and for an extent of nearly fifty zereibs around my throne, the ground was spread by my directions with the most costly brocades and gold embroidered carpets. Censors of gold and silver were disposed in different directions for the purpose of burning odoriferous drugs, and nearly three thousand camphorated wax lights, three cubits in length, in branches of gold and silver perfumed with ambergris, illuminated the scene from night till

morning. Numbers of blooming youths, beautiful as young Joseph in the pavilions of Egypt, clad in dresses of the most costly materials, woven in silk and gold, with zones and amulets sparkling with the lustre of the diamond, the emerald, the sapphire, and the ruby, awaited my commands, rank after rank, and in attitude most respectful. And finally, the Amirs of the empire, from the captain of five hundred to the commander of five thousand horse, and to the number of nine individuals, covered from head to foot in gold and jewels, and shoulder to shoulder, stood round in brilliant array, also waiting for the commands of their sovereign. For forty days and forty nights did I keep open to the world these scenes of festivity and splendour, furnishing altogether an example of imperial magnificence seldom paralleled in this stage of earthly existence.

. . . I might have been contented to the last with the title of Sultan Seleim: but to place myself on a par with the monarchs of the Turkish empire (Roum), and considering that universal conquest is the peculiar vocation of sovereign princes, I thought it incumbent on me to assume at my accession that of Jahangir Padshah, as the title which best suited my character: and I trust, with the aid of a gracious Providence, with length of life, and a favouring star, that I shall so acquit myself as to justify the appellation.

The very first ordinance which issued from me, on ascending the throne of my ancestors, was that which related to the chain of justice, one end of which I caused to be fastened to the battlements of the royal tower of the castle of Agrah, and the other to a stone pillar near the bed of the river Jumnah; to the end that, when at any time the dispensers of law under my authority might fail in the administration of justice, the injured party by applying his hand to the chain would find himself in the way of obtaining speedy redress. The chain was of gold, one hundred and forty guzz in length, with eighty small bells attached at different distances. . . .

I instituted twelve special regulations, to be applied by the different functionaries of the empire as rules of conduct, never to be deviated from in their respective stations.

1. I remitted altogether to my subjects three of the several sources of revenue. . . .

2. I ordained that wherever the property of God's people entrusted to my charge should be wrested from them, either by highway robbery or any other act of violence, the inhabitants of the district, as best knowing whence it proceeded, should be compelled to produce either the property or the depredator. I directed, when the district lay waste or destitute of inhabitants, that towns should be built, and the population registered, and every method resorted to that might contribute to protect the subject from injury. I charged the Jaguirdaurs, or feudatories of the empire, in such deserted places to erect mosques and substantial serrais, or stations for the accommodation of travellers, in order to render the district once more an inhabited country, and that wayfaring men might again be able to pass and repass in safety. For these purposes I provided that where the district was immediately dependent on the crown, and the residence of a Kroury, that officer was authorized to prosecute these works at the expense of the imperial treasury.

3. Merchants travelling through the country were not to have their bales or packages of any kind opened without their consent. But when they were perfectly willing to dispose of any article of merchandise purchasers were permitted to deal with them, without, however, offering any species of molestation.

4. When a person shall die and leave children, the individual not being in the employment of the state, no man whatever was to interfere a pin's point in his property, nor to offer the slightest molestation to the children: but when there were neither children nor direct or unquestionable heirs, the inheritance was to be applied to defray the expenses incurred for mosques and talaub, or watertanks, so as to secure perpetual blessings on the soul of the departed.

5. No person was permitted either to make or sell either wine or any other kind of intoxicating liquor. I undertook to institute this regulation, although it is sufficiently notorious that I have myself the strongest inclination for wine, in which from the age of sixteen I have liberally indulged. And in very truth, encompassed as I was with youthful associates of congenial minds, breathing the air of a delicious climate—ranging through lofty and splendid saloons, every part of which decorated with all the graces of painting and sculpture, and the floors bespread with the richest carpets of silk and gold, would it not have been a species of folly to have rejected the aid of an exhilarating cordial—and what cordial can surpass the juice of the grape? May it not happen that theriauk, or opiates, or stimulants, have been rendered habitual to the constitution and heaven forbid that this should deprive a man of the most generous feelings of his nature. With some acknowledged beneficial effects, it must however be confessed, that these indulgences to excess must expose a man's infirmities, prostrate his constitutional vigour, and awaken false desires, such being the most injurious properties belonging to the list of stimulants. At the same time, we cannot but remember that kelourica is brother's son to theriauk.

For myself, I cannot but acknowledge that such was the excess to which I had carried my indulgence, that my usual daily allowance extended to twenty, and sometimes to more than twenty cups, each cup containing half a seir [about six ounces]. . . . So far, indeed, was this baneful propensity carried, that if I were but an hour without my beverage, my hands began to shake and I was unable to sit at rest. Convinced by these symptoms, that if the habit gained upon me in this proportion my situation must soon become one of the utmost peril, I felt it full time to devise some expedient to abate the evil: and in six months I accordingly succeeded in reducing my quantity gradually from twenty to five cups a day. At entertainments I continued, however, to indulge in a cup or two more: and on most occasions I made it a rule never to commence my indulgence until about two hours before the close of the day. But now that the affairs of the empire demand my utmost vigilance and attention, my potations do not commence until after the hour of evening prayer, my quantity never exceeding five cups on any occasion; neither would more than that quantity suit the state of my stomach. Once a day I take my regular meal, and once a day seems quite sufficient to assuage my appetite for wine; but as drink seems not less necessary than meat for the sustenance of man, it appears very difficult, if not impossible, for me to discontinue altogether the use of wine. Nevertheless, I bear in mind, and I trust in heaven that, like my grandfather Homayun, who succeeded in divesting himself of the habit before he attained to the age of forty-five, I also may be supported in my resolution, some time or other to abandon the pernicious practice altogether. "In a point wherein God has pronounced his sure displeasure, let the creature exert himself ever so little towards amendment, and it may prove, in no small degree, the means of eternal salvation."

6. No person was permitted to take up his abode obtrusively in the dwelling of any subject of my realm. On the contrary, when individuals serving in the armies of the state came to any town, and could without compulsion secure an abode by rent, it were commendable; otherwise they were to pitch their tents without the place, and prepare habitations for themselves. For what grievance could be more irksome to the subject than to see a perfect stranger obtrude into the bosom of his family, and take possession most probably of the most convenient part of his dwelling, leaving to his women and children, peradventure, not space enough to stretch out an arm!

7. No person was to suffer, for any offence, the loss of a nose or ear. If the crime were theft, the offender was to be scourged with thorns, or deterred from further transgression by an attestation on the Koran.

8. The Krouries and Jaguirdaurs [local officials] were prohibited from possessing themselves by violence of the lands of the subject, or from cultivating them on their own account; neither was the Jaguirdaur or feudatory of any district to exercise any sort of authority beyond the limits of his own, nor to force either man or beast from another district into his own. On the contrary, his attention was to be wholly and exclusively devoted to the cultivation and improvement of the district allotted to himself.

9. [unintelligible]

10. The governors in all the principal cities were directed to establish infirmaries or hospitals, with competent medical aid for the relief of the sick, who were to be conveyed thither; the expense to be defrayed from the imperial exchequer until the final recovery of the patient, who was then to be discharged with a sufficient sum of money for his exigencies.

11. During the month of my birth, which was that of the former Rebbeia, the use of all animal food was prohibited both in town and country; and at equidistant periods throughout the year a day was set apart, on which all slaughtering of animals was strictly forbidden. In every week also, on Thursday, that being the day of my accession, and Sunday, was forbidden the use of animal food, it being considered unjustifiable to deprive any animal of life on that day on which the creation of the world was finished. For a period of more than eleven years was the same abstinence observed by my father, during which on no consideration would he permit himself to taste of animal food on a Sunday. On that day, therefore, I thought it right to prohibit the use of such food in every place throughout my dominions.

12. I issued a decree confirming the dignitaries and feudatories of my father's government in all that they had enjoyed while he was living; and where I found sufficient merit, I conferred an advance of rank in various gradations. Thus a commander of ten horse I advanced to the command of fifteen, and so on in proportion to the highest dignitaries of the realm.

From: Jahangir, and David Price, *Memoirs of the Emperor Jahangir*, (London: printed for the Oriental translation committee, and sold by J. Murray1829 [1605]), pp. 1–8.

QUESTIONS:

1. What practical measures does Jahangir institute at the beginning of his reign? What problems do these measures address? What symbolic acts does he undertake, and what problems or issues do those symbolic acts address?
2. What screen image does Jahangir project of himself? What audience does he seem to intend this image for? Does his confession about his weakness for wine surprise you? Why do you think he included it?

16.2: Kangxi, *Foreign Correspondence* (Kangxi, 1693, 1716, 1722)

The Kangxi Emperor (1954–1722, r. 1661–1722) established a well-deserved reputation as one of China's greatest rulers. The second Manchu Emperor to rule over all of China, his was the longest reign in Chinese history (though his son Qianlong's period of effective rule was actually longer). Under his direction, Qing China achieved high levels of economic prosperity and cultural productivity and expanded to its greatest territorial extent. Expansionism brought the Middle Kingdom into greater contact, and sometimes conflict, with other expanding hierarchies, especially Russia, while the expansion of the global trade network also expanded its relations with European merchants and their cultures. The foreign correspondence of Kangxi excerpted here illustrates how the ruler directly managed the sorts of issues China's foreign relations created.

(NOV.24, 1693) THE EMPEROR PREDICTS THAT RUSSIA COULD BE A THREAT TO CHINA

The Ch'a-han Khan of Russia sent an ambassador to present tribute. The grand secretariat had the Russian memorial of presentation translated and handed it in. Thereupon the Emperor said:

"The Kingdom of Russia has many able men, but they are narrow-minded, obstinate, and their argument is slow. From ancient times they have never communicated with China (sic.). Their country is very remote from our capital, but we can reach their territory directly by the land route. If we travel about eleven or twelve days from the Chia-yü. Pass (of the Great Wall), we arrive at Turfan, beyond which lies Russia. We hear that their territory covers more than twenty thousand li. . . .

"Although it is splendid that the foreign vassal (wai-fan) should come to present tribute, We fear that after many generations, Russia might cause trouble. In short, as long as the Middle Kingdom is at peace and is strong, foreign disturbances will not arise. Therefore, building up our strength is a matter of fundamental importance."

. . .

NEW REGULATIONS CONCERNING RUSSIAN AFFAIRS LEGISLATED

. . .

In the thirty-second year of K'ang-hsi, the Emperor approved the following deliberation of the Li-fan Yüan:

When the Russian merchants come to Peking for trade, they should number no more than two hundred and should come only once every three years. They should furnish their own horses and camels. Their commodities shall not be taxed, but they are not allowed to trade in contraband goods. After they arrive at Peking, they are to be located in Russian House (O-lo-ssu Kuan). They are not to receive government provisions. They may remain only eighty days in Peking.

Again it was deliberated and approved that the memorial of the Ch'a-han Khan of Russia was not proper according to our official forms.

Therefore, both their tribute and their memorial were ordered returned to them. However, since the location of that said country was far away and they were ignorant of Chinese institutions, we should clearly inform them why their memorial was improper. When the envoy was given an audience, he was given gracious gifts as usual. The goods which he brought with him were ordered to be traded as usual. Hereafter, when the memorial of Russia arrives at the frontier, the general of Hei-lung-chiang is ordered to open and scrutinize its form to see whether it conforms to proper specifications. If it is improper, he should stop it right there. Only after the general has scrutinized and passed its form can this memorial be submitted to the Court. On the day the envoy arrived at Peking he was ordered to present the memorial by kneeling before a table covered with yellow satin at the entrance of the Palace, Wu Gate, and to perform the three genuflections and nine kowtows.

Deliberations concerning the Russians who secretly violated the borders had been approved. They should be seized and turned over to the officials responsible for punishing them according to the degree of their guilt. There were Russians who secretly penetrated as far as the Ching-ch'i-li River to hunt sables and to explore, unknown, perhaps, to the Russian authorities. We should communicate with the chief of Ni-pu-ch'ao to investigate the facts and punish the Russians and to proclaim to the people of their own country that hereafter they are not allowed to cross the border. If the chief of this city does not strictly enforce this law, then we should communicate with the Ch'a-han Khan and let him punish the chief of the city (of Ni-pu-ch'ao).

55:10:26 (DEC. 9, 1716) THE EMPEROR PREDICTS DANGER FROM THE WEST

The Emperor decreed to the grand secretaries and ministers of the Nine Boards: "Everything on this earth begins small but grows large. We should not neglect the small things, although We must naturally pay more attention to the large ones. . . . For instance, naval defence is most important today. Because We have frequently made inquiries, We well know its origin. Perhaps the viceroys, governors, provincial commanders and brigade-generals of the various provinces do not know the details so clearly.

"When We made Our southern progress through Su-chou, We visited the shipyard and asked questions. We learned that every year seafarers, possibly over 1,000, built ships to go abroad. Only five or six out of ten returned their ships to China; the rest just sold their ships abroad, and they brought back only silver. When our government built several scores of ships, We knew the price was several ten thousand liang of silver. That is very great! How can our people afford to build so many ships (over 1,000) that will cost them millions and millions [without some secrecy]?

"Moreover, some ministers have memorialized that the keel-block of the ships must be made from the timber of T'ieh-li-li wood which grows only in Kwangtung and is not produced in foreign lands. Therefore, the merchants, seeking profit, sell it secretly. However, when We investigate, they all pretend that their ships were wrecked. This evil must stop at once.

"Beyond the ocean lie Luzon, Batavia, and other places which serve as asylum for the Chinese outlaws. From the time of the Ming dynasty, these places have been the headquarters of the Chinese pirates. However, when our government sea-patrols discover that pirate ships out-number them five to one, they cannot attack. Moreover, the sailors will not be eager to use the oars, and so our officers may become helpless. The government ships can only lag behind the pirates. How can this method achieve their annihilation?

"Chang Po-hsing had memorialized that the rice of Kiangnan and Chekiang was being mostly exported. This statement is not necessarily true, but We cannot neglect to prevent any such procedure even before it takes place. When seafarers go abroad to trade, their journey is either seven or eight keng (sea watches), or at most, twenty <u>keng.</u>

They should bring only sufficient rice for their journey and not more than that amount.

"Moreover, our commercial ships are allowed to trade in the Eastern ocean, but they are not allowed in the Southern ocean. We allow only the ships of the red-haired barbarians to come from the Southern ocean.

"Furthermore, when our ships sail for the Southern ocean, they must pass through Hai-t'an. If they are intercepted there, how can they cross the sea? The fortresses along the seacoasts are not good enough to guard against the smugglers. Therefore, We order that the fortresses built in the Ming dynasty should now be re-established in all of the provinces.

"In past years when we shipped rice from Fukien to Kwangtung, we hired 300 to 400 ships from our people, each ship manned by thirty to forty sailors, a total of several thousand. We must not neglect to guard their assembling on the sea.

"The people of T'ai-wan and the Chinese in Luzon often exchange visits; We must prevent this. Moreover, in order to gather more information on this matter, all natives of the maritime provinces, Fukien, Kwangtung, and Chekiang, who reside in the Imperial capital, should be carefully questioned by you people. We have ordered the general of Kwang-chou, Kuan Yüan-chung, the viceroy of Chekiang and Fukien, Manpao, and the viceroy of Liang-Kwang, Yang Lin, to come to Court for an audience. Then We wish to discuss this matter in person. After hundreds of years, We are afraid that the Middle Kingdom will suffer injury from the overseas countries, for example, from the European countries. This is only a prediction.

"Again We are also afraid that the hearts of the Chinese people (Hanjen) are divided. Oh! If they could unite like one person! The Manchus and the Mongols, numbering several thousand thousand people, have always had a united heart. We have reigned in the Empire so many years and found the Chinese very difficult to deal with because their hearts are divided. Now that our country has long enjoyed peace and order, We must not forget danger. We must wait until Kuan Yüan-chung and the other officials arrive at Peking; then carefully consider this matter together." (270,15a–16b)

56:4:14 (MAY 24, 1717) CH'EN MAO REQUESTS THE PROHIBITION OF CATHOLICISM

The Board of War reported their deliberation: "In a memorial Ch'en Mao, the brigade-general of Chien-shih, Kwangtung, said:

Catholicism originated in Europe; now the Westerners have set up churches in various provinces which attract bandits and rascals. The hearts of these Westerners are inconceivable. At present they have established many churches both within and without the city of Canton. Moreover, their foreign ships also throng in the harbor of Canton. How can we guarantee that the missionaries and Western merchants do not communicate with each other and cause trouble?

"Thereupon he petitioned for an edict to prohibit Catholicism early enough to prevent it from developing and spreading everywhere.

"The Board consulted a deliberation on Catholicism of the eighth year of K'ang-hsi, when the following edict had been received:

Nan Huai-jen (Verbiest) and others may exceptionally be allowed to practise Catholicism at the Court. Missionaries are still forbidden to set up churches and preach in the provinces. Our people are still strictly forbidden to follow this religion.

However, after many years had elapsed, this law was relaxed. We should order the Eight Banners and provinces of the Interior and the territories of Feng-t'ien and other places to prohibit it once more."

The Emperor approved this memorial.

(OCT. 16, 1722) T'U-LI-SHEN'S REPORT ON LANGE'S RETURN TO RUSSIA

"Your servant escorted the vice-ambassador of Russia, Lange (Lang-k'o) to Selenginsk. On the day of his return, Lange called at Your servant's residence (at Selenginsk) and kowtowed towards the southeast to return his thanks for the Imperial favor. Then he said to Your servant:

I am a petty, humble man of a remote and backward foreign land. Previously I had accompanied the Western doctor, Ka-er-fei-yin (Garvin) to Peking, and I received the extraordinary honor from the heavenly great August Emperor. Yet again, at that time when our Ch'a-han Khan specially sent us to respectfully inquire after the health of the great August Emperor and present our local products, I was loaded with great favors, such as nobody had ever enjoyed heretofore. I have lived in Peking for two years, and I have eaten the most delicious food that anybody ever tasted in his life. Moreover, I saw many places which few people in the world have seen. The great grace of the great August Emperor is as immense as the sea and the mountains. Food, clothes, and various objects His Majesty bestowed on me in such abundance that I cannot enumerate them. Therefore, I can find no words to express my thanks. As to the honor which His Majesty conferred on me and the kindness which His Majesty bestowed on me, personally, they are engraved indelibly on my heart. I shall thank and remember His Majesty all day long and only pray for long life for the great August Emperor who has given me this great happiness. May His Majesty be strong and healthy for millions and millions of years! I shall sincerely pray to Heaven and the Buddha (sic.) for His Majesty from morn till night. I, Lange, beg your Honor (Cha-er-hu-ch'i), to forward the sincere thanks of an ant-like, insignificant person to the ears of the Buddha-like great August Emperor."

This memorial was received on the seventh day of the ninth month of the sixty-first year of K'ang-hsi.

From: Fu, Lo-shu, *A documentary chronicle of Sino-Western relations, 1644–1820* (Tucson: Published for the Association for Asian Studies by the University of Arizona Press, 1966), pp. 106–7, 122–24, 136–37.

QUESTIONS:

1. What practical problems does the Kangxi Emperor face, and what measures does he take to meet them? What sources of information does he seem to have for both the problems and the possibilities for their solution?
2. What screen image does the Kangxi Emperor wish to project of China to foreigners? How, in turn, does he see foreigners? What role does image projection play in diplomacy and in relation to practical policy measures?

DECREES BY PETER THE GREAT

Kangxi's contemporary Pyotr Alexeyevech (1672–1725, r. 1682–1725), known to western Europeans as Peter the Great, was Czar of Russia during a period of imperial expansion, especially eastwards into Siberia (entailing the contact with China that we saw in the previous source). Peter also led expansion southwards, bringing Russia into conflict with the Ottoman Empire, and faced serious challenges from western European powers. It was to the latter that he turned his attention in terms of internal policy, initiating a series of reforms designed to make Russia more "western" in culture, military ability, and science. The Great Northern War (1700–21) with Charles XII's Sweden, which saw the Swedish king launch an invasion deep into Russian territory, was a key catalyst for Peter's policy decrees. The decrees excerpted here show us some of Peter's goals and the reasons he thought they were important.

16.3a: On "German" (Western) Dress (1701)

Western ["German"] dress shall be worn by all the boyars, okol'nichie, members of our councils and of our court . . . gentry of Moscow, secretaries . . . provincial gentry, deti boiarskie, gosti, government officials, strel'tsy, members of the guilds purveying for our household, citizens of Moscow of all ranks, and residents of provincial cities . . . excepting the clergy (priests, deacons, and church attendants) and peasant tillers of the soil. The upper dress shall be of French or Saxon cut, and the lower dress and underwear—[including] waistcoat, trousers, boots, shoes, and hats-shall be of the German type. They shall also ride German saddles. [Likewise] the women-folk of all ranks, including the priests', deacons', and church attendants' wives, the wives of the dragoons, the soldiers, and the strel'tsy, and their children, shall wear Western ["German"]

dresses, hats, jackets, and underwear—undervests and petticoats—and shoes. From now on no one [of the above-mentioned] is to wear Russian dress or Circassian coats, sheepskin coats, or Russian peasant coats, trousers, boots, and shoes. It is also forbidden to ride Russian saddles, and the craftsmen shall not manufacture them or sell them at the marketplaces. [Note: For a breach of this decree a fine was to be collected at the town gates: forty copecks from a pedestrian and two rubles from a mounted person.]

16.3b: On the Shaving of Beards and Moustaches (1705)

A decree to be published in Moscow and in all the provincial cities: Henceforth, in accordance with this, His Majesty's decree, all court attendants . . . provincial service men, government officials of all ranks, military men, all the gosti, members of the wholesale merchants' guild, and members of the guilds purveying for our household must shave their beards and moustaches. But, if it happens that some of them do not wish to shave their beards and moustaches, let a yearly tax be collected from such persons: from court attendants . . . provincial service men, military men, and government officials of all ranks–60 rubles per person; from the gosti and members of the wholesale merchants' guild of the first class–100 rubles per person; from

members of the wholesale merchants' guild of the middle and the lower class [and] . . . from [other] merchants and townsfolk–60 rubles per person; . . . from townsfolk [of the lower rank], boyars' servants, stagecoachmen, waggoners, church attendants (with the exception of priests and deacons), and from Moscow residents of all ranks–30 rubles per person. Special badges shall be issued to them from the Prikaz of Land Affairs [of Public Order] . . . which they must wear. . . . As for the peasants, let a toll of two half-copecks per beard be collected at the town gates each time they enter or leave a town; and do not let the peasants pass the town gates, into or out of town, without paying this toll.

16.3c: Bringing Shipbuilding to Russia (from the Preamble to the Naval Service Regulations, 1717)

Thus he [Peter] *turned all his thoughts to building a fleet; and when, on account of the Tatar attacks, Azov had been besieged, and later successfully taken,* he could not bear to deliberate long over his unalterable desire but quickly set about the work. A suitable place for shipbuilding was found on the river Voronezh just below the city of that name, skilled shipwrights were called in from England

and Holland, and a new enterprise was started in Russia in 1696–the building of ships, galleys, and other boats–at a great expense. So that this work would be established in Russia forever, he decided to introduce this art among his people. For this purpose he sent a large number of noble-born persons to Holland and to other states to study naval architecture and seamanship.

And what is even more remarkable, the monarch, as if ashamed to lag behind his subjects in this art, himself undertook a journey to Holland, and in Amsterdam, *at the East India shipyard,* he devoted himself, together with his other volunteers, to learning naval architecture; in a short time he perfected himself *in what a good ship's carpenter should know,* and with his own labor and skill he built and launched a new ship.

Then he asked Jan Pool, the master shipwright of that shipyard, to teach him the proportions of ships, which he showed him in four days. In Holland, however, this art is not perfected in accordance with the principles of geometry but is guided by a few rules only, and for the rest it is based on practical experience of long standing; the above-mentioned master shipwright also told him this and said that he was

incapable of showing him everything on a draft; then he felt disgusted that he had undertaken such a long journey without attaining the desired aim. Several days later His Majesty happened to be at a gathering at the country house of the merchant Jan Tessingh, where he sat very unhappy for the reason mentioned. When, in the midst of the conversation he was asked why he was so gloomy, he explained the reason. Among those present there said that in England naval architecture had was an Englishman who, upon hearing this, been perfected as much as any other and that it was possible to learn it in a short time. His Majesty was overjoyed at these words, and without delay he went to England, where he mastered this science within four months; and, returning from there, he brought with him two master shipwrights—John Deane and Joseph Ney.

16.3d: The Foundation of the Academy of Sciences (1724)

[The Emperor has ordered] an Academy to be instituted for the study of languages, likewise of other sciences and notable arts, and for the translation of books. . . . It will be maintained by the money collected from the customs and licenses in the cities of Narva, Derpt, Pernov, and Arensburg, namely 24,912 rubles. . . .

The growth of arts and sciences is generally furthered by means of two different systems: one being called University, the other Academy or Society of Arts and Sciences. . . .

Since at present a system for the cultivation of arts and sciences has yet to be set up in Russia, it is impossible to follow here the pattern accepted in other countries; but it is fitting, in accordance with the state of our Empire, and in the interests of both teachers and students, to institute a system through which our Empire shall gain glory in our time by the progress of science, and one that will also, in the future, bring profit to our people through the acquisition and increase of knowledge.

The institution of a mere Academy of Sciences would not fulfill this double purpose; though the progress and propagation of arts and sciences in themselves would be furthered, these would not fructify fast enough among the people. On the other hand, the organization of a University would avail us still less, since the lack of ordinary schools, gimnazii, and seminaries in which young people could learn the elements and later obtain the higher degrees of knowledge to make themselves fully capable makes it impossible for a University to be of any help in this situation.

And so it would be most desirable for us to initiate a society composed of the most learned persons who are capable (1) of advancing and perfecting science, moreover (2) of teaching young people in public, and (3) of instructing in private a few persons who in turn could teach young people the elements of all sciences.

In this manner one single institution would, at little expense, give the great profit that is obtained in other countries by three different bodies.

From: Vernadsky, George, and S. G. Pushkarev, *A Source book for Russian history from early times to 1917*, (New Haven, CT: Yale UP, 1972), pp. 313 and 347. Blinoff, Marthe, *Life and thought in old Russia* (University Park, PA: Pennsylvania State University Press, 1961), pp. 108–9.

QUESTIONS:

1. Why do you think Peter was concerned with the appearance of his elites and government officials? If these decrees shape screen image projection, who is the intended audience?
2. What does Peter's personal involvement in learning the science of shipbuilding and in establishing an Academy whose focus was on languages and translation tell you about the monarch personally? What does it tell you about Russian culture at the time? What is the connection between monarch and culture?

16.4a: *Closed Country Edict* (Tokugawa Iemitsu, 1635)

Tokugawa Ietmitsu (1604–1651, r. 1623–1651) was the third shogun of the Tokugawa Shogunate that ruled Japan during the Late Agrarian Era. His grandfather Tokugawa Ieyasu had completed the reunification of Japan after a century and a half of division and warfare. The Tokugawa Shogunate created a delicate political settlement that brought all the formerly independent domains of Japan into a federation dominated by the Tokugawa family and its allies but in which the separate political identities of the formerly independent domains remained. In that situation, the Tokugawa saw foreign influence as potentially disruptive—a potential demonstrated in reality by the Shimabara Rebellion of 1637, led by Japanese Christians protesting Iemitsu's anti-Christian policies. After suppressing the rebellion, Iemitsu issued the edicts presented here, closing the country off almost entirely to overseas network connections.

1. Japanese ships are strictly forbidden to leave for foreign countries.

2. No Japanese is permitted to go abroad. If there is anyone who attempts to do so secretly, he must be executed. The ship so involved must be impounded and its owner arrested, and the matter must be reported to the higher authority.

3. If any Japanese returns from overseas after residing there, he must be put to death.

4. If there is any place where the teachings of padres (Christianity) is practiced, the two of you must order a thorough investigation.

5. Any informer revealing the whereabouts of the followers of padres (Christians) must be rewarded accordingly. If anyone reveals the whereabouts of a high ranking padre, he must be given one hundred pieces of silver. For those of lower ranks, depending on the deed, the reward must be set accordingly.

6. If a foreign ship has an objection [to the measures adopted] and it becomes necessary to report the matter to Edo, you may ask the Omura domain to provide ships to guard the foreign ship, as was done previously.

7. If there are any Southern Barbarians (Westerners) who propagate the teachings of padres, or otherwise commit crimes, they may be incarcerated in the prison maintained by the Omura domain, as was done previously.

8. All incoming ships must be carefully searched for the followers of padres.

9. No single trading city [see 12 below] shall be permitted to purchase all the merchandise brought by foreign ships.

10. Samurai are not permitted to purchase any goods originating from foreign ships directly from Chinese merchants in Nagasaki.

11. After a list of merchandise brought by foreign ships is sent to Edo, as before you may order that commercial dealings may take place without waiting for a reply from Edo.

12. After settling the price, all white yarns (raw silk) brought by foreign ships shall be allocated to the five trading cities and other quarters as stipulated.

13. After settling the price of white yarns (raw silk), other merchandise [brought by foreign ships] may be traded freely between the [licensed] dealers. However, in view of the fact that Chinese ships are small and cannot bring large consignments, you may issue orders of sale at your discretion. Additionally, payment for goods purchased must be made within twenty days after the price is set.

14. The date of departure homeward of foreign ships shall not be later than the twentieth day of the ninth month. Any ships arriving in Japan later than usual shall depart within fifty days of their arrival. As to the departure of Chinese ships, you may use your discretion to order their departure after the departure of the Portuguese *galeota* (galleon).

15. The goods brought by foreign ships which remained unsold may not be deposited or accepted for deposit.

16. The arrival in Nagasaki of representatives of the five trading cities shall not be later than the fifth day of the seventh month. Anyone arriving later than that date shall lose the quota assigned to his city.

17. Ships arriving in Hirado must sell their raw silk at the price set in Nagasaki, and are not permitted to engage in business transactions until after the price is established in Nagasaki.

You are hereby required to act in accordance with the provisions set above. It is so ordered.

16.4b: *Completion of the Exclusion* (Tokugawa Iemitsu, 1639)

1. The matter relating to the proscription of Christianity is known [to the Portuguese], however, heretofore they have secretly transported those who are going to propagate that religion.
2. If those who believe in that religion band together in an attempt to do evil things, they must be subjected to punishment.
3. While those who believe in the preaching of padres are in hiding, there are incidents in which that country (Portugal) has sent gifts to them for their sustenance.

In view of the above, hereafter entry by the Portuguese *galeota* is forbidden. If they insist on coming [to Japan], the ships must be destroyed and anyone aboard those ships must be beheaded. We have received the above order and are thus transmitting it to you accordingly.

From: Lu, David John, *Japan: a documentary history*, (Armonk, NY: M.E. Sharpe, 1997), pp. 221–22.

QUESTIONS:

1. How do Iemitsu's decrees compare to those of Kangxi and Peter the Great in terms of their mixture of practicality and symbolism?
2. What do these edicts imply about the importance of overseas trade to the Japanese economy at the time they were issued?

16.5: *The Adventurous Simplicissimus* (Grimmelshausen, 1659)

Hans Jakob Christoffel von Grimmelshausen (1621–1676) was a German author born into the tempestuous world of the Thirty Years War (1618–1648). Mercenary soldiers (*landsknechts*) kidnapped him at the age of ten and as a result he ended up becoming a soldier himself. When the war ended he became a servant of the bishop of Strasbourg and later a magistrate in Baden. The latter allowed him to pursue a literary career. His *The Adventurous Simplicissimus* (or *Adventures of a Simpleton*) drew heavily on his own experiences to describe the religious and political conflicts of Germany during the war. The novel is narrated by a naïve hero, the Simpleton of the title, whose innocence adds ironic humor to its descriptions of horrific events. In this selection, Simplicissimus narrates a dream that shows us his view of hierarchy from below.

CHAPTER XV: HOW SIMPLICISSIMUS WAS PLUNDERED, AND HOW HE DREAMED OF THE PEASANTS AND HOW THEY FARED IN TIMES OF WAR

NOW when I came home I found that my fireplace and all my poor furniture, together with my store of provisions, which I had grown during the summer in my garden and had kept for the coming winter, were all gone. "And whither now?" thought I. And then first did need teach me heartily to pray: and I must summon all my small wits together, to devise what I should do. But as my knowledge of the world was both small and evil, I could come to no proper conclusion, only that 'twas best to commend myself to God and to put my whole confidence in Him: for otherwise I must perish. And besides all this those things which I had heard and seen that day lay heavy on my mind: and I pondered not so much upon my food and my sustenance as upon the enmity which there is ever between soldiers and peasants. Yet could my foolish mind come to no other conclusion than this—that there must of a surety be two races of men in the world, and not one only, descended from Adam, but two, wild and tame, like other unreasoning beasts, and therefore pursuing one another so cruelly.

With such thoughts I fell asleep, for mere misery and cold, with a hungry stomach. Then it seemed to me, as if in a dream, that all the trees which stood round my dwelling suddenly changed and took on another appearance: for on every treetop sat a trooper, and the trunks were garnished, in place of leaves, with all manner of folk. Of these, some had long lances, others musquets, hangers, halberts, flags, and some drums and fifes. Now this was merry to see, for all was neatly distributed and each according to his rank. The roots, moreover, were made up of folk of little worth, as mechanics and labourers, mostly, however, peasants and the like; and these nevertheless gave its strength to the tree and renewed the same when it was lost: yea more, they repaired the loss of any fallen leaves from among themselves to their own great damage: and all the time they lamented over them that sat on the tree, and that with good reason, for the whole weight of the tree lay upon them and pressed them so that all the money was squeezed out of their pockets, yea, though it was behind seven locks and keys: but if the money would not out, then did the commissaries so handle them with rods (which thing they call military execution) that sighs came from their heart, tears from their eyes, blood from their nails, and the marrow from their bones. Yet among these were some whom men call light o' heart; and these made but little ado, took all with a shrug, and in the midst of their torment had, in place of comfort, mockery for every turn.

CHAPTER XVI: OF THE WAYS AND WORKS OF SOLDIERS NOWADAYS, AND HOW HARDLY A COMMON SOLDIER CAN GET PROMOTION

SO must the roots of these trees suffer and endure toil and misery in the midst of trouble and complaint, and those upon the lower boughs in yet greater hardship: yet were these last mostly merrier than the first named, yea and moreover, insolent and swaggering, and for the most part godless folk, and for the roots a heavy unbearable burden at all times. And this was the rhyme upon them:

> "Hunger and thirst, and cold and heat, and
>   work and woe, and all we meet;
> And deeds of blood and deeds of shame, all
>   may ye put to the landsknecht's name."

Which rhymes were the less like to be lyingly invented in that they answered to the facts. For gluttony and drunkenness, hunger and thirst, wenching and dicing and playing, riot and roaring, murdering and being murdered, slaying and being slain, torturing and being tortured, hunting and being hunted, harrying and being harried, robbing and being robbed, frighting and being frighted, causing trouble and suffering trouble, beating and being beaten: in a word, hurting and harming, and in turn being hurt and harmed—this was their whole life. And in this career they let nothing hinder them: neither winter nor summer, snow nor ice, heat nor cold, rain nor wind, hill nor dale, wet nor dry; ditches, mountain-passes, ramparts and walls, fire and water, were all the same to them. Father nor mother, sister nor brother, no, nor the danger to their own bodies, souls, and consciences, nor even loss of life and of heaven itself, or aught else that can be named, will ever stand in their way, forever they toil and moil at their own strange work, till at last, little by little, in battles, sieges, attacks, campaigns, yea, and in their winter quarters too (which are the soldiers' earthly paradise, if they can but happen upon fat peasants) they perish, they die, they rot and consume away, save but a few,

who in their old age, unless they have been right thrifty reivers and robbers, do furnish us with the best of all beggars and vagabonds.

Next above these hard-worked folk sat old hen-roost-robbers, who, after some years and much peril of their lives, had climbed up the lowest branches and clung to them, and so far had had the luck to escape death. Now these looked more serious, and somewhat more dignified than the lowest, in that they were a degree higher ascended: yet above them were some yet higher, who had yet loftier imaginings because they had to command the very lowest. And these people did call coat-beaters, because they were wont to dust the jackets of the poor pikemen, and to give the musqueteers oil enough to grease their barrels with.

Just above these the trunk of the tree had an interval or stop, which was a smooth place without branches, greased with all manner of ointments and curious soap of disfavour, so that no man save of noble birth could scale it, in spite of courage and skill and knowledge, God knows how clever he might be. For 'twas polished as smooth as a marble pillar or a steel mirror. Just over that smooth spot sat they with the flags: and of these some were young, some pretty well in years: the young folk their kinsmen had raised so far: the older people had either mounted on a silver ladder which is called the Bribery Backstairs or else on a step which Fortune, for want of a better client, had left for them. A little further up sat higher folk, and these had also their toil and care and annoyance: yet had they this advantage, that they could fill their pokes with the fattest slices which they could cut out of the roots, and that with a knife which they called "War-contribution." And these were at their best and happiest when there came a commissary-bird flying overhead, and shook out a whole panfull of gold over the tree to cheer them: for of that they caught as much as they could, and let but little or nothing at all fall to the lowest branches: and so of these last more died of hunger than of the enemy's attacks, from which danger those places above seemed to be free. Therefore was there a perpetual climbing and swarming going on on those trees; for each would needs sit in those highest and happiest places: yet were there some idle, worthless rascals, not worth their commissariat-bread, who troubled themselves little about higher places, and only did their duty. So the lowest, being ambitious, hoped for the fall of the highest, that they might sit in their place, and if it happened to one among ten thousand of them that he got so far, yet would such good luck come to him only in his miserable old age when he was more fit to sit in the chimney-corner and roast apples than to meet the foe in the field. And if any man dealt honestly and carried himself well, yet was he ever envied by others, and perchance by reason of some unlucky chance of war deprived both of office and of life. And nowhere was this more grievous than at the before-mentioned smooth place on the tree: for there an officer who had had a good sergeant or corporal under him must lose him, however unwillingly, because he was now made an ensign. And for that reason they would take, in place of old soldiers, inkslingers, footmen, overgrown pages, poor noblemen, and at times poor relations, tramps and vagabonds. And these took the very bread out of the mouths of those that had deserved it, and forthwith were made Ensigns.

From: Grimmelshausen, Hans Jakob Christoph von, *The Adventurous Simplicissimus: being the description of the life of a vagabond named Melchior Sternfels von Fechshaim,* (London: William Heinemann, 1912), pp. 54–58.

QUESTIONS:

1. In this view from below, what characterizes hierarchy? What is the relationship between coercion and ideology in this view?
2. How does this view of hierarchy differ from those presented in the first three sources of this chapter? How are the two views related?

16.6: *Letters to the King of Portugal* (Nzinga Mbemba, 1526)

Nzinga Mbemba (ca. 1456–1542/3, r. 1509–1542/3), also known by his Christian name Afonso I, ruled the Kongo Empire during a period of expanded contact with Europeans, particularly the Portuguese. His father and predecessor as king had converted to Catholicism, and Afonso vigorously promoted Catholicism in his kingdom, as well as other elements of Portuguese culture such as dress and the use of coats-of-arms by the elite. But he equally vigorously opposed other aspects of Portuguese culture, especially land law: real estate in Portugal, for example, as in much of western Europe, was becoming at least to some extent a saleable commodity, but in Kongo all land belonged to the king and land sales were prohibited. Afonso also resisted the growing trade in African slaves, attempting to keep it subject to Kongolese law. He wrote many lengthy letters to kings Manuel I and João III of Portugal that express these divergent interests. The excerpts here are from those letters.

Sir, Your Highness should know how our Kingdom is being lost in so many ways that it is convenient to provide for the necessary remedy, since this is caused by the excessive freedom given by your agents and officials to the men and merchants who are allowed to come to this Kingdom to set up shops with goods and many things which have been prohibited by us, and which they spread throughout our Kingdoms and Domains in such an abundance that many of our vassals, whom we had in obedience, do not comply because they have the things in greater abundance than we ourselves; and it was with these things that we had them content and subjected under our vassalage and jurisdiction, so it is doing a great harm not only to the service of God, but the security and peace of our Kingdoms and State as well.

And we cannot reckon how great the damage is, since the mentioned merchants are taking every day our natives, sons of the land and the sons of our noblemen and vassals and our relatives, because the thieves and men of bad conscience grab them wishing to have the things and wares of this Kingdom which they are ambitious of; they grab them and get them to be sold; and so great, Sir, is the corruption and licentiousness that our country is being completely depopulated, and Your Highness should not agree with this nor accept it as in your service. And to avoid it we need from those [your] Kingdoms no more than some priests and a few people to teach in schools, and no other goods except wine and flour for the holy sacrament. That is why we beg of Your Highness to help and assist us in this matter, commanding your factors that they should not send here either merchants or wares, because it is *our will that in these Kingdoms there should not be any trade of slaves nor outlet for them.* Concerning what is referred [to] above, again we beg of Your Highness to agree with it, since otherwise we cannot remedy such an obvious damage. Pray Our Lord in His mercy to have Your Highness under His guard and let you do forever the things of His service. I kiss your hands many times.

At our town of Kongo, written on the sixth day of July, João Teixeira did it in 1526 The King. Dom Afonso.

• • •

Moreover, Sir, in our Kingdoms there is another great inconvenience which is of little service to God, and this is that many of our people, keenly desirous as they are of the wares and things of your Kingdoms, which are brought here by your people, and in order to satisfy their voracious appetite, seize many of our people, freed and exempt men, and very often it happens that they kidnap even noblemen and the sons of noblemen, and our relatives, and take them to be sold to the white men who are in our Kingdoms; and for this purpose they have concealed them; and others are brought during the night so that they might not be recognized.

And as soon as they are taken by the white men they are immediately ironed and branded with fire, and when they are carried to be embarked [on ships], if they are caught by our guards' men the whites allege that they have bought them but they cannot say from whom, so that it is our duty to do justice and to restore to the freemen their freedom, but it cannot be done if your subjects feel offended, as they claim to be.

And to avoid such a great evil we passed a law so that any white man living in our Kingdoms and wanting to purchase goods in any way should first inform three of our noblemen and officials of our court whom we rely upon in this matter, . . . who should investigate if the mentioned goods are captives or free men, and if cleared by them there will be no further doubt nor embargo [an act prohibiting the departure of a trading vessel] for them to be taken and embarked. But if the white men do not comply with it they will lose the aforementioned goods. And if we do them this favor and concession it is for the part Your Highness has in it, since we know that it is in your service too that these goods are taken from our Kingdom, otherwise we should not consent to this. . . .

• • •

Sir, Your Highness has been kind enough to write to us saying that we should ask in our letters for anything we need, and that we shall be provided with everything, and as the peace and the health of our Kingdom depend on us, and as there are among us old folks and people who have lived for many days, it happens that we have continuously many and different diseases which put us very often in such a weakness that we reach almost the last extreme; and the same happens to our children, relatives and natives owing to the lack in this country of physicians and surgeons who might know how to cure properly such diseases. And as we have got neither dispensaries nor drugs which might help us in this forlornness, many of those who had been already confirmed and instructed in the holy faith of Our Lord Jesus Christ perish and die; and the *rest* of the people in their majority cure themselves with herbs and . . . and other ancient methods, so that they put all their faith in the mentioned herbs and ceremonies if they live, and believe that they are saved if they die; and this is not much in the service of God.

And to avoid such a great error and inconvenience, since it is from God in the first place and then from your Kingdoms and from Your Highness that all the good and drugs and medicines have come to save us, we beg of you to be agreeable and kind enough to send us two phy\ians and two apothecaries and one surgeon, so that they may come with their drugstores and all the necessary things to stay in our kingdoms, because we are in extreme need of them all and each of them. We shall do them all good and shall benefit them by all means, since they are sent by Your Highness, whom we thank for your work in their coming. We beg of Your Highness as a great favor to do this for us, because besides being good in itself it is in the service of God as we have said above.

(Extracts from letter of King Afonso to the King of Portugal dated Oct. 18, 1526 By hand of Dom João Teixeira.)

From: Davidson, Basil, *The African Past: Chronicles from Antiquity to Modern Times*, (London: Longmans, 1964), pp. 191–94.

QUESTIONS:

1. What practical concerns does Afonso convey to the Portuguese ruler? What do these concerns tell you about the Kongo Empire as a hierarchy?
2. What is Afonso's attitude towards the Portuguese king? What screen image of himself and his Empire does he try to convey to the Portuguese ruler?

The Late Agrarian World III: Cultural Frames, Cultural Encounters, 1500–1750

INTRODUCTION

The growing global network connections of the Late Agrarian Era led to increased levels of cultural contact, exchange, and conflict. They also promoted new forms of knowledge. The sources presented in this chapter show these processes at work, as different peoples and cultures viewed each other through their own cultural screens and reacted according to their own frame values.

17.1:   *The True History* (Hans Staden, 1557)

The story of the life of Hans Staden (ca. 1525–ca. 1579) appears at the beginning of Chapter 17 in *Frameworks*. He was a German soldier and explorer who sailed to Brazil in 1549, was shipwrecked there, and in 1552 was captured by the Tupinamba, a local hunter-gatherer people. Three years of captivity during which he managed to avoid avoided being eaten by his captors ended when he escaped on a French ship. On his return to Germany, he wrote about his adventures in his *True History*. The excerpts here narrate Staden's capture and describe the rituals of Tupinamba cannibalism.

HOW I WAS CAPTURED BY THE SAVAGES, AND THE MANNER IN WHICH IT OCCURRED. CAP. XVIII.

I had a savage man from a group called Carios [Carijós]. He was my slave. He caught game for me, and I sometimes went along with him, into the forest.

However, after some time it so happened that a Spaniard from Sancte Vincente came to me in the bulwark where I lived, on the island of Sancte Maro that lies 5 miles away [from Bertioga]. A German called *Heliodorus Hessus*, son of the late *Eobanus*

Hessus, also came along with him. He had been stationed on the island of Sancte Vincente in an Ingenio [Engenho] where they make sugar. This Ingenio belonged to a Genoese named Josepe Ornio [Giuseppe Adorno]. He was the clerk and manager of the merchants who belonged to the Ingenio. (The houses where sugar is made are called Ingenio.)

I had had dealings with this Heliodorus before. When I was shipwrecked with the Spaniards, I met him on the Island of Sancte Vincente, and he had been friendly to me. He came to see how I was doing, for he had probably heard that I was rumored to be ill. The day before, I had sent my slave into the forest to hunt for game. I wanted to follow the next day to fetch the catch, so we might have something to eat, for in that country there is little to be had, except what comes out of the wilderness.

As I was walking through the forest, loud screaming—such as that made by savages—sounded both sides of the path. People came running towards me. Then I recognized them. They had surrounded me on all sides and were pointing their bows and arrows at me and shot at me. Then I cried out: May God now have mercy on my soul. I had scarcely uttered these words, when they beat me to the ground, and shot and stabbed at me. God be praised that they only wounded me in the leg. They tore the clothes from my body: one the jerkin, another the hat, a third the shirt, and so forth. Then they began to quarrel over me. One said that he had gotten to me first, another protested that it was he who captured me. In the meanwhile, the rest hit me with their bows. Finally, two of them seized me and lifted me up from the ground, naked as I was. One of them grabbed one of my arms, another took the other one; several stayed behind me, while others were in front. Thus they carried me swiftly through the forest towards the sea, where they had their canoes. As they brought me to the sea, I saw the canoes about a stone's throw away. They had dragged them out of the water and hidden them behind the bushes. A great crowd was gathered next to them. As soon as they saw how I was being led there, they all rushed towards me. They were all decorated with feathers according to their custom, and they bit their arms, threatening me that they wanted to eat me in this way. A king walked in front of me, carrying the club with which they kill their captives. He preached and told them how they had captured me, their slave, the Perot (that is how they name the Portuguese). They would now avenge the deaths of their friends on me. And as they brought me to

the canoes, several among them beat me with their fists. Then they hastily launched the canoes, for they feared that an alarm might be raised at Brikioka, as indeed happened.

Before launching the canoes into the water, they bound my hands together. They were not all from the same place, and since every *aldea* [settlement] disliked going home empty-handed, they began a dispute with those two holding me. Several said that they had all been just as near me when I was captured, and each of them demanded a piece of me and wanted to have me killed on the spot.

I stood there and prayed, looking around, awaiting the blow. But at last the king, who wanted to keep me, gave orders to carry me back alive, so that their women might see me alive and celebrate their feast with me. For they intended to kill me Kawewi Pepicke [cauim pepica]: that is, they wanted to make drinks and gather together for a feast where all of them would then eat me. With these words, they let it be and bound four ropes round my neck. I had to climb into a canoe while they were still standing on the ground, fastening the ends of the ropes to the canoes. Then they pushed them into the sea, to sail home.

THE CEREMONIES AT WHICH THEY KILL AND EAT THEIR ENEMIES. THE THINGS THEY USE TO SLAY THEM, AND HOW THEY HANDLE THEM.

When they bring home their enemies, these are first beaten by the women and the children. Then they decorate him [the captive enemy] with gray feathers, shave off the eyebrows above his eyes, and dance around him, binding him tight so that he cannot escape. They give him a woman who attends to him and is also doing things with him. If she becomes pregnant, they raise the child until it is grown. If it then enters their minds [to do so], they kill and eat the child.

They feed the captive well and keep him for some time, while they make preparations: they make many vessels, which they use to make drinks in, and they fire special pots, where they prepare the things with which they paint him [the captive]; they make tassels, which they tie to the club, with which he is to be killed; and they [also] make a long cord, called Mussurana, to bind him when he is going to die.

When they have made all these things ready, they then decide when he is going to die and invite the savages from the other villages, so that they come there at the given time. A couple of days in advance, they then fill all the vessels with drinks. Before the women make the drink, they lead the captive once or twice to the [open] place [between the huts] and dance round him. When all those [guests] who come from outside have now gathered together, the chief of the hut bids them welcome and says: Now come and help to eat your enemy. The day before they begin to drink, they tie the cord Mussurana about the captive's neck; on this day, they also paint the club called Iwera Pemme [Ibira-pema] with which they want to kill him. . . .

It is more than a fathom long. They [first] cover it with sticky stuff. Then they take the eggshells of a bird called Mackukawa [Macaguá], which they grind to a powder and spread upon the club. Then a woman sits down and scratches in the eggshell-powder. While she is painting, a lot of women surround her and sing. When the Iwera Pemme is as it is supposed to be–with tassels and other things–they hang it upon a pole in an empty hut, and then gather around it and sing all night.

They paint the face of the captive in the same manner; the women are also singing, while one of them is painting him. And when they begin to drink, they take their captive along and chat with him, while he drinks with them.

When the drinking has now come to an end, they rest the next day and build a small hut for the captive, on the place where he is going to die. There, he spends the night under close guard. Then, towards the morning, some time before dawn, they come and dance and sing around the club, with which they wish to slay him, until day breaks. They then take the captive away from his small hut, which they tear down and clear away. Then they remove the Mussurana from his neck, tie it around his body, and draw it tight on both sides. He is standing tied in the middle; on both ends, many of them are holding onto the cord.

They let him stand like this for a while and place small stones next to him, so that he can throw them at those women, who run about him and threaten to eat him. Now these women are painted, and when he is going to be cut up, they are meant to take the first four pieces and run with them around the hut. This provides amusement to the others.

When this [mocking and dancing] has now come to an end, they make a fire about two paces away from the slave. He has to look upon the fire. After this, a woman comes running with the club Iwera Pemme. In order to make him see it, she waves the tassels in the air, shrieks with joy, and runs past the captive.

After this has happened, a man now takes the club, goes to stand in front of the captive, and holds the club in front of him, so that he will look at it. Meanwhile, the one, who is going to slay him, goes forth with 13 or 14 others, and they all paint their bodies gray with ashes. Then he [the executioner] and his henchsmen come to the place where the captive is, and the other person, who is standing in front of the captive, gives the club to this person [the executioner]. Then the king of the hut comes and takes the club, and thrusts it once between the legs of the person who is going to slay the captive.

This is a great honor among them. Then the one, who is going to kill him, takes back the club and then says [to the captive]: Well, here I am. I will kill you, since your friends have also killed and eaten many of my friends. He answers: When I am dead, I will still have many friends, who are certainly going to avenge me. The executioner then strikes him on the back of his head and beats out his brains. The women immediately seize him and put him over the fire, where they scrape off all his skin, making him all white; they place a piece of wood in his arse to prevent a discharge.

When he [the dead captive] has then been skinned, a man takes him and cuts off the legs above the knees, and the arms at the body. Then the four women come and seize the four pieces and run around the huts with them, screaming loudly with joy. After this, they part the back, including the buttocks, from the front part and divide this [rear part] amongst themselves.

However, the women keep the innards, simmer them, and make a type of mush, called mingau [Mingáu], in the broth. They and the children drink this [mush] and eat the innards. They also eat the flesh from the head. The brain, the tongue, and whatever else is edible, is eaten by the youngsters.

When this is all done, everyone returns home, and each of them brings their piece [of meat] along. The one who has killed this [captive] gives himself another name. The king of the hut scratches him [the executioner] on the upper arm with the tooth of a wild animal. When this wound has healed properly, you can *see* the scar; this is the [sign of] honor for this act. He then has to lie all that day in a hammock, but they give him a small bow and an arrow, so that he can pass the time by shooting into [a target made of] wax. This is done to prevent his arms from becoming feeble from the shock of the slaying. I was present and have seen all of this.

Moreover, they do not know how to count beyond five. If they have to count further, they use their fingers and toes. When they want to speak about greater numbers, they point to four or five persons, referring to the number of fingers and toes that these persons have.

From: Staden, Hans, Neil L. Whitehead, and Michael Harbsmeier, *Hans Staden's true history: an account of cannibal captivity in Brazil* (Durham: Duke University Press, 2008), pp. 47–49, 129–37 passim.

QUESTIONS:

1. What are the symbolic elements of the cannibalism ritual Staden describes, and what are their significance? How does the ritual seem to fit into a broader Tupí culture that transcends particular villages and tribes?
2. Staden's book was very popular across Europe. What might audiences at the time have found interesting about Staden's stories and descriptions?

17.2:   *The Divine Narcissus* (Sor Juana Inés de la Cruz, 1689)

Sor Juana Inés de la Cruz (1651–1695) was born near Mexico City, the illegitimate daughter of a Spanish soldier and a Mexican-born Spanish woman. Though formal education of women was forbidden, she learned to read and write by the age of three and continued with her self-education throughout her life, becoming a nun and the most significant Mexican poet and scholar of the colonial period. The work excerpted here is a *loa*, or Spanish-style play, that she published in 1689. It is an allegory featuring Occident and America, male and female representations of native Aztec culture, and Zeal and Religion, male and female representations of the Spanish conquerors. There is no straightforward interpretation of the allegory, however. It can be read in terms of the conflict (and moves towards syncretism) between Aztec religion and Catholicism, and in terms of native freedom of choice in that process. But gender roles, especially female choice, play a central role as well, reflecting Sor Juana's own lifelong struggle against gender constraints and her advocacy for female equality. The play is thus a classic product of cultural encounter and exchange.

SCENE I

Enter OCCIDENT, a stately Indian wearing a crown, and AMERICA beside him, a noble Indian woman, in the *mantas* and *huipiles* worn when singing a *tocotín*. They sit in two chairs; several Indian men and women dance holding feathers and rattles in their hands, as is traditional during this celebration; as they dance, MUSIC sings:

MUSIC

Most noble Mexicans,
whose ancient origin
is found in the brilliant rays
cast like arrows by the Sun,
mark well the time of year,
this day is given to laud
and honor in our way
the highest of our gods.
Come clad in ornaments
of your station the sign,
and to your piety
let happiness be joined:
with festive pageantry
worship the all-powerful God of Seeds!

MUSIC

The riches of our lands
in copious plenteousness
are owing to the one
who makes them bounteous.
So bring your fervent thanks,
and at the harvest time,
give unto Him his due,
the first fruit of the vine.
Let flow the purest blood,
give from your own veins,
to blend with many bloods
and thus His cult sustain.
With festive pageantry
worship the all-powerful God of Seeds!
(OCCIDENT *and* AMERICA *sit, as* MUSIC
    ceases.)

OCCIDENT

So great in number are the Gods
that our religion sanctifies,
so many in this place alone
the many rites we solemnize,
that this our Royal City is
the scene of cruelest sacrifice:
two thousand gods are satisfied,
but human blood must be the price;
now see the entrails that still throb,
now see hearts that redly beat,
and though the gods are myriad,
our gods so many (I repeat),
the greatest God among them all
is our Great God, the God of Seeds!

AMERICA

And rightly so, for He alone
has long sustained our monarchy,
for all the riches of the field
we owe to Him our fealty,
and as the greatest benefice,
in which all others are contained,
is that abundance of the land,
our life and breath by it maintained,
we name Him greatest of the Gods.
What matters all the glittering gold
in which America abounds,
what value precious ores untold,
if their excrescences befoul
and sterilize a fertile earth,
if no fruits ripen, no maize grows,
and no tender buds spring forth?
But the protection of this God
is broader than continuance,
with the provision of our food,
of our daily sustenance,
He makes a paste of His own flesh,
and we partake with veneration
(though first the paste is purified
of bodily contamination),
and so our Soul he purifies

of all its blemishes and stains.
And thus in homage to His cult,
may everyone with me proclaim:

ALL *and* **MUSIC**
In festive pageantry,
worship the all-powerful God of Seeds!

SCENE II

(*They exit, dancing, and then enter* CHRISTIAN
RELIGION, *as a Spanish Lady, and* ZEAL, *as a
Captain General, armed; behind them, Spanish*
SOLDIERS.

RELIGION
How is it, then, as you are Zeal,
your Christian wrath can tolerate
that here with blind conformity
they bow before Idolatry,
and, superstitious, elevate
an Idol, with effrontery,
above our Christianity?

ZEAL
Religion, do not be dismayed:
my compassion you upbraid,
my tolerance you disavow,
but see, I stand before you now
with arm upraised, unsheathed my blade,
which I address to your revenge.
And now, retire, your cares allayed,
as their transgressions I avenge.
(*Enter, dancing,* OCCIDENT *and* AMERICA,
and from the other side, music, with accompaniment)

MUSIC
And with festive pageantry,
worship the all-powerful God of Seeds!

ZEAL
They are here. I will approach.

RELIGION
And I as well, with all compassion,
for I would go with tones of peace

(before unleashing your aggression)
to urge them to accept my word,
and in the faith be sanctified.

ZEAL
Then let us go, for even now
they practice their revolting rite.

MUSIC
And with festive pageantry,
worship the great God of Seeds!

(ZEAL *and* RELIGION *approach*)

RELIGION
Hear me, mighty Occident,
America, so beautiful,
your lives are led in misery
though your land is bountiful.
Abandon this unholy cult
which the Devil doth incite.
Open your eyes. Accept my word
and follow in the Path of Light,
fully persuaded by my love.

OCCIDENT
These unknown persons, who are they
who now before my presence stand?
Oh gods, who ventures thus to stay
the festive moment's rightful course?

AMERICA
What Nations these, which none has seen?
Do they come here to interfere,
my ancient power contravene?

OCCIDENT
Oh, Lovely Beauty, who are you,
fair Pilgrim from another nation?
I ask you now, why have you come
to interrupt my celebration?

RELIGION
Christian Religion is my name,
and I propose that all will bend
before the power of my word.

OCCIDENT
A great endeavor you intend!

AMERICA

A great madness you display!

OCCIDENT

The inconceivable you scheme!

AMERICA

She must be mad, ignore her now,
let them continue with our theme!

ALL *and* **MUSIC**

With festive pageantry,
worship the all-powerful God of Seeds!

ZEAL

How, barbaric Occident,
and you, oh blind Idolatry,
can you presume to scorn my Wife,
beloved Christianity?
For brimming to the vessel's lip
we see your sinful degradation;
the Lord our God will not allow
That you continue in transgression,
and He sends me to punish you.

OCCIDENT

And who are you, who terrorize
all those who gaze upon your face?

ZEAL

I am Zeal. Whence your surprise?
For when Religion you would scorn
with practices of vile excess,
then Zeal must enter on the scene
to castigate your wickedness.
I am a Minister from God
Who, witnessing your tyranny,
the error of these many years
of lives lived in barbarity,
has reached the limits of His grace
and sends His punishment through me.
And thus these armed and mighty Hosts
whose gleaming blades of steel you see
are His ministers of wrath,
the instruments of Holy rage.

OCCIDENT

What god, what error, what offense,
what punishment do you presage?
I do not understand your words,
nor does your argument persuade;
I know you not, who, brazenly,
would thus our rituals invade
and with such zeal that you prevent
that in just worship people say:

MUSIC

With festive pageantry,
worship the great God of Seeds!

AMERICA

Oh, mad, blind, barbaric man,
disturbing our serenity,
you bring confusing arguments
to counter our tranquillity;
you must immediately cease,
unless it is your wish to find
all here assembled turned to ash
with no trace even on the wind!
And you, Husband, and your vassals,

(to OCCIDENT)

you must close your ears and eyes,
do not heed their fantasies,
do not listen to their lies;
proceed, continue with your rites!
Our rituals shall not be banned
by these Nations, still unknown,
so newly come unto our land.

MUSIC

And with festive pageantry,
worship the great God of Seeds!

ZEAL

As our first offering of peace
you have so haughtily disdained,
accept the second, that of war,
from war we will not be restrained!
War! War! To arms! To arms!
(Sound of drums and trumpets)

OCCIDENT

What is this wrath the gods devise?
What are the weapons here displayed
that so confound my awestruck eyes?
Ho, my Soldiers, ho there, Guards!
Those arrows that you hold prepared
now send against the enemy!

AMERICA

Why have the gods their lightning bared
to strike me down? What are these spheres
that fall like fiery leaden hail?

What are these Centaurs, man and horse,
that now my followers assail?
(*Off*)

To arms! To arms! We are at war!
(*Drums and trumpets*)

Long live Spain! Her King we hail!
(*The battle is struck;* INDIANS *enter and flee
across the stage, pursued by the* SPANISH;
OCCIDENT *and* AMERICA *begin to retreat
before* RELIGION *and* ZEAL)

From: Sor Juana Ines de la Cruz, "Loa for El Divino Narciso," *Poems, Protest, and a Dream: Selected Writings,* Margaret Sayers Peden, transl. (New York: Penguin, 1997), pp. 194–239.

QUESTIONS:

1. Where do Sor Juana's sympathies seem to lie in the opening two scenes of this play? What role does her own identity as a female and a nun play in her presentation of the characters?
2. What image of Mexican identity does this play project? Who seems to be the intended audience?

17.3:   *Legal Opinions* (Khayr al-Din Ramli, late seventeenth century)

Khayr al-Din Ramli (1585–1671) was a jurist of the Hanafi school of legal interpretation, one of four major schools in the Islamic legal tradition. He lived in Palestine under Ottoman rule, working as a jurist, writer, and teacher. This means he did not work for the Ottoman state, but was an influential figure in Palestinian society as a member of the *ulema*, or body of Islamic jurists. His fatwas, or judgments, had significant influence in his own time and for several centuries afterwards. The judgments presented here concern marriage and divorce and so give insight into women's lives in the provinces of the Ottoman Empire at its height.

MARRIAGE

Question: A virgin in her legal majority and of sound mind was abducted by her brother and married off to an unsuitable man. Does her father have the right to annul the marriage contract on the basis of the [husband's] unsuitability?
Answer: Yes, if the father asks for that, then the judge should separate the spouses whether or not the marriage was consummated, so long as she has not borne children, and is not pregnant, and did not receive the *mahr* [dower] before the marriage. . . . This is the case if her brother has married her off with her consent. But if she was given in

marriage without her consent, she can reject [the marriage], and there is no need for the father [to ask for] separation [and raise] opposition, for he is not [in this case] a commissioned agent. [But] if she authorizes him to represent her, then he has the right to request from the judge an annulment [*faskh*] of the marriage and a separation, and the judge should separate them. According to al-Hasan, there is no need for [all] this because the contract is not valid in the first place. And God knows best.

. . .

Question: There is a minor girl whose brother married her off, and she came of age and chose *faskh* [annulment] in her "coming of age" choice. Her husband claimed that her brother had acted as the *wakil* [agent] of her father and she does not have a choice. She then claimed that [her brother] married her off during [her father's] brief absence on a journey. If the husband provides evidence for his claim, is her choice canceled or not? If he does not have evidence, and wants her oath on that, must she swear an oath?

Answer: Yes, if the husband proves his claim, then her choice is canceled. . . . Only the father's and grandfather's marriage arrangements cannot be canceled . . . [and] if the marriage was arranged by way of a *niyaba* [proxy] for her father, then she has no choice. If the marriage was arranged as a result of [the brother's] *wilaya* [guardianship], then she has a choice.

. . .

Question: A virgin in her majority was married by her *wali* [guardian] legally, but without her permission, to a man who was suitable and paid a fair *mahr* [dower]. Then the *wali* informed her of the marriage and of the groom and of the *mahr*, and she was silent concerning her choice and she did not reject the marriage. Is her silence acceptance of him?

Answer: Yes. But if the *wali* marries her off without consultation and then informs her after the marriage and she remains silent, and he does not mention the [name of the] groom and the [amount of the] *mahr*, then it is different and not [legally] sound. And likewise if he consults her before the marriage but fails to mention the [name of the] groom and the [amount of the] *mahr*, and she is silent, this too is not a legal marriage.

. . .

Question: A man said to his brother: "Arrange a marriage for my minor daughter and you can marry using her *mahr*," and [the uncle] married her off to a man with [the father's] permission and a *mahr* was named. And then [the uncle] married [the groom's] sister and a *mahr* was named for her. But the two marriages were consummated before the *mahrs* were received. Then the minor came of age and her father died. Can she authorize her brother or someone else to demand her *mahr* from her husband, and is the husband required to pay it? Likewise, can the husband's sister appoint an agent to collect her *mahr* from her husband, and is he obliged to pay it?

Answer: Each of them can appoint someone to receive the *mahr*, and it is not legal for the father to give the minor's *mahr* to her uncle or anyone else . . . for it is not his property, it is her property . . . and the groom must pay his debt, the *mahr*.

. . .

DIVORCE

Question: There is an evil man who harms his wife, hits her without right and rebukes her without cause. He swore many times to divorce her until she proved that a thrice divorce [a final and irrevocable divorce] had taken effect.

Answer: He is forbidden to do that, and he is rebuked and enjoined from her. If she has proved that a thrice divorce has taken place, it is permissible for her to kill him, according to many of the 'ulama' [jurists] if he is not prevented [from approaching her] except by killing.

. . .

Question: A man approached a woman, a virgin in her legal majority who was married to someone else, abducted her in the month of Ramadan, and took her to a village near her own village. He brought her to the shaykh of the village, who welcomed him and gave him hospitality and protection. There the man consummated the "marriage," saying "between us there are relations." Such is the way of the peasants. . . . What is the punishment for him and the man who helped him? . . . Should Muslim rulers halt these practices of the peasants . . . even by combat and killing?

Answer: The punishment of the abductor and his accomplice for this grave crime is severe beating and long imprisonment, and even worse punishment until they show remorse. It is conceivable that the punishment could be execution because of the severity of this act of disobedience to God. This practice—and one fears for the people of the region if it spreads and they do not halt it—will be punished by God. The one who commits this act, and those who remain silent about it, are like one who punches a hole in a ship, [an act] that will drown all the passengers. . . . It is the obligation of Muslim rulers to commit themselves to putting an end to this revolting practice . . . even if it means punishment [of the offenders] by combat and killing.

. . .

Question: There is a poor man who married a virgin in her legal majority, but he did not pay her stipulated *mahr* [dower] expeditiously, nor did he provide *nafaqa* [support], nor did he clothe her. This caused her great harm. Must he follow one of God's two commands: "Either you maintain her well or you release her with kindness?" And if the judge annuls the marriage, is it on account of the severe harm being done to her?

Answer: Yes, the husband should do one of the two things, according to God's command: "maintain her well or release her with kindness." . . . You cannot sustain [indefinitely] such needs through borrowing, and it appears that she does not have anyone to lend her money, and the husband has no actual wealth. They [the shari'a and Hanafi legal thinkers] prefer that the qadi appoint a Shafi'i *na'ib* [assistant judge] to separate [*fasakha*] them. Many of our [Hanafi] legal thinkers [*fuqaha'*] chose this path in cases of extreme necessity, and it pleases the *faqih* [legal expert] because it spares him an awkward situation and saves the woman from harm. And God knows best.

. . .

Question: There is a poor woman whose husband is absent in a remote region and he left her

without *nafaqa* or a legal provider, and she has suffered proven harm from that. She has made a claim against him for that [support], but the absent one is very poor. The resources [intended] for her *nafaqa* were left in his house and in his shop, but they are not sufficient for her to withstand her poverty. She therefore asked the Shafi'i judge to annul [*fasakha*] the marriage, and he ordered her to bring proof. Two just men testified in conformity with what she had claimed, and so the judge annulled the marriage. . . . Then, following her waiting period, she married another man. Then the first husband returned and wanted to nullify the judgment. Can that be done for him, when it was all necessary and had ample justification?

Answer: When the harm is demonstrated and the evidence for that is witnessed, the *faskh* of the absent [one's marriage] is sound. . . . It is not for the Hanafi or others to nullify this, as our *'ulama'* have said in their *fatwas*.

. . .

Question: A man was behaving at times like an insane person, to the extent that he was brought before a judge and imprisoned in an asylum [*maristan*]. But his insanity was not confirmed. Does this mean he is imbecilic [*ma'tuh*]? If he pronounced an irrevocable divorce, is the divorce valid or not?

Answer: If, when this state seizes him, his speech and actions are not proper except in rare moments, and if he hits and curses, he is insane [*majnun*]. But if he is dim witted and confused, and unable to manage but does not hit or curse, then he is imbecilic [*ma'tuh*]. At any rate, the divorce is invalid, because all divorces are invalid if pronounced by the insane, the imbecilic, the mentally confused, the unconscious [*sic*], or the epileptic during a seizure. If he had once been insane, and then he claimed under oath that he had been seized by the madness again [and had therefore pronounced an invalid divorce], then his oath is accepted. But if he had never been insane before, then his claim should not be accepted except with evidence, and God knows best.

. . .

Question: There is a man who divorced his wife with the pronouncement of a *khul'* but without [mentioning] money. He wants, after that, to take her back without her agreement, without a new marriage, and without a legal procedure. Can he not do this?

Answer: Khul' is an irrevocable divorce and he cannot take her back except with her agreement, and the holding of a new marriage and its [taking] legal effect. With or without money, it is an irrevocable divorce [*talaq*]

From: Tucker, Judith E., *In the house of the law: gender and Islamic law in Ottoman Syria and Palestine* (Berkeley: University of California Press, 1998), Chapters 2 and 3, passim.

QUESTIONS:

1. In what situations do women have control over their own lives, and when do men act as proxies for them? For example, what different types of divorces or annulments are there?
2. What is the relationship between women's legal rights and men's property rights? Which is more important?

17.4: *Narrative* (Olaudah Equiano, 1789)

Olaudah Equiano (1745–1797) was an African who became a major figure in the British antislavery movement after buying his freedom from slavery. Captured as a child and transported first to the Caribbean and then to North America, he had a series of owners who taught him practical skills and to read and write. He purchased his freedom from a Quaker merchant in about 1670 and worked in various jobs around the Atlantic, eventually settling in Britain because of the dangers of being kidnapped into slavery in the British colonies. He married an English woman and had two daughters, leaving a substantial estate when he died. His autobiography, *The Interesting Narrative of the Life of Olaudah Equiano or Gustavus Vassa the African, written by himself*, became a significant abolitionist tract. The excerpts presented here narrate his early life and his first encounters with African and European slavery.

. . . My father, besides many slaves, had a numerous family, of which seven lived to grow up, including myself and a sister, who was the only daughter. As I was the youngest of the sons, I became, of course, the greatest favourite with my mother, and was always with her; and she used to take particular pains to form my mind. I was trained up from my earliest years in the art of war; my daily exercise was shooting and throwing javelins; and my mother adorned me with emblems, after the manner of our greatest warriors. In this way I grew up till I was turned the age of eleven, when an end was put to my happiness in the following manner: . . . One day, when all our people were gone out to their works as usual, and only I and my dear sister were left to mind the house, two men and a woman got over our walls, and in a moment seized us both, and, without giving us time to cry out, or make resistance, they stopped our mouths, and ran off with us into the nearest wood. . . . The next day proved a day of greater sorrow than I had yet experienced; for my sister and I were then separated. . . . [S]he was torn from me, and immediately carried away, while I was left in a state of distraction not to be described. I cried and grieved continually; and for several days I did not eat any thing but what they forced into my mouth. At length, after many days travelling, during which

I had often changed masters, I got into the hands of a chieftain, in a very pleasant country. This man had two wives and some children, and they all used me extremely well, and did all they could to comfort me; particularly the first wife, who was something like my mother. Although I was a great many days journey from my father's house, yet these people spoke exactly the same language with us. This first master of mine, as I may call him, was a smith, and my principal employment was working his bellows, which were the same kind as I had seen in my vicinity. They were in some respects not unlike the stoves here in gentlemen's kitchens; and were covered over with leather; and in the middle of that leather a stick was fixed, and a person stood up, and worked it, in the same manner as is done to pump water out of a cask with a hand pump. I believe it was gold he worked, for it was of a lovely bright yellow colour, and was worn by the women on their wrists and ancles. . . .

From the time I left my own nation I always found somebody that understood me till I came to the sea coast. The languages of different nations did not totally differ, nor were they so copious as those of the Europeans, particularly the English. They were therefore easily learned; and, while I was journeying thus through Africa, I acquired two or three different tongues.

. . .

All the nations and people I had hitherto passed through resembled our own in their manners, customs, and language: but I came at length to a country, the inhabitants of which differed from us in all those particulars. I was very much struck with this difference, especially when I came among a people who did not circumcise, and ate without washing their hands. They cooked also in iron pots, and had European cutlasses and cross bows, which were unknown to us, and fought with their fists amongst themselves. . . .

I continued to travel, sometimes by land, sometimes by water, through different countries and various nations, till, at the end of six or seven months after I had been kidnapped, I arrived at the sea coast. . . .

The first object which saluted my eyes when I arrived on the coast was the sea, and a slave ship, which was then riding at anchor, and waiting for its cargo. These filled me with astonishment, which was soon converted into terror when I was carried on board. I was immediately handled and tossed up to see if I were sound by some of the crew; and I was now persuaded that I had gotten into a world of bad spirits, and that they were going to kill me. Their complexions too differing so much from ours, their long hair, and the language they spoke, (which was very different from any I had ever heard) united to confirm me in this belief. Indeed such were the horrors of my views and fears at the moment, that, if ten thousand worlds had been my own, I would have freely parted with them all to have exchanged my condition with that of the meanest slave in my own country.

When I looked round the ship too and saw a large furnace or copper boiling, and a multitude of black people of every description chained together, every one of their countenances expressing dejection and sorrow, I no longer doubted of my fate; and, quite overpowered with horror and anguish, I fell motionless on the deck and fainted. When I recovered a little I found some black people about me, who I believed were some of those who brought me on board, and had been receiving their pay; they talked to me in order to cheer me, but all in vain. I asked them if we were not to be eaten by those white men with horrible looks, red faces, and loose hair. They told me I was not; and one of the crew brought me a small portion of spirituous liquor in a wine glass; but, being afraid of him, I would not take it out of his hand. One of the blacks therefore took it from him and gave it to me, and I took a little down my palate, which, instead of reviving me, as they thought it would, threw me into the greatest consternation at the strange feeling it produced, having never tasted any such liquor before.

Soon after this the blacks who brought me on board went off, and left me abandoned to despair. I now saw myself deprived of all chance of returning to my native country, or even the least glimpse of hope of gaining the shore, which I now considered as friendly; and I even wished for my former slavery in preference to my present situation, which was filled with horrors of every kind, still heightened by my ignorance of what I was to undergo.

. . .

O, ye nominal Christians! might not an African ask you, learned you this from your God, who says unto you, Do unto all men as you would men should do unto you? Is it not enough that we are torn from our country and friends to toil for your luxury and lust of gain? Must every tender feeling be likewise sacrificed to your avarice? Are the dearest friends and relations, now rendered more dear by their separation from their kindred, still to be parted from each other, and thus prevented from cheering the gloom of slavery with the small comfort of being together and mingling their sufferings and sorrows? Why are parents to lose their children, brothers their sisters, or husbands their wives? Surely this is a new refinement in cruelty, which, while it has no advantage to atone for it, thus aggravates distress, and adds fresh horrors even to the wretchedness of slavery.

From: Oludah Equiano, *The Interesting Narrative of the Life of Olaudah Equiano, Or Gustavus Vassa, The African,* 1789.

QUESTIONS:

1. What does Equiano notice about people from different cultures? What in particular were his first impressions of Europeans?
2. How does he appeal to European's cultural images of themselves to argue against slavery?

17.5: *The New Organon or True Directions Concerning the Interpretation of Nature* (Francis Bacon, 1620)

Francis Bacon (1561–1626) was an English politician, philosopher, and writer, a man of many talents and interests. During his life he was best known as a member of the courts of Elizabeth I and James I, serving as Attorney General and Lord Chancellor of the kingdom. But his subsequent reputation and influence rested on his philosophical and scientific works. He was interested in everything, much like his distant predecessor Aristotle, whose continuing influence over European scientific knowledge Bacon fought against. He insisted that new knowledge would come not from deductions from authorities such as Aristotle but from induction, or conclusions drawn from the observation of nature, observation systematized by experiment. He also insisted on the social context of science and the usefulness of new knowledge, which made him one of the heralds of the Scientific Revolution of the seventeenth century. In this selection from his great work on science, the *Novum Organum*, he summarizes his principles and outlines the impediments to scientific progress that must be overcome.

APHORISMS

[Book One]

I. Man, being the servant and interpreter of Nature, can do and understand so much and so much only as he has observed in fact or in thought of the course of nature. Beyond this he neither knows anything nor can do anything.

II. Neither the naked hand nor the understanding left to itself can effect much. It is by instruments and helps that the work is done, which are as much wanted for the understanding as for the hand. And as the instruments of the hand either give motion or guide it, so the instruments of the mind supply either suggestions for the understanding or cautions.

III. Human knowledge and human power meet in one; for where the cause is not known the effect cannot be produced. Nature to be commanded must be obeyed; and that which in contemplation is as the cause is in operation as the rule.

IV. Toward the effecting of works, all that man can do is to put together or put asunder natural bodies. The rest is done by nature working within.

V. The study of nature with a view to works is engaged in by the mechanic, the mathematician, the physician, the alchemist, and the magician; but by all (as things now are) with slight endeavor and scanty success.

VI. It would be an unsound fancy and self-contradictory to expect that things which have never yet been done can be done except by means which have never yet been tried.

VII. The productions of the mind and hand seem very numerous in books and manufactures. But all this variety lies in an exquisite subtlety and derivations from a few things already known, not in the number of axioms.

VIII. Moreover, the works already known are due to chance and experiment rather than to sciences; for the sciences we now possess are merely systems for the nice ordering and setting forth of things already invented, not methods of invention or directions for new works.

IX. The cause and root of nearly all evils in the sciences is this—that while we falsely admire and extol the powers of the human mind we neglect to seek for its true helps.

X. The subtlety of nature is greater many times over than the subtlety of the senses and understanding; so that all those specious meditations, speculations, and glosses in which men indulge are quite from the purpose, only there is no one by to observe it.

. . .

XVIII. The discoveries which have hitherto been made in the sciences are such as lie close to vulgar notions, scarcely beneath the surface. In order to penetrate into the inner and further recesses of nature, it is necessary that both notions and axioms be derived from things by a more sure and guarded way, and that a method of intellectual operation be introduced altogether better and more certain.

XIX. There are and can be only two ways of searching into and discovering truth. The one flies from the senses and particulars to the most general axioms, and from these principles, the truth of which it takes for settled and immovable, proceeds to judgment and to the discovery of middle axioms. And this way is now in fashion. The other derives axioms from the senses and particulars, rising by a gradual and unbroken ascent, so that it arrives at the most general axioms last of all. This is the true way, but as yet untried.

. . .

XXIII. There is a great difference between the Idols of the human mind and the Ideas of the divine. That is to say, between certain empty dogmas, and the true signatures and marks set upon the works of creation as they are found in nature.

. . .

XXXIX. There are four classes of Idols which beset men's minds. To these for distinction's sake I have assigned names, calling the first class *Idols of the Tribe;* the second, *Idols of the Cave;* the third, *Idols of the Market Place;* the fourth, *Idols of the Theater.*

XL. The formation of ideas and axioms by true induction is no doubt the proper remedy to be applied for the keeping off and clearing away of idols. To point them out, however, is of great use; for the doctrine of Idols is to the interpretation of nature what the doctrine of the refutation of sophisms is to common logic.

XLI. The Idols of the Tribe have their foundation in human nature itself, and in the tribe or race of men. For it is a false assertion that the sense of man is the measure of things. On the contrary, all perceptions as well of the sense as of the mind are according to the measure of the individual and not according to the measure of the universe. And the human understanding is like a false mirror, which, receiving rays irregularly, distorts and discolors the nature of things by mingling its own nature with it.

XLII. The Idols of the Cave are the idols of the individual man. For everyone (besides the errors common to human nature in general) has a cave or den of his own, which refracts and discolors the light of nature, owing either to his own proper and peculiar nature; or to his education and conversation with others; or to the reading of books, and the authority of those whom he esteems and admires; or to the differences of impressions, accordingly as they take place in a mind preoccupied and predisposed or in a mind indifferent and settled; or the like. So that the spirit of man (according as it is meted out to different individuals) is in fact a thing variable and full of perturbation, and governed as it were by chance. Whence it was well observed by Heraclitus that men look for sciences in their own lesser worlds, and not in the greater or common world.

XLIII. There are also Idols formed by the intercourse and association of men with each other, which I call Idols of the Market Place, on account of the commerce and consort of men there. For it is by discourse that men associate, and words are imposed according to the apprehension of the vulgar. And therefore the ill and unfit choice of words wonderfully obstructs the understanding. Nor do the definitions or explanations wherewith in some things learned men are wont to guard and defend themselves, by any means set the matter right. But words plainly force and overrule the understanding, and throw all into confusion, and lead men away into numberless empty controversies and idle fancies.

XLIV. Lastly, there are Idols which have immigrated into men's minds from the various dogmas of philosophies, and also from wrong laws of demonstration. These I call Idols of the Theater, because in my judgment all the received systems are but so many stage plays, representing worlds of

their own creation after an unreal and scenic fashion. Nor is it only of the systems now in vogue, or only of the ancient sects and philosophies, that I speak; for many more plays of the same kind may yet be composed and in like artificial manner set forth; seeing that errors the most widely different have nevertheless causes for the most part alike. Neither again do I mean this only of entire systems, but also of many principles and axioms in science, which by tradition, credulity, and negligence have come to be received.

. . .

LIX. But the *Idols of the Market Place* are the most troublesome of all—idols which have crept into the understanding through the alliances of words and names. For men believe that their reason governs words; but it is also true that words react on the understanding; and this it is that has rendered philosophy and the sciences sophistical and inactive. Now words, being commonly framed and applied according to the capacity of the vulgar, follow those lines of division which are most obvious to the vulgar understanding. And whenever an understanding of greater acuteness or a more diligent observation would alter those lines to suit the true divisions of nature, words stand in the way and resist the change. Whence it comes to pass that the high and formal discussions of learned men end often times in disputes about words and names; with which (according to the use and wisdom of the mathematicians) it would be more prudent to begin, and so by means of definitions reduce them to order. Yet even definitions cannot cure this evil in dealing with natural and material things, since the definitions themselves consist of words, and those words beget others. So that it is necessary to recur to individual instances, and those in due series and order, as I shall say presently when I come to the method and scheme for the formation of notions and axioms.

LX. The idols imposed by words on the understanding are of two kinds. They are either names of things which do not exist (for as there are things left unnamed through lack of observation, so likewise are there names which result from fantastic suppositions and to which nothing in reality corresponds), or they are names of things which exist, but yet confused and ill-defined, and hastily and irregularly derived from realities. Of the former kind are Fortune, the Prime Mover, Planetary Orbits, Element of Fire, and like fictions which owe their origin to false and idle theories. And this class of idols is more easily expelled, because to get rid of them it is only necessary that all theories should be steadily rejected and dismissed as obsolete.

. . .

But the course I propose for the discovery of sciences is such as leaves but little to the acuteness and strength of wits, but places all wits and understandings nearly on a level. For as in the drawing of a straight line or a perfect circle, much depends on the steadiness and practice of the hand, if it be done by aim of hand only, but if with the aid of rule or compass, little or nothing; so is it exactly with my plan. But though particular confutations would be of no avail, yet touching the sects and general divisions of such systems I must say something; something also touching the external signs which show that they are unsound; and finally something touching the causes of such great infelicity and of such lasting and general agreement in error; that so the access to truth may be made less difficult, and the human understanding may the more willingly submit to its purgation and dismiss its idols.

From: Bacon, Francis. *The new organum, or, True directions concerning the interpretation of nature* (Boston: Taggard and Thompson, 1863).

QUESTIONS:

1. How does Bacon promote scientific discovery, and how does this fit into the Late Agrarian English cultural frame?
2. According to Bacon, what "Idols" inhibit the progress of science? Where do these Idols fit into the elements of the *Frameworks* model of networks, hierarchies, and cultural frames and screens?

CHAPTER 18

Late Agrarian Transitions: North Atlantic Revolutions, 1650–1800

INTRODUCTION

The developments of the Late Agrarian Era laid the foundations for the dramatic transformation into the Industrial Era, but these foundations were laid only in specific places under specific circumstances. The conjunction of lucrative global network connections, atypical hierarchy structure, and network-influenced cultural frame values in late seventeenth century Britain was the starting point for revolutionary transitions. This chapter presents sources that show some of these transitions, first in Britain, then spreading to the British colonies in North America, France, and Haiti.

ENGLAND

18.1a: *Bill of Rights of 1689*

The British state, which had been evolving into an atypical partnership between king and Parliament in the centuries since the Magna Carta in 1215, reached a crisis in the seventeenth century. The Stuart kings (James I, Chalres I, Charles II, and James II) asserted royal prerogatives at the same time that Parliament was also becoming more assertive and insisting on the principle that kings were subject to the law. The subsequent struggle to answer the question of whether king or Parliament was the ultimate authority within the state, inflamed by religious divisions, resulted in a civil war, the execution of Charles I, and then a military dictatorship under Oliver Cromwell. The restoration of Charles II in 1660 showed that this fight had failed to decide the question. The question reemerged when the Catholic James II came to the throne. The birth of an heir to James II united the opposition and in 1688 Parliament invited Mary Stuart, James' Protestant sister, and her husband William of Orange to take the throne. In what became known as The Glorious Revolution, James fled, and William and Mary signed an agreement with Parliament setting out the terms of their monarchy. This was the Bill of Rights of 1689 excerpted here.

AN ACT DECLARING THE RIGHTS AND LIBERTIES OF THE SUBJECT AND SETTLING THE SUCCESSION OF THE CROWN

Whereas the Lords Spiritual and Temporal and Commons assembled at Westminster, lawfully, fully and freely representing all the estates of the people of this realm, did upon the thirteenth day of February in the year of our Lord one thousand six hundred eighty-eight [old style date] present unto their Majesties, then called and known by the names and style of William and Mary, prince and princess of

Orange, being present in their proper persons, a certain declaration in writing made by the said Lords and Commons in the words following, viz.:

Whereas the late King James the Second, by the assistance of divers evil counsellors, judges and ministers employed by him, did endeavour to subvert and extirpate the Protestant religion and the laws and liberties of this kingdom;

By assuming and exercising a power of dispensing with and suspending of laws and the execution of laws without consent of Parliament;

By committing and prosecuting divers worthy prelates for humbly petitioning to be excused from concurring to the said assumed power;

By issuing and causing to be executed a commission under the great seal for erecting a court called the Court of Commissioners for Ecclesiastical Causes;

By levying money for and to the use of the Crown by pretence of prerogative for other time and in other manner than the same was granted by Parliament;

By raising and keeping a standing army within this kingdom in time of peace without consent of Parliament, and quartering soldiers contrary to law;

By causing several good subjects being Protestants to be disarmed at the same time when papists were both armed and employed contrary to law;

By violating the freedom of election of members to serve in Parliament;

By prosecutions in the Court of King's Bench for matters and causes cognizable only in Parliament, and by divers other arbitrary and illegal courses;

And whereas of late years partial corrupt and unqualified persons have been returned and served on juries in trials, and particularly divers jurors in trials for high treason which were not freeholders;

And excessive bail hath been required of persons committed in criminal cases to elude the benefit of the laws made for the liberty of the subjects;

And excessive fines have been imposed;

And illegal and cruel punishments inflicted;

And several grants and promises made of fines and forfeitures before any conviction or judgment against the persons upon whom the same were to be levied;

All which are utterly and directly contrary to the known laws and statutes and freedom of this realm;

And whereas the said late King James the Second having abdicated the government and the throne being thereby vacant, his Highness the prince of Orange (whom it hath pleased Almighty God to make the glorious instrument of delivering this kingdom from popery and arbitrary power) did (by the advice of the Lords Spiritual and Temporal and divers principal persons of the Commons) cause letters to be written to the Lords Spiritual and Temporal being Protestants, and other letters to the several counties, cities, universities, boroughs and cinque ports, for the choosing of such persons to represent them as were of right to be sent to Parliament, to meet and sit at Westminster upon the two and twentieth day of January in this year one thousand six hundred eighty and eight [old style date], in order to such an establishment as that their religion, laws and liberties might not again be in danger of being subverted, upon which letters elections having been accordingly made;

And thereupon the said Lords Spiritual and Temporal and Commons, pursuant to their respective letters and elections, being now assembled in a full and free representative of this nation, taking into their most serious consideration the best means for attaining the ends aforesaid, do in the first place (as their ancestors in like case have usually done) for the vindicating and asserting their ancient rights and liberties declare

That the pretended power of suspending the laws or the execution of laws by regal authority without consent of Parliament is illegal;

That the pretended power of dispensing with laws or the execution of laws by regal authority, as it hath been assumed and exercised of late, is illegal;

That the commission for erecting the late Court of Commissioners for Ecclesiastical Causes, and all other commissions and courts of like nature, are illegal and pernicious;

That levying money for or to the use of the Crown by pretence of prerogative, without grant of Parliament, for longer time, or in other manner than the same is or shall be granted, is illegal;

That it is the right of the subjects to petition the king, and all commitments and prosecutions for such petitioning are illegal;

That the raising or keeping a standing army within the kingdom in time of peace, unless it be with consent of Parliament, is against law;

That the subjects which are Protestants may have arms for their defence suitable to their conditions and as allowed by law;

That election of members of Parliament ought to be free;

That the freedom of speech and debates or proceedings in Parliament ought not to be impeached or questioned in any court or place out of Parliament;

That excessive bail ought not to be required, nor excessive fines imposed, nor cruel and unusual punishments inflicted;

That jurors ought to be duly impanelled and returned, and jurors which pass upon men in trials for high treason ought to be freeholders;

That all grants and promises of fines and forfeitures of particular persons before conviction are illegal and void;

And that for redress of all grievances, and for the amending, strengthening and preserving of the laws, Parliaments ought to be held frequently.

. . . And the Lords Spiritual and Temporal and Commons do pray the said prince and princess to accept the same accordingly.

Upon which their said Majesties did accept the crown and royal dignity of the kingdoms of England, France and Ireland, and the dominions thereunto belonging, according to the resolution and desire of the said Lords and Commons contained in the said declaration. . . . And whereas it hath been found by experience that it is inconsistent with the safety and welfare of this Protestant kingdom to be governed by a popish prince, or by any king or queen marrying a papist, the said Lords Spiritual and Temporal and Commons do further pray that it may be enacted, that all and every person and persons that is, are or shall be reconciled to or shall hold communion with the see or Church of Rome, or shall profess the popish religion, or shall marry a papist, shall be excluded and be for ever incapable to inherit, possess or enjoy the crown and government of this realm and Ireland and the dominions thereunto belonging or any part of the same, or to have, use or exercise any regal power, authority or jurisdiction within the same. . . . All which their Majesties are contented and pleased shall be declared, enacted and established by authority of this present Parliament, and shall stand, remain and be the law of this realm for ever; and the same are by their said Majesties, by and with the advice and consent of the Lords Spiritual and Temporal and Commons in Parliament assembled and by the authority of the same, declared, enacted and established accordingly.

From: http://avalon.law.yale.edu/17th_century/england.asp.

QUESTIONS:

1. What provisions of the Bill of Rights demonstrate that Parliament, not the king, is now the ultimate authority in the British state?
2. What screen image of "Britishness" does the Bill of Rights project? What values does it assert as fundamental?

18.1b: *Second Treatise of Government* (John Locke, 1690)

John Locke (1632–1704) was an English doctor and philosopher who, along with Isaac Newton, is one of the fountainheads of the Enlightenment. He wrote about epistemology, or the theory of knowledge, building on Francis Bacon's work to create a British school of empiricism. He also wrote on political philosophy in his *Second Treatise of Government,* which was written before but published after the Glorious Revolution of 1688. In providing a justification for the actions of 1688, the *Second Treatise* became one of the most influential theories in the modern world about the origins and proper limits of government.

CHAPTER II. OF THE STATE OF NATURE

Sect. 4. TO understand political power right, and derive it from its original, we must consider, what state all men are naturally in, and that is, a state of perfect freedom to order their actions, and dispose of their possessions and persons, as they think fit, within the bounds of the law of nature, without asking leave, or depending upon the will of any other man.

A state also of equality, wherein all the power and jurisdiction is reciprocal, no one having more than another; there being nothing more evident, than that creatures of the same species and rank, promiscuously born to all the same advantages of nature, and the use of the same faculties, should also be equal one amongst another without subordination or subjection, unless the lord and master of them all should, by any manifest declaration of his will, set one above another, and confer on him, by an evident and clear appointment, an undoubted right to dominion and sovereignty. . . .

Sect. 6. But though this be a state of liberty, yet it is not a state of licence: though man in that state have an uncontroulable liberty to dispose of his person or possessions, yet he has not liberty to destroy himself, or so much as any creature in his possession, but where some nobler use than its bare

preservation calls for it. The state of nature has a law of nature to govern it, which obliges every one: and reason, which is that law, teaches all mankind, who will but consult it, that being all equal and independent, no one ought to harm another in his life, health, liberty, or possessions: for men being all the workmanship of one omnipotent, and infinitely wise maker; all the servants of one sovereign master, sent into the world by his order, and about his business; they are his property, whose workmanship they are, made to last during his, not one another's pleasure: and being furnished with like faculties, sharing all in one community of nature, there cannot be supposed any such subordination among us, that may authorize us to destroy one another, as if we were made for one another's uses, as the inferior ranks of creatures are for our's. Every one, as he is bound to preserve himself, and not to quit his station wilfully, so by the like reason, when his own preservation comes not in competition, ought he, as much as he can, to preserve the rest of mankind, and may not, unless it be to do justice on an offender, take away, or impair the life, or what tends to the preservation of the life, the liberty, health, limb, or goods of another.

Sect. 8. And thus, in the state of nature, one man comes by a power over another; but yet no absolute or arbitrary power, to use a criminal, when he has got him in his hands, according to the passionate heats, or boundless extravagancy of his own will; but only to retribute to him, so far as calm reason and conscience dictate, what is proportionate to his transgression, which is so much as may serve for reparation and restraint: for these two are the only reasons, why one man may lawfully do harm to another, which is that we call punishment. In transgressing the law of nature, the offender declares himself to live by another rule than that of reason and common equity, which is that measure God has set to the actions of men, for their mutual security; and so he becomes dangerous to mankind, the tye, which is to secure them from injury and violence, being slighted and broken by him. Which being a trespass against the whole species, and the peace and safety of it, provided for by the law of nature, every man upon this score, by the right he hath to preserve mankind in general, may restrain, or where it is necessary, destroy things noxious to them, and so may bring such evil on any one, who hath transgressed that law, as may make him repent the doing of it, and thereby deter him, and by his example others, from doing the like mischief. And in the case, and upon this ground, EVERY MAN HATH A RIGHT TO PUNISH THE OFFENDER, AND BE EXECUTIONER OF THE LAW OF NATURE.

CHAPTER V. OF PROPERTY

Sect. 25. Whether we consider natural reason, which tells us, that men, being once born, have a right to their preservation, and consequently to meat and drink, and such other things as nature affords for their subsistence: or revelation, which gives us an account of those grants God made of the world to Adam, and to Noah, and his sons, it is very clear, that God, as king David says, Psal. cxv. 16. has given the earth to the children of men; given it to mankind in common. But this being supposed, it seems to some a very great

difficulty, how any one should ever come to have a property in any thing: I will not content myself to answer, that if it be difficult to make out property, upon a supposition that God gave the world to Adam, and his posterity in common, it is impossible that any man, but one universal monarch, should have any property upon a supposition, that God gave the world to Adam, and his heirs in succession, exclusive of all the rest of his posterity. But I shall endeavour to shew, how men might come to have a property in several parts of that which God gave to mankind in common, and that without any express compact of all the commoners.

Sect. 26. God, who hath given the world to men in common, hath also given them reason to make use of it to the best advantage of life, and convenience. The earth, and all that is therein, is given to men for the support and comfort of their being. And tho' all the fruits it naturally produces, and beasts it feeds, belong to mankind in common, as they are produced by the spontaneous hand of nature; and no body has originally a private dominion, exclusive of the rest of mankind, in any of them, as they are thus in their natural state: yet being given for the use of men, there must of necessity be a means to appropriate them some way or other, before they can be of any use, or at all beneficial to any particular man. The fruit, or venison, which nourishes the wild Indian, who knows no enclosure, and is still a tenant in common, must be his, and so his, i.e. a part of him, that another can no longer have any right to it, before it can do him any good for the support of his life.

Sect. 27. Though the earth, and all inferior creatures, be common to all men, yet every man has a property in his own person: this no body has any right to but himself. The labour of his body, and the work of his hands, we may say, are properly his. Whatsoever then he removes out of the state that nature hath provided, and left it in, he hath mixed his labour with, and joined to it something that is his own, and thereby makes it his property.

It being by him removed from the common state nature hath placed it in, it hath by this labour something annexed to it, that excludes the common right of other men: for this labour being the unquestionable property of the labourer, no man but he can have a right to what that is once joined to, at least where there is enough, and as good, left in common for others.

Sect. 28. He that is nourished by the acorns he picked up under an oak, or the apples he gathered from the trees in the wood, has certainly appropriated them to himself. No body can deny but the nourishment is his. I ask then, when did they begin to be his? when he digested? or when he eat? or when he boiled? or when he brought them home? or when he picked them up? and it is plain, if the first gathering made them not his, nothing else could. That labour put a distinction between them and common: that added something to them more than nature, the common mother of all, had done; and so they became his private right. And will any one say, he had no right to those acorns or apples, he thus appropriated, because he had not the consent of all mankind to make them his? Was it a robbery thus to assume to himself what belonged to all in common? If such a consent as that was necessary, man had starved, notwithstanding the plenty God had given him. We see in commons, which remain so by compact, that it is the taking any part of what is common, and removing it out of the state nature leaves it in, which begins the property; without which the common is of no use. And the taking of this or that part, does not depend on the express consent of all the commoners. Thus the grass my horse has bit; the turfs my servant has cut; and the ore I have digged in any place, where I have a right to them in common with others, become my property, without the assignation or consent of any body. The labour that was mine, removing them out of that common state they were in, hath fixed my property in them.

Sect. 32. But the chief matter of property being now not the fruits of the earth, and the beasts that subsist on it, but the earth itself; as that which takes in and carries with it all the rest; I think it is plain, that property in that too is acquired as the former. As much land as a man tills, plants, improves, cultivates, and can use the product of, so much is his property. He by his labour does, as it were, inclose it from the common. Nor will it invalidate his right, to say every body else has an equal title to it; and therefore he cannot appropriate, he cannot inclose, without the consent of all his fellow-commoners, all mankind. God, when he gave the world in common to all mankind, commanded man also to labour, and the penury of his condition required it of him. God and his reason commanded him to subdue the earth, i.e. improve it for the benefit of life, and therein lay out something upon it that was his own, his labour. He that in obedience to this command of God, subdued, tilled and sowed any part of it, thereby annexed to it something that was his property, which another had no title to, nor could without injury take from him.

CHAPTER VIII. OF THE BEGINNING OF POLITICAL SOCIETIES

Sect. 95. MEN being, as has been said, by nature, all free, equal, and independent, no one can be put out of this estate, and subjected to the political power of another, without his own consent. The only way whereby any one divests himself of his natural liberty, and puts on the bonds of civil society, is by agreeing with other men to join and unite into a community for their comfortable, safe, and peaceable living one amongst another, in a secure enjoyment of their properties, and a greater security against any, that are not of it. This any number of men may do, because it injures not the freedom of the rest; they are left as they were in the liberty of the state of nature. When any number of men have so consented to make one community or government, they are thereby presently incorporated, and make one body politic, wherein the majority have a right to act and conclude the rest.

Sect. 96. For when any number of men have, by the consent of every individual, made a community, they have thereby made that community one body, with a power to act as one body, which is only by the will and determination of the majority: for that which acts any community, being only the consent of the individuals of it, and it being necessary to that which is one body to move one way; it is necessary the body should move that way whither the greater force carries it, which is the consent of the majority: or else it is impossible it should act or continue one body, one community, which the consent of every individual that united into it, agreed that it should; and so every one is bound by that consent to be concluded by the majority. And therefore we see, that in assemblies, impowered to act by positive laws, where no number is set by that positive law which impowers them, the act of the majority passes for the act of the whole, and of course determines, as having, by the law of nature and reason, the power of the whole.

From: Locke, John, 1690, *The Project Gutenberg eBook of Second Treatise Of Government by John Locke.*

QUESTIONS:

1. How, according to Locke, does government come about? What fundamental rights does Locke assert?
2. What is the significance of the fact that government is formed by a contract? As a theory of hierarchy, what network values are embedded in the *Second Treatise?* Why might this theory be threatening to rulers of more traditional hierarchies?

THE UNITED STATES

18.2a: *The Zenger Trial* (1735)

The screen image of "The Rights of Englishmen" created by the Bill of Rights and the theories of John Locke traveled with colonists to British North America along with the ancient English institution of trial by jury. These elements combined in the faction-ridden politics of the New York colony to create new developments in self-government. Opponents of William Cosby, the appointed British governor of the colony, published attacks on his actions in a newspaper printed by John Peter Zenger. Cosby issued "an information" (something like an indictment) against Zenger and had him arrested and tried for seditious libel, which under British law required no proof of falsehood. Damage to reputation and any threat to stable government, even if the charges were true, were sufficient for conviction. But at the jury trial of Zenger, Zenger's attorney, Andrew Hamilton, argued that juries could reach conclusions not just about fact (Zenger's actions were uncontested) but about law. The jury agreed and found Zenger innocent in defiance of Cosby's hand-picked judge's instructions. This led to the divergence of American colonial legal tradition from British precedent on both libel and jury power, the latter of which was reinforced as an avenue of just self-government.

[HAMILTON REITERATES THE TASK OF THE JURY. CLOSING STATEMENTS]

Mr. Hamilton. . . . I must insist that where matter of law is complicated with matter of fact, the jury have a right to determine both. As for instance; upon indictment for murder, the jury may, and almost constantly do, take upon them to judge whether the evidence will amount to murder or manslaughter, and find accordingly; and I must say I cannot see why in our case the jury have not at least as good a right to say whether our newspapers are a libel or not libel as another jury has to say whether killing of a man is murder or manslaughter. The right of the jury to find such a verdict as they in their conscience do think is agreeable to their evidence is supported by the authority of Bushel's case, in Vaughan's

Reports, pag. 135, beyond any doubt. . . . The reason given in the same book is *because the judge (as judge) cannot know what the evidence is which the jury have,* that is, *he can only know the evidence given in court; but the evidence which the jury have may be of their own knowledge, as they are returned of the neighborhood. They may also know from their own knowledge that what is sworn in court is not true; and they may know the witnesses to be stigmatized, to which the Court may be strangers.* But what is to my purpose is that suppose that the Court did really know all the evidence which the jury know, yet in that case it is agreed *that the judge and jury may differ in the result of their evidence as well as two judges may,* which often happens. And in pag. 148, the judge subjoins the reason why it is no crime for a jury to differ in opinion from the Court, where he *says that a man cannot see with another's eye, nor hear by another's ear; no more can a man conclude or infer the thing by another's understanding or reasoning.* From all which (I insist) it is very plain *that the jury are by law at liberty (without any affront to the judgment of the Court) to find both the law and the fact in our case* . . . .

. . .

. . . I sincerely believe that were some persons to go through the streets of New York nowadays, and read a part of the Bible, if it was not known to be such, Mr. Attorney, with the help of his *innuendoes,* would easily turn it into a libel. As for instance, *Is.* IX. 16, *The leaders of the people cause them to err, and they that are led by them are destroyed.* But should Mr. Attorney go about to make this libel, he would read it thus; *The leaders of the people* [*innuendo,* the Governor and Council of New York] *cause them* [*innuendo,* the people of this Province] *to err, and they* [the people of this Province meaning] *that are led by them* [the Governor and Council meaning] *are destroyed* [*innuendo,* are deceived into the loss of their liberty] which is the worst kind of destruction. . . . Then if Mr. Attorney is at liberty to come into court, and file an information in the King's name without leave, who is secure whom he

is pleased to prosecute as a libeler? And as the Crown law is contended for in bad times, there is no remedy for the greatest oppression of this sort, even though the party prosecuted is acquitted with honor. And give me leave to say as great men as any in Britain have boldly asserted that the mode of prosecuting by information (when a Grand Jury will not find *billa vera*) is a national grievance, and greatly inconsistent with that freedom which the subjects of England enjoy in most other cases. . . .

Gentlemen; the danger is great in proportion to the mischief that may happen through our too great credulity. A proper confidence in a court is commendable; but as the verdict (whatever it is) will be yours, you ought to refer no part of your duty to the discretion of other persons. If you should be of opinion that there is no falsehood in Mr. Zenger's papers, you will, nay (pardon me for the expression) you ought to say so; because you don't know whether others (I mean the Court) may be of that opinion. It is your right to do so, and there is much depending upon your resolution as well as upon your integrity.

. . .

. . . [T]he question before the Court and you gentlemen of the jury is not of small nor private concern, it is not the cause of a poor printer, nor of New York alone, which you are now trying: No! It may in its consequence affect every freeman that lives under a British government on the main of America. It is the best cause. It is the cause of liberty; and I make no doubt but your upright conduct this day will not only entitle you to the love and esteem of your fellow citizens; but every man who prefers freedom to a life of slavery will bless and honor you as men who have baffled the attempt of tyranny; and by an impartial and uncorrupt verdict, have laid a noble foundation for securing to ourselves, our posterity, and our neighbors that to which nature and the laws of our country have given us a right—the liberty—both of exposing and opposing arbitrary power (in these parts of the world, at least) by speaking and writing truth.

[Here Mr. Attorney observed that Mr. Hamilton had gone very much out of the way, and had made himself and the people very merry: But that he had been citing cases not at all to the purpose; . . . All that the jury had to consider of was Mr. Zenger's printing and publishing two scandalous libels, which very highly reflected on His Excellency and the principal men concerned in the administration of this government, which is confessed. That is, the printing and publishing of the *Journals* set forth in the information is confessed. And concluded that as Mr. Hamilton had confessed the printing and there could be no doubt but they were scandalous papers . . . therefore he made no doubt but the jury would find the Defendant guilty, and would refer to the Court for their direction.]

Mr. Chief Justice. Gentlemen of the jury. The great pains Mr. Hamilton has taken to show how little regard juries are to pay to the opinion of the judges, and his insisting so much upon the conduct of some judges in trials of this kind, is done no doubt with a design that you should take but very little notice of what I might say upon this occasion. I shall therefore only observe to you that as the facts or words in the information are confessed: The only thing that can come in question before you is whether the words as set forth in the information make a libel. And that is a matter of law, no doubt, and which you may leave to the Court. But I shall trouble you no further with anything more of my own, but read to you the words of a learned and upright judge in a case of the like nature.

To say that corrupt officers are appointed to administer affairs is certainly a reflection on the government. If people should not be called to account for possessing the people with an ill opinion of the government, no government can subsist, for it is very necessary for all governments that the people should have a good opinion of it. And nothing can be worse to any government than to endeavor to procure animosities; as to the management of it, this has been always looked upon as a crime, and no government can be safe without it be punished.

Now you are to consider whether these words I have read to you, do not tend to beget an ill opinion of the administration of the government? To tell us, that those that are employed know nothing of the matter, and those that do know are not employed. Men are not adapted to offices, but offices to men, out of a particular regard to their interest, and not to their fitness for the places; this is the purport of these papers.

Mr. Hamilton. I humbly beg Your Honor's pardon: I am very much misapprehended, if you suppose what I said was so designed.

Sir, you know; I made an apology for the freedom I found myself under a necessity of using upon this occasion. I said there was nothing personal designed; it arose from the nature of our defense.

The jury withdrew and in a small time returned and being asked by the Clerk whether they were agreed of their verdict, and whether John Peter Zenger was guilty of printing and publishing the libels in the information mentioned? They answered by Thomas Hunt, their foreman, *Not Guilty,* upon which there were three huzzas in the hall which was crowded with people and the next day I was discharged from my imprisonment.

From: Presser, Stephen B., and Jamil S. Zainaldin, *Law and jurisprudence in American history: cases and materials* (St. Paul: Thomson Reuters/West, 2009), pp. 41–62.

QUESTIONS:

1. How do Hamilton and Chief Justice Delancey argue the case? What is the balance between tradition and precedent on one hand and abstract principles of good government on the other for each?
2. What screen image of British government does Hamilton project in his arguments? What does the public reaction at the end of the trial tell you about the reception of this screen image?

18.2b: *American Declaration of Independence* (1776)

Colonial resentment over instances of "British tyranny" that simmered just below the surface of the Zenger trial grew over the next forty years. Britain and its colonies clashed over tax policy, American freedom to conduct trade on its own terms, and continental expansion. These various conflicts exploded in 1776 and a Continental Congress made up of representative of all thirteen colonies met that summer to declare independence. The declaration of this intent, drafted by Thomas Jefferson, became one of the foundational documents of the new United States of America. With the successful conclusion of its war for independence in 1783, the new country became the leading model of the still radical idea of democratic government.

DECLARATION OF INDEPENDENCE: IN CONGRESS, JULY 4, 1776. THE UNANIMOUS DECLARATION OF THE THIRTEEN UNITED STATES OF AMERICA

When in the Course of human events, it becomes necessary for one people to dissolve the political bands which have connected them with another, and to assume among the powers of the earth, the separate and equal station to which the Laws of Nature and of Nature's God entitle them, a decent respect to the opinions of mankind requires that they should declare the causes which impel them to the separation.

We hold these truths to be self-evident, that all men are created equal, that they are endowed by their Creator with certain unalienable Rights, that among these are Life, Liberty and the pursuit of Happiness.—That to secure these rights, Governments are instituted among Men, deriving their just powers from the consent of the governed,—That whenever any Form of Government becomes destructive of these ends, it is the Right of the People to alter or to abolish it, and to institute new Government, laying its foundation on such principles and organizing its powers in such form, as to them shall seem most likely to effect their Safety and Happiness. Prudence, indeed, will dictate that Governments long established should not be changed for light and transient causes; and accordingly all experience hath shewn, that mankind are more disposed to suffer, while evils are sufferable, than to right themselves by abolishing the forms to which they are accustomed. But when a long train of abuses and usurpations, pursuing invariably the same Object evinces a design to reduce them under absolute Despotism, it is their right, it is their duty, to throw off such Government, and to provide new Guards for their future security.— Such has been the patient sufferance of these Colonies; and such is now the necessity which constrains them to alter their former Systems of Government. The history of the present King of Great Britain is a history of repeated injuries and usurpations, all having in direct object the establishment of an absolute Tyranny over these States. To prove this, let Facts be submitted to a candid world.

He has refused his Assent to Laws, the most wholesome and necessary for the public good.

He has forbidden his Governors to pass Laws of immediate and pressing importance, unless suspended in their operation till his Assent should be obtained; and when so suspended, he has utterly neglected to attend to them.

He has refused to pass other Laws for the accommodation of large districts of people, unless those people would relinquish the right of Representation in the Legislature, a right inestimable to them and formidable to tyrants only.

He has called together legislative bodies at places unusual, uncomfortable, and distant from the depository of their public Records, for the sole purpose of fatiguing them into compliance with his measures.

He has dissolved Representative Houses repeatedly, for opposing with manly firmness his invasions on the rights of the people.

He has refused for a long time, after such dissolutions, to cause others to be elected; whereby the Legislative powers, incapable of Annihilation, have returned to the People at large for their exercise; the State remaining in the mean time exposed to all the dangers of invasion from without, and convulsions within.

He has endeavoured to prevent the population of these States; for that purpose obstructing the Laws for Naturalization of Foreigners; refusing to pass others to encourage their migrations hither, and raising the conditions of new Appropriations of Lands.

He has obstructed the Administration of Justice, by refusing his Assent to Laws for establishing Judiciary powers.

He has made Judges dependent on his Will alone, for the tenure of their offices, and the amount and payment of their salaries.

He has erected a multitude of New Offices, and sent hither swarms of Officers to harrass our people, and eat out their substance.

He has kept among us, in times of peace, Standing Armies without the Consent of our legislatures.

He has affected to render the Military independent of and superior to the Civil power.

He has combined with others to subject us to a jurisdiction foreign to our constitution, and unacknowledged by our laws; giving his Assent to their Acts of pretended Legislation:

For Quartering large bodies of armed troops among us:

For protecting them, by a mock Trial, from punishment for any Murders which they should commit on the Inhabitants of these States:

For cutting off our Trade with all parts of the world:

For imposing Taxes on us without our Consent:

For depriving us in many cases, of the benefits of Trial by Jury:

For transporting us beyond Seas to be tried for pretended offences

For abolishing the free System of English Laws in a neighbouring Province, establishing therein an Arbitrary government, and enlarging its Boundaries so as to render it at once an example and fit instrument for introducing the same absolute rule into these Colonies:

For taking away our Charters, abolishing our most valuable Laws, and altering fundamentally the Forms of our Governments:

For suspending our own Legislatures, and declaring themselves invested with power to legislate for us in all cases whatsoever.

He has abdicated Government here, by declaring us out of his Protection and waging War against us.

He has plundered our seas, ravaged our Coasts, burnt our towns, and destroyed the lives of our people.

He is at this time transporting large Armies of foreign Mercenaries to compleat the works of death, desolation and tyranny, already begun with circumstances of Cruelty & perfidy scarcely paralleled in the most barbarous ages, and totally unworthy the Head of a civilized nation.

He has constrained our fellow Citizens taken Captive on the high Seas to bear Arms against their Country, to become the executioners of their friends and Brethren, or to fall themselves by their Hands.

He has excited domestic insurrections amongst us, and has endeavoured to bring on the inhabitants of our frontiers, the merciless Indian

Savages, whose known rule of warfare, is an un-distinguished destruction of all ages, sexes and conditions.

In every stage of these Oppressions We have Petitioned for Redress in the most humble terms: Our repeated Petitions have been answered only by repeated injury. A Prince whose character is thus marked by every act which may define a Tyrant, is unfit to be the ruler of a free people.

Nor have We been wanting in attentions to our Brittish brethren. We have warned them from time to time of attempts by their legislature to extend an unwarrantable jurisdiction over us. We have reminded them of the circumstances of our emigration and settlement here. We have appealed to their native justice and magnanimity, and we have conjured them by the ties of our common kindred to disavow these usurpations, which, would inevitably interrupt our connections and correspondence. They too have been deaf to the voice of justice and of consanguinity. We must, therefore, acquiesce in the necessity, which denounces our Separation, and hold them, as we hold the rest of mankind, Enemies in War, in Peace Friends.

We, therefore, the Representatives of the united States of America, in General Congress, Assembled, appealing to the Supreme Judge of the world for the rectitude of our intentions, do, in the Name, and by Authority of the good People of these Colonies, solemnly publish and declare, That these United Colonies are, and of Right ought to be Free and Independent States; that they are Absolved from all Allegiance to the British Crown, and that all political connection between them and the State of Great Britain, is and ought to be totally dissolved; and that as Free and Independent States, they have full Power to levy War, conclude Peace, contract Alliances, establish Commerce, and to do all other Acts and Things which Independent States may of right do. And for the support of this Declaration, with a firm reliance on the protection of divine Providence, we mutually pledge to each other our Lives, our Fortunes and our sacred Honor.

From: http://www.archives.gov/exhibits/charters/declaration_transcript.html.

QUESTIONS:

1. What similarities exist between the Declaration of Independence and the Bill of Rights of 1689? Why does the Declaration focus on the actions of King George? What screen image of British rule does the Declaration project?
2. What debt does the Declaration owe to John Locke for its statement of the principles of government? What are the differences in fundamental rights between the two? What is the significance of the difference?

FRANCE

18.3a: *The Declaration of the Rights of Man and Citizen* (1789)

The contradictions between traditional hierarchy values, especially the idea of absolute royal power, and ideas about natural political rights, whose origins lay in the growing influence of network values filtered through the British political experience and Enlightenment philosophy, came to a head in France when the royal government went bankrupt (again) in 1789. King Louis XVI called the Estates General, the long dormant analogue of the

British Parliament; its Third Estate, or the representative of commoners (in actuality dominated by merchant and urban "middle class" interests) declared itself the National Constituent Assembly and launched the French Revolution. One of its first acts was to publish a Declaration of the Rights of Man and Citizen stating the ideals at which the Revolution aimed.

The Representatives of the French people, organized in National Assembly, considering that ignorance, forgetfulness, or contempt of the rights of man are the sole causes of public miseries and the corruption of governments, have resolved to set forth in a solemn declaration the natural, inalienable, and sacred rights of man, so that this declaration, being ever present to all the members of the social body, may unceasingly remind them of their rights and duties; in order that the acts of the legislative power, and those of the executive power, may at each moment be compared with the aim and of every political institution and thereby may be more respected; and in order that the demands of the citizens, grounded henceforth upon simple and incontestable principles, may always take the direction of maintaining the constitution and welfare of all.

In consequence, the National Assembly recognizes and declares, in the presence and under the auspices of the Supreme Being, the following rights of man and citizen:

Articles:

1. Men are born free and remain free and equal in rights. Social distinctions can be based only on public utility.
2. The aim of every political association is the preservation of the natural and imprescriptible rights of man. These rights are liberty, property, security, and resistance to oppression.
3. The sources of all sovereignty resides essentially in the nation; no body, no individual can exercise authority that does not proceed from it in plain terms.
4. Liberty consists in the power to do anything that does not injure others; accordingly, the exercise of the rights of each man has no limits except those that secure the enjoyment of these same rights to the other members of society. These limits can be determined only by law.
5. The law has only the rights to forbid such actions as are injurious to society. Nothing can be forbidden that is not interdicted by the law, and no one can be constrained to do that which it does not order.
6. Law is the expression of the general will. All citizens have the right to take part personally, or by their representatives, and its formation. It must be the same for all, whether it protects or punishes. All citizens, being equal in its eyes, art equally eligible to all public dignities, places, and employments, according to their capacities, and without other distinction than that of their virtues and talents.
7. No man can be accused, arrested, or detained, except in the cases determined by the law and according to the forms it has prescribed. Those who procure, expedite, execute, or cause arbitrary orders to be executed, ought to be punished: but every citizen summoned were seized in virtue of the law ought to render instant obedience; he makes himself guilty by resistance.
8. The law ought only to establish penalties that are strict and obviously necessary, and no one can be punished except in virtue of a law established and promulgated prior to the offense and legally applied.
9. Every man being presumed innocent until he has been pronounced guilty, if it is thought indispensable to arrest him, all severity that may not be necessary to secure his person ought to be strictly suppressed by law.
10. No one should be disturbed on account of his opinions, even religious, provided their

manifestation does not upset the public order established by law.

11. The free communication of ideas and opinions is one of the most precious of the rights of man; every citizen can then freely speak, write, and print, subject to responsibility for the abuse of this freedom in the cases is determined by law.

12. The guarantee of the rights of man and citizen requires a public force; this force then is instituted for the advantage of all and not for the personal benefit of those to whom it is entrusted.

13. A general tax is indispensable for the maintenance of the public force and for the expenses of administration; it ought to be equally apportioned among all citizens according to their means.

14. All the citizens have a right to ascertain, by themselves or by their representatives, the necessity of the public tax, to consent to it freely, to follow the employment of it, and to determine the quota, the assessment, the collection, and the duration of it.

15. Society has the right to call for an account of his administration by every public agent.

16. Any society in which the guarantee of the rights is not secured, or the separation of powers not determined, has no constitution at all.

17. Property being a sacred to and inviolable right, no one can be deprived of it, unless illegally established public necessity evidently demands it, under the condition of a just and prior indemnity.

From: Frank Maloy Anderson, ed., *The Constitution and Other Select Documents Illustrative of the History of France, 1789–1907* (New York: Russell and Russell, 1908), pp. 59–61.

QUESTIONS:

1. Compare this Declaration to the British Bill of Rights and the American Declaration of Independence. What are the similarities? Where do they diverge?

2. The French system of government in 1788 was very different from the British system of 1687 or the American system of 1775, neither of which had to be radically altered as a result of their Revolutions. How does the different French context shape the French statement of rights?

18.3b: *Declaration of the Rights of Woman and the Female Citizen* (Olympe de Gouges, 1791)

As early as October 1789, French women joined the Revolution and petitioned the National Assembly with a declaration of women's equality, protesting that the male representative, while eliminating almost every other form of inequality, "would leave standing the oldest and most general of all abuses." The failure of this petition led Olympe de Gouges (1748–1793), a playwright and political activist who was the daughter of a butcher and a cloth merchant mother, to write another declaration that called men to task again for excluding women from their Revolution. Olympe fell victim to the Revolution in 1793, when she went under the guillotine during the Reign of Terror.

Man, are you capable of being just? It is a woman who poses the question; you will not deprive her of that right at least. Tell me, what gives you sovereign empire to oppress my sex? Your strength? Your talents? Observe the Creator in his wisdom; survey in all her grandeur that nature with whom you seem to want to be in harmony, and give me, if you dare, an example of this tyrannical empire. Go back to animals, consult the elements, study plants, finally glance at all the modifications of organic matter, and surrender to the evidence when I offer you the means; search, probe, and distinguish, if you can, the sexes in the administration of nature. Everywhere, you will find them mingled; everywhere they cooperate in harmonious togetherness in this immortal masterpiece.

Man alone has raised his exceptional circumstances to a principle. Bizarre, blind, bloated with science and degenerated—in a century of enlightenment and wisdom—into the crassest ignorance, he wants to command as a despot a sex which is in full possession of its intellectual faculties; he pretends to enjoy the Revolution and to claim his rights to equality in order to say nothing more about it.

DECLARATION OF THE RIGHTS OF WOMAN AND THE FEMALE CITIZEN

For the National Assembly to decree in its last sessions, or in those of the next legislature:

Preamble:

Mothers, daughters, sisters [and] representatives of the nation demand to be constituted into a national assembly. Believing that ignorance, omission, or scorn for the rights of woman are the only causes of public misfortunes and of the corruption of governments, [the women] have resolved to set forth in a solemn declaration the natural, inalienable, and sacred rights of woman in order that this declaration, constantly exposed before all the members of the society, will ceaselessly remind them of their rights and duties; in order that the authoritative acts of women and the authoritative acts of men may be at any moment compared with and respectful of the purpose of all political institutions; and in order that citizens' demands, henceforth based on simple and incontestable principles, will

always support the constitution, good morals, and the happiness of all.

Consequently, the sex that is as superior in beauty as it is in courage during the sufferings of maternity recognizes and declares in the presence and under the auspices of the Supreme Being, the following Rights of Woman and of Female Citizens.

1. Woman is born free and lives equal to man in her rights. Social distinctions can be based only on the common utility.

2. The purpose of any political association is the conservation of the natural and imprescriptible rights of woman and man,; these rights are liberty, property, security, and especially resistance to oppression.

3. The principle of all sovereignty rests essentially with the nation, which is nothing but the union of woman and man; no body and no individual can exercise any authority which does not come expressly from it [the nation].

4. Liberty and justice consist of restoring all that belongs to others; thus, the only limits on the exercise of the natural rights of woman are perpetual male tyranny; these limits are to be reformed by the laws of nature and reason.

5. Laws of nature and justice proscribe all acts harmful to society; everything which is not prohibited by these wise and divine laws cannot be prevented, and no one can be constrained to do what they do not command.

6. The law must be the expression of the general will; all female and male citizens must contribute either personally or through their representatives to its formation; it must be the same for all; male and female citizens, being equal in the eyes of the law, must be equally admitted to all honors, positions, and public employment according to their capacity and without other distinctions besides those of their virtues and talents.

7. No woman is an exception; she is accused, arrested, and detained in cases determined by law. Women, like men, obey this rigorous law.

8. The law must establish only those penalties that are strictly and obviously necessary, and no one can be punished except by virtue of a law established and promulgated prior to the crime and legally applicable to women.

9. Once any woman is declared guilty, complete rigor is [to be] exercised by the law.

10. No one is to be disquieted for his very basic opinions; woman has the right to mount the scaffold; she must equally have the right to mount the rostrum, provided that her demonstrations do not disturb the legally established public order.

11. The free communication of thoughts and opinions is one of the most precious rights of woman, since that liberty assures the recognition of children by their fathers. Any female citizen thus may say freely, I am the mother of a child which belongs to you, without being forced by a barbarous prejudice to hide the truth; [an exception may be made] to respond to the abuse of this liberty in cases determined by the law.

12. The guarantee of the rights of woman and the female citizen implies a major benefit; this guarantee must be instituted for the advantage of all, and not for the particular benefit of those to whom it is entrusted.

13. For the support of the public force and the expenses of administration, the contributions of woman and man are equal; she shares all the duties [corvees] and all the painful tasks; therefore, she must have the same share in the distribution of positions, employment, offices, honors and jobs [industrie].

14. Female and male citizens have the right to verify, either by themselves or through their representatives, the necessity of the public contribution. This can only apply to women in they are granted an equal share, not only of wealth, but also of public administration, and in the determination of the proportion, the base, the collection, and the duration of the tax.

15. The collectivity of women, joined for tax purposes to the aggregate of men, has the right to demand an accounting of his administration from any public agent.

16. No society has a constitution without the guarantee of rights and the separation of powers; the constitution is null if the majority of individuals comprising the nation have not cooperated in drafting it.

17. Property belongs to both sexes whether united or separate; for each it is an inviolable and sacred right; no one can be deprived of it, since it is the true patrimony of nature, unless the legally determined public need obviously dictates it, and then only with a just and prior indemnity.

Postscript

Woman, wake up; the tocsin [warning bell] of reason is being heard throughout the whole universe; discover your rights. The powerful empire of nature is no longer surrounded by prejudice, fanaticism, superstition, and lies. The flame of truth has dispersed all the clouds of folly and usurpation. Enslaved man has multiplied his strength and needs recourse to yours to break his chains. Having become free, he has become unjust to his companion. Oh, women, women! When will you cease to be blind? What advantage have you received from the Revolution? A more pronounced scorn, a more marked disdain. In the centuries of corruption you ruled only over the weakness of men. The reclamation of your patrimony, based on the wise decrees of nature—what have you to dread from such a fine undertaking? . . .

From: Levy, Darline Gay, Harriet Branson Applewhite, and Mary Durham Johnson, *Women in Revolutionary Paris, 1789–1795: selected documents translated with notes and commentary* (Urbana: University of Illinois Press, 1979), pp. 87–92.

QUESTIONS:

1. The Declaration is clearly modeled on the declaration of 1789 in the previous source. What differences in language does it contain, especially in the preamble? What is the significance of those differences?
2. What frame value uniting all the preceding documents in this chapter does this Declaration reveal? What does this say about the history of Agrarian societies, especially the divisions of the Agrarian social pyramid?

HAITI

18.4:   *Speeches and Letters on the Haitian Revolution* (Toussaint Louverture, 1801)

Toussaint Louverture (1743–1803) was a military leader who led the French colony of Sant-Domingue to independence as Haiti. He was born into slavery on a Haitian plantation to royal African parents who had been enslaved. Somehow he obtained some education, perhaps from Jesuit priests—he was a devout Catholic. Freed in 1776, he rose in the island's society, obtaining property and wealth and even renting a plantation worked by slaves. The outbreak of the French Revolution in 1789 destabilized Saint-Domingue. Major slave revolts became a general rebellion against French rule in 1791. Louverture assumed a leading role, negotiating with Spain for support. The war lasted through several French regimes. Louverture proposed a Constitution in 1801 to Napoleon Bonaparte, excerpted below with the letter Louverture sent with it. But it was not until 1804, after several disastrous campaigns by French troops on the island, that Napoleon finally conceded Haitian independence.

27 Messidor, year IX

Citizen Consul

The Minister of the Navy, in the account he gave you of the political situation of this colony, which I devoted myself to making known to him, should have submitted to you my proclamation of last 16 Pluviôse [5 February 1801] on the convocation of a Central Assembly, which would be able to set the destiny of St-Domingue through wise laws modelled on the mores of its inhabitants. I today have the satisfaction of announcing to you that the final touch has just been put to this work. I hasten to send it to you in order to have your approval and the sanction of my government.

Given the absence of laws, and the Central Assembly having requested to have this constitution provisionally executed, which will more quickly lead St-Domingue to its future prosperity, I have surrendered to its wishes. This constitution was received by all classes of citizens with transports of joy that will not fail to be reproduced when it is sent back bearing the sanction of the government.

Greetings and profound respect

Toussaint L'Ouverture

. . .

The representatives of the colony of St-Domingue, gathered in Central Assembly, have identified and established the constitutional bases of the regime of the French colony of St-Domingue as follows:

TITLE I OF THE TERRITORY

Art. 1. St-Domingue in its entire expanse, and Samana, La Tortue, La Gonave, Les Cayemites, L'Ile-a-Vache, La Saone and other adjacent islands form the territory of a single colony, which is part of the French Empire, but ruled under particular laws.

Art. 2. The territory of this colony is divided in departments, *arrondissements* (districts) and parishes.

TITLE II OF THE INHABITANTS

Art. 3. There cannot exist slaves on this territory, servitude is therein forever abolished. All men are born, live and die free and French.

Art. 4. All men, regardless of colour, are eligible for all employment.

Art. 5. There shall exist no distinction other than those based on virtue and talent, and other superiority afforded by law in the exercise of a public function.

The law is the same for all whether in punishment or in protection.

TITLE III OF THE RELIGION

Art. 6. The Catholic, apostolic, Roman faith shall be the only publicly professed faith.

Art. 7. Each parish shall provide for the maintenance of the cult of religion and of its ministers. The wealth of the factories shall be especially allocated to this expense, and the residences to the housing of ministers.

Art. 8. The Governor of the colony shall assign to each minister of religion the extent of his spiritual administration, and said ministers can never, under any circumstance, form a corps in the colony.

TITLE IV OF THE MORES

Art. 9. Marriage, by its civic and religious institution, supports the purity of mores; spouses who will practise the virtues required by their condition shall always be distinguished and specially protected by the government.

Art. 10. Divorce shall not take place in the colony.

Art. 11. Laws that will tend to expand and maintain social virtues, and to encourage and cement family bonding, shall fix the condition and rights of children born in wedlock.

TITLE V OF MEN IN SOCIETY

Art. 12. The Constitution guarantees freedom and individual security. No one shall be arrested unless by a formally expressed mandate, issued from a functionary to whom the law grants the right to order arrest and detention in a publicly designated location.

Art. 13. Property is sacred and inviolable. Each person, either by himself, or by his representatives, has the free right to dispose of and to administer property that is recognized as belonging to him. Anyone who attempts to deny this right shall become guilty of crime towards society and responsible towards the person whose property is troubled.

TITLE VI OF CULTURES AND COMMERCE

Art. 14. The colony being essentially agricultural cannot suffer the least disruption in the works of its cultivation.

Art. 15. Each plantation shall constitute a manufacture that requires the gathering of cultivators and workers; it shall represent the quiet haven of an active and constant family, of which the owner of the land or his representative shall be the father.

Art. 16. Each cultivator and each worker is a member of the family and is entitled to a share in the revenues.

Every change in domicile on the part of the cultivator threatens the ruin of the crops. In order to repress a vice as disruptive to the colony as it is to public order, the Governor issues all policy requirements necessary in the circumstances and in conformance with the bases of the rules of police of 20 Vendémiaire, year IX [12 October 1800], and of the proclamation of the following 19th Pluviôse [9 February 1801] of the Chief General Toussaint-L'Ouverture.

Art. 17. The introduction of cultivators indispensable to the reestablishment and to the growth of agriculture shall take place in St-Domingue. The Constitution charges the Governor to take convenient measures to encourage and favour the increase in manpower, to stipulate and balance the diverse interests, to ensure and guarantee the execution of respective engagements resulting from this process.

Art. 18. Commerce in the colony consists uniquely of exchange goods produced on its territory; consequently. the introduction of goods similar in nature is and shall remain prohibited.

TITLE VII OF THE LEGISLATION AND LEGISLATIVE AUTHORITY

Art. 19. The colonial regime is determined by laws proposed by the Governor and rendered by a gathering of inhabitants, who shall meet at fixed periods at the central seat of the colony under the title Central Assembly of St-Domingue.

Art. 20. No law relative to the internal administration of the colony shall be promulgated unless it contains the following formula:

The Central Assembly of St-Domingue. upon the proposition of the Governor, renders the following law:

Art. 21. No law shall be obligatory to the citizen until the day it is promulgated in the chief town of each department.

The promulgation of law shall take place as follows: In the name of the French colony of St-Domingue, the Governor orders that the subsequent law be sealed, promulgated and executed in all of the colony.

Art 22. The Central Assembly of St-Domingue shall be composed of two representatives of each department, whom, to be eligible, shall be at least thirty years of age and have resided for five years in the colony.

Art. 23. The Assembly shall be renewed every two years by half; no one shall be a member for six consecutive years. The election shall proceed as follows: every two years each municipality nominates one deputy each, on the 10th Ventôse [1 March], each of the deputies, who shall meet ten days thereafter at the chief town of their respective departments, where they shall form as

many departmental electoral assemblies that will each nominate one representative to the Central Assembly.

The next election shall take place on the 10th Ventôse of the eleventh year of the French Republic [1 March 1803]. In case of death, resignation or other vacancy of one or several members of the Assembly, the Governor shall provide a replacement.

He shall equally designate the members of the current Central Assembly who, at the time of its first renewal, shall remain members of the Assembly for two additional years.

Art. 24. The Central Assembly shall vote the adoption or the rejection of laws that are proposed to it by the Governor; it shall express its vote on rules made and on the application of laws already made, on abuses to correct, on improvements to undertake in all parts of service of the colony

. . .

Art. 26. On the state of revenues and spending that are proposed to the Assembly by the Governor, the Central Assembly shall determine, when appropriate, establishment of rates, quotas, the duration and mode of tax collection, its increase or decrease; these conditions shall be summarily printed

TITLE VIII OF THE GOVERNMENT

Art. 27. The administrative direction of the government shall be entrusted to a Governor who corresponds directly with the government of the Metropole, on all matters relative to the interests of the colony.

Art. 28. The Constitution nominates the citizen Toussaint-L'Ouverture, Chief General of the army of St-Domingue. and, in consideration for important services rendered to the colony, in the most critical circumstances of the revolution, and upon the wishes of the grateful inhabitants, he is entrusted the direction thereof for the remainder of his glorious life.

Art. 29. In the future, each Governor shall be nominated for five years, and shall continue every five years for reasons of his good administration.

Art. 30. In order to strengthen the tranquillity that the colony owes to the steadfastness, activity, indefatigable zeal and rare virtues of General Toussaint L'Ouverture, and as a sign of the unlimited trust of the inhabitants of St-Domingue. the constitution attributes exclusively to this general the right to designate the citizen who, in the unfortunate event of the general's death, shall immediately replace him. . . .

TITLE XI OF THE ARMED FORCES

Art. 52. The Armed Forces are essentially obedient, they can never deliberate; they are at the disposition of the Governor who can mobilize them only to maintain public order, protection due to all citizens, and the defence of the colony.

Art. 53. They are divided into the paid colonial guard and the unpaid colonial guard.

Art. 54. The unpaid colonial guard shall not go outside the limits of its parish unless there is a case of imminent danger, and upon the order and the responsibility of the local military commander.

Outside of its parish it shall be compensated; and shall submit, in this case, to military discipline, and in all other cases it is only subject to the law.

Art. 55. The state police force of the colony shall be part of the Armed Forces; it shall be divided into a mounted force and a pedestrian force. The mounted force is instituted for the policing of the countryside; it has charge of the wealth of the colony.

The pedestrian force is instituted for the policing of cities and towns; it shall be at the charge of the city or town for which it performs services.

Art. 56. The army is recruited upon the request of the Governor to the Central Assembly, according to the mode established by law.

. . .

TITLE XIII GENERAL DISPOSITIONS

Art. 63. The residence of any person shall constitute an inviolable abode. During night-time, no one shall have the right to enter therein unless in case of fire, flooding or upon request from within. During the day, authorities shall have access for a particular objective determined either by a law or by an order issued by a public authority.

Art. 64. For an act ordering the arrest of a person to be executed, it must

(1) formally express the motive of the arrest and the law in virtue of which it is ordered;
(2) be issued by a functionary whom the law formally empowers to do so;
(3) be presented to the person in the form of a copy of the warrant.

Art. 65. Anyone who, without the authority of the law to make an arrest, gives, signs, executes or causes to be executed the arrest of a person shall be guilty of the crime of arbitrary detention.

Art. 66. Any person shall have the right to address individual petitions to all constitutional authorities and especially to the Governor.

. . .

Made at Port Républicain, this 19th Floréal, year IX [10 May 1801] of the French Republic, one and indivisible.

Signed:

Borgella, President,

Raymond Collet Gaston Nogérée,

Lacour,

Roxas,

Munos,

Mancebo,

E. Viert, secretary

After having taken knowledge of the Constitution, I give it my approval. The invitation of the Central Assembly is for me an order; consequently, I shall pass it to the French government in order to obtain its sanction; as for its execution in the colony, the wish expressed by the Central Assembly shall be fulfilled as well and executed.

Given at Cap Français, this 14th Messidor, year IX [3 July 1801] of the French Republic, one and indivisible.

The General in Chief:

Signed: Toussaint L'Ouverture

From: Toussaint Louverture, Jean-Bertrand Aristide, and Nick Nesbitt, *The Haitian revolution* (London: Verso, 2008), pp. 42–61.

QUESTIONS:

1. What aspects of the Haitian Constitution reflect French influence? How is it similar to the earlier sources in this chapter, and how does it differ?
2. What kind of hierarchy does this Constitution establish?

CHAPTER 19

The Industrial Revolution: Overview, Networks, Economics

INTRODUCTION

The transitions of the Late Agrarian Era paved the way for the Industrial Revolution and the beginning of a new industrial era in world history. The Industrial Revolution began in England in the late eighteenth century and became a global phenomenon over the next two hundred years. The transition to the Industrial Era led to massive changes in all areas of societal organization, network activity, and culture. The sources presented in this chapter focus on the early nineteenth century and show the early causes and effects of that transformation.

19.1: *Patent Application for Steam Engine* (James Watt, 1782)

James Watt (1736–1819) was a Scottish inventor whose story is told at the beginning of *Frameworks* Chapter 19. He is best known for his improvements to Thomas Newcomen's steam engine (invented 1712). Watt's improvements worked so well that steam power became the practical engine of industrialization. In 1775 he partnered with Matthew Boulton, an entrepreneur and investor, to market his invention, which he also attempted to protect from commercial competition by patenting. One of his many patent applications is excerpted below. To measure the work output of his engines, he invented the concept of horsepower, and the watt, a standard unit of energy in the International System of Units (SI) is named in honor of him.

WHEREAS His Most Excellent Majesty King George the Third, by His Letters Patent, under the Great Seal of Great Britain, bearing date at Westminster, the twelfth day of March, in the twenty-second year of His reign [1782], did give and grant unto me, the said JAMES WATT, His especial licence, full power, sole privilege and authority, that I, the said JAMES WATT, my executors, administrators and assigns, should, and lawfully might, during the term of years therein expressed, make, use, exercise, and vend, within that part of his Majesty's Kingdom of Great

Britain called England, his Dominion of Wales, and Town of Berwick upon Tweed, my invention of 'CERTAIN NEW IMPROVEMENTS UPON STEAM OR FIRE ENGINES FOR RAISING WATER, AND OTHER MECHANICAL PURPOSES, AND CERTAIN NEW PIECES OF MECHANISM APPLICABLE TO THE SAME;' in which said recited Letters Patent is contained a Proviso obliging me, the said JAMES WATT, by an instrument in writing under my hand and seal, to cause a particular description of the nature of my said invention, and in what manner the same is to be performed, to be inrolled in his Majesty's High Court of Chancery within four calendar months after the date of the said Letters Patent, as in and by the said Letters Patent, relation being hereunto had, may more at large appear.

. . .

I PERFORM THIS [new improvement of steam or fire engines], FIRST, by means of two wheels or sectors of circles, one of which is attached to the pump rods, and the other to the piston rod of the engine, and which are connected together by means of rods or chains, or otherwise, so that the levers whereby they act upon one another decrease and increase respectively during the ascent

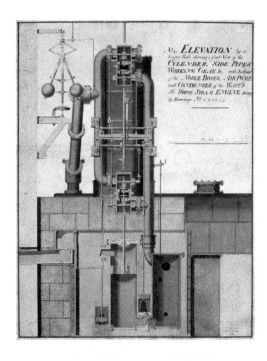

or descent of the piston, in, or nearly in, the ratios required. This method, mechanism, or contrivance, is delineated in fig. 2nd and also its application to one of my new invented steam engines, the sole use and benefit of which was granted to me by an Act of Parliament passed in the fifteenth year of the reign of his present Majesty [1775].

From: Robinson, Eric, and A. E. Musson, *James Watt and the steam revolution: a documentary history* (London: Adams & Dart, 1969), pp. 96–107, passim.

QUESTIONS:

1. What frame values shape the form and content of this patent application? What is the central function of the patent for Watt?
2. What does the form and content of this patent tell you about the operations of the British state? Characterize and explain, for example the style of writing in the patent. (Does Watt sound more like Jahangir [Chapter 16] or an IRS tax form?)

19.2: *The Sadler Committee Report* (Michael Sadler, 1832)

Early industrialization in England created unprecedented working conditions for great masses of laborers, including women and children. (Whether "unprecedented" means better or worse than working conditions in most Agrarian economies is a matter of debate, though in the long run, the answer is clear.) Michael Sadler

(1780–1835), a member of the House of Commons of the British Parliament, introduced legislation in 1831 to limit the working hours of children and otherwise ameliorate some of the harsh working conditions (especially for children and women) that industrialization had abruptly created. Although his initial legislation failed, he chaired a committee of parliament that investigated the problem. The testimony of 89 workers was published in *The Sadler Report*, which ultimately led to labor reforms, but only after Sadler's death. Some of the testimony in the report is excerpted here.

EVIDENCE GIVEN BEFORE THE SADLER COMMITTEE

Joshua Drake, called in; and Examined.

You say you would prefer moderate labour and lower wages; are you pretty comfortable upon your present wages?

—I have no wages, but two days a week at present; but when I am working at some jobs we can make a little, and at others we do very poorly.

When a child gets 3s. a week, does that go much towards its subsistence?

—No, it will not keep it as it should do.

When they got 6s. or 7s. when they were pieceners, if they reduced the hours of labor, would they not get less?

—They would get a halfpenny a day less, but I would rather have less wages and less work.

Do you receive any parish assistance?

—No.

Why do you allow your children to go to work at those places where they are ill-treated or over-worked?

—Necessity compels a man that has children to let them work.

Then you would not allow your children to go to those factories under the present system, if it was not from necessity?

—No.

Supposing there was a law passed to limit the hours of labour to eight hours a day, or something of that sort, of course you are aware that a manufacturer could not afford to pay them the same wages?

—No, I do not suppose that they would, but at the same time I would rather have it, and I believe that it would bring me into employ; and if I lost 5d. a day from my children's work, and I got half-a-crown myself, it would be better.

How would it get you into employ?

—By finding more employment at the machines, and work being more regularly spread abroad, and divided amongst the people at large. One man is now regularly turned off into the street, whilst another man is running day and night.

You mean to say, that if the manufacturers were to limit the hours of labour, they would employ more people?

—Yes.

Mr. Matthew Crabtree, called in; and Examined.

What age are you?

—Twenty-two.

What is your occupation?

—A blanket manufacturer.

Have you ever been employed in a factory?

—Yes.

At what age did you first go to work in one?

—Eight.

How long did you continue in that occupation?

—Four years.

Will you state the hours of labour at the period when you first went to the factory, in ordinary times?

—From 6 in the morning to 8 at night.

Fourteen hours?
—Yes.

With what intervals for refreshment and rest?
—An hour at noon.

When trade was brisk what were your hours?
—From 5 in the morning to 9 in the evening.

Sixteen hours?
—Yes.

With what intervals at dinner?
—An hour.

How far did you live from the mill?
—About two miles.

Was there any time allowed for you to get your breakfast in the mill?
—No.

Did you take it before you left your home?
—Generally.

During those long hours of labour could you be punctual; how did you awake?
—I seldom did awake spontaneously; I was most generally awoke or lifted out of bed, sometimes asleep, by my parents.

Were you always in time?
—No.

What was the consequence if you had been too late?
—I was most commonly beaten.

Severely?
—Very severely, I thought.

In those mills is chastisement towards the latter part of the day going on perpetually?
—Perpetually.

So that you can hardly be in a mill without hearing constant crying?
—Never an hour, I believe.

Do you think that if the overlooker were naturally a humane person it would still be found necessary for him to beat the children, in order to keep up their attention and vigilance at the termination of those extraordinary days of labour?
—Yes; the machine turns off a regular quantity of cardings, and of course, they must keep as regularly to their work the whole of the day; they must keep with the machine, and therefore however humane the slubber may be, as he must keep up with the machine or be found fault with, he spurs the children to keep up also by various means but that which he commonly resorts to is to strap them when they become drowsy.

At the time when you were beaten for not keeping up with your work, were you anxious to have done it if you possibly could?
—Yes; the dread of being beaten if we could not keep up with our work was a sufficient impulse to keep us to it if we could.

When you got home at night after this labour, did you feel much fatigued?
—Very much so.

Had you any time to be with your parents, and to receive instruction from them?
—No.

What did you do?
—All that we did when we got home was to get the little bit of supper that was provided for us and go to bed immediately. If the supper had not been ready directly, we should have gone to sleep while it was preparing.

Did you not, as a child, feel it a very grievous hardship to be roused so soon in the morning?
—I did.

Were the rest of the children similarly circumstanced?
—Yes, all of them; but they were not all of them so far from their work as I was.

And if you had been too late you were under the apprehension of being cruelly beaten?
—I generally was beaten when I happened to be too late; and when I got up in the morning the apprehension of that was so great, that I used to run, and cry all the way as I went to the mill.

Elizabeth Bentley, called in; and Examined.

What age are you?
—Twenty-three.

Where do you live?
—At Leeds.

What time did you begin to work at a factory?
—When I was six years old.

At whose factory did you work?
—Mr. Busk's.

What kind of mill is it?
—Flax-mill.

What was your business in that mill?
—I was a little doffer.

What were your hours of labour in that mill?
—From 5 in the morning till 9 at night, when they were thronged.

For how long a time together have you worked that excessive length of time?
—For about half a year.

What were your usual hours when you were not so thronged?
—From 6 in the morning till 7 at night.

What time was allowed for your meals?
—Forty minutes at noon.

Had you any time to get your breakfast or drinking?
—No, we got it as we could.

And when your work was bad, you had hardly any time to eat it at all?

—No; we were obliged to leave it or take it home, and when we did not take it, the overlooker took it, and gave it to his pigs.

Do you consider doffing a laborious employment?
—Yes.

Explain what it is you had to do?
—When the frames are full, they have to stop the frames, and take the flyers off, and take the full bobbins off, and carry them to the roller; and then put empty ones on, and set the frame going again.

Does that keep you constantly on your feet?
—Yes, there are so many frames, and they run so quick.

Your labour is very excessive?
—Yes; you have not time for any thing.

Suppose you flagged a little, or were too late, what would they do?
—Strap us.

Are they in the habit of strapping those who are last in doffing?
—Yes.

Constantly?
—Yes.

Girls as well as boys?
—Yes.

Have you ever been strapped?
—Yes.

Severely?
—Yes.

Could you eat your food well in that factory?
—No, indeed I had not much to eat, and the little I had I could not eat it, my appetite was so poor, and being covered with dust; and it was no use to take it home, I could not eat it, and the overlooker took it, and gave it to the pigs.

You are speaking of the breakfast?
—Yes.

How far had you to go for dinner?
—We could not go home to dinner.

Where did you dine?
—In the mill.

Did you live far from the mill?
—Yes, two miles.

Had you a clock?
—No, we had not.

Supposing you had not been in time enough in the morning at these mills, what would have been the consequence?
—We should have been quartered.

What do you mean by that?
—If we were a quarter of an hour too late, they would take off half an hour; we only got a penny an hour, and they would take a halfpenny more.

The fine was much more considerable than the loss of time?
—Yes.

Were you also beaten for being too late?
—No, I was never beaten myself, I have seen the boys beaten for being too late.

Were you generally there in time?
—Yes; my mother had been up at 4 o'clock in the morning, and at 2 o'clock in the morning; the colliers used to go to their work about 3 or 4 o'clock, and when she heard them stirring she has got up out of her warm bed, and gone out and asked them the time; and I have sometimes been at Hunslet Car at 2 o'clock in the morning, when it was streaming down with rain, and we have had to stay until the mill was opened.

Peter Smart, called in; and Examined.

You say you were locked up night and day?
—Yes.

Do the children ever attempt to run away?
—Very often.

Were they pusued and brought back again?
—Yes, the overseer pursued them, and brought them back.

Did you ever attempt to run away?
—Yes, I ran away twice.

And you were brought back?
—Yes; and I was sent up to the master's loft, and thrashed with a whip for running away.

Were you bound to this man?
—Yes, for six years.

By whom were you bound?
—My mother got 15s. for the six years.

Do you know whether the children were, in point of fact, compelled to stop during the whole time for which they were engaged?
—Yes, they were.

By law?
—I cannot say by law; but they were compelled by the master; I never saw any law used there but the law of their own hands.

To what mill did you next go?
—To Mr. Webster's, at Battus Den, within eleven miles of Dundee.

In what situation did you act there?
—I acted as overseer.

At 17 years of age?
—Yes.

Did you inflict the same punishment that you yourself had experienced?
—I went as an overseer; not as a slave, but as a slave-driver.

What were the hours of labour in that mill?
—My master told me that I had to produce a certain quantity of yarn; the hours were at that time fourteen; I said that I was not able to produce

the quantity of yarn that was required; I told him if he took the timepiece out of the mill I would produce that quantity, and after that time I found no difficulty in producing the quantity.

How long have you worked per day in order to produce the quantity your master required?
—I have wrought nineteen hours.

Was this a water-mill?
—Yes, water and steam both.

To what time have you worked?
—I have seen the mill going till it was past 12 o'clock on the Saturday night.

So that the mill was still working on the Sabbath morning?
—Yes.

Were the workmen paid by the piece, or by the day?
—No, all had stated wages.

Did not that almost compel you to use great severity to the hands then under you?
—Yes; I was compelled often to beat them, in order to get them to attend to their work, from their being over-wrought.

Were not the children exceedingly fatigued at that time?
—Yes, exceedingly fatigued.

Were the children bound in the same way in that mill?
—No; they were bound from one year's end to another, for twelve months.

Did you keep the hands locked up in the same way in that mill?
—Yes, we locked up the mill; but we did not lock the bothy.

Did you find that the children were unable to pursue their labour properly to that extent?
—Yes; they have been brought to that condition, that I have gone and fetched up the doctor to them, to see what was the matter with them, and to know whether they were able to rise or not able to rise; they were not at all able to rise; we have had great difficulty in getting them up.

When that was the case, how long have they been in bed, generally speaking?
—Perhaps not above four or five hours in their beds.

From: "Parliamentary Papers, 1831–1832, vol. XV", reprinted in Jonathan F. Scott and Alexander Baltzly, eds. *Readings in European History Since 1814* (New York: Appleton-Century-Crofts, 1930), pp. 44, 95–97, 115, 195, 197, 339, 341–342.

QUESTIONS:

1. Characterize the sorts of people and the conflicting interests that appear before the Saddler Commission. Who wants what and why?
2. Relate the issues raised in the question above as well as the very fact of a parliamentary commission into working conditions to the diagram in *Frameworks* Figure 18.11 (Britain ca. 1780: a new model of hierarchy).

19.3: *The Philosophy of Manufactures* (Andrew Ure, 1835)

Andrew Ure (1778–1857), a Scottish physician and chemist, was known in his own time and well after his death as the author of encyclopedic reference works, such as *A Dictionary of Arts, Manufactures, and Mines* (1837), which covered a vast range of technical subjects, including chemistry, geology, astronomy, technology, manufacturing, and so forth. His unusually broad scientific interests, as for example in his early experiments in inducing muscles response to electrical stimulation in human corpses in 1818, turned in the 1830s toward advances in technology and the conditions of factory work. He conducted extensive investigations and published his findings in *The Philosophy of Manufactures*. The excerpt below reveals his interest in the welfare of people, technological progress, and the connection he saw between the two.

This island is pre-eminent among civilized nations for the prodigious development of its factory wealth, and has been therefore long viewed with a jealous admiration by foreign powers. This very pre-eminence, however, has been contemplated in a very different light by many influential members of our own community, and has been even denounced by them as the certain origin of innumerable evils to the people, and of revolutionary convulsions to the state. If the affairs of the kingdom be wisely administered, I believe such allegations and fears will prove to be groundless, and to proceed more from the envy of one ancient and powerful order of the commonwealth, towards another suddenly grown into political importance than from the nature of things.

In the recent discussions concerning our factories, no circumstance is so deserving of remark, as the gross ignorance evinced by our leading legislators and economists, gentlemen well informed in other respects, relative to the nature of those stupendous manufactures which have so long provided the rulers of the kingdom with the resources of war, and a great body of the people with comfortable subsistence; which have, in fact made this island the arbiter of many nations, and the benefactor of the globe itself.* Till this ignorance be dispelled, no sound legislation need be expected on manufacturing subjects. . . .

The blessings which physico-mechanical science has bestowed on society, and the means it has still in store for ameliorating the lot of mankind, have been too little dwelt upon; while, on the other hand, it has been accused of lending itself to the rich capitalists as an instrument for harassing the poor, and of exacting from the operative an accelerated rate of work. It has been said, for example, that the steam-engine now drives the power-looms with such velocity as to urge on their attendant weavers at the same rapid pace; but that the hand-weaver, not being subjected to this restless agent, can throw his shuttle and move his treadles at his convenience. There is, however, this difference in the two cases, that in the factory, every member of the loom is so adjusted, that the driving force leaves the attendant nearly nothing at all to do, certainly no muscular fatigue to sustain, while it procures for him good, unfailing wages, besides a healthy workshop *gratis:* whereas the non-factory weaver, having everything to execute by muscular exertion, finds the labour irksome, makes in consequence innumerable short pauses, separately of little account, but great when added together; earns therefore proportionally low wages, while he loses his health by poor diet and the dampness of his hovel. Dr. Carbutt of Manchester says, "With regard to Sir Robert Peel's assertion a few evenings ago, that. the hand-loom weavers are mostly small farmers, nothing can be a greater mistake; they live, or rather they just keep life together, in the most miserable manner, in the cellars and garrets of the town, working sixteen or eighteen hours for the merest pittance."

The constant aim and effect of scientific improvement in manufactures are philanthropic, as they tend to relieve the workmen either from niceties of adjustment which exhaust his mind and fatigue his eyes, or from painful repetition of effort which distort or wear out his frame. At every step of each manufacturing process described in this volume, the humanity of science will be manifest. . . .

*Even the eminent statesman lately selected by his Sovereign to wield the destinies of this commercial empire–Sir Robert Peel, who derives his family consequence from the cotton trade, seems to be but little conversant with its nature and condition. . . .

The term *Factory,* in technology, designates the combined operation of many orders of work-people, adult and young, in tending with assiduous skill a system of productive machines continuously impelled by a central power. This definition includes such organizations as cotton-mills, flax-mills, silk-mills, woollen-mills, and certain engineering works; but it excludes those in which the mechanisms do not form a connected series, nor are dependent on one prime mover. Of the latter class, examples occur in ironworks, dye-works, soap-works, brass-foundries, &c. Some authors, indeed, have comprehended under the title *factory,* all extensive establishments wherein a number of people co-operate towards a common purpose of art; and would therefore rank breweries, distilleries, as well as the workshops of carpenters, turners, coopers, &c., under the factory system. But I conceive that this title, in its strictest sense, involves the idea of a vast automaton, composed of various mechanical and intellectual organs, acting in uninterrupted concert for the production of a common object, all of them being subordinated to a self-regulated moving force. If the marshalling of human beings in systematic order for the execution of any technical enterprise were allowed to constitute a factory, this term might embrace every department of civil and military engineering; a latitude of application quite inadmissible.

. . .

In my recent tour, continued during several months, through the manufacturing districts, I have seen tens of thousands of old, young, and middle-aged of both sexes, many of them too feeble to get their daily bread by any of the former modes of industry, earning abundant food, raiment, and domestic accommodation, without perspiring at a single pore, screened meanwhile from the summer's sun and the winter's frost, in apartments more airy and salubrious than those of the metropolis, in which our legislative and fashionable aristocracies assemble. In those spacious halls the benignant power of steam summons around him his myriads of willing menials, and assigns to each the regulated task, substituting for painful muscular effort on their part, the energies of his own gigantic arm, and demanding in return only attention and. dexterity to correct such little aberrations as casually occur in his workmanship. The gentle docility of this moving force qualifies it for impelling the tiny bobbins of the lace-machine with a precision and speed. inimitable by the most dexterous hands, directed by the sharpest eyes. Hence, under its auspices, and in obedience to Arkwright's polity., magnificent edifices, surpassing far in number, value, usefulness, and ingenuity of construction, the boasted monuments of Asiatic, Egyptian, and Roman despotism, have, within the short period of fifty years, risen up in this kingdom, to show to what extent, capital, industry, and science may augment the resources of a state, while they meliorate the condition of its citizens. Such is the factory system, replete with prodigies in mechanics and political economy, which promises, in its future growth, to become the great minister of civilization to the terraqueous globe, enabling this country, as its heart, to diffuse along with its commerce, the life-blood of science and religion to myriads of people still lying "in the region and shadow of death."

When Adam Smith wrote his immortal elements of economics, automatic machinery being hardly known, he was properly led to regard the division of labour as the grand principle of manufacturing improvement; and he showed, in the example or pin-making, how each handicraftsman, being thereby enabled to perfect himself by practice in one point, became a quicker and cheaper workman. In each branch of manufacture he saw that some parts were, on that principle, of easy execution, like the cutting of pin wires into uniform lengths, and sonic were comparatively difficult, like the formation and fixation of their heads; and therefore he concluded that to each a workman of appropriate value and cost was naturally assigned.

This appropriation forms the very essence of the division of labour, and has been constantly made since the origin of society. The ploughman, with powerful hand and skilful eye, has been always hired at high wages to form the furrow, and the ploughboy at low wages, to lead the team. But what was in Dr. Smith's time a topic of useful illustration, cannot now be used without risk of misleading the public mind as to the right principle of manufacturing industry. In fact, the division, or rather adaptation of labour to the different talents of men, is little thought of in factory employment. On the contrary, wherever a process requires peculiar dexterity and steadiness of hand, it is withdrawn as soon as possible from the *cunning* workman, who is prone to irregularities of many kinds, and it is placed in charge of a peculiar mechanism, so self-regulating, that a child may superintend it. . . .

From: Ure, Andrew, *The philosophy of manufactures or, An exposition of the scientific, moral, and commercial economy of the factory system of Great Britain* (London: Ca. Knight, 1835), pp. 6, 7–8, 13–14, 17–19.

QUESTIONS:

1. Compare Ure's account of factory work to the testimony in the Sadler commission. Are they incompatible? Why or why not?
2. What is the role of the state in industry as portrayed by Ure? What screen image of the state does Ure's writing present?

19.4: *The Communist Manifesto* (Karl Marx, 1848)

Karl Marx (1818–1883) was a German economist, philosopher, and social scientist (although that term did not yet exist in his day). In 1848 Marx and his English collaborator Fredrick Engels (1820–1895) published *The Communist Manifesto,* which laid out Marx's theory of history upon which the political program of the Communist Party came to be based. This excerpt outlines that theory and uses it to analyze the historical development and current conditions of capitalist industry. Marx is an acute observer whose perhaps mistaken prediction of a socialist utopia should not detract from the accuracy of his diagnosis.

MANIFESTO OF
THE COMMUNIST PARTY

[From the English edition of 1888, edited by Friedrich Engels]

A spectre is haunting Europe—the spectre of Communism. All the Powers of old Europe have entered into a holy alliance to exorcise this spectre: Pope and Czar, Metternich and Guizot, French Radicals and German police-spies.

Where is the party in opposition that has not been decried as Communistic by its opponents in power? Where is the Opposition that has not hurled back the branding reproach of Communism, against the more advanced opposition parties, as well as against its reactionary adversaries?

Two things result from this fact.

I. Communism is already acknowledged by all European Powers to be itself a Power.
II. It is high time that Communists should openly, in the face of the whole world, publish their views, their aims, their tendencies, and meet this nursery tale of the Spectre of Communism with a Manifesto of the party itself.

To this end, Communists of various nationalities have assembled in London, and sketched the following Manifesto, to be published in the English,

French, German, Italian, Flemish and Danish languages.

I. BOURGEOIS AND PROLETARIANS

The history of all hitherto existing societies is the history of class struggles.

Freeman and slave, patrician and plebeian, lord and serf, guild-master and journeyman, in a word, oppressor and oppressed, stood in constant opposition to one another, carried on an uninterrupted, now hidden, now open fight, a fight that each time ended, either in a revolutionary re-constitution of society at large, or in the common ruin of the contending classes.

In the earlier epochs of history, we find almost everywhere a complicated arrangement of society into various orders, a manifold gradation of social rank. In ancient Rome we have patricians, knights, plebeians, slaves; in the Middle Ages, feudal lords, vassals, guild-masters, journeymen, apprentices, serfs; in almost all of these classes, again, subordinate gradations.

The modern bourgeois society that has sprouted from the ruins of feudal society has not done away with class antagonisms. It has but established new classes, new conditions of oppression, new forms of struggle in place of the old ones. Our epoch, the epoch of the bourgeoisie, possesses, however, this distinctive feature: it has simplified the class antagonisms. Society as a whole is more and more splitting up into two great hostile camps, into two great classes, directly facing each other: Bourgeoisie and Proletariat.

From the serfs of the Middle Ages sprang the chartered burghers of the earliest towns. From these burgesses the first elements of the bourgeoisie were developed.

The discovery of America, the rounding of the Cape, opened up fresh ground for the rising bourgeoisie. The East-Indian and Chinese markets, the colonisation of America, trade with the colonies, the increase in the means of exchange and in commodities generally, gave to commerce, to navigation, to industry, an impulse never before known, and thereby, to the revolutionary element in the tottering feudal society, a rapid development.

The feudal system of industry, under which industrial production was monopolised by closed guilds, now no longer sufficed for the growing wants of the new markets. The manufacturing system took its place. The guild-masters were pushed on one side by the manufacturing middle class; division of labour between the different corporate guilds vanished in the face of division of labour in each single workshop.

Meantime the markets kept ever growing, the demand ever rising. Even manufacture no longer sufficed. Thereupon, steam and machinery revolutionised industrial production. The place of manufacture was taken by the giant, Modern Industry, the place of the industrial middle class, by industrial millionaires, the leaders of whole industrial armies, the modern bourgeois.

Modern industry has established the world-market, for which the discovery of America paved the way. This market has given an immense development to commerce, to navigation, to communication by land. This development has, in its time, reacted on the extension of industry; and in proportion as industry, commerce, navigation, railways extended, in the same proportion the bourgeoisie developed, increased its capital, and pushed into the background every class handed down from the Middle Ages.

We see, therefore, how the modern bourgeoisie is itself the product of a long course of development, of a series of revolutions in the modes of production and of exchange.

Each step in the development of the bourgeoisie was accompanied by a corresponding political advance of that class. An oppressed class under the sway of the feudal nobility, an armed and self-governing association in the mediaeval commune; here independent urban republic (as in Italy and

Germany), there taxable "third estate" of the monarchy (as in France), afterwards, in the period of manufacture proper, serving either the semi-feudal or the absolute monarchy as a counterpoise against the nobility, and, in fact, corner-stone of the great monarchies in general, the bourgeoisie has at last, since the establishment of Modern Industry and of the world-market, conquered for itself, in the modern representative State, exclusive political sway. The executive of the modern State is but a committee for managing the common affairs of the whole bourgeoisie.

The bourgeoisie, historically, has played a most revolutionary part.

The bourgeoisie, wherever it has got the upper hand, has put an end to all feudal, patriarchal, idyllic relations. It has pitilessly torn asunder the motley feudal ties that bound man to his "natural superiors," and has left remaining no other nexus between man and man than naked self-interest, than callous "cash payment." It has drowned the most heavenly ecstasies of religious fervour, of chivalrous enthusiasm, of philistine sentimentalism, in the icy water of egotistical calculation. It has resolved personal worth into exchange value, and in place of the numberless and indefeasible chartered freedoms, has set up that single, unconscionable freedom—Free Trade. In one word, for exploitation, veiled by religious and political illusions, naked, shameless, direct, brutal exploitation.

The bourgeoisie has stripped of its halo every occupation hitherto honoured and looked up to with reverent awe. It has converted the physician, the lawyer, the priest, the poet, the man of science, into its paid wage labourers.

The bourgeoisie has torn away from the family its sentimental veil, and has reduced the family relation to a mere money relation.

. . . The bourgeoisie cannot exist without constantly revolutionising the instruments of production, and thereby the relations of production, and with them the whole relations of society. Conservation of the old modes of production in unaltered form, was, on the contrary, the first condition of existence for all earlier industrial classes. Constant revolutionising of production, uninterrupted disturbance of all social conditions, everlasting uncertainty and agitation distinguish the bourgeois epoch from all earlier ones. All fixed, fast-frozen relations, with their train of ancient and venerable prejudices and opinions, are swept away, all new-formed ones become antiquated before they can ossify. All that is solid melts into air, all that is holy is profaned, and man is at last compelled to face with sober senses, his real conditions of life, and his relations with his kind.

The need of a constantly expanding market for its products chases the bourgeoisie over the whole surface of the globe. It must nestle everywhere, settle everywhere, establish connexions everywhere.

The bourgeoisie has through its exploitation of the world-market given a cosmopolitan character to production and consumption in every country. To the great chagrin of Reactionists, it has drawn from under the feet of industry the national ground on which it stood. All old-established national industries have been destroyed or are daily being destroyed. They are dislodged by new industries, whose introduction becomes a life and death question for all civilised nations, by industries that no longer work up indigenous raw material, but raw material drawn from the remotest zones; industries whose products are consumed, not only at home, but in every quarter of the globe. In place of the old wants, satisfied by the productions of the country, we find new wants, requiring for their satisfaction the products of distant lands and climes. In place of the old local and national seclusion and self-sufficiency, we have intercourse in every direction, universal inter-dependence of nations. And as in material, so also in intellectual production. The intellectual creations of individual nations become common property. National one-sidedness and narrow-mindedness become more and more impossible, and from the numerous national and local literatures, there arises a world literature.

The bourgeoisie, by the rapid improvement of all instruments of production, by the immensely facilitated means of communication, draws all, even the most barbarian, nations into civilisation. The cheap prices of its commodities are the heavy artillery with which it batters down all Chinese walls, with which it forces the barbarians' intensely obstinate hatred of foreigners to capitulate. It compels all nations, on pain of extinction, to adopt the bourgeois mode of production; it compels them to introduce what it calls civilisation into their midst, i.e., to become bourgeois themselves. In one word, it creates a world after its own image.

The bourgeoisie has subjected the country to the rule of the towns. It has created enormous cities, has greatly increased the urban population as compared with the rural, and has thus rescued a considerable part of the population from the idiocy of rural life. Just as it has made the country dependent on the towns, so it has made barbarian and semi-barbarian countries dependent on the civilised ones, nations of peasants on nations of bourgeois, the East on the West.

. . .

II. PROLETARIANS AND COMMUNISTS

The weapons with which the bourgeoisie felled feudalism to the ground are now turned against the bourgeoisie itself.

But not only has the bourgeoisie forged the weapons that bring death to itself; it has also called into existence the men who are to wield those weapons—the modern working class—the proletarians.

. . .

In this sense, the theory of the Communists may be summed up in the single sentence: Abolition of private property.

We Communists have been reproached with the desire of abolishing the right of personally acquiring property as the fruit of a man's own labour, which property is alleged to be the groundwork of all personal freedom, activity and independence.

Hard-won, self-acquired, self-earned property! Do you mean the property of the petty artisan and of the small peasant, a form of property that preceded the bourgeois form? There is no need to abolish that; the development of industry has to a great extent already destroyed it, and is still destroying it daily.

Or do you mean modern bourgeois private property?

But does wage-labour create any property for the labourer? Not a bit. It creates capital, i.e., that kind of property which exploits wage-labour, and which cannot increase except upon condition of begetting a new supply of wage-labour for fresh exploitation. Property, in its present form, is based on the antagonism of capital and wage-labour. Let us examine both sides of this antagonism.

To be a capitalist, is to have not only a purely personal, but a social status in production. Capital is a collective product, and only by the united action of many members, nay, in the last resort, only by the united action of all members of society, can it be set in motion.

Capital is, therefore, not a personal, it is a social power.

When, therefore, capital is converted into common property, into the property of all members of society, personal property is not thereby transformed into social property. It is only the social character of the property that is changed. It loses its class-character.

. . .

Nevertheless in the most advanced countries, the following will be pretty generally applicable.

1. Abolition of property in land and application of all rents of land to public purposes.
2. A heavy progressive or graduated income tax.
3. Abolition of all right of inheritance.
4. Confiscation of the property of all emigrants and rebels.
5. Centralisation of credit in the hands of the State, by means of a national bank with State capital and an exclusive monopoly.

6. Centralisation of the means of communication and transport in the hands of the State.

7. Extension of factories and instruments of production owned by the State; the bringing into cultivation of waste-lands, and the improvement of the soil generally in accordance with a common plan.

8. Equal liability of all to labour. Establishment of industrial armies, especially for agriculture.

9. Combination of agriculture with manufacturing industries; gradual abolition of the distinction between town and country, by a more equable distribution of the population over the country.

10. Free education for all children in public schools. Abolition of children's factory labour in its present form. Combination of education with industrial production, &c., &c.

From: Marx, Karl, and Friedrich Engels, *Manifesto of the Communist party* (London: William Reeves Bookseller, 1888).

QUESTIONS:

1. How does Marx explain the rise of industry? What global effects of industry does he describe, and how accurate do these descriptions seem to you?

2. Consider the list of proposals at the end of the Manifesto. Do they strike you as radical in today's terms? Why was Communism a "spectre haunting Europe"?

CHAPTER 20

Industrial Hierarchies: Society, State, Culture

INTRODUCTION

The sources in this chapter represent a range of nineteenth-century cultural and political consequences of industrialization. Industrialization transformed the social sphere and greatly expanded means of mass communication. As a result, more people from previously mute and invisible groups were able to project images onto the cultural screen. In this context ideology, artistic expression, and political assertions became more self-conscious and more numerous, leading to a world of "isms".

20.1: *Self-Help* (Samuel Smiles, 1859)

Samuel Smiles (1812–1904) was a Scottish author and reformer. He began to advocate for parliamentary reform while still a medical student at the University of Edinburgh. After his father's death, he was able to continue his studies because of the thrift and hard work of his widowed mother, who was an early example of the kind of self-reliance he promoted in his writings. After his studies, he was for a time the editor of the progressive *Leeds Times* newspaper and then secretary to a railway company. Through this work he came to know George Stephenson, the early railway engineer who built some of the first railways that used steam locomotives. Smiles admired Stephenson and wrote a biography of him in 1855. Smiles believed that material progress was possible for the working and middle classes through individual enterprise and free trade, and he did not believe that business owners and laborers were inherent adversaries. The ideas of utilitarian philosophers Jeremy Bentham influenced Smiles, though his writings generally and *Self-Help* in particular are far more practical. *Self-Help* was a popular and well-known work in Smiles' own lifetime (it sold twenty thousand copies in its first year of publication) and for many years after. In the excerpt below, Smiles introduces his idea of self-help.

**CHAPTER I—SELF-HELP—
NATIONAL AND INDIVIDUAL**

"The worth of a State, in the long run, is the worth of the individuals composing it."

—*J. S. Mill.*

"We put too much faith in systems, and look too little to men."

—*B. Disraeli.*

"Heaven helps those who help themselves" is a well-tried maxim, embodying in a small compass the results of vast human experience. The spirit of self-help is the root of all genuine growth in the individual; and, exhibited in the lives of many, it constitutes the true source of national vigour and strength. Help from without is often enfeebling in its effects, but help from within invariably invigorates. Whatever is done *for* men or classes, to a certain extent takes away the stimulus and necessity of doing for themselves; and where men are subjected to over-guidance and over-government, the inevitable tendency is to render them comparatively helpless.

Even the best institutions can give a man no active help. Perhaps the most they can do is, to leave him free to develop himself and improve his individual condition. But in all times men have been prone to believe that their happiness and well-being were to be secured by means of institutions rather than by their own conduct. Hence the value of legislation as an agent in human advancement has usually been much over-estimated. To constitute the millionth part of a Legislature, by voting for one or two men once in three or five years, however conscientiously this duty may be performed, can exercise but little active influence upon any man's life and character. Moreover, it is every day becoming more clearly understood, that the function of Government is negative and restrictive, rather than positive and active; being resolvable principally into protection—protection of life, liberty, and property. Laws, wisely administered, will secure men in the enjoyment of the fruits of their labour, whether of mind or body, at a comparatively small personal sacrifice; but no laws, however stringent, can make the idle industrious, the thriftless provident, or the drunken sober. Such reforms can only be effected by means of individual action, economy, and self-denial; by better habits, rather than by greater rights.

The Government of a nation itself is usually found to be but the reflex of the individuals composing it. The Government that is ahead of the people will inevitably be dragged down to their level, as the Government that is behind them will in the long run

be dragged up. In the order of nature, the collective character of a nation will as surely find its befitting results in its law and government, as water finds its own level. The noble people will be nobly ruled, and the ignorant and corrupt ignobly. Indeed all experience serves to prove that the worth and strength of a State depend far less upon the form of its institutions than upon the character of its men. For the nation is only an aggregate of individual conditions, and civilization itself is but a question of the personal improvement of the men, women, and children of whom society is composed.

National progress is the sum of individual industry, energy, and uprightness, as national decay is of individual idleness, selfishness, and vice. What we are accustomed to decry as great social evils, will, for the most part, be found to be but the outgrowth of man's own perverted life; and though we may endeavour to cut them down and extirpate them by means of Law, they will only spring up again with fresh luxuriance in some other form, unless the conditions of personal life and character are radically improved. If this view be correct, then it follows that the highest patriotism and philanthropy consist, not so much in altering laws and modifying institutions, as in helping and stimulating men to elevate and improve themselves by their own free and independent individual action.

It may be of comparatively little consequence how a man is governed from without, whilst everything depends upon how he governs himself from within. The greatest slave is not he who is ruled by a despot, great though that evil be, but he who is the thrall of his own moral ignorance, selfishness, and vice. Nations who are thus enslaved at heart cannot be freed by any mere changes of masters or of institutions; and so long as the fatal delusion prevails, that liberty solely depends upon and consists in government, so long will such changes, no matter at what cost they may be effected, have as little practical and lasting result as the shifting of the figures in a phantasmagoria. The solid foundations of liberty must rest upon individual character;

which is also the only sure guarantee for social security and national progress. John Stuart Mill truly observes that "even despotism does not produce its worst effects so long as individuality exists under it; and whatever crushes individuality *is* despotism, by whatever name it be called."

Old fallacies as to human progress are constantly turning up. Some call for Caesars, others for Nationalities, and others for Acts of Parliament. We are to wait for Caesars, and when they are found, "happy the people who recognise and follow them." This doctrine shortly means, everything *for* the people, nothing *by* them,—a doctrine which, if taken as a guide, must, by destroying the free conscience of a community, speedily prepare the way for any form of despotism. Caesarism is human idolatry in its worst form—a worship of mere power, as degrading in its effects as the worship of mere wealth would be. A far healthier doctrine to inculcate among the nations would be that of Self-Help; and so soon as it is thoroughly understood and carried into action, Caesarism will be no more. The two principles are directly antagonistic; and what Victor Hugo said of the Pen and the Sword alike applies to them, "Ceci tuera cela." [This will kill that.]

The power of Nationalities and Acts of Parliament is also a prevalent superstition. What William Dargan, one of Ireland's truest patriots, said at the closing of the first Dublin Industrial Exhibition, may well be quoted now. "To tell the truth," he said, "I never heard the word independence mentioned that my own country and my own fellow townsmen did not occur to my mind. I have heard a great deal about the independence that we were to get from this, that, and the other place, and of the great expectations we were to have from persons from other countries coming amongst us. Whilst I value as much as any man the great advantages that must result to us from that intercourse, I have always been deeply impressed with the feeling that our industrial independence is dependent upon ourselves. I believe that with

simple industry and careful exactness in the utilization of our energies, we never had a fairer chance nor a brighter prospect than the present. We have made a step, but perseverance is the great agent of success; and if we but go on zealously, I believe in my conscience that in a short period we shall arrive at a position of equal comfort, of equal happiness, and of equal independence, with that of any other people."

All nations have been made what they are by the thinking and the working of many generations of men. Patient and persevering labourers in all ranks and conditions of life, cultivators of the soil and explorers of the mine, inventors and discoverers, manufacturers, mechanics and artisans, poets, philosophers, and politicians, all have contributed towards the grand result, one generation building upon another's labours, and carrying them forward to still higher stages. This constant succession of noble workers—the artisans of civilisation—has served to create order out of chaos in industry, science, and art; and the living race has thus, in the course of nature, become the inheritor of the rich estate provided by the skill and industry of our forefathers, which is placed in our hands to cultivate, and to hand down, not only unimpaired but improved, to our successors.

The spirit of self-help, as exhibited in the energetic action of individuals, has in all times been a marked feature in the English character, and furnishes the true measure of our power as a nation. Rising above the heads of the mass, there were always to be found a series of individuals distinguished beyond others, who commanded the public homage. But our progress has also been owing to multitudes of smaller and less known men. Though only the generals' names may be remembered in the history of any great campaign, it has been in a great measure through the individual valour and heroism of the privates that victories have been won. And life, too, is "a soldiers' battle,"—men in the ranks having in all times been amongst the greatest of workers. Many are the lives of men unwritten, which have nevertheless as powerfully influenced civilisation and progress as the more fortunate Great whose names are recorded in biography. Even the humblest person, who sets before his fellows an example of industry, sobriety, and upright honesty of purpose in life, has a present as well as a future influence upon the well-being of his country; for his life and character pass unconsciously into the lives of others, and propagate good example for all time to come.

From: Smiles, Samuel, *Self-help: with illustrations of character and conduct* (London: John Murray, 1859), pp. 1–2.

QUESTIONS:

1. In what ways does Smiles' advice apply more to an Industrial-Era fluid social sphere than to a rigid Agrarian-Era pyramid?
2. What is the role of nationalism in shaping Smiles' advice? What is the relationship between nations and individuals that Smiles puts forth? Is his argument about nations consistent?

WOMEN AND SOCIAL CHANGE

20.2a: *Resolutions* from *The Proceedings of The Woman's Rights Convention, Worcester* (1850)

Over a thousand people gathered for the Woman's Rights Convention of 1850 in October in Worcester, Massachusetts. The convention, which had its beginnings in a meeting at the end of an Anti-Slavery Society meeting, included among its attendees many prominent feminists and abolitionists such as Lucretia Mott, Sojourner Truth, and Frederick Douglass. The delegates discussed issues including women's property rights, female suffrage, and women's education. The proceedings of the convention included an address by Lucy Stone on women's property rights that so impressed Horace Greeley that he wrote about it in *The New York Herald* with approval if also condescending bemusement. Despite this, the article inspired Susan B. Anthony to work for women's issues and it inspired the Englishwoman Harriet Taylor to write *The Enfranchisement of Women*. The excerpt from the proceedings here are the resolutions from the convention, which the attendees unanimously approved.

Whereas, The very contracted sphere of action prescribed for woman, arising from an unjust view of her nature, capacities, and powers, and from the infringement of her just rights as an equal with man,—is highly injurious to her physical, mental, and moral development; therefore, Resolved, That we will not cease our earnest endeavors to secure for her political, legal, and social equality with man, until her proper sphere is determined, by what alone should determine it, her Powers and Capacities, strengthened and refined by an education in accordance with her nature.

Resolved, That every human being of full age, and resident for a proper length of time on the soil of the nation, who is required to obey law, is entitled to a voice in its enactments; that every such person, whose property or labor is taxed for the support of government, is entitled to a direct share in such government. Therefore, Resolved, That women are clearly entitled to the right of suffrage, and to be considered eligible to office; the omission to demand which, on her part, is a palpable recreancy to duty; and the denial of which is a gross usurpation, on the part of man, no longer to be endured; and that every party which claims to represent the humanity, civilization, and progress of the age, is bound to inscribe on its banners, Equality before the law, without distinction of sex or color. Resolved, That political rights acknowledge no sex, and therefore the word "male" should be stricken from every State Constitution. Resolved, That the laws of property, as affecting married parties, demand a thorough revisal, so that all rights may be equal between them;—that the wife may have, during life, an equal control over the property gained by their mutual toil and sacrifices, be heir to her husband precisely to the extent that he is heir to her, and entitled, at her death, to dispose by will of the same share of the joint property as he is.

Resolved, That since the prospect of honorable and useful employment, in after life, for the faculties we are laboring to discipline, is the keenest stimulus to fidelity in the use of educational advantages, and since the best education is what we give ourselves in the struggles, employments, and discipline of life; therefore, it is impossible that woman should make full use of the instruction already accorded to her, or that her career should do justice to her faculties, until the avenues to the various civil and professional employments are thrown open to arouse her ambition and call forth all her nature.

Resolved, That every effort to educate woman, until you accord to her her rights, and arouse her conscience by the weight of her responsibilities, is futile, and a waste of labor.

Resolved, That the cause we are met to advocate,—the claim for woman of all her natural and civil rights,—bids us remember the million and a half of slave women at the South, the most grossly wronged and foully outraged of all women; and in every effort for an improvement in our civilization, we will bear in our heart of hearts the memory of the trampled womanhood of the plantation, and omit no effort to raise it to a share in the rights we claim for ourselves.

From: Woman's Rights Convention, *The proceedings of the Woman's Rights Convention held at Worcester, October 23rd & 24th, 1850* (Boston: Prentiss & Sawyer, 1851).

QUESTIONS:

1. Which triad frames this document more powerfully in your opinion: Jefferson's "life, liberty, & the pursuit of happiness" or Locke's "life, liberty, & property"?
2. How do the resolutions from this convention in 1851 in the United States compare to the ten points of the Communist Manifesto (Chapter 19) of 1848? What common demands do you find? Where do they differ over fundamentals?

20.2b: From *The Wives of England* (Sarah Stickney Ellis, 1843)

Sarah Stickney Ellis (1799–1872) was a prolific Victorian author of novels, poems, short fiction, and advice books. Her advice books exemplify the Cult of True Womanhood, which held that the proper "sphere" for women was one of domesticity and private life, and separate from the "public sphere" of business, politics, and so forth, which was the proper place for men. "True women" were characterized by the four virtues of piety, purity, submission, and domesticity. Advocates of True Womanhood condemned women who spoke publically on women's issues, such as Mary Wollstonecraft, as unfeminine and "unnatural." The ideology of Separate Spheres emerged with the Industrial Revolution, and opposition to it was a factor in the emergence of nineteenth-century feminism. In this excerpt, Sarah Stickney Ellis describes some aspects of what she considers proper comportment for "the mistress of the house".

The mistress of a house should always appear calm, and perfectly self-possessed, whether she feels so or not; and if form an accumulation of household disasters, particularly such as mal-occurrences before her guests, the agitation of her feelings should be too great for her powers of self-control, she may always find a natural and appropriate outlet for them, by sympathizing with other suffers in the same calamity, and thus evincing her regard for them, rather than for herself.

Nor ought we to class this species of self-discipline with those artificial manners which are assumed merely for the sake of effect. If the same individual who controlled her feelings before her guests, should go out amongst her servants and give full vent to them there, such a case would certainly deserve to be so classed. But the self-control I would gladly recommend, is of a widely different order, extending to a mastery over the feelings, as well as the expressions. In the former case, a lady seated at the head of her table, will sometimes speak in a sharp whisper to a servant, with a countenance in which all the furies might be represented as one; when suddenly turning to her guests, she will address them with the blandest smiles, even before the cloud has had time to vanish from her brow. In the latter case, the mistress of the house will recollect, that others have been made to suffer perhaps more than herself, and that whatever the cause of vexation or distress may be, it can only be making that distress greater, for her to appear angry or disturbed. By such habits of reflection, and by the mastery of judgment over impulse, she will be able in time, not only to appear calm, but really to feel so; or if there should be just as much excitement as may be agreeably carried off in condolence with her friends, there will never be sufficient really to destroy either their comfort, or her own peace of mind.

. . .

Forethought, then, is a most essential quality in the mistress of a house, if she wishes to maintain throughout her establishment the principle of order. Whatever others *do*, she must *think*. It is not possible for order to exist, where many minds are employed in directing a variety of movements. There must be one presiding intellect to guide the whole; and whether the household to be governed belong to a mansion or a cottage, whether the servants to be directed be many or few, that presiding power must be vested in the mistress, or in some one individual deputed to act in her stead. It is form leaving the thinking and contriving part, along with the executive, to servants, that we see perpetuated so many objectionable and absurd methods of transacting the business of domestic life; methods handed down from one generation to another, and acted upon sometimes with great inconvenience and equal waste, simply because habit has rendered it a sort of established thing, that whatever is done, should be done in a certain manner; for servants are a class of people who think but little, and many of them would rather take double pains, and twice the necessary length of time in doing their work the old way, than risk the experiment of a new one, even if it should ever occur to them to make it.

. . .

The word justice has a somewhat startling sound to female ears, and I might perhaps be induced to use a softer expression, could I find one suited to my purpose; though after all, I fancy we should none of us be much the worse for having the word justice in its simple and imperative strictness, more frequently applied to our relative and social duties. It is, in fact, a good old-fashioned notion, that of doing justice, which has fallen a little too much into disuse; or perhaps, I ought rather to say, has been dismissed from its place amongst female duties, and considered too exclusively as belonging to points of law and cases of public trial.

I am well aware that justice in its highest sense belongs not to creatures frail, short-sighted, and liable to deception like ourselves; but that strong sense of truth, and honesty, and individual right, which, we naturally include in our idea of the love of justice, was surely given us to be exercised in our dealings with each other, and in the general conduct of our domestic affairs. This regard to what is just in itself, necessarily including what is due to others, and what is due from them also, is the moral basis upon which all good management depends; for when once this foundation is removed, an inlet is opened for innumerable lower motives, such as selfishness, vanity, caprice, and a host of others of the same unworthy character, to enter and mix themselves up with the conduct of daily life.

From: Ellis, Sarah Stickney, *The Wives of England: their relative duties, domestic influence, and social obligations* (New York: Appleton, 1843), pp. 194–95, 198, 199–200.

QUESTIONS:

1. What role does class play in Ellis's advice about proper womanly behavior? What frame value can you detect behind her writing?
2. How is this an argument in favor of female power?

20.3:   *Our Views* (Heinrich von Treitschke, 1879-80)

Heinrich Gotthard von Treitschke (1834–1896) was a German political writer and historian who advocated for German nationalism, imperialism, and authoritarian rule. His most well-known work is his *History of Germany in the Nineteenth Century*, a five-volume work published from 1879–94. In stark contrast to the work of his predecessor Leopold von Ranke (1795–1886), arguably the founder of the modern discipline of history, von Treitschke's writings are polemical and agenda driven. The essay excerpted here, "Our Views" ("Unsere Aussichten") was first published in 1879 as a "review" of Heinrich Graetz's *History of the Jews* in the *Preußische Jahrbücher,* but it was subsequently republished several times as a pamphlet called "A Word about Our Jews" (Ein Wort über unser Judentum). Scholars have noted that von Treitschke gets many of his facts in this essay simply wrong, but factual content is not the point of this antisemitic diatribe.

. . . Among the symptoms of a deep change of heart going through our nation, none appears so strange as the passionate movement against Jewry. A few months ago the oft-heard cry "Hep-Hep" [a call to pogrom later used by Nazi storm troopers] still echoed in Germany. Anyone is permitted to say unabashedly the harshest things about the national shortcomings of the Germans, the French, and all the other peoples, but any who dared to speak about the undeniable weaknesses of the Jewish character, no matter how moderately or justly, was immediately branded by almost the entire press as a barbarian and a religious bigot. Today we have progressed so far that a majority of the voters of Breslau have sworn under no circumstances to elect a Jew to the state parliament—and this apparently not in wild agitation but with calm forethought. Antisemitic leagues are banding together. The "Jewish question" is being discussed in excited meetings. A flood of anti-Jewish libels is inundating the book market. There is all too much dirt and crudity in these activities, and it is nauseating to note that many of those inflammatory writings apparently stem from Jewish pens. . . . But is all that hides behind this noisome activity really just the coarseness of the mob and business envy? Are these outbreaks of deep, long-restrained anger merely an ephemeral excrescence, as hollow and baseless as the Teutonic Jew baiting of 1819? No; in fact, the instinct of the masses has correctly identified a serious danger, a critical defect in the new German life. It is no empty formula when we speak today of a German Jewish question.

When, with disdain, the English and French talk of German prejudice against Jews, we must answer: You don't know us. You live in fortunate circumstances that make the emergence of such "prejudices" impossible. The number of Jews in western Europe is so small that it cannot exert a palpable influence upon your national mores. However, year after year, out of the inexhaustible Polish cradle there streams over our eastern border a host of hustling, pants-peddling youths, whose children and children's children will someday command Germany's stock exchanges and newspapers. The immigration grows visibly, and the question becomes more and more grave: how can we amalgamate this alien people? The Israelites of the west and south belong mostly to the Spanish branch of Jewry, which looks back on a comparatively proud history and has always adapted rather easily to Western ways. In fact, they have become for the most part good Frenchmen, Englishmen, and Italians. This is true to the extent that we can appropriately expect from a people of such pure blood and such pronounced peculiarity. But we Germans have to deal with that Polish branch of Jewry, which has been deeply scarred by centuries of Christian tyranny. As a result of this experience, it is incomparably more alien to the European and, especially, the German essence.

What we have to demand of our Israelite fellow citizens is simple: they should become Germans. They should feel themselves, modestly and properly, Germans—and this without prejudicing their faith and their ancient, holy memories, which we all hold in reverence. For we do not want to see millennia of Germanic morality followed by an era of German-Jewish hybrid culture. It would be sinful to forget that a great many Jews, baptized and unbaptized, were German men in the best sense. Felix Mendelssohn, Veit, Riesser, etc.—to say nothing of the living—were men in whom we honor the noble and good traits of the German spirit. But it is equally undeniable that numerous and mighty circles among our Jews simply lack the goodwill to become thoroughly German. It is painful to speak of these things. Even conciliatory words will be easily misunderstood. Nevertheless, I believe that many of my Jewish friends will concede, though with deep regret, that I am right when I assert that in recent times a dangerous spirit of arrogance has arisen in Jewish circles. The influence of Jewry on our national life, which created much good in earlier times, nowadays shows itself in many ways harmful. Just read the *History of the Jews* by Graetz. What fanatical rage against the "arch-enemy," Christianity. What lethal hatred against the purest and mightiest representatives of the Germanic essence from Luther right up to Goethe and Fichte! And what empty, insulting self-glorification! [In Graetz] it is demonstrated in constant, spiteful tirades that the nation of Kant was educated to humanity only through the Jews, that the language of Lessing and Goethe has become receptive to beauty, intelligence, and wit through Heine and Börne. What English Jew would dare defame the land that shielded and protected him in such a way? And this benighted contempt against the German goyim is in no way merely the attitude of an isolated fanatic.

There is no German commercial city that does not count many honorable and respectable Jewish firms. But undoubtedly, the Semites bear a heavy share of guilt for the falsehood and deceit, the insolent greed of fraudulent business practices, and that base materialism of our day. [That materialism] regards all labor as pure business and threatens to stifle our people's traditional good-natured joy in labor. In thousands of German villages sits the Jew who sells out his neighbors with usury. Among the leading men in the arts and sciences, the number of Jews is not very great; all the stronger do the Semitic talents constitute the host of the third rate.

And how firmly these scribblers stick together. How securely they work on the tested business principle of reciprocity, whereby, as in some insurance company dealing in immortality, every Jewish poetaster receives free and clear one day of fame, paid out by the newspapers, without having to pay the premium.

Most dangerous, however, is the improper preponderance of Jewry in the daily press, a fateful consequence of our narrow-minded old laws forbidding Israelites entry to most of the learned professions. For ten years the public opinion of many German cities was largely "created" by Jewish pens. It was a misfortune for the Liberal party, and one of the reasons for its fall, to have afforded too free a scope to Jewry in its press. The present-day weakness of the press is the result of a backlash against this unnatural condition. The little man can no longer be talked out of the fact that the Jews write the newspapers. Therefore, he won't believe them any longer. Our newspaper system owes a great deal to Jewish talents. From the first the trenchancy and acuity of the Jewish spirit found a fruitful field. But here, too, the effect was ambiguous. [Ludwig] Börne was the first to introduce a characteristically shameless tone into our journalism. [He wrote] from abroad with no respect for the Fatherland, as though he was not part of it at all, as though his scorn for Germany did not cut each and every German to the quick. Add to this the unfortunate bustling intrusion into all and sundry, which does not even shy away from magisterially passing judgment on the innermost matters of the Christian churches. The anti-Christian defamations and witticisms of Jewish journalists are simply shocking, and such blasphemies are put up for sale in its own language as the latest achievements of "German" enlightenment! Scarcely had emancipation been achieved before they brazenly insisted on its pretext. They demanded literal parity in everything and did not want to see that we Germans are still a Christian people and that the Jews are only a minority among us. We have experienced their demands that

Christian images be set aside and that their sabbath be celebrated in mixed schools.

Overlooking all these circumstances—and how many others could be added!—this noisy agitation of the moment, though brutal and hateful, is nonetheless a natural reaction of Germanic racial feeling against an alien element that has assumed all too large a space in our life. [The agitation] has inadvertently performed a useful service: it has lifted the ban on a quiet untruth. An evil that everyone felt but no one wanted to touch upon is now openly discussed. Let's not deceive ourselves. The movement is very deep and strong. A few jokes by Christian Social politicos will not suffice to stem it. Among the circles of highly educated men who reject any idea of church intolerance or national arrogance there rings with one voice: *the Jews are our misfortune!*

There can be no talk, among those with any understanding, of a revocation or even an abridgment of the completed emancipation. It would be an open injustice, a falling away from the good traditions of our state, and would sharpen rather than ameliorate the national conflict that pains us. The Jews in France and England have become a harmless and in many ways beneficial, element of civil society. That is in the last analysis the result of the energy and national pride of these two ancient culture-bearing peoples. Our culture is a young one. Our being still lacks a national style, an instinctive pride, a thoroughly imprinted character. That is why for so long we stood defenseless against alien essences. Now, however, we are at the point of acquiring those goods. We can only wish that our Jews recognize in time the transformation that is the logical consequence of the rise of the German state. Quietly, here and there, Jewish associations against usury do much good. They are the work of insightful Israelites who understand that their racial brothers must adapt to the morality and ideas of their Christian fellow citizens.

There is still a great deal to be done in this direction. To make hard German heads into Jewish ones is surely impossible. Thus, only one possibility remains: Our Jewish fellow citizens must resolve to be German without qualification, as so many of them have already done, to our benefit and their own. The task can never be wholly completed. A cleft has always existed between Occidental and Semitic essences [. . .]; there will always be Jews who are nothing more than German-speaking Orientals. A specific Jewish civilization will also always flourish, as befits a historically cosmopolitan power. But the conflict will lessen when the Jews, who speak so much of tolerance, really become tolerant and show respect for the faith, customs, and feelings of the German people, who have atoned for the old injustice and bestowed upon them the rights of man and citizen. That this respect is wholly missing in a section of our commercial and literary Jewry is the ultimate basis for the passionate embitterment of today.

It is not a pretty picture—this storming and wrangling, this bubbling and boiling of half-baked ideas in the new Germany. But we are now the most passionate of peoples, even though we often berate ourselves as phlegmatic. New ideas have never established themselves among us without convulsive twitches. May God grant that we emerge from the rashness and ill humor of these restless years with a stricter conception of the state and its duties, a more powerful national feeling.

From: Levy, Richard S., *Antisemitism in the modern world: an anthology of texts* (Lexington, MA: D.C. Heath, 1991), pp. 69–73. Original German source: Heinrich von Treitschke, 1879, "Unsere Aussichten" in *Preußische Jahrbücher* 44, Heft 5 (November), pp. 572–76.

QUESTIONS:

1. How does the nationalism in von Treitschke compare to the nationalism in Smiles? What relationship between individuals and nations does von Treitschke posit?
2. What are the characteristics of a "proper German"? Why in von Treitschke's view are German Jews not "proper Germans"? What does von Treitschke's view of hybridity imply about connections between nationality and biology?

ROMANTICISM TO EXPRESSIONISM

The rise of self-conscious "isms" in the early nineteenth century is especially evident in the realm of the arts. One of the first and arguably most important of the new ideologies was Romanticism, which criticized the Enlightenment focus on rationality by emphasizing the importance of emotions alongside rationality. "She Was a Phantom of Delight", a poem by the British poet William Wordsworth, and the painting "The Death of Sardanapalus" by Eugene Delacroix represent Romanticism in literature and painting. Subsequent artistic movements, usually named by those who invented and promoted them, are represented in the other paintings.

20.4a: *"She Was a Phantom of Delight"* (William Wordsworth, 1807)

She was a Phantom of delight
When first she gleamed upon my sight;
A lovely Apparition, sent
To be a moment's ornament;
Her eyes as stars of Twilight fair;

Like Twilight's, too, her dusky hair;
But all things else about her drawn
From May-time and the cheerful Dawn;
A dancing Shape, an Image gay,
To haunt, to startle, and way-lay.

I saw her upon nearer view,
A Spirit, yet a Woman too!
Her household motions light and free,
And steps of virgin-liberty;
A countenance in which did meet
Sweet records, promises as sweet;
A Creature not too bright or good
For human nature's daily food;
For transient sorrows, simple wiles,
Praise, blame, love, kisses, tears, and smiles.

And now I see with eye serene
The very pulse of the machine;
A Being breathing thoughtful breath,
A Traveller between life and death;
The reason firm, the temperate will,
Endurance, foresight, strength, and skill;
A perfect Woman, nobly planned,
To warn, to comfort, and command;
And yet a Spirit still, and bright
With something of angelic light.

From: Wordsworth, William, and John Morley, *The complete poetical works of William Wordsworth* (New York: Crowell, 1888), p. 236, http://catalog.hathitrust.org/api/volumes/oclc/10698999.html.

20.4b: *Art Isms* (Delacroix, 1827; Cezanne, 1904; Vlaminck, 1906; Picasso, 1910; Boccioni, 1913; Oppenheim, 1936)

Romanticism; Eugene Delacroix, *The Death of Sardanopalus,* 1827; Louvre Museum.

Post-Impressionism; Paul Cezanne, *Mont Sainte-Victoire,* 1904.

Fauvism; Maurice de Vlaminck, *André Derain*, 1906.

Cubism; Pablo Picasso, *Girl with a Mandolin,* 1910.

Dadaism; Meret Oppenheim, *Fur Lined Teacup,* 1936.

Futurism; Umberto Boccioni, *Unique Forms of Continuity in Space*, 1913.

QUESTIONS:

1. What unites the Romanticism of Wordsworth's poem and of Delacroix's painting? Where do you see emotion in each work, and how do the emotions compare?
2. What visual characteristics of the images proclaim a self-conscious approach to the making of art (indeed, perhaps to identity)?

CHAPTER 21

Imperialism: Structures and Patterns

INTRODUCTION

Industrialization started first in Britain and spread in the second half of the nineteenth century to other parts of western Europe and the United States. Industrialized hierarchies began competing for political and economic position against each other on a global scale, with the wealth and weapons of industry backing them. The result was an age of imperialism. The sources in this chapter show us some of the motives of the imperial powers as well as some of the results of their conquests.

21.1: *Letter to Queen Victoria* (Lin Zexu, 1839)

Lin Zexu (1785–1850) was a highly respected official and scholar during the Qing dynasty who is known in particular for his opposition to British importation of opium to China. Like other European countries, Britain had difficulty establishing favorable trade conditions with China. With the huge demand for tea in Britain and China as the only supplier, Britain found itself in a continual deficit to China until the British hit on the strategy of importing opium from India. The narcotic was initially tolerated by the Chinese, even though it had been outlawed for all but medical uses in 1729. When the British began to plant tea in Africa and India, however, the trade balance tipped away from China's favor. By 1820 trade was out of firm Chinese control—even the Qing navy brought the contraband into the country illegally—and the viceroy of Guangdong tried without success to suppress the opium trade. This aroused the concern of many officials who in memorial letters urged the Emperor to take action against trade in opium. In this context Lin Zexu wrote an open memorial letter to the British monarch (published in Canton in 1839) describing the unfairness and immorality of the situation and appealing to her conscience to stop it. Later that same year, the first of two year-long opium wars between Britain and China broke out.

A communication: magnificently our great emperor soothes and pacifies China and the foreign countries, regarding all with the same kindness. If there is profit, then he shares it with the peoples of the world; if there is harm, then he removes it on behalf of the world. This is because he takes the mind of Heaven and earth as his mind.

The kings of your honorable country by a tradition handed down from generation to generation have always been noted for their politeness and submissiveness. We have read your successive tributary memorials saying: "In general our countrymen who go to trade in China have always received His Majesty the Emperor's gracious treatment and equal justice," and so on. Privately we are delighted with the way in which the honorable rulers of your country deeply understand the grand principles and are grateful for the Celestial grace. For this reason the Celestial Court in soothing those from afar has redoubled its polite and kind treatment. The profit from trade has been enjoyed by them continuously for two hundred years. This is the source from which your country has become known for its wealth.

But after a long period of commercial intercourse, there appear among the crowd of barbarians both good persons and bad, unevenly. Consequently there are those who smuggle opium to seduce the Chinese people and so cause the spread of the poison to all provinces. Such persons who only care to profit themselves, and disregard their harm to others, are not tolerated by the laws of Heaven and are unanimously hated by human beings. His Majesty the Emperor, upon hearing of this, is in a towering rage. He has especially sent me, his commissioner, to come to Kwangtung, and together with the governor-general and governor jointly to investigate and settle this matter. . . .

We find that your country is sixty or seventy thousand *li* from China. Yet there are barbarian ships that strive to come here for trade for the purpose of making a great profit. The wealth of China is used to profit the barbarians. That is to say, the great profit made by barbarians is all taken from the rightful share of China. By what right do they then in return use the poisonous drug to injure the Chinese people? Even though the barbarians may not necessarily intend to do us harm, yet in coveting profit to an extreme, they have no regard for injuring others. Let us ask, where is your conscience? I have heard that the smoking of opium is very strictly forbidden by your country; that is because the harm caused by opium is clearly understood. Since it is not permitted to do harm to your own country, then even less should you let it be passed on to the harm of other countries—how much less to China! Of all that China exports to foreign countries, there is not a single thing which is not beneficial to people; they are of benefit when eaten, or of benefit when used, or of benefit when resold: all are beneficial. Is there a single article from China which has done any harm to foreign countries? Take tea and rhubarb, for example; the foreign countries cannot get along for a single day without them. If China cuts off these benefits with no sympathy for those who are to suffer, then what can the barbarians rely upon to keep themselves alive? Moreover the woolens, camlets, and longells [i.e., textiles] of foreign countries cannot be woven unless they obtain Chinese silk. If China, again, cuts off this beneficial export, what profit can the barbarians expect to make? As for other foodstuffs, beginning with candy, ginger, cinnamon, and so forth, and articles for use, beginning with silk, satin, chinaware, and so on, all the things that must be had by foreign countries are innumerable. On the other hand, articles coming from the outside to China can only be used as toys. We can take them or get along without them. Since they are not needed by China, what difficulty would there be if we closed the frontier and stopped the trade? Nevertheless our Celestial Court lets tea, silk, and other goods be shipped without limit and circulated everywhere without begrudging it in the slightest. This is for no other reason but to share the benefit with the people of the whole world.

The goods from China carried away by your country not only supply your own consumption and use, but also can be divided up and sold to other countries, producing a triple profit. Even if you do not sell opium, you still have this threefold profit. How can you bear to go further, selling products injurious to others in order to fulfill your insatiable desire? . . .

We have further learned that in London, the capital of your honorable rule, and in Scotland

(Ssu-ko-lan), Ireland (Ai-lun), and other places originally no opium has been produced. Only in several places of India under your control such as Bengal, Madras, Bombay, Patna, Benares, and Malwa has opium been planted from hill to hill, and ponds have been opened for its manufacture. For months and years work is continued in order to accumulate the poison. The obnoxious odor ascends, irritating Heaven and frightening the spirits. Indeed you, O King, can eradicate the opium plant in these places, hoe over the fields entirely, and sow in its stead the five grains [i.e., millet, barley, wheat, etc.]. Anyone who dares again attempt to plant and manufacture opium should be severely punished. This will really be a great, benevolent government policy that will increase the common weal and get rid of evil. For this, Heaven must support you and the spirits must bring you good fortune, prolonging your old age and extending your descendants. All will depend on this act. . . .

Now we have set up regulations governing the Chinese people. He who sells opium shall receive the death penalty and he who smokes it also the death penalty. Now consider this: if the barbarians do not bring opium, then how can the Chinese people resell it, and how can they smoke it? The fact is that the wicked barbarians beguile the Chinese people into a death trap. How then can we grant life only to these barbarians? He who takes the life of even one person still has to atone for it with his own life; yet is the harm done by opium limited to the taking of one life only? Therefore in the new regulations, in regard to those barbarians who bring opium to China, the penalty is fixed at decapitation or strangulation. This is what is called getting rid of a harmful thing on behalf of mankind.

Moreover we have found that in the middle of the second month of this year [April 9] Consul [Superintendent] Elliot of your nation, because the opium prohibition law was very stern and severe, petitioned for an extension of the time limit. He requested a limit of five months for India and its adjacent harbors and related territories, and ten months for England proper, after which they would act in conformity with the new regulations. Now we, the commissioner and others, have memorialized and have received the extraordinary Celestial grace of His Majesty the Emperor, who has redoubled his consideration and compassion. All those who within the period of the coming one year (from England) or six months (from India) bring opium to China by mistake, but who voluntarily confess and completely surrender their opium, shall be exempt from their punishment. After this limit of time, if there are still those who bring opium to China then they will plainly have committed a willful violation and shall at once be executed according to law, with absolutely no clemency or pardon. This may be called the height of kindness and the perfection of justice.

Our Celestial Dynasty rules over and supervises the myriad states, and surely possesses unfathomable spiritual dignity. Yet the Emperor cannot bear to execute people without having first tried to reform them by instruction. Therefore he especially promulgates these fixed regulations. The barbarian merchants of your country, if they wish to do business for a prolonged period, are required to obey our statutes respectfully and to cut off permanently the source of opium. They must by no means try to test the effectiveness of the law with their lives. May you, O King, check your wicked and sift out your vicious people before they come to China, in order to guarantee the peace of your nation, to show further the sincerity of your politeness and submissiveness, and to let the two countries enjoy together the blessings of peace. How fortunate, how fortunate indeed! After receiving this dispatch will you immediately give us a prompt reply regarding the details and circumstances of your cutting off the opium traffic. Be sure not to put this off. The above is what has to be communicated. [Vermilion endorsement:] This is appropriately worded and quite comprehensive *(Te-t'i chou-tao)*.

From: DeBary, William Theodore, *Sources of Chinese tradition* (New York: Columbia University Press, 1960), pp. 668–71.

QUESTIONS:

1. What screen image does Lin Zexu project of his Emperor and countrymen on the hand and of the British king and of "the barbarians" or British people on the other? How effective were these screen images as a diplomatic communication? How do you think the British received this letter?
2. Examine carefully the Chinese attitude toward trade and the implied British attitude toward trade. This is a key instance of network-hierarchy clash, but the two cultures have different screen images of merchant activity in particular. Are the Chinese and British mutually comprehensible hierarchies? Why (not)?

JUSTIFYING IMPERIALISM

21.2a: *Speech before the French National Assembly* (Jules Ferry, 1883)

Jules Ferry (1832–1893) was a statesman who had two terms as President of the Council (Prime Minister) of France. A freethinker and freemason, Ferry was in the political sphere a vehement laïcist (he opposed any religious involvement in government). He led an education policy for free, nonclerical, and compulsory education for both sexes—and in the French language. In the wake of the French defeat by the Germans in the Franco-Prussian War, Ferry emphatically supported French imperialist expansion, which is the topic of the speech excerpted below. Note that Ferry's position on colonialism are not unopposed, a reminder that a culture can produce multiple—and conflicting—screen images.

FRANCE MUST BE A GREAT COUNTRY!

JULES FERRY: Gentlemen, it embarrasses me to make such a prolonged demand upon the gracious attention of the Chamber, but I believe that the duty I am fulfilling upon this platform is not a useless one: it is as strenuous for me as for you, but I believe that there is some benefit in summarizing and condensing, in the form of arguments, the principles, the motives, and the various interests by which a policy of colonial expansion may be justified. . . .

In the area of economics, I will allow myself to place before you, with the support of some figures, the considerations which justify a policy of colonial expansion from the point of view of that need, felt more and more strongly by the industrial populations of Europe and particularly those of our won rich and hard working country: the need for export markets. . . .

Gentlemen, there is a second point, as second order of ideas to which I have to give equal attention, but as quickly as possible, believe me; it is the humanitarian and civilizing side of the question. On this point the honorable Camille Pelletan [a conservative politician] has jeered in his own refined and clever manner; he jeers, he condemns, and he says "What is this civilization which you impose with cannon-ball? What is it but another form or barbarism? Don't these populations, these inferior races, have the same rights as you? Aren't they masters of their own houses? Have they called upon you? You come to them against their will, you offer them violence, but not civilization." There, gentlemen is the thesis. . . . But, I must speak from a higher and more truthful plane. It must be stated openly that, in effect, superior races have rights over inferior races.

JULES MAIGNE: Oh! You dare to say this in the country which has proclaimed the rights of man!

M. DE GULLOUTET: This is a justification of slavery and the slave trade!

JULES FERRY: If M. Maigne is right, if the declaration of the rights of man was written for the black of equatorial Africa, then by what right do you impose regular commerce upon them? They have not called upon you.

RAOUL DUVAN: We do not want to impose anything upon them. It is you who wish to do so!

JULES MAIGNE: To propose and to impose are two different things!

GEORGES PERIN: In any case, you cannot bring about commerce by force.

JULES FERRY: I repeat that superior races have a right, because they have a duty. They have the duty to civilize inferior races. . . . Gentlemen, in Europe as it is today, in this competition of so many rivals which we see growing around us, some by perfecting their military or maritime forces, others by the prodigious development of an ever growing population; in a Europe, or rather in a universe of this sort, a policy of peaceful seclusion or abstention is simply the highway to decadence! Nations are great in our times only by means of the activities which they develop; it is not simply "by the peaceful shining froth of institutions" that they are great at this hour. . . .

[The Republican Party] has shown that it is quite aware that one cannot impose upon France a political ideal conforming to that of nations like independent Belgium and the Swiss Republic; that something else is needed for France; that she cannot be merely a free country, that she must also be a great country, exercising all of her rightful influence over the destiny of Europe, that she ought to propagate this influence throughout the world and carry everywhere that she can her language, her customs, her flag, her arms, and her genius.

From: Austen, Ralph A., *Modern imperialism, Western overseas expansion, and its aftermath, 1776–1965* (Lexington, MA: Heath, 1969), pp. 70–73.

QUESTIONS:

1. What justifications for a colonial policy do Ferry and his supporters present? On what basis do others in the assembly disagree with him?
2. Who might be the intended audience—other than the assembly members before him—for Ferry's assertions of French might?

21.2b: *The White Man's Burden* (Rudyard Kipling, 1899)

Rudyard Kipling (1865–1936) was an English writer of stories, poems, and novels for both children and adults. He was a one of the most popular writers in England during his lifetime, and he was the first English recipient of the Nobel Prize in literature (1907). Kipling was born in India but sent to England at age five to be boarded with an English family and educated. He returned to India at age sixteen and worked for newspapers until his return to England in 1889 via Singapore, Hong Kong, Japan and the United States and Canada. During his extensive journey across the United States, he met Mark Twain, whose own writings on colonialism offer a strong contrast to Kipling's. For his entire life, Kipling was a prolific writer, and he was known for his stories for children and for his sympathetic portraits of British soldiers in India. Like Ferry, Kipling was a freemason and a supporter of colonialism. The poem included here, addressed to the Americans on the eve of the United States war in the Philippines, is a cautionary note about the duties and costs, as he saw them, of being a colonial power.

Take up the White Man's burden—
Send forth the best ye breed—
Go bind your sons to exile
To serve your captives' need;
To wait in heavy harness,
On fluttered folk and wild—
Your new-caught, sullen peoples,
Half-devil and half-child.

Take up the White Man's burden—
In patience to abide,
To veil the threat of terror
And check the show of pride;
By open speech and simple,
An hundred times made plain
To seek another's profit,
And work another's gain.

Take up the White Man's burden—
The savage wars of peace—
Fill full the mouth of Famine
And bid the sickness cease;
And when your goal is nearest
The end for others sought,
Watch sloth and heathen Folly
Bring all your hopes to nought.

Take up the White Man's burden—
No tawdry rule of kings,
But toil of serf and sweeper—
The tale of common things.

The ports ye shall not enter,
The roads ye shall not tread,
Go mark them with your living,
And mark them with your dead.

Take up the White Man's burden—
And reap his old reward:
The blame of those ye better,
The hate of those ye guard—
The cry of hosts ye humour
(Ah, slowly!) toward the light:—
"Why brought he us from bondage,
Our loved Egyptian night?"

Take up the White Man's burden—
Ye dare not stoop to less—
Nor call too loud on Freedom
To cloke your weariness;
By all ye cry or whisper,
By all ye leave or do,
The silent, sullen peoples
Shall weigh your gods and you.

Take up the White Man's burden—
Have done with childish days—
The lightly proffered laurel,
The easy, ungrudged praise.
Comes now, to search your manhood
Through all the thankless years
Cold, edged with dear-bought wisdom,
The judgment of your peers!

From: Kipling, Rudyard, 1899, "The White Man's Burden: The United States and the Philippine Islands," *McClure's Magazine* p. 290.

QUESTIONS:

1. What is Kipling's attitude toward imperialism? Why is it a "burden" to the "White Man" and what does he claim the effects for the colonized are?
2. Who are the peers who will judge the United States, and how does this compare to Ferry's presentation of judgment?

BRITISH INDIA

21.3a: *Letter to Lord Amherst* (Rammohun Roy, 1823)

Rammohun Roy (1772–1833) was an Indian scholar and reformer who is sometimes called the Father of Modern India. A monotheist, he wrote one of the first translations of Vedic scripture into English. In addition to his work as a pandit, or Indian legal scholar, he was employed by the East India Company. Roy favored English education in India, and he advocated for property rights for women and against the misogynist traditions of widow burning and child marriage. Roy wrote the letter below to William Pitt Amherst, 1st Earl Amherst (1773–1857), who was the Governor-General (or the head of the East India Company and effectively the ruler of India) from 1823 to 1828.

Address from Rammohan Roy, December 11, 1823

Address, dated 11th December 1823, from Raja Rammohan Roy.

Sir,

I beg leave to send you the accompanying address and shall feel obliged if you will have the goodness to lay it before the Right Hon'ble the Governor-General in Council.

I have, etc., RAMMOHUN ROY

CALCUTTA The 11th December 1823
To His Excellency the Right Hon'ble William Pitt, Lord Amherst
My Lord,

Humbly reluctant as the natives of India are to obtrude upon the notice of Government the sentiments they entertain on any public measure there are circumstances when silence would be carrying this respectful feeling to culpable excess. The present Rulers of India, coming from a distance of many thousand miles to govern a people whose language, literature, manners, customs, and ideas are almost entirely new and strange to them, cannot easily become so intimately acquainted with their real circumstances, as the natives of the country are themselves. We should therefore be guilty of a gross dereliction of duty to ourselves, and afford our Rulers just ground of complaint at our apathy, did we omit on occasions of importance like the present to supply them with such accurate information as might enable them to devise and adopt measures calculated to be beneficial to the country, and thus second by our local knowledge and experience their declared benevolent intentions for its improvement.

The establishment of a new Sangscrit School in Calcutta evinces the laudable desire of Government to improve the Natives of India by Education,—a blessing for which they must ever be grateful; and every well wisher of the human race must be desirous that the efforts made to promote it should be guided by the most enlightened principles, so that the stream of intelligence may flow into the most useful channels.

When this Seminary of learning was proposed, we understood that the Government in England had ordered a considerable sum of money to be annually devoted to the instruction of its Indian Subjects. We were filled with sanguine hopes that this sum would be laid out in employing European Gentlemen of talents and education to instruct the natives of India in Mathematics, Natural Philosophy, Chemistry, Anatomy and other useful Sciences, which the Nations of Europe have carried to a degree of perfection that has raised them above the inhabitants of other parts of the world.

While we looked forward with pleasing hope to the dawn of knowledge thus promised to the rising generation, our hearts were filled with mingled feelings of delight and gratitude; we already offered up thanks to Providence for inspiring the most generous and enlightened of the Nations of the West with the glorious ambitions of planting in Asia the Arts and Sciences of modern Europe.

We now find that the Government are establishing a Sangscrit school under Hindoo Pundits to impart such knowledge as is already current in India. This Seminary (similar in character to those which existed in Europe before the time of Lord Bacon) can only be expected to load the minds of youth with grammatical niceties and metaphysical distinctions of little or no practicable use to the possessors or to society. The pupils will there acquire what was known two thousand years ago, with the addition of vain and empty subtilties [*sic*] since produced by speculative men, such as is already commonly taught in all parts of India.

The Sangscrit language, so difficult that almost a life time is necessary for its perfect acquisition, is well known to have been for ages a lamentable check on the diffusion of knowledge; and the learning concealed under this almost impervious veil is far from sufficient to reward the labour of acquiring it. But if it were thought necessary to perpetuate this language for the sake of the portion of the valuable information it contains, this might be much more easily accomplished by other means than the establishment of a new Sangscrit College; for there have been always and are now numerous professors of Sangscrit in the different parts of the country, engaged in teaching this language as well as the other branches of literature which are to be the object of the new Seminary. Therefore their more diligent cultivation, if desirable, would be effectually promoted by holding out premiums and granting certain allowances to those most eminent Professors, who have already undertaken on their own account to teach them, and would by such rewards be stimulated to still greater exertions.

From these considerations, as the sum set apart for the instruction of the Natives of India was intended by the Government in England, for the improvement of its Indian subjects, I beg leave to state, with due deference to your Lordship's exalted situation, that if the plan now adopted be followed, it will completely defeat the object proposed; since no improvement can be expected from inducing young men to consume a dozen of years of the most valuable period of their lives in acquiring the niceties of the Byakurun or Sangscrit Grammar. For instance, in learning to discuss such points as the following: *Khad* signifying to eat, *khaduti*, he or she or it eats. Query, whether does the word *khaduti*, taken as a whole, convey the meaning *he*, *she*, or *it eats*, or are separate parts of this meaning conveyed by distinct

portions of the word? As if in the English language it were asked, how much meaning is there in the *eat*, how much in the *s*? and is the whole meaning of the word conveyed by those two portions of it distinctly, or by them taken jointly?

Neither can much improvement arise from such speculations as the following, which are the themes suggested by the Vedant:—In what manner is the soul absorbed into the deity? What relation does it bear to the divine essence? Nor will youths be fitted to be better members of society by the Vedantic doctrines, which teach them to believe that all visible things have no real existence; that as father, brother, etc., have no actual entirety, they consequently deserve no real affection, and therefore the sooner we escape from them and leave the world the better. Again, no essential benefit can be derived by the student of the Meemangsa from knowing what it is that makes the killer of a goat sinless on pronouncing certain passages of the Veds, and what is the real nature and operative influence of passages of the Ved, etc.

Again the student of the Nyaya Shastra cannot be said to have improved his mind after he has learned from it into how many ideal classes the objects in the Universe are divided, and what speculative relation the soul bears to the body, the body to the soul, the eye to the ear, etc.

In order to enable your Lordship to appreciate the utility of encouraging such imaginary learning as above characterised, I beg your Lordship will be pleased to compare the state of science and literature in Europe before the time of Lord Bacon, with the progress of knowledge made since he wrote.

If it had been intended to keep the British nation in ignorance of real knowledge the Baconian philosophy would not have been allowed to displace the system of the schoolmen, which was the best calculated to perpetuate ignorance. In the same manner the Sangscrit system of education would be the best calculated to keep this country in darkness, if such had been the policy of the

British Legislature. But as the improvement of the native population is the object of the Government, it will consequently promote a more liberal and enlightened system of instruction, embracing mathematics, natural philosophy, chemistry and anatomy, with other useful sciences which may be accomplished with the sum proposed by employing a few gentlemen of talents and learning educated in Europe, and providing a college furnished with the necessary books, instruments and other apparatus.

In representing this subject to your Lordship I conceive myself discharging a solemn duty which I owe to my countrymen and also to that enlightened Sovereign and Legislature which have extended their benevolent cares to this distant land actuated by a desire to improve its inhabitants and I therefore humbly trust you will excuse the liberty I have taken in thus expressing my sentiments to your Lordship.

I have, etc., RAMMOHUN ROY
CALCUTTA; The 11th December 1823

From: Bureau of Education, *Selections from Educational Records, Part I (1781–1839)*, Edited by H. Sharp, ed. (Calcutta: Superintendent Government Printing, 1920), reprint. (Delhi: National Archives of India, 1965), pp. 98–101.

QUESTIONS:

1. What constitutes ignorance and what constitutes knowledge for Roy? How might his view of learning contribute to the success of European imperialism?
2. What image of himself does Roy's style of writing project? How might this screen image appeal to Roy's audience?

21.3b: *On the Commerce of India* (Dadbhai Naoroji, 1871)

Dadbhai Naoroji (1825–1917) was a Parsi, or Persian Zoroastrian in India, a professor of mathematics and natural science, and a prominent Indian political reformer. He was among the establishers of the East India Association, an organization which brought the Indian perspective to the attention of the British Public. Having first travelled to Britain as a businessman for a few years in the 1850s—he opened the first Indian company in Britain—he later returned and successfully stood for parliament for the Liberal Party in 1892. He was the first Asian member of the British Parliament, from 1892 to 1895. In his book *Poverty and Un-British Rule in India* (1901), Naoroji described what he called a drain, or several hundred million pound loss of revenue from India to Britain. In the excerpt below Naoroji tabulates the "credits and debits" of British rule in a speech before a meeting of the Society of Arts in London on February 15, 1871.

Cr. [Credit]—*In the Cause of Humanity.*—Abolition of suttee and infanticide.

Destruction of Dacoits, Thugs, Pindarees, and other such pests of Indian society.

Allowing remarriage of Hindu widows, and charitable aid in time of famine.

Glorious work all this, of which any nation may well be proud, and such as has not fallen to the lot of any people in the history of mankind.

In the Cause of Civilization.—Education, both male and female. Though yet only partial, an ines-

timable blessing as far as it has gone, and leading gradually to the destruction of superstition, and many moral and social evils. Resuscitation of India's own noble literature, modified and refined by the enlightenment of the West.

   . . .

Politically—Peace and order. Freedom of speech and liberty of the press. Higher political knowledge and aspirations. Improvement of government in the native states. Security of life and property. Freedom from oppression caused by the caprice or greed of despotic rulers, and from devastation by war. Equal justice between man and man (sometimes vitiated by partiality to Europeans). Services of highly educated administrators, who have achieved the above-mentioned results.

Materially.—Loans for railways and irrigation. . . . [D]evelopment of a few valuable products, such as indigo, tea, coffee, silk, etc. Increase of exports. Telegraphs.

Generally.—A slowly growing desire of late to treat India equitably, and as a country held in trust. Good intentions.

No nation on the face of the earth has ever had the opportunity of achieving such a glorious work as this. I hope in the credit side of the account I have done no injustice, and if I have omitted any item which anyone may think of importance, I shall have the greatest pleasure in inserting it. I appreciate, and so do my countrymen, what England has done for India, and I know that it is only in British hands that her regeneration can be accomplished. Now for the debit side.

Dr. [Detriment]—*In the Cause of Humanity.*—Nothing. Everything, therefore, is in your favor under this heading.

In the Cause of Civilization: As I have said already, there has been a failure to do as much as might have been done, but I put nothing to the debit. Much has been done, or I should not be standing here this evening.

Politically—Repeated breach of pledges to give the natives a fair and reasonable share in the higher administration of their own country, which has much shaken confidence in the good faith of the British word. Political aspirations and the legitimate claim to have a reasonable voice in the legislation and the imposition and disbursement of taxes, met to a very slight degree, thus treating the natives of India not as British subjects, in whom representation is a birthright.

. . .

Consequent on the above, an utter disregard of the feelings and views of the natives. The great

moral evil of the drain of wisdom and practical administration, leaving none to guide the rising generation. . . .

Financially—All attention is engrossed in devising new modes of taxation, without any adequate effort to increase the means of the people to pay; and the consequent vexation and oppressiveness of the taxes imposed, imperial and local. Inequitable financial relations between England and India, i.e., the political debt of £100,000,000 clapped on India's shoulders, and all home charges also, though the British Exchequer contributes nearly £3,000,000 to the expense of the colonies. . . .

Materially.—The political drain, up to this time, from India to England, of above £500,000,000, at the lowest computation, in principal alone, which with interest would be some thousands of millions. The further continuation of this drain at the rate, at present, of above £12,000,000 [yearly], with a tendency to increase. . . .

The consequent continuous impoverishment and exhaustion of the country, except so far as it has been very partially relieved and replenished by the railway and irrigation loans, and the windfall of the consequences of the American war, since 1850. Even with this relief, the material condition of India is such that the great mass of the poor have hardly *2d.* [two pence] a day and a few rags, or a scanty subsistence.

The famines that were in their power to prevent, if they had done their duty, as a good and intelligent government. The policy adopted during the last fifteen years of building railways, irrigation works, etc., is hopeful, has already resulted in much good to your credit, and if persevered in, gratitude and contentment will follow.

Contra.—An increase of exports without adequate compensation; loss of manufacturing industry and skill. Here I end the debit side.

. . .

. . . To sum up the whole, the British rule has been—morally, a great blessing; politically, peace and order on one hand, blunders on the other; materially, impoverishment, relieved as far as the railway and other loans go. The natives call the British system "Sakar ki Churi," the knife of sugar. That is to say, there is no oppression, it is all smooth and sweet, but it is the knife, notwithstanding. I mention this that you should know these feelings. Our great misfortune is that you do not know our wants. When you will know our real wishes, I have not the least doubt that you would do justice. The genius and spirit of the British people is fair play and justice. . . .

From: Naoroji, Dadabhai, *Essays, Speeches, Addresses and Writings* (Bombay: Caxton Printing Works, 1887), pp. 131–36.

QUESTIONS:

1. How does Naoroji characterize the British? How does he account for the detriments that have resulted from their rule in India?
2. What do you think Naoroji's vision for the future of India looks like?

21.4: *Open Letter to King Leopold II of Belgium* (George Washington Williams, 1890)

George Washington Williams (1849–91) was a free black minister, historian, and politician born in Pennsylvania. He is the author of *A History of Negro Troops in the War of Rebellion* and *The History of the Negro Race in America 1619–1880* (1882). Williams fought in the US Civil War on the Union side, as well as in the Mexican Republican army against Emperor Maximilian. After he returned to the United States in 1867, he served in Indian Territory, where he was wounded in his first year of service. He attended Howard University for a time and finished his studies at Newton Theological College. He served as a Baptist minister in several places before he went to law school in Cincinnati, where he became the first black member of the Ohio State Legislature. He went in 1889 to meet with King Leopold II of Belgium, after which he traveled to the Congo to see the situation there firsthand. Williams wrote the letter below after this trip. He died in England in 1891 on his return trip from Africa.

An Open Letter to His Serene Majesty Leopold II, King of the Belgians and Sovereign of the Independent State of Congo By Colonel, The Honorable Geo. W. Williams, of the United States of America.

Good and Great Friend,

I have the honor to submit for your Majesty's consideration some reflections respecting the Independent State of Congo, based upon a careful study and inspection of the country and character of the personal Government you have established upon the African Continent.

It afforded me great pleasure to avail myself of the opportunity afforded me last year, of visiting your State in Africa; and how thoroughly I have been disenchanted, disappointed and disheartened, it is now my painful duty to make known to your Majesty in plain but respectful language. . . .

FIRST.—Your Majesty's Government is deficient in the moral military and financial strength, necessary to govern a territory o 1,508,000 square miles, 7,251 miles of navigation, and 31,694 square miles of lake surface. Cruelties of the most astounding character are practiced by the natives, such as burying slaves alive in the grave of a dead chief, cutting off the heads of captured warriors in native combats, and no effort is put forth by your Majesty's Government to prevent them. Between 800 and 1,000 slaves are sold to be eaten by the natives of the Congo State annually; and slave raids, accomplished by the most cruel and murderous agencies, are carried on within the territorial limits of your Majesty's Government which is impotent. There are only 2,300 soldiers in the Congo. . . .

FOURTH.—The Courts of your Majesty's Government are abortive, unjust, partial and delinquent. I have personally witnessed and examined their clumsy operations. The laws printed and circulated in Europe "for the Protection of the blacks" in the Congo, are a dead letter and a fraud. I have heard an officer of the Belgian Army pleading the cause of a white man of low degree who had been guilty of beating and stabbing a black man, and urging race distinctions and prejudices as good and sufficient reasons why his client should be adjudged innocent. I know of prisoners remaining in custody for six and ten months because they were not judged. . . .

. . .

SEVENTH.—Your Majesty's Government is engaged in trade and commerce, competing with the organized trade companies of Belgium, England, France, Portugal and Holland. It taxes all trading companies and exempts its own goods from export-duty, and makes many of its officers ivory-traders, with the promise of a liberal commission upon all they can buy or get for the State. State soldiers patrol many villages forbidding the natives to trade with any person but a State official, and when the natives refuse to accept the price of the State, their goods are seized by the Government that promised them "protection". When natives have persisted in trading with the trade-companies the State has punished their independence by burning the villages in the vicinity of the trading houses and driving the natives away. . . .

NINTH.—Your Majesty's Government has been, and is now, guilty of waging unjust and cruel wars against natives, with the hope of securing slaves and women, to minister to the behests of the officers of your Government.

TENTH.—Your Majesty's Government is engaged in the slave-trade, wholesale and retail. It buys and sells and steals slaves. Your Majesty's Government gives £3 per head for able-bodied slaves for military service. Officers at the chief stations get the men and receive the money when they are transferred to the State; but there are some middle-men who only get from twenty to twenty-five francs per head. Three hundred and sixteen slaves were sent down the river recently, and others are to follow . . .

From: Williams, George Washington, "An Open Letter to His Serene Majesty Leopold II, King of the Belgians and Sovereign of the Independent State of Congo," John Hope Franklin, ed. (Chicago: The University of Chicago Press, 1985), pp. 243–54.

QUESTIONS:

1. This letter is addressed to King Leopold II of Belgium, but it is an open letter. Who do you think Williams' intended audience was? How persuasive is the letter?
2. What is Williams' attitude toward imperialism? How does this compare to the attitudes of Kipling, Roy, and Naoroji? Does Williams believe that Leopold should be out of the Congo or ruling it more humanely?

CHAPTER 22

Imperialism: Reactions and Consequences

INTRODUCTION

This chapter looks at the age of imperialism from the perspective of the colonized. Imperialism was characterized by encounters between new Industrial Era hierarchies and mature Agrarian hierarchies, with harsh consequences for the latter. Policymakers in the Agrarian world faced a difficult range of options. One was traditionalist resistance—possibly futile given the technological and organizational gap opening between themselves and the Industrial powers—that involved attempting to reject any western influence. Westernizers, on the other hand, wished to adopt the technologies and the values of the Industrial powers, but such a path threatened to undermine the cultural identity of their societies. Modernizers aimed at a narrow middle path of adopting western technology but retaining their own culture. Every path was fraught with difficulties, as these documents show.

22.1: *Reflections on My Errors* (Sakuma Shozan, 1860)

Sakuma Shozan (1811–1864), the offspring of a samurai family and a controversial Japanese politician, technological expert, and writer, is featured in the opening story of *Frameworks* Chapter 22. A student of western science well before the opening of Japan by the fleet of American Admiral Perry in 1853, his study of the results of the Opium War led him to advocate the adoption of western military technology. He was a paradigmatic modernizer, however, as he thought Japan should remain Japanese in cultural spirit. His slogan, "Western science, Eastern ethics" became, in effect, the mission statement of the Meiji Restoration of 1868, several of whose leaders had been Shozan's students. Shozan himself was under house arrest for the last years of the Tokugawa Shogunate that fell to the Restoration for his association with a student who tried to smuggle himself aboard one of Perry's ships. The selection below comes from *Reflection on My Errors,* which was in fact anything but an admission of error.

In the summer of Kaei 7, the fourth month [May 1854], I, Taisei, because of an incident, went down into prison. During my seven months of imprisonment I pondered my errors, and as a result, there were things that I should have liked to say concerning them. However, brush and inkstone were forbidden in the prison, and I was therefore unable to keep a manuscript. Over that long period, then, I forgot much. Now that I have come out, I shall record what I remember, deposit the record in a cloth box, and bequeath it to my descendants. As for publicizing what I have to say, I dare do no such thing.

2. Take, for example, a man who is grieved by the illness of his lord or his father and who is seeking medicine to cure it. If he is fortunate enough to secure the medicine and is certain that it will be efficacious, then, certainly, without questioning either its cost or the quality of its name, he will beg his lord or father to take it. Should the latter refuse on the grounds that he dislikes the name, does the younger man make various schemes to give the medicine secretly, or does he simply sit by and wait for his master to die? There is no question about it: the feeling of genuine sincerity and heartfelt grief on the part of the subject or son makes it absolutely impossible for him to sit idly and watch his master's anguish; consequently, even if he knows that he will later have to face his master's anger, he cannot help but give the medicine secretly.

16. Although my family branch was poor, I grew up with plenty to eat and with warm clothing to wear. I never underwent the tempering of cold and hardship. I was therefore always afraid that in the event of a national emergency I would have difficulty bearing the attendant difficulties in everyday living, such as privations in food and drink. However, last summer, when the American ships suddenly arrived, and Edo was put on strict guard, I managed military affairs in the mansion belonging to my *han*, and although I got no sleep for seven days and nights, my spirits grew higher and higher. This year, I was condemned and sent to prison. For several weeks I have eaten meager food, licked salt, and received the same treatment as men under heavy punishment. However, I have kept calm and have managed to become content with my lot. Moreover, my spirit is active, and my body is healthy. To have tried myself somewhat on these two points is of no small profit. My ordeal can thus be called a heavenly blessing.

20. The noble man has five pleasures, but wealth and rank are not among them. That his house un-

derstands decorum and rightness and remains free from family rifts—this is one pleasure. That exercising care in giving to and taking from others, he provides for himself honestly, free, internally, from shame before his wife and children, and externally, from disgrace before the public—this is the second pleasure. That he expounds and glorifies the learning of the sages, knows in his heart the great Way, and in all situations contents himself with his duty, in adversity as well as in prosperity—this is the third pleasure. That he is born after the opening of the vistas of science by the Westerners and can therefore understand principles not known to the sages and wise men of old—this is the fourth pleasure. That he employs the ethics of the East and the scientific technique of the West, neglecting neither the spiritual nor material aspects of life, combining subjective and objective and thus bringing benefit to the people and serving the nation—this is the fifth pleasure.

27. All learning is cumulative. It is not something that one comes to realize in a morning or an evening. Effective maritime defense is in itself a great field of study. Since no one has yet thoroughly studied its fundamentals, it is not easy to learn rapidly its essential points. Probably this fact explains why even if you take hold of a man's ear and explain these essential points to him, he does not understand.

30. Of the men who now hold posts as commanders of the army, those who are not dukes or princes or men of noble rank are members of wealthy families. As such, they find their daily pleasure in drinking wine, singing, and dancing; and they are ignorant of military strategy and discipline. Should a national emergency arise, there is no one who could command the respect of the warriors and halt the enemy's attack. This is the great sorrow of our times. For this reason, I have wished to follow in substance the Western principles of armament and, by banding together loyal, valorous, strong men of old, established families not in the military class—men of whom one would be equal to ten ordinary men—to form a voluntary group that would be made to have as its sole aim that of

guarding the nation and protecting the people. Anyone wishing to join the society would be tested and his merits examined; and if he did not shrink from hardship, he would then be permitted to join. Men of talent in military strategy, planning, and administration would be advanced to positions of leadership, and then if the day should come when the country must be defended, this group could be gathered together and organized into an army to await official commands. It is to be hoped that they could drive the enemy away and perform greater service than those who now form the military class.

35. Mathematics is the basis for all learning. In the Western world after this science was discovered, military tactics advanced greatly, far outstripping that of former times. This development accords with the statement that "one advanced from basic studies to higher learning." In Sunzi's *Art of War,* the statement about "estimation, determination of quantity, calculation, judgment, and victory" refers to mathematics. However, since Sunzi's time, neither we nor the Chinese have ceased to read, study, and memorize his teachings, and our art of war remains exactly as it was then. It consequently cannot be compared with that of the West. There is no reason for this other than that we have not devoted ourselves to basic studies. At the present time, if we wish really to complete our military preparations, we must develop this branch of study.

. . .

44. We say that this nation has an abundance of gold, rice, and millet. However, our territory is not large, and after the country's internal needs have been met, there is hardly any surplus of the materials produced here. Such things as the need for coastal defense arise from without. To install several hundred defense barriers, to construct several hundred large warships, and to cast several thousand large artillery pieces call for vast expenditures. Again, all these things are not permanent: every ten or twenty years they must be repaired, reconstructed, or improved. Externally, we will need funds to carry on relations with foreign countries and, internally,

[to cover] the expense of necessary food supplies for our own country. Where can the money for these sorts of things be obtained? If a family in financial distress receives many guests and frequently prepares feasts for them, its resources will be dissipated to the point that it no longer can continue to carry on these activities. How does the present position of the nation differ from the plight of this poor family? With what tactics can such a situation be overcome? Those who sincerely wish to conduct the affairs of state well must make careful plans in advance.

46. At the time when my former lord assumed office in the government, and later, when he took charge of coastal defense, the English barbarians were invading the Qing empire, and news of the war was sensational. I, greatly lamenting the events of the day, submitted a plan in a memorial. That was, actually, in Tenpō 13, the eleventh month [December 1842—January 1843]. Later I saw the *Shengwu-ji* of the Chinese writer Wei Yuan [1784–1856]. Wei had also written out of sorrow over recent events. The preface to the book was composed in the seventh month of the same year [August—September 1842]; and although Wei thus wrote only four months before I submitted my memorial, the two of us, without having had any previous consultation, were often in complete agreement. Ah! Wei and I were born in different places and did not even know each other's name. Isn't it interesting that we both wrote lamenting the times during the same year and that our views were in accord without our having met? We really must be called comrades from separate lands. However, Wei says that from ancient tunes until the present, China has had a naval defense but has had no naval warfare; therefore as the method of defense against attacks from the sea, it should strengthen fortified towns and clear fields in order to be able to push back the landing invaders. I, on the other hand, wish to promote to the full the teaching of techniques for using armored warships and to form a plan of attack whereby an enemy could be intercepted and destroyed, in order that the death sentence may be

given to the plunderers before they have reached the country's shores. That is the only point of difference between Wei and me.

47. In order to master the barbarians, there is nothing so effective as to ascertain in the beginning the conditions among them. To do this, there is no better first step than to be familiar with barbarian tongues. Thus, learning a barbarian language is not only a step toward knowing the barbarians but also the groundwork for mastering them. When the various nations on one pretext or another began sending ships frequently to the territory around Sagami and Awa, I thought it genuinely difficult to find out facts about them. As a result, I felt the desire to compile a lexicon in several volumes, translating other languages into Japanese, in order to teach the tongues of the various European countries. Also, since we have long had trade relations with Holland and since many of us already know how to read the books used in that country, I wished to publish the Dutch section first. Before this, the government had ordered to the effect that all books to be published must be officially inspected. Therefore, in the winter of Kaei 2 [1849–1850], I came to Edo, submitted my manuscript, and requested permission to publish it. The affair dragged on for a year, and I was ultimately unable to obtain permission. During the time I was in the capital, I first secured Wei's book and read it. He also wished to set up schools in his country primarily to translate foreign documents and to promote a clear understanding of conditions among the enemy nations, in order to further the cause of mastering the enemies. In this, too, his opinion concurred with mine. I do not know, however, whether or not his country has put his words into effect.

48. The main requirement for maritime defense are guns and warships, but the more important item is guns. Wei included an article on guns in his *Haiguo tushi*. It is for the most part inaccurate and unfounded; it is like the doings of a child at play. No one can learn the essentials of a subject without engaging personally in the study of it. That a man

of Wei's talent should fail to understand this is unfortunate. I deeply pity Wei that in the world of today, he, ignorant of artillery, should have unwittingly perpetrated these errors and foisted these mistakes on later generations.

49. Last summer the American barbarians arrived in the Bay of Uraga with four warships, bearing their president's message. Their deportment and manner of expression were exceedingly arrogant, and the resulting insult to our national dignity was not small. Those who heard could only gnash their teeth. A certain person on guard in Uraga suffered this insult in silence, and having been ultimately unable to do anything about it, after the barbarians had retired, he drew his knife and slashed to bits a portrait of their leader, which they had left as a gift. Thus, he gave vent to his rage. In former times Cao Wei of Song, having been demoted, was serving as an official in Shensi, and when he heard of the character of Zhao Yuanhao, he had a person skillful in drawing paint Zhao's image. Cao looked at this portrait and knew from its manly appearance that Zhao would doubtless make trouble on the border in the future. Therefore Wei wished to take steps toward preparing the border in advance and toward collecting together and examining men of ability. Afterward, everything turned out as he had predicted. Thus, by looking at the portrait of his enemy, he could see his enemy's abilities and thereby aid himself with his own preparations. It can only be regretted that the Japanese guard did not think of this. Instead of using the portrait, he tore it up. In both cases it was a barbarian; in both cases it was a portrait. But one man, lacking the portrait, sought to obtain it, while the other, having it, destroyed it. Their depth of knowledge and farsightedness in planning were vastly different.

52. Formerly, with one or two friends, I took a trip to Kamakura; . . . having stayed a time at Uraga, we went up to Sarujima, viewed Kanazawa, went out to Honmoku, and returned to Edo. In the course of this trip I stopped at about ten places where barricades had been set up in preparation

against an invasion from the sea. However, the arrangement of them made no sense, and none of them could be depended on as a defense fortification. Upon discovering this, I unconsciously looked up to Heaven and sighed deeply; I struck my chest and wept for a long time. Edo is the throat of the nation, and while Futtsu, as its lip, may be called a natural barrier, the mouth opening into the sea is still broad. From the outset, it would be difficult without warships and naval troops to halt an enemy transgression or attack. Now, without any real effort, these foolish walls and mock parapets have been thrown up high above the surface of the sea, only to display to the foreign nations our lack of planning. If during these times the nations to east and west sent ships to pay us a visit, how could they take us seriously? There is no point in criticizing the mediocrity of the lower officials. But what is to be done if even those who ride on golden saddles with ornate saddle cloths, who wear brocade and feast on meat, and who call themselves high class, fail to recognize the great plan for the nation but instead use up the country's wealth on this useless construction work? If barbarian ships arrived in force, how could we either defend against them or defeat them? After my trip, I felt the urge to write a petition discussing the things that should and should not be done in maritime defense, with the hope that I might be of assistance in this time of emergency. I completed my manuscript and requested my former lord for permission to submit it. He refused, and I gave up my plan. This was in the early summer of Kaei 3 [1850]. Four years later, as I had predicted, the affair of the American barbarians arose. At the time my former lord stopped my memorial, he was probably acting out of the fear that I might be punished for impertinence. His benevolence in protecting me was truly great. If he were in the world today and were informed that I have been imprisoned, his grief would be profound!

From: De Bary, William Theodore, Yoshiko Kurata Dykstra, William M. Bodiford, J. S. A. Elisonas, and Philip B. Yampolsky, *Sources of Japanese tradition* (New York: Columbia University Press, 2001), pp. 633–38.

QUESTIONS:

1. What "scientific techniques of the West" does Shozan advocate? How does he want to apply these? To what end?
2. What does "ethics of the East" mean to Shozan in concrete terms? What role do Eastern ethics play in his proposals?

22.2: *Letter to Emperor Tu Duc* and *Last Message to His Administration* (Phan Thanh Gian, 1867)

Phan Thanh Gian (1796–1867) was a leading advisor and Confucian-trained official in the court of king Tự Đứ'c of the Nguyen Dynasty of Vietnam. In this capacity he had to deal with the incursions of French imperialist troops into Indochina starting in the 1860s. He was a leading Vietnamese negotiator of the Treaty of Saigon in 1862 that ceded several provinces of southern Vietnam to France, for which Phan received criticism. He then led a large diplomatic mission to Paris the next year to negotiate the return of the provinces with Napoleon III. He was initially successful, but Napoleon reversed his decision under criticism from his own ministers. The more important result of the trip for Phan was that it exposed him to the vast technological and economic gap between France and his home country. Thus, when French troops invaded the remaining provinces of southern Vietnam in 1867, over which Phan had been installed as governor, and his king refused to listen to his warnings about French superiority, he decided not to command resistance. Instead, he surrendered a key fortification and committed suicide. He wrote the notes excerpted here to his king and his subordinates before his death.

8, July 1867

I, Phan Thanh Gian, make the following report, in expressing frankly, with my head bowed, my humble sentiments, and in soliciting, with my head raised, your discerning scrutiny.

During the period of difficulties and misfortunes that we are presently undergoing, rebellion is rising around the capital, the pernicious [French] influence is expanding on our frontiers. . . .

My duty compels me to die. I would not dare to live thoughtlessly, leaving a heritage of shame to my Sovereign and my Father. Happily, I have confidence in my Emperor, who has extensive knowledge of ancient times and the present and who has studied profoundly the causes of peace and of dissension: . . . In respectfully observing the warnings of Heaven and in having pity on the misery of man . . . in changing the string of the guitar, in modifying the track of the governmental chariot, it is still possible for you to act in accordance with your authority and means.

At the last moment of life, the throat constricted, I do not know what to say, but, in wiping my tears and in raising my eyes toward you affectionately, I can only ardently hope that this wish will be realized. With respect, I make this report, Tu Duc, twentieth year, sixth moon, seventh day, Phan Thanh Gian.

Last Message to His Administrators

It is written: He who lives in accordance with the will of Heaven lives in virtue; he who does not live according to the will of Heaven lives in evil. To work according to the will of Heaven is to listen to natural reason. . . . Man is an intelligent animal created by Heaven. Every animal lives according to his nature, as water flows to low ground, as fire goes out on dry ground. . . .

The empire of our king is ancient. Our gratitude toward our kings is complete and always ardent; we cannot forget them. Now, the French are come, with their powerful weapons of war to cause dissension among us. We are weak against them; our commanders and our soldiers have been vanquished. Each battle adds to our misery. . . . The French have immense warships, filled with soldiers and armed with huge cannons. No one can resist them. They go where they want, the strongest ramparts fall before them.

I have raised my spirit toward Heaven and I have listened to the voice of reason. And I have said: "It would be as senseless for you to wish to defeat your enemies by force of arms as for a young fawn to attack a tiger. You attract uselessly great misfortunes upon the people whom Heaven has confided to you. I have thus written to all the mandarins and to all the war commanders to break their lances and surrender the forts without fighting.

"But, if I have followed the Will of Heaven by averting great evils from the head of the people, I am a traitor to our king in delivering without resistance the provinces which belong to him. . . . I deserve death. Mandarins and people, you can live under the command of the French, who are only terrible during the battle, but their flag must never fly above a fortress where Phan Thanh Gian still lives."

From: Sully, François, and Marjorie Weiner Normand, *We the Vietnamese; voices from Vietnam* (New York: Praeger, 1971), pp. 132–34.

QUESTIONS:

1. What moral conflict does Phan Thanh Gian face as an administrator? Why does he feel its solution lies in suicide?
2. What does his reaction say about choices facing the targets of European imperialism? How does his response compare to Shozan's?

22.3: *Imperial Rescript* (Sultan Abdülmecid I, 1856)

Abdülmecid I (1823–61, r. 1839–61) was Sultan of the Ottoman Empire during a critical period of its relations with the rising industrial powers of western Europe. Upon his succession to the throne, the European-educated sultan, who spoke fluent French, immediately implemented a number of measures designed by his father Sultan Mahmud II to improve the administration and economy of the empire along European lines. The implementation of these reforms helped Abdülmecid's diplomatic advances toward leading European powers, especially England and France. But the rise of nationalist movements in the empire's Balkan provinces continued to pose problems. Abdülmecid issued the Imperial Rescript (proclamation) excerpted here in 1856. It abolished the special tax on non-Muslims and granted full religious toleration to all subjects of the Empire. In contrast to the relative success of the administrative reforms, this measure did little to quell Balkan nationalist resistance.

It has always been my most earnest desire to insure the happiness of all classes of the subjects whom Divine Providence has placed under my imperial scepter, and since my accession to the throne I have not ceased to direct all my efforts to the attainment of that end.

. . .

It being now my desire to renew and enlarge still more the new institutions ordained with a view of establishing a state of things conformable with the dignity of my empire and the position which it occupies among civilized nations, and the rights of my empire having, by the fidelity and praiseworthy efforts of all my subjects, and by the kind and friendly assistance of the great powers, my noble allies, received from abroad a confirmation which will be the commencement of a new era, it is my desire to augment its well being and prosperity, to effect the happiness of all my subjects, who in my sight are all equal, and equally dear to me, and who are united to each other by the cordial ties of patriotism, and to insure the means of daily increasing the prosperity of my empire.

I have therefore resolved upon, and I order the execution of the following measures:

The guarantees promised on our part by the Hatti-Hamayonn of Gulhané (No. 188), and in conformity with the Tanzimat, to all the subjects of my empire, without distinction of classes or of religion, for the security of their persons and property, and the preservation of their honor, are to-day confirmed and consolidated, and efficacious measures

shall be taken in order that they may have their full entire effect.

All the privileges and spiritual immunities granted by my ancestors *ab antique*, and at subsequent dates, to all Christian communities or other non-Mussulman persuasions established in my empire, under my protection, shall be confirmed and maintained.

Every Christian or other non-Mussulman community shall be bound within a fixed period, and with the concurrence of a commission composed *ad hoo* of members of its own body, to proceed, with my high approbation and under the inspection of my Sublime Porte, to examine into its actual immunities and privileges, and to discuss and submit to my Sublime Porte the reforms required by the progress of civilization and of the age. The powers conceded to the Christian patriarchs and bishops by the Sultan Mahomet II and to his successors shall be made to harmonize with the new position which my generous and beneficent intentions insure to these communities.

The principle of nominating the patriarchs for life, after the revision of the rule of election now in force, shall be exactly carried out, conformably to the tenor of their firmans of investiture.

The patriarchs, metropolitans, archbishops, bishops, and rabbins shall take an oath, on their entrance into office, according to a form agreed upon in common by my Sublime Porte and the spiritual heads of the different religious communities. The ecclesiastical dues, of whatever sort or nature they by abolished and replaced by fixed revenues of the patriarchs and heads of communities, and by the allocations of allowances and salaries equitably proportioned to the importance, the rank, and the dignity of the different members of the clergy.

. . .

As all forms of religion are and shall be freely professed in my dominions, on subject of my empire shall be hindered in the exercise of the religion that he professes, nor shall he be in any way annoyed on this account. No one shall be compelled to change their religion.

The nomination and choice of all functionaries and other employees of my empire being wholly dependent upon my sovereign will, all the subjects of my empire, without distinction of nationality, shall be admissible to public employments, and qualified to till them according to their capacity and merit, and conformably with rules to be generally applied.

All the subjects of my empire, without distinction, shall be received into the civil and military schools of the governments, if they otherwise satisfy the conditions as to age and examination which are specified in the organic regulations of the said schools. Moreover, every community is authorized to establish public schools of science, are, and industry. Only the method of instructions and the choice of professors in schools of this class shall be under the control of a mixed council of public instruction, the members of which shall be named by my sovereign command.

. . .

The organization of the police in the capital, in the provincial towns and in the rural districts, shall be revised in such a manner as to give to all the peaceable subjects of my empire the strongest guarantees for the safety both of their persons and property.

The equality of taxes entailing equality of burdens, as equality of duties entails that of rights, Christian subjects, and those of other non-Mussulman sects, as it has been already decided, shall, as well as Mussulmans, be subjects to the obligations of the law of recruitment.

. . .

Proceedings shall be taken for a reform in the constitution of the provincial and communal councils in order to insure fairness in the choice of the deputies of the Mussulman, Christian, and other communities and freedom of voting in the councils.

. . .

Steps shall be taken for the formation of banks and other similar institutions, so as to effect a reform in the monetary and financial system, as well as to create funds to be employed in augmenting the sources of the material walth of my empire. Steps shall also be taken for the formation of roads and canals to increase the facilities of communication and increase the sources of the wealth of the country.

Everything that can impede commerce or agriculture shall be abolished. To accomplish these objects means shall be sought to profit by the science, the art and the funds of Europe, and thus gradually to execute them.

. . .

10 Dzemaziul, 1272 (February 18, 1856).

From: United States, and Edward Abbott Van Dyck, *Report of Edward A. Van Dyck, consular clerk of the United States at Cairo, upon the capitulations of the Ottoman Empire since the year 1150,* Pt. 1 (Washington: Govt. Print. Off. 1881), pp. 109–11, passim.

QUESTIONS:

1. Why do you think Abdülmecid's proclamation of religious toleration met with less success than other parts of his modernization program? How does this Rescript compare to Sakuma Shozan's plan for modernization?
2. How do you think his proposals were received among different elites and commoners in Ottoman society? Who benefits and who is threatened by this plan?

22.4:   *Secret Memorandum on Industrialization* (Sergei Witte, 1899)

Sergei Witte (1849–1915) was one of the most influential government ministers of late imperial Russia, serving in a number of top posts under the last two czars. Born into a noble family with German connections through his father, he began his career in the railway industry. His success there brought him to the attention of the state, and in 1883 he became Director of State Railways. Czar Alexander III appointed him Minister of Finance in 1892, a position he held for the next eleven years. He used the position to greatly expand the Russian railway network, including pushing the completion of the Trans-Siberian Railway, to negotiate favorable trade agreements with Germany, and to encourage the industrialization of Russia in order to keep up with the western European Great Powers, of which Russia was nominally one. He wrote his 1899 *Secret Memorandum on Industrialization* to Czar Nicholas II as part of this general program. After 1902 Witte lost influence with Nicholas. He died of a brain tumor in 1915, having unsuccessfully argued against Russia's participation in World War I.

REPORT OF THE MINISTER OF FINANCE TO HIS MAJESTY ON THE NECESSITY OF FORMULATING AND THEREAFTER STEADFASTLY ADHERING TO A DEFINITE PROGRAM OF A COMMERCIAL AND INDUSTRIAL POLICY OF THE EMPIRE. EXTREMELY SECRET

The measures taken by the government for the promotion of national trade and industry have at present a far deeper, and broader significance than they had at any time before. Indeed, the entire economic structure of the empire has been transformed in the course of the second half of the current century, so that now the market and its price structure represent the collective interest of all private enterprises which constitute our national economy. Buying and selling and wage labor penetrate now into much deeper layers of our national existence than was the case at the time of serf economy, when the landlord in his village constituted a self-sufficient economic little world, leading an independent life, almost without relation to the market. The division of labor; the specialization of skills; the increased exchange of goods among a population increasingly divided among towns, village, factories, and mines; the greater complexity of the demands of the population—all these processes rapidly developed in our fatherland under the influence of the emancipation of the serfs, the construction of a railroad network, the development of

credit., and the extraordinary growth of foreign trade. Now all organs and branches of our national economy are drawn into a common economic life, and all its individual exits have become far more sensitive and responsive to the economic activation of the government. Because of the extremely interlaced network of contemporary economic relationships, any change in the conditions of one or the other industry, of one or the other branch of trade, credit, or communications, touches and influences, often in hidden ways, the fate of a considerable majority of our enterprises.

As a result of such fundamental transformation of the economic interests of the country, every major measure of the government more or less affects the life of the entire economic organism. The solicitude shown to various branches of industry, a new railroad, the discovery of a new field for Russian enterprise, these and other measures, even if partial and of local application only, touch the entire ever more complicated network and upset the established equilibrium. . . .

In view of these facts, the minister of finance concludes that the country, which in one way or the other is nurtured by the commercial and industrial policy of the government, requires above all that this policy be carried out according to a definite plan, with strict system and continuity. Isolated and uncoordinated acts of encouragement can never offset the pernicious and painful shocks which the economic organism suffers from a change of the guiding policy. Even the most beneficial measures of the government in the realm of economic policy during the first years of their operation often seem to impose a hardship on the population. It is a difficult matter; years, even decades, must pass before the sacrifices can bear fruit. Wise statesmanship requires, then, that these difficult years be suffered patiently, as the experience of other peoples shows that the sacrifices demanded by the coherent and steadfast adherence to a firm and just economic system are always rewarded a hundred fold. Any change of basic policy before the fruits of sacrifice have had time to mature leads to the complete loss of all capital invested in the previous system, or it leads to new sacrifices in the pursuit of a new system. A government with an unsteady commercial and industrial policy is like a businessman who constantly reorganizes his production without producing anything. No matter how great the technical perfection of such a business, it always ends in ruin.

When I became minister of finance, I acted on the conviction that the government, no matter which commercial and industrial system it follows, is guided by the property interests of the entire people and that in order to compensate them for their losses one has merely to wait for the positive results of the government's economic system. This lasts years and sometimes decades. In taking over the ministry of finance in 1892, I felt obliged to make clear to myself the foundations of the commercial and industrial policy of my predecessors and to bend all efforts toward continuing and finishing what they had begun or had taken over from their predecessors.

. . .

The coming renewal of our trade treaties on favorable terms will be a difficult matter economically as well as politically. In dealing with countries which buy our agricultural exports, we should insist on their lowering their tariffs for our goods. But this time the conflict with the interests of native agriculture in these countries with whom we must

deal may be even more bitter than at the time of the memorable tariff war with Germany. It will be possible to obtain from them better conditions for our exports only if we, on our part, are in a position to offer them lowered tariffs for their industries. A trade agreement is nothing but a mutual exchange of such tariff reductions. If we voluntarily reduce our tariff before 1904 without receiving compensation from foreign governments, then we cannot induce them to reciprocate at the time of the conclusion of a new treaty. They not only will not agree to making concessions to our exports but under pressure from their native agrarians might even raise their barriers. That is the reason why our protective tariff should stand unchanged until 1904.

If we carry our commercial and industrial system, begun in the reign of Alexander III, consistently to the end, then Russia will at last come of age economically. Then her prosperity, her trade and finance, will be based on two reliable pillars, agriculture and industry; and the relations between them, profitable to both, will be the chief motive power in our economy. Russia will move closer to that goal with the help of foreign capital, which, anyway is required to make the protective tariff of 1891 effective.

Your Imperial Highness may see from the foregoing that the economic policy which the Russian government has followed for the last eight years is a carefully planned system, in which all parts are inseparably interconnected. Other persons, perhaps, can devise a better system to establish the needed equilibrium more successfully in a different way. Upon assuming the direction of the ministry of finance, I found a protective system almost in full operation. This system seemed to me then, and still seems to me now, completely justified. I bent all my efforts to speed its beneficial results and to alleviate, principally with the help of foreign capital, the hardships of the transition period. It is possible that we could have pursued a different policy. But in following the directives of Your Imperial Highness in such an intimately interdependent matter as our national economy, I believed it my duty as minister of finance to ask Your Majesty, to consider this point: even if it were possible to follow a different economic policy, it would, no matter how beneficial its ultimate results, produce in the immediate future a sharp break. Such an unnecessary shock would aggravate, the hardships now existing. Only by a system strictly sustained, and not by isolated measures, can a healthy development be guaranteed to our national economy.

Pledging all my efforts to fulfill still better the will of my sovereign, I make bold to ask that it may please Your Imperial Highness to lend your firm support to the foundations of our economic system as I have analyzed them. They form, in essence, the following programs:

1. To keep the tariff of 1891 unchanged until the renewal of our trade treaties.
2. To work in the meantime by all means for reducing the prices of industrial goods, not by increasing the import goods from abroad but by the development of our domestic production, which makes mandatory the influx of foreign capital.
3. To postpone a lowering of our tariff until the time of the renewal of our trade treaties, so that, in turn, we can insist upon favorable terms for our agricultural exports.
4. Not to impose in the meantime new restraints on the influx of foreign capital, either through new laws or new interpretations of existing laws or, *especially, through administrative decrees.*
5. To maintain unchanged our present policy toward foreign capital until 1904, so that with its help our domestic industries can develop in the meantime to a position of such strength that in the renewal of trade treaties we may be able to make genuine reductions on several of our tariff rates.
6. To review in 1904, at the time of the renewal of the trade treaties, the problem of foreign capital and to decide then whether new safeguards should be added to existing legislation.

In submitting this program to favorable consideration by Your Imperial Highness, I respectfully ask that it may please you, my sovereign, to make certain that it may not be endangered henceforth by waverings and changes, because our industries, and our national economy in general, require a firm and consistent system carried to its conclusion.

If this program does not find the support of Your Imperial Highness, then, pray, tell me which economic policy I am to pursue.

STATE SECRETARY S. IU. WITTE III/22/1899

From: Riha, Thomas, *Readings in Russian civilization* (Chicago: University of Chicago Press, 1964), pp. 428–41, passim.

QUESTIONS:

1. What benefits of a modernized economic policy does Witte tout? What main obstacles to the modernization of Russia's trade and industry does he fear?
2. Why does Witte make this proposal top secret? Whose interests might be threatened by the reforms he proposes to the Czar?

22.5: *Edicts and Proclamations* (King Chulalongkorn, 1873)

Phra Bat Somdet Phra Poraminthra Maha Chulalongkorn Phra Chunla Chom Klao Chao Yu Hua (1853–1910, and how's that for a full name?!), known as Chulalongkorn or by his reign name Rama V, was one of the great kings in Siamese history. The son of Mongut, or Rama IV, who had himself begun dealing with the encroachments of Western imperial powers, the Western-educated Chulalongkorn successfully led Siam, or modern Thailand, through the period of imperialism with its independence intact, though at the cost of some territorial losses.

The key to his modernization policies was to modernize the Thai state without any military emphasis, so as to avoid worrying English and French interests in the region, while building up a new Thai national identity. The selections below include a short piece of advice his father Mongut gave him near the end of his life, a brief statement by Chulalongkorn on his principle of modernization, and a speech on education, one of the centerpieces of his program. Finally, we present a table that shows the number of Thai students in the state-sponsored schools where the program was implemented that shows the impact of the king's program.

[King Mongkut's deathbed advice to his government, 1851]

I personally think that for whoever is chief of the king's ministers, there will be no more wars with Vietnam and Burma. We will have them only with the West. Take care, and do not lose any opportunity to them. Anything which they propose should be held up to close scrutiny before acceptance; and do not blindly believe in them.

. . .

[January 1898] I have convinced myself in Europe of the great benefit which Asiatic nations may derive from the acquisition of European science, [but] I am convinced also that there exists no incompatibility between such acquisition and the maintenance of our individuality as an independent Asiatic nation.

. . .

[September 1898] We meet today to confer on how education might best be organized so as to be more securely established and widespread in the future. We all know that Thailand's education cannot compete with that of other countries, for we began our work much later than all of them except Japan; and although Japan may be considered as having begun her modernization at about the same time as we did, our progress has been very dissimilar, inasmuch as Japan was a special case, as its educational system had come from China, and was already very well developed, and the Japanese have worked very hard to improve it. Our late development is due to the fact that we have not been able to find skilled people, and to the fact that those skilled people that we possess have not had the drive to do this work. In short, we have not found the skilled people for the job. It is important to realize that an educational system cannot be established quickly, and takes ten or twenty years. If we

do not hurry now to lay down the basis of one, we will still not have it in another "generation," and a great deal of time will have been wasted. The government will in the future require educated men for the public service. The education system established by Prince Damrong was very good, but it could not be taken as a basis for a general system for the entire kingdom. After the ministry of Prince Damrong, the officials [in the Ministry of Public Instruction] continued to follow Prince Damrong's plan, but they misunderstood it and even deviated from it, or to their own self-deception they sought only to establish large numbers of schools, and by entering into their reports statistics as to the numbers of items of correspondence handled sought to convey the impression that these were an index of the respect with which their office was regarded. The present schools are only quantities, and as such are not meaningful. The work that the Education Department has accomplished to the present moment is only as good as that which preceded it, and represents no advances. The flowerpot plant has grown larger and filled the pot, but it is no more beautiful or healthy. In the future, we would like to make this work more like a tree planted firmly in the earth, growing up healthy and beautiful, extending further outward. It is no wonder that people say our present education is no good. There is only the Mahamakut Academy, which Prince Wachirayan has organized and supported with all his vigor it is good because of him. If Chaophraya Phat has supported it, he can be credited with that, but it cannot be said that he has organized it. It is a good example of how education has been organized in conjunction with Buddhism. No education can be established which is not connected with the monastery, because to the teaching of reading and writing must be added instruction in religion. This is a goal of the first order, and if we meet without referring to it we ignore the fact that most of the Thai people do not know the Five Precepts. I have investigated in the provinces, and we have seen the great decay of a Thai people without religion, which has caused them to lose their "morals." I would like to have the educational system connected with religion. Thus I ask you to organize education in such a manner that it will be as strong and wide spreading as a banyan tree, with a firm grounding, healthy, beautiful, and splendid, and not like a potted plant.

SUMMARY EDUCATIONAL STATISTICS, 1885–1912

Year	Bangkok		Provinces		Total	
	Schools	Students	Schools	Students	Schools	Students
1885/86	19	1,504	10	510	29	2,014
1886/87	21	1,500	13	488	34	1,988
1887/88	21	1,476	16	602	37	2,078
1888/89	22	1,474	17	568	39	2,042
1889/90	25	1,595	20	730	45	2,325
1890/91	24	1,800	27	915	51	2,715
1891/92	24	1,584	24	841	48	2,425
1892/93					98	2,515
1893/94		Not Available			94	2,640
1894/95					75	2,565
1895/96					61	2,336
1896/97	34	1,634	26	986	60	2,620
1897/98	49	2,364	43	1,825	92	4,189
1898/99	56	3,430	43	1,990	99	5,420
1899/00	(55)	(4,000)	202	6,147	257	10,147
1900/01	55	4,956	348	12,258	403	17,214
1901/02	79	7,560	350	14,106	429	21,666
1902/03	(76)	(7,200)	300	14,917	376	22,117
1903/04	(75)	(7,900)	306	16,817	381	24,717
1904/05	(74)	(8,700)	336	19,082	410	27,782
1905/06	81	8,175	330	19,881	411	28,056
1906/07	90	8,660	328	19,997	418	28,657
1907/08	91	9,894	340	20,244	431	30,138
1908/09	137	13,359	307	16,603	444	29,962
1909/10	131	14,174	1,347	29,899	1,478	44,073
1910/11	179	13,933	2,936	70,033	3,115	83,966
1911/12	437	18,006	3,235	115,438	3,672	133,444

From: Wyatt, David K., *The politics of reform in Thailand: education in the reign of King Chulalongkorn* (New Haven: Yale University Press, 1969), pp. 30, 224–25, 232, 387.

QUESTIONS:

1. How does King Chulalongkorn's statement about the benefits of European science reflect his father's advice? How does his education proposal put his statement into action?
2. What do the statistics in the table at the end of the selection indicate about the success of King Chulalongkorn's education program? What do the gender restrictions built into the program imply about the limits of Thai modernization?

22.6: *The Restriction of Immigration* (Henry Cabot Lodge, 1891)

Henry Cabot Lodge (1850–1924) was a historian and Republican Senator from Massachusetts. He is best known for his positions in foreign policy: in favor of American intervention in Cuba and the Philippines, for building up a strong navy, for early entry into World War I, and (in opposition to his fellow academic Woodrow Wilson) against United States entry into the League of Nations. His views on domestic policy connected to his foreign policy focus on the topic of immigration. Lodge was a "100% Americanist", meaning that he became increasingly worried about the ability of the American economy and culture to absorb and assimilate immigrants from areas such as southern and eastern Europe and Asia. To warn against too simple a reading of Lodge's motives, it should be noted that he led an (ultimately unsuccessful) Senate effort to pass stronger protections for the voting rights of African Americans. Still, as the excerpt from one of his articles on immigration shows, he was a product of his cultural times.

[I]mmigration to this country is increasing, and . . . it is making its greatest relative increase from races most alien to the body of the American people and from the lowest and most illiterate classes among those races. In other words, it is apparent that, while our immigration is increasing, it is showing at the same time a marked tendency to deteriorate in character.

It has been the policy of the United States until very recent years to encourage immigration in all possible ways, which was, under the circumstances, a wise and obvious course to pursue. The natural growth of the people established in the thirteen colonies was not sufficient to occupy or develop the vast territory and valuable resources of the Union. We therefore opened our arms to the people of every land and invited them to come in, and when all the region beyond the Alleghanies, or even beyond the Mississippi, was still a wilderness, the general wisdom of this policy could not be gainsaid. To the practical advantages to be gained from the rapid filling-up of the country we also joined the sentimental and generous reason that this free country was to be a haven of refuge for the unfortunate of every land.

This liberality toward immigration, combined with the normal growth of the population, in the course of the present century rapidly filled the country, and the conditions under which, at the outset we had opened our doors and asked every one to come in changed radically. The first sign of an awakening to this altered state of things was in the movement against the Chinese. When that great reservoir of cheap labor was opened and when its streams began to pour into the United States, the American people, first on the western coast and then elsewhere, suddenly were roused to the fact that they were threatened with a flood of low-class labor which would absolutely destroy good rates of wages among American workingmen by a competition which could not be met, and which at the same time threatened to lower the quality of American citizenship. The result was the Chinese-Exclusion Act, much contested in its inception, but the wisdom of which everybody now admits. The next awakening came upon the discovery that employers of labor were engaged in making contracts with large bodies of working people in other countries, and importing them into the United States to work for a remuneration far below that which American workmen were accustomed to receive. This resulted in the passage of the Alien Contract-Labor law, intended to stop the importation of this low-priced labor. No one doubts to-day that the general principle of that law is sound, although its details are defective and its enforcement so imperfect that it has little practical effect.

. . .

In a word, the continued introduction into the labor market of four hundred thousand persons annually, half of whom have no occupation and most of whom represent the rudest form of labor, has a very great effect in reducing the rates of wages and disturbing the labor market. This, of course, is too obvious to need comment, and this tendency to constantly lower wages by the competition of an increasing and deteriorating immigration is a danger to the people of the United States the gravity of which can hardly be overestimated. Moreover, the shifting of the sources of the immigration is unfavourable, and is bringing to the country people whom it is very difficult to assimilate and who do not promise well for the standard of civilization in the United States—a matter as serious as the effect on the labor market.

The question, therefore, arises,—and there is no more important question before the American people,—what shall be done to protect our labor against this undue competition, and to guard our citizenship against an infusion which seems to threaten deterioration? We have the power, of course, to prohibit all immigration, or to limit the number of persons to be admitted to the country

annually, or—which would have the same effect—to impose upon immigrants a heavy capitation tax. Such rough and stringent measures are certainly neither necessary nor desirable if we can overcome the difficulties and dangers of the situation by more moderate legislation. These methods, moreover, are indiscriminate; and what is to be desired, if possible, is restriction which shall at the same time discriminate. We demand now that immigrants shall not be paupers or diseased or criminals, but these and all other existing requirements are vague, and the methods provided for their enforcement are still more indefinite and are perfectly ineffective. Any law, to be of use, must require, in the first place, that immigrants shall bring from their native country, from the United States consul or other diplomatic representative, an effective certificate that they are not obnoxious to any of the existing laws of the United States. We ought, in addition, to make our test still more definite by requiring a medical certificate in order to exclude unsound and diseased persons.

. . .

It is a truism to say that one of the greatest dangers to our free government is ignorance. Every one knows this to be the case, and that the danger can be overcome only by constant effort and vigilance. We spend millions annually in educating our children that they may be fit to be citizens and rulers of the Republic. We are ready to educate also the children who come to us from other countries; but it is not right to ask us to take annually a large body of persons who are totally illiterate and who are for the most part beyond the age at which education can be imparted. We have the right to exclude illiterate persons from our immigration, and this test, combined with the others of a more general character, would in all probability shut out a large part of the undesirable portion of the present immigration. It would reduce in a discriminating manner the total number of immigrants, and would thereby greatly benefit the labor market and help to maintain the rate of American wages. At the same time it would sift the immigrants who come to this country, and would shut out in a very large measure those elements which tend to lower the quality of American citizenship, and which now in many cases gather in dangerous masses in the slums of our great cities.

The measure proposed would benefit every honest immigrant who really desired to come to the United States and become an American citizen, and would stop none. It would exclude many, if not all, of those persons whose presence no one desires, and whose exclusion is demanded by our duty to our own citizens and to American institutions. Above all, it would be a protection and a help to our workingmen, who are more directly interested in this great question than any one else can possibly be.

From: Henry Cabot Lodge, "The Restriction of Immigration", *The North American Review* vol. 152, no. 410 (January 1891), pp. 32–36, passim.

QUESTIONS:

1. What economic arguments does Lodge make in favor of immigration restriction?
2. What do you think his real reasons are for restricting immigration? What frame values lie behind his views?

CHAPTER 23

"The West" in Crisis: 1914 to 1937

INTRODUCTION

The growing competition between the small number of industrialized, imperialist powers that characterized the imperialist age came to a head in 1914 in the catastrophe of World War I. The war initiated a series of crises that would dominate the twentieth century and that were characterized by increasing levels of combative ideology. The sources in this chapter present two views of the Great War, a narrative of the Mexican Revolution, and selections from one of the horrifying proclamations of ideology to emerge from the Great War, Adolph Hitler's *Mein Kampf*.

23.1: World War I Narratives

The first two sources in this chapter are both excerpted from book-length first-person narratives by the German veterans of World War I described at the beginning of Chapter 23 in *Frameworks*. The first is from *Storm of Steel* by Ernst Jünger (1895–1998), a controversial author who expressed extreme right-wing views and glorified war in his writings. Although he shared many of the antisemitic and antidemocratic views expressed by Hitler and served in the German army in World War II, he refused invitations to join the Nazis and was even distantly involved in the Stauffenberg plot to assassinate Hitler. At a joint French-German ceremony at Verdun in 1984, Jünger declared that the German "ideology of war" was a "calamitous mistake". The second excerpt is from *All Quiet on the Western Front* (1929) by Erich Maria Remarque (1898–1970). Whereas Hitler's party courted Jünger, they persecuted Remarque. His works were burned by Nazis, and while they were in power he fled to Switzerland and eventually to the United States. He had romantic involvements with two other German exiles, Hedy Lamarr and Marlene Dietrich, and in 1958 he finally married another actress, Paulette Goddard, with whom he divided his time between Switzerland and the United States until his death.

23.1a: *Storm of Steel* (Ernst Jünger, 1920)

We resolved to be on the alert for anything the coming night, and agreed that anyone who didn't give his name in response to a 'Hallo!' would be immediately fired at. Every officer had his pistol loaded with a red flare, to alert the artillery.

The night was still wilder than the last. In particular, one concentration of fire at quarter past two outdid anything there had been up to that point. A hail of heavy shells struck all round my dugout. We stood fully armed on the shelter steps, while the light of our little candle stumps reflected glitteringly off the wet, from the wet, mildewed walls. Blue smoke streamed in through the entrances and earth crumbled off the ceiling. 'Boom!' 'Good God!' 'A light! A light!' 'Get everything ready!' Everyone's hearts were in their mouths. Hands darted to release the pins on bombs. 'That was the last of them!' 'Let's go!' As we charged out of the entrance, a mine with a delay fuse went off, and hurled us back inside. All the same, as the last of the iron birds came whooshing down, all the sentry positions were manned by us. Bright as day, a firework display of flares lit the cloud-swathed field. These instants, in which the entire complement of men stood behind the traverses, tensed and ready, had something magical about them; they were like the last breathless second before a hugely important performance, as the music is turned off and the big lights go up.

. . .

We were coming downhill. Indistinct figures moved against a background of red-brown clay. A machine-gun spat out its gouts of bullets. The feeling of hopelessness increased. Even so, we broke into a run, while the gunners were finding their range.

We jumped over several snipers' nests and hurriedly excavated trenches. In mid-jump over a slightly better-made trench, I felt a piercing jolt in the chest—as though I had been hit like a game-bird. With a sharp cry that seemed to cost me all the air I had, I spun on my axis and crashed to the ground.

It had got me at last. At the same time as feeling I had been hit, I felt the bullet taking away my life. I had felt Death's hand once before, on the road at Mory—but this time his grip was firmer and more determined. As I came down heavily on the bottom of the trench, I was convinced it was all over. Strangely, that moment is one of very few in my life of which I am able to say they were utterly happy. I understood, as in a flash of lightning, the true inner purpose and form of my life. I felt surprise and disbelief that it was to end there and then, but this surprise had something untroubled and almost merry to it. Then I heard the firing grow less, as if I were a stone sinking under the surface of some turbulent water. Where I was going, there was neither war nor enmity.

From: Jünger, Ernst, and Michael Hofmann, *Storm of steel* (London: Penguin Books, 2004), pp. 276–77, 281–82.

23.1b: *All Quiet on the Western Front* (Erich Maria Remarque, 1929)

There are rumours of an offensive. We go up to the front two days earlier than usual. On the way we pass a shelled school-house. Stacked up against its longer side is a high double wall of yellow, unpolished, brand-new coffins. They still smell of resin, and pine, and the forest. There are at least a hundred.

"That's a good preparation for the offensive," says Müller astonished.

"They're for us," growls Detering.

"Don't talk rot," says Kat to him angrily.

"You be thankful if you get so much as a coffin," grins Tjaden, "they'll slip you a waterproof sheet for your old Aunt Sally of a carcase."

. . .

During the day we loaf about and make war on the rats. Ammunition and hand-grenades become more plentiful. We overhaul the bayonets—that is to say, the ones that have a saw on the blunt edge. If the fellows over there catch a man with one of those he's killed at sight. In the next sector some of our men were found whose noses were cut off and their eyes poked out with their own sawbayonets. Their mouths and noses were stuffed with sawdust so that they suffocated.

Some of the recruits have bayonets of this sort; we take them away and give them the ordinary kind.

But the bayonet has practically lost its importance. It is usually the fashion now to charge with bombs and spades only. The sharpened spade is a more handy and many-sided weapon; not only can it be used for jabbing a man under the chin, but it is much better for striking with because of its greater weight; and if one hits between the neck and shoulder it easily cleaves as far down as the chest. The bayonet frequently jams on the thrust and then a man has to kick hard on the other fellow's belly to pull it out again; and in the interval he may easily get one himself. And what's more the blade often gets broken off.

At night they send over gas. We expect the attack to follow and lie with our masks on, ready to tear them off as soon as the first shadow appears.

Dawn approaches without anything happening— only the everlasting, nerve-wracking roll behind the enemy lines, trains, trains, lorries, lorries; but what are they concentrating? Our artillery fires on it continually, but still it does not cease.

. . .

The night is unbearable. We cannot sleep, but stare ahead of us and doze. Tjaden regrets that we wasted the gnawed pieces of bread on the rats. We would gladly have them again to eat now. We are short of water, too, but not seriously yet.

Towards morning, while it is still dark, there is some excitement. Through the entrance rushes in a swarm of fleeing rats that try to storm the walls. Torches light up the confusion. Everyone yells and curses and slaughters. The madness and despair of many hours unloads itself in this outburst. Faces are distorted, arms strike out, and the beasts scream; we just stop in time to avoid attacking one another.

The onslaught has exhausted us. We lie down to wait again. It is a marvel that our post has had no casualties so far. It is one of the less deep dugouts.

A corporal creeps in; he has a loaf of bread with him. Three people have had the luck to get through during the night and bring some provisions. They say the bombardment extends undiminished as far as the artillery lines. It is a mystery where the enemy gets all his shells.

We wait and wait. By midday what I expected happens. One of the recruits has a fit. I have been watching him for a long time, grinding his teeth and opening and shutting his fists. These hunted, protruding eyes, we know them too well. During the last few hours he has had merely the appearance of calm. He had collapsed like a rotten tree.

Now he stands up, stealthily creeps across the floor, hesitates a moment and then glides towards the door. I intercept him and say: "Where are you going?"

"I'll be back in a minute," says he, and tries to push past me.

"Wait a bit, the shelling will stop soon."

He listens for a moment and his eyes become clear. Then again he has the glowering eyes of a mad dog, he is silent, he shoves me aside.

"One minute, lad," I say. Kat notices. Just as the recruit shakes me off Kat jumps in and we hold him.

Then he begins to rave: "Leave me alone, let me go out, I will go out!"

He won't listen to anything and hits out, his mouth is wet and pours out words, half choked, meaningless words. It is a case of claustrophobia, he feels as though he is suffocating here and wants to get out at any price. If we let him go he would run about everywhere regardless of cover. He is not the first.

Though he raves and his eyes roll, it can't be helped, we have to give him a hiding to bring him to his senses. We do it quickly and mercilessly, and at last he sits down quietly. The others have turned pale; let's hope it deters them. This bombardment is too much for the poor devils, they have been sent straight from a recruiting-depot into a barrage that is enough to turn an old soldier's hair grey.

After this affair the sticky, close atmosphere works more than ever on our nerves. We sit as if in our graves waiting only to be closed in.

Suddenly it howls and flashes terrifically, the dug-out cracks in all its joints under a direct hit, fortunately only a light one that the concrete blocks are able to withstand. It rings metallically, the walls reel, rifles, helmets, earth, mud, and dust fly everywhere. Sulphur fumes pour in.

If we were in one of those light dug-outs that they have been building lately instead of this deeper one, none of us would be alive.

But the effect is bad enough even so. The recruit starts to rave again and two others follow suit. One jumps up and rushes out, we have trouble with the other two. I start after one who escapes and wonder whether to shoot him in the leg—then it shrieks again, I fling myself down and when I stand up the wall of the trench is plastered with smoking splinters, lumps of flesh, and bits of uniform. I scramble back.

The first recruit seems actually to have gone insane. He butts his head against the wall like a goat. We must try to-night to take him to the rear. Meanwhile we bind him, but in such a way that in case of attack he can be released at once.

Kat suggests a game of skat: it is easier when a man has something to do. But it is no use, we listen for every explosion that comes close, miscount the tricks, and fail to follow suit. We have to give it up. We sit as though in a boiler that is being belaboured from without on all sides.

Night again. We are deadened by the strain—a deadly tension that scrapes along one's spine like a gapped knife. Our legs refuse to move, our hands tremble, our bodies are a thin skin stretched painfully over repressed madness, over an almost irresistible, bursting roar. We have neither flesh nor muscles any longer, we dare not look at one another for fear of some miscalculable thing. So we shut our teeth—it will end—it will end—perhaps we will come through.

Suddenly the nearer explosions cease. The shelling continues but it has lifted and falls behind us, our trench is free. We seize the hand-grenades, pitch them out in front of the dug-out and jump after them. The bombardment has stopped and a heavy barrage now falls behind us. The attack has come.

No one would believe that in this howling waste there could still be men; but steel helmets now appear on all sides out of the trench, and fifty yards from us a machine-gun is already in position and barking.

The wire entanglements are torn to pieces. Yet they offer some obstacle. We see the storm-troops coming. Our artillery opens fire. Machine-guns rattle, rifles crack. The charge works its way across. Haie and Kropp begin with the hand-grenades. They throw as fast as they can, others pass them, the handles with the strings already pulled. Haie throws seventy-five yards, Kropp sixty, it has been measured, the distance is important. The enemy as they run cannot do much before they are within forty yards.

We recognize the smooth distorted faces, the helmets; they are French. They have already suffered heavily when they reach the remnants of the barbed wire entanglements. A whole line has gone down before our machine-guns; then we have a lot of stoppages and they come nearer.

I see one of them, his face upturned, fall into a wire cradle. His body collapses, his hands remain suspended as though he were praying. Then his body drops clean away and only his hands with the stumps of his arms, shot off, now hang in the wire.

· · ·

We have become wild beasts. We do not fight, we defend ourselves against annihilation. It is not against men that we fling our bombs, what do we know of men in this moment when Death is hunting us down—now, for the first time in three days we can see his face, now for the first time in three days we can oppose him; we feel a mad anger. No longer do we lie helpless, waiting on the scaffold, we can destroy and kill, to save ourselves, to save ourselves and to be revenged.

From: Remarque, Erich Maria, *All quiet on the Western front* (New York: Ballantine Books, 1982), pp. 99, 103–4, 108–13.

QUESTIONS:

1. How do Jünger's and Remarque's narrations of their experiences as soldiers in World War I resemble each other? How do they corroborate each other? What implications does this corroboration have for the use of personal narratives as historical evidence?
2. How on the other hand do the accounts by the two authors differ? What different screen images of war are they projecting? What are the ideological implications of these images?

23.2: *The Underdogs* (Mariano Azuela, 1915)

Mariano Azuela (1873–1952) was a Mexican author and doctor who is known for his stories of the Mexican Revolution of 1910. During the revolution Azuela served as an army doctor with Pancho Villa and wrote *The Underdogs* (the Spanish title is *Los de abajo*). After the war, Azuela had to flee to the United States, where the novel was published as a series in the newspaper *El Paso del Norte*. He returned to Mexico later, where he continued to write. He won the Mexican National Prize for Literature in 1942. The excerpt from *The Underdogs* here reflects his view that the complexity of the revolution—the varied social situations and motives of its participants and their lack of ideological clarity—rendered it ineffective as a moment of true social change.

XVIII

On the day General Natera began his advance against the town of Zacatecas, Demetrio with a hundred men went to meet him at Fresnillo.

The leader received him cordially.

"I know who you are and the sort of men you bring. I heard about the beatings you gave the Federals from Tepic to Durango."

Natera shook hands with Demetrio effusively while Luis Cervantes said:

"With men like General Natera and Colonel Demetrio Macias, we'll cover our country with glory."

Demetrio understood the purpose of those words, after Natera had repeatedly addressed him as "Colonel."

Wine and beer were served; Demetrio and Natera drank many a toast. Luis Cervantes proposed: "The triumph of our cause, which is the sublime triumph of Justice, because our ideal—to free the noble, long-suffering people of Mexico—is about to be realized and because those men who have watered the earth with their blood and tears will reap the harvest which is rightfully theirs."

Natera fixed his cruel gaze on the orator, then turned his back on him to talk to Demetrio. Presently, one of Natera's officers, a young man with a frank open face, drew up to the table and stared insistently at Cervantes.

"Are you Luis Cervantes?"

"Yes. You're Solis, eh?"

"The moment you entered I thought I recognized you. Well, well, even now I can hardly believe my eyes!"

"It's true though!"

"Well, but . . . look here, let's have a drink, come along." Then:

"Hm," Solís went on, offering Cervantes a chair, "since when have you turned rebel?"

"I've been a rebel the last two months!"

"Oh, I see! That's why you speak with such faith and enthusiasm about things we all felt when we joined the revolution."

"Have you lost your faith or enthusiasm?"

"Look here, man, don't be surprised if I confide in you right off. I am so anxious to find someone intelligent among this crowd, that as soon as I get hold of a man like you I clutch at him as eagerly as

I would at a glass of water, after walking mile after mile through a parched desert. But frankly, I think you should do the explaining first. I can't understand how a man who was correspondent of a Government newspaper during the Madero regime, and later editorial writer on a Conservative journal, who denounced us as bandits in the most fiery articles, is now fighting on our side."

"I tell you honestly: I have been converted," Cervantes answered.

"Are you absolutely convinced?"

Solís sighed, filled the glasses; they drank.

"What about you? Are you tired of the revolution?" asked Cervantes sharply.

"Tired? My dear fellow, I'm twenty-five years old and I'm fit as a fiddle! But am I disappointed? Perhaps!"

"You must have sound reasons for feeling that way."

"I hoped to find a meadow at the end of the road, I found a swamp. Facts are bitter; so are men. That bitterness eats your heart out; it is poison, dry rot. Enthusiasm, hope, ideals, happiness—vain dreams, vain dreams. . . . When that's over, you have a choice. Either you turn bandit, like the rest, or the timeservers will swamp you. . . ."

Cervantes writhed at his friend's words; his argument was quite out of place . . . painful. . . . To avoid being forced to take issue, he invited Solís to cite the circumstances that had destroyed his illusions.

"Circumstances? No—it's far less important than that. It's a host of silly, insignificant things that no one notices except yourself . . . a change of expression, eyes shining—lips curled in a sneer— the deep import of a phrase that is lost! Yet take these things together and they compose the mask of our race . . . terrible . . . grotesque . . . a race that awaits redemption!"

He drained another glass. After a long pause, he continued:

"You ask me why I am still a rebel? Well, the revolution is like a hurricane: if you're not a man . . . you're a leaf, a dead leaf, blown by the wind."

Demetrio reappeared. Seeing him, Solís relapsed into silence.

"Come along," Demetrio said to Cervantes. "Come with me."

Unctuously, Solís congratulated Demetrio on the feats that had won him fame and the notice of Pancho Villa's northern division.

Demetrio warmed to his praise. Gratefully, he heard his prowess vaunted, though at times he found it difficult to believe he was the hero of the exploits the other narrated. But Solís' story proved so charming, so convincing, that before long he found himself repeating it as gospel truth.

"Natera is a genius!" Luis Cervantes said when they had returned to the hotel. "But Captain Solís is a nobody . . . a timeserver."

Demetrio Macías was too elated to listen to him.

"I'm a colonel, my lad! And you're my secretary!"

Demetrio's men made many acquaintances that evening; much liquor flowed to celebrate new friendships. Of course, men are not necessarily even tempered, nor is alcohol a good counselor; quarrels naturally ensued. Yet many differences that occurred were smoothed out in a friendly spirit, outside the saloons, restaurants, or brothels.

On the morrow, casualties were reported. Always a few dead. An old prostitute was found with a bullet through her stomach; two of Colonel Macías' new men lay in the gutter, slit from ear to ear.

Anastasio Montáñez carried an account of the events to his chief. Demetrio shrugged his shoulders.

"Bury them!" he said.

XX .

"Villa is coming!"

The news spread like lightning. Villa—the magic word! The Great Man, the salient profile, the unconquerable warrior who, even at a distance, exerts the fascination of a reptile, a boa constrictor.

"Our Mexican Napoleon!" exclaimed Luis Cervantes.

"Yes! The Aztec Eagle! He buried his beak of steel in the head of Huerta the serpent!" Solís, Natera's chief of staff, remarked somewhat ironically, adding: "At least, that's how I expressed it in a speech I made at Ciudad Juárez!"

The two sat at the bar of the saloon, drinking beer. The "high hats," wearing mufflers around their necks and thick rough leather shoes on their feet, ate and drank endlessly. Their gnarled hands loomed across table, across bar. All their talk was of Villa and his men. The tales Natera's followers related won gasps of astonishment from Demetrio's men. Villa! Villa's battles! Ciudad Juárez . . . Tierra Blanca . . . Chihuahua . . . Torreón. . . .

The bare facts, the mere citing of observation and experience meant nothing. But the real story, with its extraordinary contrasts of high exploits and abysmal cruelties was quite different. Villa, indomitable lord of the sierra, the eternal victim of all governments . . . Villa tracked, hunted down like a wild beast . . . Villa the reincarnation of the old legend; Villa as Providence, the bandit, that passes through the world armed with the blazing torch of an ideal: to rob the rich and give to the poor. It was the poor who built up and imposed a legend about him which Time itself was to increase and embellish as a shining example from generation to generation.

"Look here, friend," one of Natera's men told Anastasio, "if General Villa takes a fancy to you, he'll give you a ranch on the spot. But if he doesn't, he'll shoot you down like a dog! God! You ought to see Villa's troops! They're all northerners and dressed like lords! You ought to see their wide-brimmed Texas hats and their brand-new outfits and their four-dollar shoes, imported from the U.S.A."

As they retailed the wonders of Villa and his men, Natera's men gazed at one another ruefully, aware that their own hats were rotten from sunlight and moisture, that their own shirts and trousers were tattered and barely fit to cover their grimy, lousy bodies.

"There's no such a thing as hunger up there. They carry boxcars full of oxen, sheep, cows! They've got cars full of clothing, trains full of guns, ammunition, food enough to make a man burst!"

Then they spoke of Villa's airplanes.

"Christ, those planes! You know when they're close to you, be damned if you know what the hell they are! They look like small boats, you know, or tiny rafts . . . and then pretty soon they begin to rise, making a hell of a row. Something like an automobile going sixty miles an hour. Then they're like great big birds that don't even seem to move sometimes. But there's a joker! The Goddamn things have got some American fellow inside with hand grenades by the thousand. Now you try and figure what that means! The fight is on, see? You know how a farmer feeds corn to his chickens, huh? Well, the American throws his lead bombs at the enemy just like that. Pretty soon the whole damn field is nothing but a graveyard . . . dead men all over the dump . . . dead men here. . . . dead men there . . . dead men everywhere!"

Anastasio Montáñez questioned the speaker more particularly. It was not long before he realized that all this high praise was hearsay and that not a single man in Natera's army had ever laid eyes on Villa.

"Well, when you get down to it, I guess it doesn't mean so much! No man's got much more guts than any other man, if you ask me. All you need to be a good fighter is pride, that's all. I'm not a professional soldier even though I'm dressed like hell, but let me tell you. I'm not forced to do this kind of bloody job, because I own . . ."

"Because I own over twenty oxen, whether you believe it or not!" Quail said, mocking Anastasio.

From: Azuela, Mariano, *The underdogs: a novel of the Mexican Revolution* (New York: Signet, 1996), pp. 69–72, 76–78.

1. What do the characters in Azuela's novel think or say they are fighting for?
2. What image of the Mexican Revolution does Azuela project in this novel, and what does this say about the role of ideology in the struggle?

23.3: *Mein Kampf* (Adolph Hitler, 1925–26)

Adolph Hitler (1889–1945) was an Austrian-born politician who as the leader of the Nazis, the National Socialist German Workers Party (NSDAP or Nationalsozialistische Deutsche Arbeiterpartei), became the fascist dictator in Germany from 1933 to 1945, when he committed suicide as it became clear that Germany was losing World War II. Hitler espoused a racist, profoundly antisemitic, and anticommunist nationalism that he and his followers made into a horrific, genocidal reality. Before Hitler's rise to power, there were about nine million Jews living in Europe, and in addition to the murder of six million of these people, the execution of Nazi policy resulted in the deaths of hundreds of thousands of Sinti and Roma ("gypsy") people, disabled people, Communists, and others who threatened the ostensible racial purity of the German nation according to Nazi ideology. In this excerpt from his exposition of that ideology, *Mein Kampf* ("my struggle"), Hitler describes his view of the dangers of democracy and of "race", both in terms very similar to—indeed, likely influenced by or even taken from—von Treitschke's writing, which is excerpted in Chapter 20.

This invention of democracy is most intimately related to a quality which in recent times has grown to be a real disgrace, to wit, the cowardice of a great part of our so-called 'leadership.' What luck to be able to hide behind the skirts of a so-called majority in all decisions of any real importance!

Take a look at one of these political bandits. How anxiously he begs the approval of the majority for every measure, to assure himself of the necessary accomplices, so he can unload the responsibility at any time. And this is one of the main reasons why this type of political activity is always repulsive and hateful to any man who is decent at heart and hence courageous, while it attracts all low characters—and anyone who is unwilling to take personal responsibility for his acts, but seeks a shield, is a cowardly scoundrel. When the leaders of a nation consist of such vile creatures, the results will soon be deplorable. Such a nation will be unable to muster the courage for any determined act; it will prefer to accept any dishonor, even the most shameful, rather than rise to a decision; for there is no one who is prepared of his own accord

to pledge his person and his head for the execution of a dauntless resolve.

For there is one thing which we must never forget: in this, too, the majority can never replace the man. It is not only a representative of stupidity, but of cowardice as well. And no more than a hundred empty heads make one wise man will an heroic decision arise from a hundred cowards.

The less the responsibility of the individual leader, the more numerous will be those who, despite their most insignificant stature, feel called upon to put their immortal forces in the service of the nation. Indeed, they will be unable to await their turn; they stand in a long line, and with pain and regret count the number of those waiting ahead of them, calculating almost the precise hour at which, in all probability, their turn will come. Consequently, they long for any change in the office hovering before their eyes, and are thankful for any scandal which thins out the ranks ahead of them. And if some man is unwilling to move from the post he holds, this in their eyes is practically a breach of a holy pact of solidarity. They grow vindictive, and they do not rest until the impudent fellow is at last overthrown, thus turning his warm place back to the public. And, rest assured, he won't recover the position so easily. For as soon as one of these creatures is forced to give up a position, he will try at once to wedge his way into the 'waiting-line' unless the hue and cry raised by the others prevents him.

. . .

Gravely as certain evils of the pre-War period corroded and threatened to undermine the inner strength of the nation, it must not be forgotten that other states suffered even more than Germany from most of these ailments and yet in the critical hour of danger did not flag and perish. But if we consider that the German weaknesses before the War were balanced by equally great strengths, the ultimate cause of the collapse can and must lie in a different field; and this is actually the case.

The deepest and ultimate reason for the decline of the old Reich lay in its failure to recognize the racial problem and its importance for the historical development of peoples. For events in the lives of peoples are not expressions of chance, but processes related to the self-preservation and propagation of the species and the race and subject to the laws of Nature, even if people are not conscious of the inner reason for their actions.

There are some truths which are so obvious that for this very reason they are not seen or at least not recognized by ordinary people. They sometimes pass by such truisms as though blind and are most astonished when someone suddenly discovers what everyone really ought to know. . . .

. . .

Even the most superficial observation shows that Nature's restricted form of propagation and increase is an almost rigid basic law of all the innumerable forms of expression of her vital urge. Every animal mates only with a member of the same species. . . .

. . .

Any crossing of two beings not at exactly the same level produces a medium between the level of the two parents. This means: the offspring will probably stand higher than the racially lower parent, but not as high as the higher one. Consequently, it will later succumb in the struggle against the higher level. Such mating is contrary to the will of Nature for a higher breeding of all life. The precondition for this does not lie in associating superior and inferior, but in the total victory of the former. The stronger must dominate and not blend with the weaker, thus sacrificing his own greatness. Only the born weakling can view this as cruel, but he after all is only a weak and limited man; for if this law did not prevail, any conceivable higher development of organic living beings would be unthinkable.

The consequence of this racial purity, universally valid in Nature, is not only the sharp outward delimitation of the various races, but their uniform character in themselves. . . .

Therefore, here, too, the struggle among themselves arises less from inner aversion than from hunger and love. In both cases, Nature looks on calmly, with satisfaction, in fact. In the struggle for daily bread all those who are weak and sickly or less determined succumb, while the struggle of the males for the female grants the right or opportunity to propagate only to the healthiest. And struggle is always a means for improving a species' health and power of resistance and, therefore, a cause of its higher development.

If the process were different, all further and higher development would cease and the opposite would occur. For, since the inferior always predominates numerically over the best, if both had the same possibility of preserving life and propagating, the inferior would multiply so much more rapidly that in the end the best would inevitably be driven into the background, unless a correction of this state of affairs were undertaken. Nature does just this by subjecting the weaker part to such severe living conditions that by them alone the number is limited, and by not permitting the remainder to increase promiscuously, but making a new and ruthless choice according to strength and health.

No more than Nature desires the mating of weaker with stronger individuals, even less does she desire the blending of a higher with a lower race, since, if she did, her whole work of higher breeding, over perhaps hundreds of thousands of years, night be ruined with one blow.

Historical experience offers countless proofs of this. It shows with terrifying clarity that in every mingling of Aryan blood with that of lower peoples the result was the end of the cultured people. North America, whose population consists in by far the largest part of Germanic elements who mixed but little with the lower colored peoples, shows a different humanity and culture from Central and South America, where the predominantly Latin immigrants often mixed with the aborigines on a large scale. By this one example, we can clearly and distinctly recognize the effect of racial mixture. The Germanic inhabitant of the American continent, who has remained racially pure and unmixed, rose to be master of the continent; he will remain the master as long as he does not fall a victim to defilement of the blood.

The result of all racial crossing is therefore in brief always the following:

(a) Lowering of the level of the higher race;

(b) Physical and intellectual regression and hence the beginning of a slowly but surely progressing sickness.

To bring about such a development is, then, nothing else but to sin against the will of the eternal creator.

And as a sin this act is rewarded.

When man attempts to rebel against the iron logic of Nature, he comes into struggle with the principles to which he himself owes his existence as a man. And this attack must lead to his own doom.

Here, of course, we encounter the objection of the modern pacifist, as truly Jewish in its effrontery as it is stupid! 'Man's role is to overcome Nature!'

Millions thoughtlessly parrot this Jewish nonsense and end up by really imagining that they themselves represent a kind of conqueror of Nature; though in this they dispose of no other weapon than an idea, and at that such a miserable one, that if it were true no world at all would be conceivable.

. . .

In actual fact the pacifistic-humane idea is perfectly all right perhaps when the highest type of man has previously conquered and subjected the world to an extent that makes him the sole ruler of this earth. Then this idea lacks the power of producing evil effects in exact proportion as its practical application becomes rare and finally impossible. Therefore, first struggle and then we shall see what can be done. Otherwise mankind has passed the high point of its development and the end is not the domination of any ethical idea but barbarism and consequently chaos. . . .

Everything we admire on this earth today—science and art, technology and inventions—is only the creative product of a few peoples and originally perhaps of one race. On them depends the existence of this whole culture. If they perish, the beauty of this earth will sink into the grave with them.

However much the soil, for example, can influence men, the result of the influence will always be different depending on the races in question. The low fertility of a living space may spur the one race to the highest achievements; in others it will only be the cause of bitterest poverty and final undernourishment with all its consequences. The inner nature of peoples is always determining for the manner in which outward influences will be effective. What leads the one to starvation trains the other to hard work.

All great cultures of the past perished only because the originally creative race died out from blood poisoning.

The ultimate cause of such a decline was their forgetting that all culture depends on men and not conversely; hence that to preserve a certain culture the man who creates it must be preserved. This preservation is bound up with the rigid law of necessity and the right to victory of the best and stronger in this world.

Those who want to live, let them fight, and those who do not want to fight in this world of eternal struggle do not deserve to live.

. . .

It is idle to argue which race or races were the original representative of human culture and hence the real founders of all that we sum up under the word 'humanity.' It is simpler to raise this question with regard to the present, and here an easy, clear answer results. All the human culture, all the results of art, science, and technology that we see before us today, are almost exclusively the creative product of the Aryan. . . .

From: Hitler, Adolf, and John Chamberlain, *Mein Kampf: complete and unabridged, fully annotated* (New York: Reynal & Hitchcock, 1939), pp. 104–5, 388–97 passim.

QUESTIONS:

1. How does Hitler characterize democracy as weak? How in particular does he portray it as cowardly, and what are the practical political implications of this view?
2. Why does Hitler frame his discussion of race and the Jews in pseudoscientific terminology? What tensions between tradition and modernization in the ideology of Fascism does this language reveal?

CHAPTER 24

The World in Crisis: 1929 to 1945

INTRODUCTION

The world's age of crisis deepened a decade after the end of World War I when the global network suffered a catastrophic breakdown in the Great Depression. The economic collapse created serious political uncertainty in liberal democracies, which highlighted the apparent success of the Soviet Union in building its own economy and joining the list of industrial powers with little to no outside assistance. It also contributed to the spread of fascism. The toxic mixture ignited into World War II, during which technological advance reached an explosive moral turning point with the invention of the atomic bomb. The sources presented here give us samples of these issues and events and the choices they posed to those living through them.

24.1: *First Inaugural Address* (Franklin Delano Roosevelt, 1932)

Franklin Delano Roosevelt (1882–1945) was elected thirty-second president of the United States in 1932, in the depths of the Great Depression, on the strength of his promise of a "New Deal" for American workers suffering with unemployment rates as high as 25%. He went on to be elected three more times, serving longer in the office than any other president and leading his country through the Great Depression and World War II. What he faced when he assumed the office in 1932 was a country not just in economic crisis but in a crisis of confidence and simmering social unrest. Roosevelt's policies, especially the measures of his famous "First 100 Days", began to deal with the economic crisis and laid the foundations of the United States' modern social safety net, but the depression in fact lingered until the outbreak of World War II. But after Roosevelt's First Inaugural Address, reproduced here in full, the crisis of confidence and the threat of radical political unrest was effectively over. Roosevelt, in the words of some historians, had saved America for capitalism.

Inaugural Speech of Franklin Delano Roosevelt
Given in Washington, D.C.
March 4th, 1933

President Hoover, Mr. Chief Justice, my friends: This is a day of national consecration, and I am certain that my fellow-Americans expect that on my induction into the Presidency I will address them with a candor and a decision which the present situation of our nation impels.

This is pre-eminently the time to speak the truth, the whole truth, frankly and boldly. Nor need we shrink from honestly facing conditions in our country today. This great nation will endure as it has endured, will revive and will prosper.

So first of all let me assert my firm belief that the only thing we have to fear . . . is fear itself . . . nameless, unreasoning, unjustified terror which paralyzes needed efforts to convert retreat into advance.

In every dark hour of our national life a leadership of frankness and vigor has met with that understanding and support of the people themselves which is essential to victory. I am convinced that you will again give that support to leadership in these critical days. In such a spirit on my part and on yours we face our common difficulties. They concern, thank God, only material things. Values have shrunken to fantastic levels: taxes have risen, our ability to pay has fallen, government of all kinds is faced by serious curtailment of income, the means of exchange are frozen in the currents of trade, the withered leaves of industrial enterprise lie on every side, farmers find no markets for their produce, the savings of many years in thousands of families are gone.

More important, a host of unemployed citizens face the grim problem of existence, and an equally great number toil with little return. Only a foolish optimist can deny the dark realities of the moment.

Yet our distress comes from no failure of substance. We are stricken by no plague of locusts. Compared with the perils which our forefathers conquered because they believed and were not afraid, we have still much to be thankful for. Nature still offers her bounty and human efforts have multiplied it. Plenty is at our doorstep, but a generous use of it languishes in the very sight of the supply.

Primarily, this is because the rulers of the exchange of mankind's goods have failed through their own stubbornness and their own incompetence, have admitted their failures and abdicated. Practices of the unscrupulous money changers stand indicted in the court of public opinion, rejected by the hearts and minds of men.

True, they have tried, but their efforts have been cast in the pattern of an outworn tradition.

Faced by failure of credit, they have proposed only the lending of more money.

Stripped of the lure of profit by which to induce our people to follow their false leadership, they have resorted to exhortations, pleading tearfully for restored conditions. They know only the rules of a generation of self-seekers.

They have no vision, and when there is no vision the people perish.

The money changers have fled their high seats in the temple of our civilization. We may now restore that temple to the ancient truths.

The measure of the restoration lies in the extent to which we apply social values more noble than mere monetary profit.

Happiness lies not in the mere possession of money, it lies in the joy of achievement, in the thrill of creative effort.

The joy and moral stimulation of work no longer must be forgotten in the mad chase of evanescent profits. These dark days will be worth all they cost us if they teach us that our true destiny is not to be ministered unto but to minister to ourselves and to our fellow-men.

Recognition of the falsity of material wealth as the standard of success goes hand in hand with the abandonment of the false belief that public office and high political position are to be valued only by the standards of pride of place and personal profit, and there must be an end to a conduct in banking and in business which too often has given to a sacred trust the likeness of callous and selfish wrongdoing.

Small wonder that confidence languishes, for it thrives only on honesty, on honor, on the sacredness of obligations, on faithful protection, on unselfish performance. Without them it cannot live.

Restoration calls, however, not for changes in ethics alone. This nation asks for action, and action now.

Our greatest primary task is to put people to work. This is no unsolvable problem if we face it wisely and courageously.

It can be accompanied in part by direct recruiting by the government itself, treating the task as we would treat the emergency of a war, but at the same time, through this employment, accomplishing greatly needed projects to stimulate and reorganize the use of our national resources.

Hand in hand with this, we must frankly recognize the over-balance of population in our industrial centers and, by engaging on a national scale in a redistribution, endeavor to provide a better use of the land for those best fitted for the land.

The task can be helped by definite efforts to raise the values of agricultural products and with this the power to purchase the output of our cities.

It can be helped by preventing realistically the tragedy of the growing loss, through foreclosure, of our small homes and our farms.

It can be helped by insistence that the Federal, State, and local governments act forthwith on the demand that their cost be drastically reduced.

It can be helped by the unifying of relief activities which today are often scattered, uneconomical and unequal. It can be helped by national planning for and supervision of all forms of transportation and of communications and other utilities which have a definitely public character.

There are many ways in which it can be helped, but it can never be helped merely by talking about it. We must act, and act quickly.

Finally, in our progress toward a resumption of work we require two safeguards against a return of the evils of the old order: there must be a strict supervision of all banking and credits and investments; there must be an end to speculation with other people's money, and there must be provision for an adequate but sound currency.

These are the lines of attack. I shall presently urge upon a new Congress in special session detailed measures for their fulfillment, and I shall seek the immediate assistance of the several States.

Through this program of action we address ourselves to putting our own national house in order and making income balance outgo.

Our international trade relations, though vastly important, are, to point in time and necessity, secondary to the establishment of a sound national economy.

I favor as a practical policy the putting of first things first. I shall spare no effort to restore world trade by international economic readjustment, but the emergency at home cannot wait on that accomplishment.

The basic thought that guides these specific means of national recovery is not narrowly nationalistic.

It is the insistence, as a first consideration, upon the interdependence of the various elements in and parts of the United States . . . a recognition of the old and permanently important manifestation of the American spirit of the pioneer.

It is the way to recovery. It is the immediate way. It is the strongest assurance that the recovery will endure.

In the field of world policy I would dedicate this nation to the policy of the good neighbor . . . the neighbor who resolutely respects himself and, because he does so, respects the rights of others . . . the neighbor who respects his obligations and respects the sanctity of his agreements in and with a world of neighbors.

If I read the temper of our people correctly, we now realize, as we have never realized before, our interdependence on each other: that we cannot merely take, but we must give as well, that if we are to go forward we must move as a trained and loyal army willing to sacrifice for the good of a common discipline, because, without such discipline, no progress is made, no leadership becomes effective.

We are, I know, ready and willing to submit our lives and property to such discipline because it makes possibly a leadership which aims at a larger good.

This I propose to offer, pledging that the larger purposes will bind upon us all as a sacred obligation with a unity of duty hitherto evoked only in time of armed strife.

With this pledge taken, I assume unhesitatingly the leadership of this great army of our people, dedicated to a disciplined attack upon our common problems.

Action in this image and to this end is feasible under the form of government which we have inherited from our ancestors.

Our Constitution is so simple and practical that it is possible always to meet extraordinary needs by changes in emphasis and arrangement without loss of essential form.

That is why our constitutional system has proved itself the most superbly enduring political mechanism the modern world has produced. It has met every stress of vast expansion of territory, of foreign wars, of bitter internal strife, of world relations.

It is to be hoped that the normal balance of executive and legislative authority may be wholly adequate to meet the unprecedented task before us. But it may be that an unprecedented demand and need for undelayed action may call for temporary departure from that normal balance of public procedure.

I am prepared under my constitutional duty to recommend the measures that a stricken nation in the midst of a stricken world may require.

But in the event that the Congress shall fail to take one of these courses, and in the event that the national emergency is still critical, I shall not evade the clear course of duty that will then confront me.

I shall ask the Congress for the one remaining instrument to meet the crisis . . . broad executive power to wage a war against the emergency as great as the power that would be given to me if we were in fact invaded by a foreign foe.

For the trust reposed in me I will return the courage and the devotion that befit the time. I can do no less.

We face the arduous days that lie before us in the warm courage of national unity, with the clear consciousness of seeking old and precious moral values, with the clean satisfaction that comes from the stern performance of duty by old and young alike.

We aim at the assurance of a rounded and permanent national life.

We do not distrust the future of essential democracy. The people of the United States have not failed. In their need they have registered a mandate that they want direct, vigorous action.

They have asked for discipline and direction under leadership. They have made me the present instrument of their wishes. In the spirit of the gift I will take it.

In this dedication of a nation we humbly ask the blessing of God. May He protect each and every one of us! May He guide me in the days to come!

From: http://www.archives.gov/education/lessons/fdr-inaugural/#documents.

QUESTIONS:

1. How does Roosevelt characterize the economic situation of the United States in 1932? What is his vision of the place of the United States in the global economic network?
2. How does Roosevelt package his economic prescriptions rhetorically and ideologically? To what cultural screen images or frame values does he appeal?

24.2: *The Results of the First Five Year Plan* (Josef Stalin, 1932)

At the same time that Roosevelt was rescuing liberalism and capitalism in the United States, Joseph Stalin (1878–1953) was leading an equally dramatic but far more radical, wrenching, and bloody transformation of the economy and society of the new Soviet Union, the world's first avowedly communist power. Stalin, an ethnic Georgian, had risen through the Communist Party ranks during the Russian Revolution to become Party Secretary in 1922. When Lenin died in 1924 Stalin consolidated his hold on power (mostly by executing political rivals) and remained leader of the Soviet Union until his death in 1953. He reversed Lenin's New Economic Policy, which had encouraged individual initiative, and instituted a massive collectivization of agriculture and a centrally controlled command economy outlined in the First Five Year Plan of 1928. The plan largely succeeded in transforming the Soviet economy from an Agrarian to an Industrial one, but at a huge cost. The collectivization of agriculture disrupted production badly enough to create a vast famine in 1932–33, for example. In the speech to Party representatives excerpted below, Stalin gives his own view of the success of the Plan.

THE RESULTS OF THE FIRST FIVE-YEAR PLAN

Report Delivered on January 7, 1933

I THE INTERNATIONAL SIGNIFICANCE OF THE FIVE-YEAR PLAN

Comrades, when the five-year plan was published, people hardly anticipated that it could be of tremendous international significance. On the contrary, many thought that the five-year plan was the private affair of the Soviet Union—an important and serious affair, but nevertheless the private, national affair of the Soviet Union.

History has shown, however, that the international significance of the five-year plan is immeasurable. History has shown that the five-year plan is not the private affair of the Soviet Union, but the concern of the whole international proletariat.

Long before the five-year plan appeared on the scene, in the period when we were finishing our struggle against the interventionists and were going over to the work of economic construction—even in that period Lenin said that our economic construction was of profound international significance; that every step forward taken by the Soviet Government along the path of economic construction was finding a powerful response among the most varied strata in capitalist countries and dividing people into two camps—the camp of the supporters of the proletarian revolution and the camp of its opponents.

. . .

This was said at the time when we were bringing to a close the war against the interventionists, when we were passing from the military struggle against capitalism to the struggle on the economic front, to the period of economic development.

Many years have elapsed since then, and every step taken by the Soviet Government in the sphere of economic development, every year, every quarter, has brilliantly confirmed Comrade Lenin's words.

. . .

II THE FUNDAMENTAL TASK OF THE FIVE-YEAR PLAN AND THE WAY TO ITS FULFILMENT

We pass to the question of the essence of the five-year plan.

What is the five-year plan?

What was the fundamental task of the five-year plan?

The fundamental task of the five-year plan was to transfer our country, with its backward, and in part medieval, technology, on to the lines of new, modern technology.

The fundamental task of the five-year plan was to convert the U.S.S.R. from an agrarian and weak country, dependent upon the caprices of the capitalist countries, into an industrial and powerful country, fully self-reliant and independent of the caprices of world capitalism.

The fundamental task of the five-year plan was, in converting the U.S.S.R. into an industrial country, to completely oust the capitalist elements, to widen the front of socialist forms of economy, and to create the economic basis for the abolition of classes in the U.S.S.R., for the building of a socialist society.

The fundamental task of the five-year plan was to create in our country an industry that would be capable of re-equipping and reorganising, not only industry as a whole, but also transport and agriculture—on the basis of socialism.

The fundamental task of the five-year plan was to transfer small and scattered agriculture on to the lines of large-scale collective farming, so as to ensure the economic basis of socialism in the countryside and thus to eliminate the possibility of the restoration of capitalism in the U.S.S.R.

Finally, the task of the five-year plan was to create all the necessary technical and economic prerequisites for increasing to the utmost the defence capacity of the country, enabling it to organise determined resistance to any attempt at military intervention from abroad, to any attempt at military attack from abroad.

What dictated this fundamental task of the five-year plan; what were the grounds for it?

The necessity of putting an end to the technical and economic backwardness of the Soviet Union, which doomed it to an unenviable existence; the necessity of creating in the country the prerequisites that would enable it not only to overtake but in time to outstrip, technically and economically, the advanced capitalist countries.

Consideration of the fact that the Soviet regime could not maintain itself for long on the basis of a backward industry; that only a modern large-scale industry, one not merely not inferior to but capable in time of surpassing the industries of the capitalist countries, can serve as a real and reliable foundation for the Soviet regime.

Consideration of the fact that the Soviet regime could not for long rest upon two opposite foundations: on large-scale socialist industry, which *destroys* the capitalist elements, and on small, individual peasant farming, which *engenders* capitalist elements.

Consideration of the fact that until agriculture was placed on the basis of large-scale production, until the small peasant farms were united into large collective farms, the danger of the restoration of capitalism in the U.S.S.R. was the most real of all possible dangers.

· · ·

That is how matters stand with regard to the fundamental task of the five-year plan.

But the execution of such a gigantic plan cannot be started haphazardly, just anyhow. In order to carry out such a plan it is necessary first of all to find its main link; for only after finding and grasping this main link could a pull be exerted on all the other links of the plan.

What was the main link in the five-year plan?

The main link in the five-year plan was heavy industry, with machine building as its core. For only heavy industry is capable of reconstructing both industry as a whole, transport and agriculture, and of putting them on their feet. It was necessary to begin the fulfilment of the five-year plan with heavy industry. Consequently, the restoration of heavy industry had to be made the basis of the fulfilment of the five-year plan.

· · ·

But the restoration and development of heavy industry, particularly in such a backward and poor country as ours was at the beginning of the five-year plan period, is an extremely difficult task; for, as is well known, heavy industry calls for enormous financial expenditure and the existence of a certain minimum of experienced technical forces, without which, generally speaking, the restoration of heavy industry is impossible. Did the Party know this, and did it take this into account? Yes, it did. Not only did the Party know this, but it announced it for all to hear. The Party knew how heavy industry had been built in Britain, Germany and America. It knew that in those countries heavy industry had been built either with the aid of big loans, or by plundering other countries, or by both methods simultaneously. The Party knew that those paths were closed to our country. What, then, did it count on? It counted on our country's own resources. It counted on the fact that, with a Soviet government at the helm, and the land, industry, transport, the banks and trade nationalised, we could pursue a regime of the strictest economy in order to accumulate sufficient resources for the restoration and development of heavy industry. The Party declared frankly that this would call for serious sacrifices, and that it was our duty openly and consciously to make these sacrifices if we wanted to achieve our goal. The Party counted on carrying through this task with the aid of the internal resources of our country—without enslaving credits and loans from abroad.

. . .

To establish a regime of the strictest economy and to accumulate the resources necessary for financing the industrialisation of our country—such was the path that had to be taken in order to succeed in creating heavy industry and in carrying out the five-year plan.

. . .

III THE RESULTS OF THE FIVE-YEAR PLAN IN FOUR YEARS IN THE SPHERE OF INDUSTRY

. . .

We did not have an iron and steel industry, the basis for the industralisation of the country. Now we have one.

We did not have a tractor industry. Now we have one.

We did not have an automobile industry. Now we have one.

We did not have a machine-tool industry. Now we have one.

We did not have a big and modern chemical industry. Now we have one.

We did not have a real and big industry for the production of modern agricultural machinery. Now we have one.

We did not have an aircraft industry. Now we have one.

In output of electric power we were last on the list. Now we rank among the first.

In output of oil products and coal we were last on the list. Now we rank among the first.

We had only one coal and metallurgical base—in the Ukraine—and it was with difficulty that we made do with that. We have not only succeeded in improving this base, but have created a new coal and metallurgical base—in the East—which is the pride of our country.

We had only one centre of the textile industry—in the North of our country. As a result of our efforts we shall have in the very near future two new centres. . . .

VIII GENERAL CONCLUSIONS

. . .

1. The results of the five-year plan have refuted the assertion of the bourgeois and Social-Democratic leaders that the five-year plan was a fantasy, delirium, an unrealisable dream. The results of the five-year plan show that the five-year plan has already been fulfilled.

2. The results of the five-year plan have shattered the well-known bourgeois "article of faith" that the working class is incapable of building something new, that it is capable only of destroying the old. The results of the five-year plan have shown that the working class is just as well able to build the new as to destroy the old.

3. The results of the five-year plan have shattered the thesis of the Social-Democrats that it is impossible to build socialism in one country taken separately. The results of the five-year plan have shown that it is quite possible to build a socialist society in one country; for the economic foundations of such a society have already been laid in the U.S.S.R.

4. The results of the five-year plan have refuted the assertion of bourgeois economists that the capitalist system of economy is the best of all systems—that every other system of economy is unstable and incapable of standing the test of the difficulties of economic development. The results of the five-year

plan have shown that the capitalist system of economy is bankrupt and unstable; that it has outlived its day and must give way to another, a higher, Soviet, socialist system of economy; that the only system of economy that has no fear of crises and is able to overcome the difficulties which capitalism cannot solve—is the Soviet system of economy.

5. Finally, the results of the five-year plan have shown that the Communist Party is invincible, *if* it knows its goal, and *if* it is not afraid of difficulties.

(Stormy and prolonged applause, increasing to an ovation. All rise to greet Comrade Stalin.)

From: Stalin, Joseph, *Works*, vol. 13 (Moscow: Foreign Languages Pub. House, 1952), pp. 161–220.

QUESTIONS:

1. How does Stalin's economic plan compare to Roosevelt's? What different economic conditions did each leader inherit, and how did those different backgrounds shape their respective responses?
2. How do the two audiences influence how the speakers frame their messages? Who else (in addition to Soviet Communist Party members) does Stalin have in mind in his address?

24.3: *Night* (Elie Wiesel, 1958)

Elie Wiesel (1928–) is a Romanian-born Jewish professor, writer, and policial activist and United States citizen and resident since 1955. When he was fifteen, in May 1944, the Nazis deported Wiesel and the rest of the Jews from his hometown of Sighet, including his mother, father, and three sisters, to the concentration camp at Auschwitz. He was separated from his mother and sisters, who died at Auschwitz, but managed to stay with his father for eight months at Auschwitz and the associated work camp at Buna. When advancing Soviet forces approached Auschwitz, the prisoners at Auschwitz there were force marched in the snow in January 1945 to Buchenwald. Wiesel's father, weakened, was beaten by the Nazis and by fellow prisoners for his bread ration, and was sent to the crematorium weeks before the American army liberated the camp in April 1945. Wiesel survived, became an agnostic, and in the mid-1950s wrote a memoir of his experiences. It was published in the United States in 1960 under the title *Night*, and though it initially sold slowly is now a perennial best-seller. Wiesel won the Nobel Peace Prize in 1986.

Lying down was out of the question, and we were only able to sit by deciding to take turns. There was very little air. The lucky ones who happened to be near a window could see the blossoming countryside roll by.

After two days of traveling, we began to be tortured by thirst. Then the heat became unbearable.

Free from all social constraint, young people gave way openly to instinct, taking advantage of the darkness to flirt in our midst, without caring about anyone else, as though they were alone in the world. The rest pretended not to notice anything.

We still had a few provisions left. But we never ate enough to satisfy our hunger. To save was our rule; to save up for tomorrow. Tomorrow might be worse.

The train stopped at Kaschau, a little town on the Czechoslovak frontier. We realized then that we were not going to stay in Hungary. Our eyes were opened, but too late.

The door of the car slid open. A German officer, accompanied by a Hungarian lieutenant-interpreter, came up and introduced himself.

"From this moment, you come under the authority of the German army. Those of you who still have gold, silver, or watches in your possession must give them up now Anyone who is later found to have kept anything will be shot on the spot. Secondly, anyone who feels ill may go to the hospital car. That's all."

The Hungarian lieutenant went among us with a basket and collected the last possessions from those who no longer wished to taste the bitterness of terror.

"There are eighty of you in this wagon," added the German officer. "If anyone is missing, you'll all be shot, like dogs. . . ."

They disappeared. The doors were closed. We were caught in a trap, right up to our necks. The doors were nailed up; the way back was finally cut off. The world was a cattle wagon hermetically sealed.

We had a woman with us named Madame Schächter. She was about fifty; her ten-year-old son was with her, crouched in a corner. Her husband and two eldest sons had been deported with the first transport by mistake. The separation had completely broken her.

I knew her well. A quiet woman with tense, burning eyes, she had often been to our house. Her husband, who was a pious man, spent his days and nights in study, and it was she who worked to support the family.

Madame Schächter had gone out of her mind. On the first day of the journey she had already begun to moan and to keep asking why she had been separated from her family. As time went on, her cries grew hysterical.

On the third night, while we slept, some of us sitting one against the other and some standing, a piercing cry split the silence:

"Fire! I can see a fire! I can see a fire!"

There was a moment's panic. Who was it who had cried out? It was Madame Schächter. Standing in the middle of the wagon, in the pale light from the windows, she looked like a withered tree in a cornfield. She pointed her arm toward the window, screaming:

"Look! Look at it! Fire! A terrible fire! Mercy! *Oh, that fire!*"

Some of the men pressed up against the bars. There was nothing there; only the darkness.

The shock of this terrible awakening stayed with us for a long time. We still trembled from it. With every groan of the wheels on the rail, we felt that an abyss was about to open beneath our bodies. Powerless to still our own anguish, we tried to console ourselves:

"She's mad, poor soul. . . ."

Someone had put a damp cloth on her brow, to calm her, but still her screams went on:

"Fire! Fire!"

Her little boy was crying, hanging onto her skirt, trying to take hold of her hands. "It's all right, Mummy! There's nothing there. . . . Sit down. . . ." This shook me even more than his mother's screams had done.

Some women tried to calm her. "You'll find your husband and your sons again . . . in a few days. . . ."

She continued to scream, breathless, her voice broken by sobs. "Jews, listen to me! I can see a fire! There are huge flames! It is a furnace!"

It was as though she were possessed by an evil spirit which spoke from the depths of her being.

We tried to explain it away, more to calm ourselves and to recover our own breath than to comfort her: "She must be very thirsty, poor thing! That's why she keeps talking about a fire devouring her."

But it was in vain. Our terror was about to burst the sides of the train. Our nerves were at breaking point. Our flesh was creeping. It was as though madness were taking possession of us all. We could stand it no longer. Some of the young men forced her to sit down, tied her up, and put a gag in her mouth.

Silence again. The little boy sat down by his mother, crying. I had begun to breathe normally again. We could hear the wheels churning out that monotonous rhythm of a train traveling through the night. We could begin to doze, to rest, to dream. . . .

An hour or two went by like this. Then another scream took our breath away. The woman had broken loose from her bonds and was crying out more loudly than ever:

"Look at the fire! Flames, flames everywhere. . . ."

Once more the young men tied her up and gagged her. They even struck her. People encouraged them:

"Make her be quiet! She's mad! Shut her up! She's not the only one. She can keep her mouth shut . . . ."

They struck her several times on the head—blows that might have killed her. Her little boy clung to her; he did not cry out; he did not say a word. He was not even weeping now.

   . . .

The cherished objects we had brought with us thus far were left behind in the train, and with them, at last, our illusions.

Every two yards or so an SS man held his tommy gun trained on us. Hand in hand we followed the crowd.

An SS noncommissioned officer came to meet us, a truncheon in his hand. He gave the order:

"Men to the left! Women to the right!"

Eight words spoken quietly, indifferently, without emotion. Eight short, simple words. Yet that was the moment when I parted from my mother. I had not had time to think, but already I felt the pressure of my father's hand: we were alone. For a part of a second I glimpsed my mother and my sisters moving away to the right. Tzipora held Mother's hand. I saw them disappear into the distance; my mother was stroking my sister's fair hair, as though to protect her, while I walked on with my father and the other men. And I did not know that in that place, at that moment, I was parting from my mother and Tzipora forever. I went on walking. My father held onto my hand.

Behind me, an old man fell to the ground. Near him was an SS man, putting his revolver back in its holster.

My hand shifted on my father's arm. I had one thought—not to lose him. Not to be left alone.

The SS officers gave the order:

"Form fives!"

Commotion. At all costs we must keep together.

"Here, kid, how old are you?"

It was one of the prisoners who asked me this. I could not see his face, but his voice was tense and weary.

"I'm not quite fifteen yet."

"No. Eighteen."

"But I'm not," I said. "Fifteen."

"Fool. Listen to what *I* say."

Then he questioned my father, who replied:

"Fifty."

The other grew more furious than ever.

"No, not fifty. Forty. Do you understand? Eighteen and forty."

He disappeared into the night shadows.

   . . .

The wind of revolt died down. We continued our march toward the square. In the middle stood the notorious Dr. Mengele (a typical SS officer: a cruel face, but not devoid of intelligence, and wearing a monocle); a conductor's baton in his hand, he was standing among the other officers. The baton moved unremittingly, sometimes to the right, sometimes to the left.

I was already in front of him:

"How old are you?" he asked, in an attempt at a paternal tone of voice.

"Eighteen." My voice was shaking.

"Are you in good health?"

"Yes."

"What's your occupation?"

Should I say that I was a student?

"Farmer," I heard myself say.

This conversation cannot have lasted more than a few seconds. It had seemed like an eternity to me.

The baton moved to the left. I took half a step forward. I wanted to see first where they were sending my father. If he went to the right, I would go after him.

The baton once again pointed to the left for him too. A weight was lifted from my heart.

We did not yet know which was the better side, right or left; which road led to prison and which to the crematory. But for the moment I was happy; I was near my father. Our procession continued to move slowly forward.

· · ·

My father's voice drew me from my thoughts:

"It's a shame . . . a shame that you couldn't have gone with your mother. . . . I saw several boys of your age going with their mothers. . . ."

His voice was terribly sad. I realized that he did not want to see what they were going to do to me. He did not want to see the burning of his only son.

My forehead was bathed in cold sweat. But I told him that I did not believe that they could burn people in our age, that humanity would never tolerate it. . . .

"Humanity? Humanity is not concerned with us. Today anything is allowed. Anything is possible, even these crematories. . . ."

His voice was choking.

"Father," I said, "if that is so, I don't want to wait here. I'm going to run to the electric wire. That would be better than slow agony in the flames."

He did not answer. He was weeping. His body was shaken convulsively. Around us, everyone was weeping. Someone began to recite the Kaddish, the prayer for the dead. I do not know if it has ever happened before, in the long history of the Jews, that people have ever recited the prayer for the dead for themselves.

"*Yitgadal veyitkadach shmé raba*. . . . May His Name be blessed and magnified. . . ." whispered my father.

For the first time, I felt revolt rise up in me. Why should I bless His name? The Eternal, Lord of the Universe, the All-Powerful and Terrible, was silent. What had I to thank Him for?

We continued our march. We were gradually drawing closer to the ditch, from which an infernal heat was rising. Still twenty steps to go. If I wanted to bring about my own death, this was the moment. Our line had now only fifteen paces to cover. I bit my lips so that my father would not hear my teeth chattering. Ten steps still. Eight. Seven. We marched slowly on, as though following a hearse at our own funeral. Four steps more. Three steps. There it was now, right in front of us, the pit and its flames. I gathered all that was left of my strength, so that I could break from the ranks and throw myself upon the barbed wire. In the depths of my heart, I bade farewell to my father, to the whole universe; and, in spite of myself, the words formed themselves and issued in a whisper from my lips: *Yitgadal veyitkadach shmé raba*. . . . May His name be blessed and magnified. . . . My heart was bursting. The moment had come. I was face to face with the Angel of Death. . . .

No. Two steps from the pit we were ordered to turn to the left and made to go into a barracks.

I pressed my father's hand. He said:

"Do you remember Madame Schächter, in the train?"

Never shall I forget that night, the first night in camp, which has turned my life into one long night, seven times cursed and seven times sealed. Never shall I forget that smoke. Never shall I forget the little faces of the children, whose bodies I saw turned into wreaths of smoke beneath a silent blue sky.

Never shall I forget those flames which consumed my faith forever.

Never shall I forget that nocturnal silence which deprived me, for all eternity, of the desire to live. Never shall I forget those moments which murdered my God and my soul and turned my dreams to dust. Never shall I forget these things, even if I am condemned to live as long as God Himself. Never.

· · ·

"Everyone outside!"

Ten gypsies had come and joined our supervisor. Whips and truncheons cracked round me. My feet were running without my being aware of it. I tried to hide from the blows behind the others. The spring sunshine.

"Form fives!"

The prisoners whom I had noticed in the morning were working at the side. There was no guard near them, only the shadow of the chimney. . . . Dazed by the sunshine and by my reverie, I felt someone tugging at my sleeve. It was my father. "Come on, my boy."

We marched on. Doors opened and closed again. On we went between the electric wires. At each step, a white placard with a death's head on it stared us in the face. A caption: "Warning. Danger of death." Mockery: was there a single place here where you were not in danger of death?

The gypsies stopped near another barracks. They were replaced by SS, who surrounded us. Revolvers, machine guns, police dogs.

The march had lasted half an hour. Looking around me, I noticed that the barbed wires were behind us. We had left the camp.

It was a beautiful April day. The fragrance of spring was in the air. The sun was setting in the west.

But we had been marching for only a few moments when we saw the barbed wire of another camp. An iron door with this inscription over it:

"Work is liberty!"

Auschwitz.

First impression: this was better than Birkenau. There were two-storied buildings of concrete instead of wooden barracks. There were little gardens here and there. We were led to one of these prison blocks. Seated on the ground by the entrance, we began another session of waiting. Every now and then, someone was made to go in. These were the showers, a compulsory formality at the entrance to all these camps. Even if you were simply passing from one to the other several times a day, you still had to go through the baths every time.

After coming out from the hot water, we stayed shivering in the night air. Our clothes had been left behind in the other block, and we had been promised other outfits.

Toward midnight, we were told to run.

"Faster," shouted our guards. "The faster you run, the sooner you can go to bed."

After a few minutes of this mad race we arrived in front of another block. The prisoner in charge was waiting for us. He was a young Pole, who smiled at us. He began to talk to us, and, despite our weariness, we listened patiently.

"Comrades, you're in the concentration camp of Auschwitz. There's a long road of suffering ahead of you. But don't lose courage. You've already escaped the gravest danger: selection. So now, muster your strength, and don't lose heart. We shall all see the day of liberation. Have faith in life. Above all else, have faith. Drive out despair, and you will keep death away from yourselves. Hell is not for eternity. And now, a prayer—or rather, a piece of advice: let there be comradeship among you. We are all brothers, and we are all suffering the same fate. The same smoke floats over all our heads. Help one another. It is the only way to survive. Enough said. You're tired. Listen. You're in Block 17. I am responsible for keeping order here. Anyone with a complaint against anyone else can come and see me. That's all. You can go to bed. Two people to a bunk. Good night." The first human words.

From: Wiesel, Elie, *Night* (New York: Bantam Books, 1989), pp. 21–39, passim.

QUESTIONS:

1. What practical measures do the Nazis running the prison camps take to dehumanize their victims?
2. What responses do the prisoners have to maintain elements of their own humanity intact?

24.4:   The Bomb

Albert Einstein (1879–1955), whose story is told at the beginning of *Frameworks* Chapter 24, was a German Jewish physicist whose work laid the foundations for the invention of atomic and nuclear weaponry. When he was visiting the United States in 1933 Adolph Hitler came to power in Germany, and Einstein never returned, becoming a United States citizen in 1940. In 1939 he signed a letter written by Leo Slizard (1898–1964), a Hungarian born American physicist, to President Roosevelt urging him to fund the development of atomic weaponry, as they feared that Nazi Germany would get there first. But in 1945, with the success of the resulting Manhattan Project, Szilard and Einstein joined many other scientists in urging President Truman not to actually use the weapon against Japan, Germany having already been defeated. Both the letter and the Szilard Petition are reproduced here.

24.4a: *Letter to Roosevelt* (Albert Einstein, 1939)

Old Grove Rd. Nassau Point Peconic, Long Island
    August 2nd, 1939
    F.D. Roosevelt, President of the United States,
White House, Washington, D.C.
    Sir:

Some recent work by E. Fermi and L. Szilard, which has been communicated to me in manuscript, leads me to expect that the element uranium may be turned into a new and important source of energy in the immediate future. Certain aspects of the situation which has arisen seem to call for watchfulness and, if necessary, quick action on the part of the administration. I believe therefore that it is my duty to bring to your attention the following facts and recommendations:

In the course of the last four months it has been made probable—through the work of Joliot in France as well as Fermi and Szilard in America—that it may become possible to set up a nuclear chain reaction in a large mass of uranium, by which vast amounts of power and large quantities of new radium like elements would be generated. Now it appears almost certain that this could be achieved in the immediate future.

This new phenomenon would also lead to the construction of bombs, and it is conceivable—though much less certain—that extremely powerful bombs of a new type may thus be constructed. A single bomb of this type, carried by boat and exploded in a port, might very well destroy the whole port together with some of the surrounding territory. However, such bombs might very well prove to be too heavy for transportation by air.

The United States has only very poor [illegible] of uranium in moderate quantities. There is some good ore in Canada and the former Czechoslovakia, while the most important source of Uranium is Belgian Congo.

In view of this situation you may think it desirable to have some permanent contact maintained between the Administration and the group of physicists working on chain reactions in America. One possible way of achieving this might be for you to entrust with this task a person who has your confidence and who could perhaps serve in an unofficial capacity. His task might comprise the following:

a) To approach Government Departments, keep them informed of the further development, and out forward recommendations for Government action, giving particular attention to the problem of uranium ore for the United States;

b) To speed up the experimental work, which is at present being carried on within the limits of the budgets of University laboratories, by providing funds, if such funds be required, through his contacts with private persons who are willing to make a contribution for this cause, and perhaps also by obtaining the co-operation of industrial laboratories which have the necessary equipment.

I understand that Germany has actually stopped the sale of uranium from the Czechoslovakian mines, which she has taken over. That she should have taken such early action might perhaps be understood on the ground that the son of the German Under-Secretary of State, Von Weishlicker [sic], is attached to the Kaiser Wilhelm Institute in Berlin where some of the American work on uranium is now being repeated.

Yours very truly,

(Albert Einstein)

From: Argonne National Laboratory, http://www.pbs.org/wgbh/americanexperience/features/primary-resources/truman-ein39/.

24.4b: *Szilard Petition* (1945)

July 17, 1945

A PETITION TO THE PRESIDENT OF THE UNITED STATES

Discoveries of which the people of the United States are not aware may affect the welfare of this nation in the near future. The liberation of atomic power which has been achieved places atomic bombs in the hands of the Army. It places in your hands, as Commander-in-Chief, the fateful decision whether or not to sanction the use of such bombs in the present phase of the war against Japan.

We, the undersigned scientists, have been working in the field of atomic power. Until recently, we have had to fear that the United States might be attacked by atomic bombs during this war and that her only defense might lie in a counterattack by the same means. Today, with the defeat of Germany, this danger is averted and we feel impelled to say what follows:

The war has to be brought speedily to a successful conclusion and attacks by atomic bombs may very well be an effective method of warfare. We feel, however, that such attacks on Japan could not be justified, at least not unless the terms which will be imposed after the war on Japan were made public in detail and Japan were given an opportunity to surrender.

If such public announcement gave assurance to the Japanese that they could look forward to a life devoted to peaceful pursuits in their homeland and if Japan still refused to surrender our nation might then, in certain circumstances, find itself forced to resort to the use of atomic bombs. Such a step, however, ought not to be made at any time without seriously considering the moral responsibilities which are involved.

The development of atomic power will provide the nations with new means of destruction. The atomic bombs at our disposal represent only the first step in this direction, and there is almost no limit to the destructive power which will become available in the course of their future development. Thus a nation which sets the precedent of using these newly liberated forces of nature for purposes of destruction may have to bear the responsibility of opening the door to an era of devastation on an unimaginable scale.

If after this war a situation is allowed to develop in the world which permits rival powers to be in uncontrolled possession of these new means of destruction, the cities of the United States as well as the cities of other nations will be in continuous danger of sudden annihilation. All the resources of the United States, moral and material, may have to be mobilized to prevent the advent of such a world situation. Its prevention is at present the solemn responsibility of the United States—singled out by virtue of her lead in the field of atomic power.

The added material strength which this lead gives to the United States brings with it the obligation of restraint and if we were to violate this obligation our moral position would be weakened in the eyes of the world and in our own eyes. It would then be more difficult for us to live up to our responsibility of bringing the unloosened forces of destruction under control.

In view of the foregoing, we, the undersigned, respectfully petition: first, that you exercise your power as Commander-in-Chief, to rule that the United States shall not resort to the use of atomic bombs in this war unless the terms which will be imposed upon Japan have been made public in detail and Japan knowing these terms has refused to surrender; second, that in such an event the question whether or not to use atomic bombs be decided by you in light of the considerations presented in this petition as well as all the other moral responsibilities which are involved.

Leo Szilard and 69 co-signers

From: U.S. National Archives, Record Group 77, Records of the Chief of Engineers, Manhattan Engineer District, Harrison-Bundy File, folder #76, online at http://www.dannen.com/decision/45-07-17.html.

QUESTIONS:

1. How do the different contexts of 1939 and 1945 influence the scientists' presentation of their work?
2. How do the results of their own work (as they become a potentially devastating reality) change the scientists' attitudes toward scientific and technological "progress"—and even toward science itself?

CHAPTER 25

Crisis Institutionalized and Transformed: 1945 to 1989

INTRODUCTION

This chapter presents sources from the nearly fifty years after the end of World War II. These were years dominated by the Cold War, the great bipolar struggle between the capitalist world led by the United States and the communist world led by the Soviet Union, though bipolarity was never complete. Indeed the emergence of communist China as a rival to the Soviet Union and a self-proclaimed leader of the "Third World" of unaligned nations complicated the Cold War and intersected with the other trend of the period, decolonization, or the breakup of the European empires that had been built in the nineteenth century. The sources in this chapter present some of the complexities of this period.

25.1: *Speech on the Granting of Indian Independence* (Jawaharlal Nehru, 1947)

Jawaharlal Nehru (1889–1964) was the first Prime Minister of India from 1947 to 1964 as well as father and grandfather respectively of subsequent Indian Prime Ministers Indira and Rajiv Gandhi. A nationalist from boyhood, Nehru was active in Indian independence movements from the time he returned to India after his education at Cambridge University and as a barrister at the Inner Temple in England. Until he was assassinated, Mahatma Gandhi, India's most famous advocate for nonviolence, civil rights, and Indian independence, was Nehru's mentor. Nehru agreed, with reluctance and against the advice of Gandhi, to a partition between India and a separate Muslim state of Pakistan, but this plan was not announced until after Nehru was inaugurated as Prime Minister on August 15, 1947. The phrase "not wholly or in full measure" is an indirect reference to the plan for partitoning, just as "pains that continue even now" refers to violence between Hindus and Muslims. Nehru gave this speech before the Constituent Assembly of India in New Delhi at midnight on August 14, 1947.

Long years ago we made a tryst with destiny, and now the time comes when we shall redeem our pledge, not wholly or in full measure, but very substantially. At the stroke of the midnight hour, when the world sleeps, India will awake to life and freedom. A moment comes, which comes but rarely in history, when we step out from the old to the new, when an age ends, and when the soul of a nation, long suppressed, finds utterance. It is fitting that at this solemn moment we take the pledge of dedication to the service of India and her people and to the still larger cause of humanity.

At the dawn of history India started on her unending quest, and trackless centuries are filled with her striving and the grandeur of her success and her failures. Through good and ill fortune alike she has never lost sight of that quest or forgotten the ideals which gave her strength. We end today a period of ill fortune and India discovers herself again. The achievement we celebrate today is but a step, an opening of opportunity, to the greater triumphs and achievements that await us. Are we brave enough and wise enough to grasp this opportunity and accept the challenge of the future?

Freedom and power bring responsibility. The responsibility rests upon this Assembly, a sovereign body representing the sovereign people of India. Before the birth of freedom we have endured all the pains of labor and our hearts are heavy with the memory of this sorrow. Some of those pains continue even now. Nevertheless, the past is over and it is the future that beckons to us now.

That future is not one of ease or resting but of incessant striving so that we may fulfill the pledges we have so often taken and the one we shall take today. The service of India means the service of the millions who suffer. It means the ending of poverty and ignorance and disease and inequality of opportunity. The ambition of the greatest man of our generation has been to wipe every tear from every eye. That may be beyond us, but as long as there are tears and suffering, so long our work will not be over.

And so we have to labor and to work, and work hard, to give reality to our dreams. Those dreams are for India, but they are also for the world, for all the nations and peoples are too closely knit together today for any one of them to imagine that it can live apart Peace has been said to be indivisible; so is freedom, so is prosperity now, and so also is disaster in this One World that can no longer be split into isolated fragments.

To the people of India, whose representatives we are, we make an appeal to join us with faith and confidence in this great adventure. This is no time for petty and destructive criticism, no time for ill-will or blaming others. We have to build the noble mansion of free India where all her children may dwell.

II

The appointed day has come—the day appointed by destiny—and India stands forth again, after long slumber and struggle, awake, vital, free and independent. The past clings on to us still in some measure and we have to do much before we redeem the pledges we have so often taken. Yet the turning-point is past, and history begins anew for us, the history which we shall live and act and others will write about.

It is a fateful moment for us in India, for all Asia and for the world. A new star rises, the star of freedom in the East, a new hope comes into being, a vision long cherished materializes. May the star never set and that hope never be betrayed!

We rejoice in that freedom, even though clouds surround us, and many of our people are sorrow-stricken and difficult problems encompass us. But freedom brings responsibilities and burdens and we have to face them in the spirit of a free and disciplined people.

On this day our first thoughts go to the architect of this freedom, the Father of our Nation [Gandhi], who, embodying the old spirit of India, held aloft the torch of freedom and lighted up the darkness that surrounded us. We have often been unworthy followers of his and have strayed from his message, but not only we but succeeding generations will remember this message and bear the imprint in their hearts of this great son of India, magnificent in his faith and strength and courage and humility. We shall never allow that torch of freedom to be blown out, however high the wind or stormy the tempest.

Our next thoughts must be of the unknown volunteers and soldiers of freedom who, without praise or reward, have served India even unto death.

We think also of our brothers and sisters who have been cut off from us by political boundaries and who unhappily cannot share at present in the freedom that has come. They are of us and will remain of us whatever may happen, and we shall be sharers in their good [or] ill fortune alike.

The future beckons to us. Whither do we go and what shall be our endeavour? To bring freedom and opportunity to the common man, to the peasants and workers of India; to fight and end poverty and ignorance and disease; to build up a prosperous, democratic and progressive nation, and to create social, economic and political institutions which will ensure justice and fullness of life to every man and woman.

We have hard work ahead. There is no resting for any one of us till we redeem our pledge in full, till we make all the people of India what destiny intended them to be. We are citizens of a great country on the verge of bold advance, and we have to live up to that high standard. All of us, to whatever religion we may belong, are equally the children of India with equal rights, privileges and obligations. We cannot encourage communalism or narrow-mindedness, for no nation can be great whose people are narrow in thought or in action.

To the nations and peoples of the world we send greetings and pledge ourselves to cooperate with them in furthering peace, freedom and democracy.

And to India, our much-loved motherland, the ancient, the eternal and the ever-new, we pay our reverent homage and we bind ourselves afresh to her service.

JAI HIND.

From: Nehru, Jawaharlal, and Mushirul Hasan, *Nehru's India: select speeches* (New Delhi: Oxford University Press, 2007), pp. 76–78.

QUESTIONS:

1. What image of Indian identity does Nehru project in this speech? What frame values does he draw on—or indeed try to create?
2. How does the heritage of India's colonial past show up in Nehru's speech?

25.2: *Report on an Investigation of the Peasant Movement in Hunan (Mao Zedong, 1927)*

Mao Zedong (1893–1976) was the first chairman of the Communist Party of China from the founding of the People's Republic of China in 1949 to his death. Born into a wealthy peasant family, Mao became one of the first members of the Communist Party of China in 1921 while working at Beijing University. Sun Yat-sen, the cofounder of the larger and militarized Kuomintang (Chinese Nationalist Party), began to cooperate with the Communist Party of China in 1923, but after Sun Yat-sen's death in 1925, the military leader of the Kuomintang and successor to Sun Yat-sen, Chiang Kai-shek, broke cooperation with the Communists. Chiang Kai-shek purged Communists in areas under his military control. In response and thus beginning the Chinese Civil War, Mao Zedong raised and led a small peasant army against the Kuomintang in the Hunan province in 1927, but it was defeated.

During my recent visit to Hunan I made a firsthand investigation of conditions in the five counties of Hsiangtan, Hsianghsiang, Hengshan, Liling and Changsha. In the thirty-two days from January 4 to February 5, I called together fact-finding conferences in villages and county towns, which were attended by experienced peasants and by comrades working in the peasant movement, and I listened attentively to their reports and collected a great deal of material. Many of the hows and whys of the peasant movement were the exact opposite of what the gentry in Hankow and Changsha are saying. I saw and heard of many strange things of which I had hitherto been unaware. I believe the same is true of many other places, too. All talk directed against the peasant movement must be speedily set right. All the wrong measures taken by the revolutionary authorities concerning the peasant movement must be speedily changed. Only thus can the future of the revolution be benefited. For the present upsurge of the peasant movement is a colossal event. In a very short time, in China's central, southern and northern provinces, several hundred million peasants will rise like a mighty storm, like a hurricane, a force so swift and violent that no power, however great, will be able to hold it back. They will smash all the trammels that bind them and rush forward along the road to liberation. They will sweep all the imperialists, warlords, corrupt officials, local tyrants and evil gentry into their graves. Every revolutionary party and every revolutionary comrade will be put to the test, to be accepted or rejected as they decide. There are three alternatives. To march at their head and lead them? To trail behind them, gesticulating and criticizing? Or to stand in their way and oppose them? Every Chinese is free to choose, but events will force you to make the choice quickly.

. . .

The main targets of attack by the peasants are the local tyrants, the evil gentry and the lawless landlords, but in passing they also hit out against patriarchal ideas and institutions, against the corrupt officials in the cities and against bad practices and customs in the rural areas. In force and momentum the attack is tempestuous; those who bow before it survive and those who resist perish. As a result, the privileges which the feudal landlords enjoyed for thousands of years are being shattered

to pieces. Every bit of the dignity and prestige built up by the landlords is being swept into the dust. With the collapse of the power of the landlords, the peasant associations have now become the sole organs of authority and the popular slogan "All power to the peasant associations" has become a reality. Even bides such as a quarrel between husband and wife are brought to the peasant association. Nothing can be settled unless someone from the peasant association is present. The association actually dictates all rural affairs, and, quite literally, "whatever it says, goes". Those who are outside the associations can only speak well of them and cannot say anything against them. The local tyrants, evil gentry and lawless landlords have been deprived of all right to speak, and none of them dares even mutter dissent. In the face of the peasant associations' power and pressure, the top local tyrants and evil gentry have fled to Shanghai, those of the second rank to Hankow, those of the third to Changsha and those of the fourth to the county towns, while the fifth rank and the still lesser fry surrender to the peasant associations in the villages.

"Here's ten yuan. Please let me join the peasant association," one of the smaller of the evil gentry will say.

"Ugh! Who wants your filthy money?" the peasants reply.

. . . [W]hat was looked down upon four months ago as a "gang of peasants" has now become a most honorable institution. Those who formerly prostrated themselves before the power of the gentry now bow before the power of the peasants. No matter what their identity, all admit that the world since last October is a different one.

. . .

The right-wing of the Kuomintang says, "The peasant movement is a movement of the riffraff, of the lazy peasants." This view is current in Changsha. When I was in the countryside, I heard the gentry say, "It is all right to set up peasant associations, but the people now running them are no good. They ought to be replaced!" This opinion comes to the same thing as what the right-wingers are saying; according to both it is all right to have a peasant movement (the movement is already in being and no one dare say otherwise), but they say that the people running it are no good and they particularly hate those in charge of the associations at the lower levels, calling them "riffraff." In short, all those whom the gentry had despised, those whom they had trodden into the dirt, people with no place in society, people with no right to speak, have now audaciously lifted up their heads. They have not only lifted up their heads but taken power into their hands. They are now running the township peasant associations (at the lowest level), which they have turned into something fierce and formidable. They have raised their rough, work-soiled hands and laid them on the gentry. They tether the evil gentry with ropes, crown them with tall paper-hats and parade them through the villages. (In Hsiangtan and Hsianghsiang they call this "parading through the township" and in Liling "parading through the fields".) Not a day passes but they drum some harsh, pitiless words of denunciation into these gentry's ears. They are issuing orders and are running everything. Those who used to rank lowest now rank above everybody else; and so this is called "turning things upside down."

· · ·

From: http://www.marxists.org/reference/archive/mao/selected-works/volume-1/mswv1_2.htm.

QUESTIONS:

1. Why does Mao want to characterize the peasants as revolutionary? How does this compare with Marx's theory in the Communist Manifesto (Chapter 19)? How does it compare with Stalin's Five-Year Plan (Chapter 24)?
2. What audience(s) does Mao seem to be addressing here? Is he talking to the peasants?

25.3: *"Suffern on the Steppes"* (Walt Kelly, 1955)

Walt Kelly (1913–73) was a great American artist whose comic strip *Pogo* pioneered a path of humor and political commentary later followed by Garry Trudeau's strip *Doonesbury*. *Pogo* featured animal characters from the Okefenokee Swamp in Georgia: the title character Pogo Possum, Albert Alligator, Howland Owl, the turtle Churchy La Femme, Beauregard the Dog, and Porky Porcupine, among others. Kelly also put out special Pogo books with stories that did not appear in daily strips. "The Man from Suffern on the Steppes," from *The Pogo Peek-a-Book,* is one of those. In it, he makes fun of both sides of the Cold War by putting his characters in his version of Soviet Russia, which includes a "Madisonav" building where the characters break into a hilarious sendup of 1950s advertising speak. Kelly's language is full of puns, wordplay, and complex cultural references. As one example, the "Kenesaw Mountain Somebody", who the characters think might have been czar in 1923, refers to Kenesaw Mountain Landis, first Commissioner of Baseball, who ruled the sport like a czar. (In 1923, nobody was czar, naturally, as another bit player points out, only to be seriously misunderstood.) This may not be your standard historical source, but as Albert Alligator says in the middle of this story, "well, as sausages they make perty good cigars."

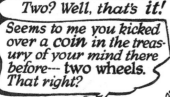

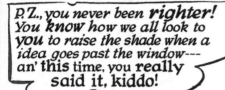

From: Kelly, Walt, *The Pogo peek-a-book* (New York: Simon and Schuster, 1955), n.p.

QUESTIONS:

1. According to Kelly's satire, what is the Cold War about? What does he portray as the key flaws of the Soviet system? What does he think is wrong with the American capitalist system? Which set of flaws is worse?
2. How does Kelly manage to make difficult issues entertaining?

VIETNAM

25.4a: *Vietnamese Declaration of Independence* (Ho Chi Minh, 1945)

Ho Chi Minh (1890–1969) led the Democratic Republic of Vietnam (North Vietnam) in its war of liberation against France and the subsequent war against the United States that ended with the unification of North and South Vietnam. The son of a Confucian bureaucrat in the French Vietnamese government, Ho left Vietnam in 1911 to pursue further education in France. This became a long series of travels and work, often as a waiter or other restaurant work, in the United States, the United Kingdom, France, the Soviet Union, and China. Along the way, he became a communist. He returned to Vietnam in 1941 to lead Vietnamese resistance against both Vichy French and Japanese occupation forces. At the end of World War II he issued the Declaration reproduced here and appealed to President Truman repeatedly for recognition and support. Receiving no reply, he turned in 1950 to the Soviet Union and Mao's China for support, which he received. He died in 1969 of heart failure, with war against the United States still going on.

"All men are created equal. They are endowed by their Creator with certain inalienable rights; among these are Life, Liberty, and the pursuit of Happiness."

This immortal statement was made in the Declaration of Independence of the United States of America in *1776*. In a broader sense, this means: All the peoples on the earth are equal from birth, all the peoples have a right to live, to be happy and free.

The Declaration of the French Revolution made in *1791* on the Rights of Man and the Citizen also states: "All men are born free and with equal rights, and must always remain free and have equal rights."

Those are undeniable truths.

Nevertheless, for more than eighty years, the French imperialists, abusing the standard of Liberty, Equality, and Fraternity, have violated our Fatherland and oppressed our fellow-citizens. They have acted contrary to the ideals of humanity and justice.

In the field of politics, they have deprived our people of every democratic liberty.

They have enforced inhuman laws; they have set up three distinct political regimes in the North, the Center, and the South of Vietnam in order to wreck our national unity and prevent our people from being united.

They have built more prisons than schools. They have mercilessly slain our patriots; they have drowned our uprisings in rivers of blood.

They have fettered public opinion; they have practiced obscurantism against our people.

To weaken our race they have forced us to use opium and alcohol.

In the field of economics, they have fleeced us to the backbone, impoverished our people, and devastated our land.

They have robbed us of our rice fields, our mines, our forests, and our raw materials. They have monopolized the issuing of banknotes and the export trade.

They have invented numerous unjustifiable taxes and reduced our people, especially our peasantry, to a state of extreme poverty.

They have hampered the prospering of our national bourgeoisie; they have mercilessly exploited our workers.

In the autumn of 1940, when the Japanese Fascists violated Indochina's territory to establish new bases in their fight against the Allies, the French imperialists went down on their bended knees and handed over our country to them.

Thus, from that date, our people were subjected to the double yoke of the French and the Japanese. Their sufferings and miseries increased. The result was that from the end of last year to the beginning of this year, from Quang Tri province to the North of Vietnam, more than two million of our fellow citizens died from starvation. On March 9, the French troops were disarmed by the Japanese. The French colonialists either fled or surrendered showing that not only were they incapable of "protecting" us, but that, in the span of five years, they had twice sold our country to the Japanese.

On several occasions before March 9, the Vietminh League urged the French to ally themselves with it against the Japanese. Instead of agreeing to this proposal, the French colonialists so intensified their terrorist activities against the Vietminh members that before fleeing they massacred a great number of our political prisoners detained at Yen Bay and Caobang.

Notwithstanding all this, our fellow-citizens have always manifested toward the French a tolerant and humane attitude. Even after the Japanese putsch of March 1945, the Vietminh League helped many Frenchmen to cross the frontier, rescued some of them from Japanese jails, and protected French lives and property.

From the autumn of 1940, our country had in fact ceased to be a French colony and had become a Japanese possession.

After the Japanese had surrendered to the Allies, our whole people rose to regain our national sovereignty and to found the Democratic Republic of Vietnam.

The truth is that we have wrested our independence from the Japanese and not from the French.

The French have fled, the Japanese have capitulated, Emperor Bao Dai has abdicated. Our people have broken the chains which for nearly a century have fettered them and have won independence for the Fatherland. Our people at the same time have overthrown the monarchic regime that has reigned supreme for dozens of centuries. In its place has been established the present Democratic Republic.

For these reasons, we, members of the Provisional Government, representing the whole Vietnamese people, declare that from now on we break off all relations of a colonial character with France; we repeal all the international obligation that France has so far subscribed to on behalf of Vietnam and we abolish all the special rights the French have unlawfully acquired in our Fatherland.

The whole Vietnamese people, animated by a common purpose, are determined to fight to the bitter end against any attempt by the French colonialists to reconquer their country.

We are convinced that the Allied nations, which at Tehran and San Francisco have acknowledged the principles of self-determination and equality of nations, will not refuse to acknowledge the independence of Vietnam.

A people who have courageously opposed French domination for more than eight years, a people who have fought side by side with the Allies against the Fascists during these last years, such a people must be free and independent.

For these reasons, we, members of the Provisional Government of the Democratic Republic of Vietnam, solemnly declare to the world that Vietnam has the right to be a free and independent country-and in fact is so already. The entire Vietnamese people are determined to mobilize all their physical and mental strength, to sacrifice their lives and property in order to safeguard their independence and liberty.

From: Minh, Ho Chi, "Declaration of Independence of the Democratic Republic of Vietnam", in *Selected Writings* (Hanoi: Foreign Languages Publishing House, 1977), pp. 53–56.

QUESTIONS:

1. Who is Ho Chi Minh addressing in this declaration? What screen image does he appeal to?
2. Vietnam in the colonial era was known as "French Indo-China", a name that contains not a single reference to Vietnam. How does this document project an image of Vietnamese identity?

25.4b: *People's War* (Vo Nguyen Giap, 1962)

Vo Nguyen Giap (1911–2013) was a general of the Vietnam People's Army. He was a protégé of Ho Chi Minh and was the second in command behind Ho in North Vietnam's war with the United States that ended with the reunification of North and South Vietnam in 1975. His first combat experience was at Nha Trang against the French in 1946, and he knew the military strengths of his enemies well. He made this knowledge available to other anticolonialist movements when he published his insights into how a small, underdeveloped country could fight a major western military power in his 1962 book *People's war, People's Army: the Viet Công insurrection manual for underdeveloped countries*. He greatly admired the advice of the Chinese military manual *Sunzi* and of Napoleon I. Vo Nguyen Giap's advice is excerpted below.

The Vietnamese people's war of liberation was, a just war, aiming to win back the independence and unity of the country, to bring land to our peasants and guarantee them the right to it, and to defend the achievements of the August Revolution. That is why it was first and foremost a people's war. To educate, mobilize, organize and arm the whole people in order that they might take part in the Resistance was a crucial question.

The enemy of the Vietnamese nation was aggressive imperialism, which had to be overthrown. But the latter having long since joined up with the feudal landlords, the anti-imperialist struggle could definitely not be separated from anti-feudal action. On the other hand, in a backward colonial country such as ours where the peasants make up the majority of the population, a people's war is essentially a peasant's war under the leadership of the working class. Owing to this fact, a general mobilization of the whole people is neither more nor less than the mobilization of the rural masses. The problem of land is of decisive importance. From an exhaustive analysis, the Vietnamese people's war of liberation was essentially a people's national democratic revolution carried out under armed form and had twofold fundamental task: the overthrowing of imperialism and the defeat of the feudal landlord class, the anti-imperialist struggle being the primary task.

A backward colonial country which had only just risen up to proclaim its independence and install people's power, Viet Nam only recently possessed armed forces, equipped with still very mediocre arms and having no combat experience. Her enemy, on the other hand, was an imperialist power which has retained a fairly considerable economic and military potentiality despite the recent German occupation and benefited, furthermore, from the active support of the United States. The balance of forces decidedly showed up our weaknesses against the enemy's power. The Vietnamese people's war of liberation had, therefore, to be a hard and long-lasting war in order to succeed in creating conditions for victory. All the conceptions born of impatience and aimed at obtaining speedy victory could only be gross errors. It was necessary to firmly grasp the strategy of a long-term resistance, and to exalt the will to be self-supporting in order to maintain and gradually augment our forces, while nibbling at and progressively destroying those of the enemy; it was necessary to accumulate thousands of small victories to turn them into a great success, thus gradually altering the balance of forces, in transforming our weakness into power and carrying off final victory.

At an early stage, our Party was able to discern the characteristics of this war: a people's war and a long-lasting war, and it was by proceeding from these premises that, during the whole of hostilities and in particularly difficult conditions, the Party solved all the problems of the Resistance. This judicious leadership by the Party led us to victory.

From the point of view of directing operations, our strategy and tactics had to be those of a people's war and of a long-term resistance.

Our strategy was, as we have stressed, to wage a long-lasting battle. A war of this nature in general entails several phases; in principle, starting from a stage of contention, it goes through a period of equilibrium before arriving at a general counter-offensive. In effect, the way in which it is carried on can be more subtle and more complex, depending on the particular conditions obtaining on both sides during the course of operations. Only a long-term war could enable us to utilize to the maximum our political trump cards, to overcome our material handicap and to transform our weakness into strength. To maintain and increase our forces, was the principle to which we adhered, contenting ourselves with attacking when success was certain, refusing to give battle likely to incur losses to us or to engage in hazardous actions. We had to apply the slogan: to build up our strength during the actual course of fighting.

The forms of fighting had to be completely adapted that is, to raise the fighting spirit to the maximum and rely on heroism of our troops to overcome the enemy's material superiority. In the main, especially at the outset of the war, we had recourse to guerrilla fighting. In the Vietnamese theatre of operations, this method carried off great victories: it could be used in the mountains as well as in the delta, it could be waged with good or mediocre material and even without arms, and was to enable us eventually to equip ourselves at the cost of the enemy. Wherever the Expeditionary Corps came, the entire population took part in the fighting; every commune had its fortified village, every district had its regional troops fighting under the command of the local branches of the Party and the people's administration, in liaison with the regular forces in order to wear down and annihilate the enemy forces.

Thereafter, with the development of our forces, guerrilla warfare changed into a mobile warfare—a form of mobile warfare still strongly marked by guerrilla warfare—which would afterwards become the essential form of operations on the main front, the northern front. In this process of development of guerrilla warfare and of accentuation of the mobile warfare, our people's army constantly grew and passed from the stage of combats involving a section or company, to fairly large-scale campaigns bringing into action several divisions. Gradually, its equipment improved, mainly by the seizure of arms from the enemy—the material of the French and American imperialists.

From the military point of view, *the Vietnamese people's war of liberation proved that an insufficiently equipped people's army, but an army fighting for a just cause, can, with appropriate strategy and tactics, combine the conditions needed to conquer a modern army of aggressive imperialism.* [italics in original]

From: Võ Nguyên Giáp, *People's war, People's Army: the Viet Công insurrection manual for underdeveloped countries* (New York: Praeger, 1962), pp. 27–30.

QUESTIONS:

1. How do the goals and language of Giap's statement differ from Minh's Declaration?
2. What strengths and weaknesses in Vietnam's military resources does Giap outline? How does his plan for a "people's war" take account of them?

CHAPTER 26

The Modern Global Network:
Environment and Economy since 1970

INTRODUCTION

This chapter presents sources that illustrate aspects of the global network in the world since 1970. These include the worldwide environmental impact of modern industrial activity, evidence of the continuing unevenness of economic development, and reactions to the capitalist culture of a global network dominated by corporations. They show that the tense intersection between networks and hierarchies, a theme of world history since the rise of complex Agrarian societies, remains tense even as the nature of the intersection changes.

26.1: *Speech on the 25th Anniversary of Earth Day* (Gaylord Nelson, 1995)

Gaylord Nelson (1916–2005) was a Democratic United States senator from Wisconsin who proclaimed the first Earth Day on April 22, 1970. Nelson, drawing on and working with a wide range of environmental activists, conceived of Earth Day as a day for teach-ins and peaceful gatherings to raise awareness of environmental issues. It worked brilliantly, as tens of thousands of students from grade schools through colleges participated. The event became annual and in the 1980s spread globally. Today it is celebrated in 192 countries worldwide and over one billion people participate each year, making it the largest secular celebration in the world. On the twenty-fifth anniversary of Earth Day, Nelson delivered the speech excerpted here, reviewing the successes and looking forward to the future of environmentalism.

WHERE DO WE GO FROM HERE?

by

GAYLORD NELSON, FOUNDER OF EARTH DAY

Twenty five years ago that remarkable phenomenon Earth Day burst onto the political scene. In October 1993 American Heritage magazine reflected on that event in these words:

". . . on April 22, 1970, Earth Day was held, one of the most remarkable happenings in the history of democracy. Fully 10 percent of the population of the country, twenty million people, demonstrated their support for redeeming the American environment. . . . American politics and public policy would never be the same again."

The idea of Earth Day was a national demonstration of environmental concern big enough to shake up the political establishment-get its attention, get some action, force the environmental issue onto the political agenda of national priorities. That was the goal. Magically it worked, thanks to the spontaneous response of millions of concerned Americans. Suddenly the environment became a national political priority by public demand. That was the vital first step. At last the political establishment woke up and began the process of responding to public concerns about the deteriorating condition of the environment.

Now, after twenty five years of debating, researching, learning, there has evolved a pretty general understanding that the state of the environment is the key factor in determining our way of life and the quality of it.

The history of man has been influenced by many revolutions but none more important than the Agricultural Revolution followed by the Industrial Revolution. We are now at the threshold of a third great revolution, the transition to a sustainable society . . . which is described as "one that meets the needs of the present without compromising the ability of future generations to meet their own needs."

There is a profound moral question that revolves around the issue of how we treat the life-giving resources of the planet. Do we who are here today owe anything to future generations of people and other living things? If our answer is in the negative, as current and past practices would seem to indicate, then we are squarely on course travelling down the road to massive environmental degradation. If, however, we have a moral obligation to the future then we must move expeditiously to preserve all environmental options for those who will follow.

The problem is this. Until recently, we haven't recognized the existence of any environmental limits or problems that might impose a moral duty on this generation to preserve opportunities and choices for future generations. From the time our ancestors landed on these shores, we have lived by the belief that the gifts of nature were inexhaustible. So, there was no need to worry about the future.

Now that we know there are finite limits to the bounty of the land, we also must know we have a moral obligation to pass that bounty on to future generations. That is what sustainability is all about.

The most encouraging phenomenon evolving in the big and real world of politics and ecology is the growing recognition that forging and maintaining a sustainable society is the challenge and the ultimate goal for this and all generations to come.

At this point in history, no nation has managed, either by design or accident, to evolve into a sustainable society. We are all pursuing a self destructive course of fueling our economies by consuming our capital—that is to say, by degrading and depleting our resource base—and counting it on the income side of the ledger. That, obviously, is not a sustainable situation over the long term.

The bottom line question is obvious and critical. Can we as a nation evolve into a sustainable society during the next four or five decades? That is to say, a sustainable society which we would view with approval. The answer is yes—if we have strong political leadership and the support of a society imbued with a guiding environmental ethic. The evolution of such an ethic within our culture is happening now at an accelerating pace.

Increasingly, we have come to understand that the wealth of the nation is its air, water, soil, forests, minerals, rivers, lakes, oceans, scenic beauty, wildlife habitats and biodiversity. Take this resource base away and all that is left is a wasteland.

The Worldwatch Institute states the same case in another way.

"Three biological systems—croplands. forests, and grasslands—support the world economy. Except for fossil fuels and minerals, they supply all the raw materials for industry; except for seafood, they provide all our food.

In short, that's all there is. That's the whole economy. That's where all the economic activity and all the jobs come from. These biological systems contain the sustaining wealth of the world. All around the planet these systems are under varying degrees of stress and degradation in almost all places including the United States. As we continue to degrade them we are consuming our capital. And, in the process, we erode living standards and compromise the quality of our habitat. It is a dangerous and slippery slope.

On December 5, 1962, Dean Achison, in a speech at West Point, observed that "Britain has lost an empire and has not yet found a goal." That describes the current American dilemma. The Soviet superpower has disintegrated, the Communist menace has dissolved and the Cold War is over. Still, the United States has yet to find a unifying theme, a moral cause to replace it. This despite the fact that a monumental moral cause is near at hand and a far more serious challenge than the Cold War ever was. It's the war against the planet. How do we bring it to an end and where do we start? It must start in the United States. We cannot and should not wait for the rest of the world.

From: http://www.nelsonearthday.net/collection/tradition-25th-speech.htm.

QUESTIONS:

1. How and why does Nelson redefine "economy"?
2. Why does Nelson compare the challenge of saving the environment to the Cold War?

26.2: *Thinking Past Ourselves* (Bill McKibben, 2007)

Bill McKibben (1960–) is an American writer, environmentalist, and political activist who is best known for his writings on global warming and climate change. The article presented here lays out his views in concise form. Starting with his 1989 book *The End of Nature,* McKibben has been influential in bringing scientific findings about global warming to the attention of the general public and in leading rallies, often organized via his online organizations such as 350.org, to call for changes to address the problem. It should be noted that there is no serious scientific *debate* about global warming: the overwhelming consensus is that human-generated greenhouse emissions are making the planet warmer. Debate is about how to limit warming and what to do about its effects.

LET ME DESCRIBE AN EXPERIMENT I PERFORMED once— not a very scientific experiment, but an extremely laborious one. I found what in 1990 was the largest cable television system on Earth, in Fairfax, Virginia. It had 100 channels, and I found 100 volunteers to tape for me everything that came across each of those channels for a 24-hour period. They shipped me a cardboard box with 2,400 hours of VHS tape, a day in the life of the information age, pre-internet. So, I went to Sears, bought a recliner, and settled in and watched, about eight hours a day for a year.

The results of that experiment became a book, *The Age of Missing Information.* It was filled with my sense of how the world would look to individuals if the TV were the main window through which they apprehended it (which, for a great many people, it is; we're the first generations to live a mostly mediated life, our experience predominantly prechewed). I wrote about how it affects our sense of time, sufficiency, history, and war. But if you had to boil down everything that came through that coaxial cable into a single idea, it would be this: *You are at the center of everything, you sitting there*

*on the couch with the remote control in your hand.
You're the heaviest object in the known universe, and
everything should orbit around you.* Advertisers pander
and cajole; entertainers truckle and flatter. Certainly,
there is much mention on television of human shortcomings—but always with a product that can cure
the problem. Basically, this Bud's for you.

It's the same message that comes from every
organ of our consumer culture. The suburb, for instance, the institution to which we've devoted the
largest share of our economy for half a century,
speaks by its very design to our isolation. In recent
years, more and more upper-end houses come with
a new design feature: dual master bedrooms. The
husband snores, the wife steals the covers, and our
solution is 900 square feet more house—and one
final layer of hyperindividualism. We've gotten so
used to the idea that our own individual selves
should be the center of our lives that we've taken to
calling it "human nature."

Hence, it is easy to fear that we simply will not
be able to rise to the challenge presented by our
environmental dilemmas, which, after all, require
us to think past ourselves. If we were serious about
controlling carbon dioxide in the atmosphere, for
instance, the first thing we would do is make carbon
more expensive, either by directly taxing fossil fuel
or by implementing some form of cap-and-trade
system that would impose a less obvious tax. But
that would require foregoing some consumption
right now—we'd have less money to spend on ourselves. In some way, we'd be sending that cash into
the future, making the investment that would allow
the future to prosper at the slight expense of the
present. That kind of sacrifice, some maintain,
simply goes against the "human nature" I've described. As the late philosopher Norman Care once
put it, "Certain familiar sorts of motivation are not
available to support policies demanding serious
sacrifice for the sake of future generations, and we
may well be discouraged by the further apparent
fact that the cultivation of a form of motivation
directly supportive of such policies might require

something close to an overhaul of main elements in
the makeup of our society which influence the
moral psychology of citizens." In other words,
we're stuck in the realm of *what's in it for me?,* and
getting out of that realm would require some kind
of soul transplant. I'm not an optimist by tempera-
ment. (I wrote the first book for a general audience
on global warming, and called it, cheerfully, *The
End of Nature.*) But on this question of human
nature, it seems to me quite possible that we've
mistaken our particular culture for the whole of
humanity and, in so doing, have limited our sense
of the possibilities for real change.

Anthropological evidence indicates that for
almost all of human civilization, most people in
most cultures have had something other than their
own selves close to the center of their identity. That
is, they understood themselves much more strongly
in relation to something else than we do: their tribe
or community, their God, the natural world around
them. (A Native American tenet concerning the
stewardship of land was, "In our every deliberation, we should consider the impact of our decisions on the next seven generations.") And this
sense of identity was useful in that it let them more
easily place limits on their behavior; that is, if you
really understand yourself to be a part of a community, then there are things you won't do because
they harm that community. We've spent 500 years
doing away with those limits in the Western
world—that's been the central theme of our ongo-
ing project of "liberation," and much of it has been
good and useful. We've developed a strong sense of
personhood, mobility, and freedom of thought and
action; no one expects us to live in the same spot as
our parents or follow the same career.

But in the United States in recent decades,
we've gone further: As the most fully realized consumer society in history, we've defined ourselves
almost entirely as individuals, without any limits on
what we should want. Any call to group action is
dismissed as interfering with economic growth, with
our personal quest for more. Even in emergencies,

we're urged to keep thinking of ourselves as atomized individuals. In the wake of 9/11, for instance, there was a bit of flag-waving and fellow-feeling, but President George W. Bush's only real request was that we resume normal life, which he defined as returning to shopping.

But was that because a particular (powerful and largely nonpartisan) ideology has gained great sway in our society, or was it because of human nature? That's a key question, so perform this thought experiment. Say that President Bush, on September 12, 2001, had spoken to us from the Oval Office and said: "Job No. 1 is to catch Osama bin Laden. But job No. 2 is to make sure we're never in this situation again—that no future generation of Americans ever again is involved in the tortuous politics of places we don't understand simply because we need the oil beneath their sand. Beginning tomorrow, there will be a $1 tax on every gallon of gasoline pumped in the United States, and that money will be used to make sure every American is driving a plug-in hybrid car by the time I leave office." Or say he'd taken the occasion of the horror that we felt in the wake of Hurricane Katrina to say: "Job No. 1 is to succor the victims of this tragedy. But job No. 2 is to try to lower the odds that these superstorms will become commonplace for our descendants. From now on, every ton of coal burned to power our lives will come with enough of a tax to make sure that when I leave office, there will be 10 million solar panels on the roofs of our houses."

My guess is that there remains in us enough of the other facets of human nature—those predilections for community, for moral responsibility—that we would have responded. Not all of us: Peabody Coal and General Motors would have raised holy hell because their identities truly are only about the quarter ahead. But actual people are more complex than the model of *homo economicus* driven by utility-maximizing single-mindedness that economists have proffered in recent decades.

Where's my evidence? This is not an area subject to easy empirical proofs, but take this anecdote

as one small sign: Earlier this year, a few of us decided that there wasn't enough political protest about climate change—that though polls showed that most Americans knew about the problem, little action was being taken in Washington because politicians perceived scant pressure. So we—and in this case "we" means me and six kids who had just graduated from Middlebury College—launched a website on January 10, 2007. We asked people to organize rallies in their communities for April 14, rallies demanding that Congress pledge to cut carbon emissions 80 percent by 2050. That is, we were demanding that our leaders spend our money and our attention as a nation in the next half century trying to accomplish the energy transformation that science now tells us is our only hope for preventing completely catastrophic changes in Earth's condition. (James Hansen of NASA, our foremost climatologist, says his computer modeling gives us less than a decade to reverse the flow of carbon dioxide into the atmosphere before we're committed to the melting of the Greenland and West Antarctic ice sheets and, his words, "a completely different planet.")

We began this effort, which we called Stepitup07.org, with neither any money nor any organization—we didn't even have a mailing list. As a result, our expectations were low; we hoped we might organize 100 demonstrations, but that sounded grandiose, so we didn't tell anyone. Instead, twelve weeks later, on April 14, there were 1,400 demonstrations in all 50 states, one of the biggest days of grassroots environmental protest since the first Earth Day in 1970. It wasn't because of any organizational genius on our part—it was because all over the United States, people were in despair about climate change and looking for some kind of signal about what to do with that despair. Given a lead, they ran with it: Scuba divers organized underwater demonstrations off the endangered coral reefs of Key West, and skiers put together mass descents of the glaciated western slopes that won't be glaciated in a few decades' time. In Lower Manhattan, thousands of people in blue shirts formed a "sea of people" around the Battery showing where the new tide line would fall; in Jacksonville, Florida, they winched a yacht 20 feet into the air to show where the sea level was headed. On beaches and mountaintops, on church steps and in public parks, people came together and made enough noise that, in combination with new scientific reports and new Supreme Court rulings, started to put real pressure on the system. Within weeks, the leading Democratic presidential contenders had all endorsed carbon emission cuts of 80 percent by 2050, and legislation to that end was suddenly on a fast track in the House and Senate.

Large number of Americans, in other words, were clearly willing to put their own lives on hold for weeks to organize rallies and to advocate policies that would cost them in the short run; their action were impressive enough that seasoned politicians were willing to start endorsing similar ideas, albeit less vigorously. Put differently, it is possible to envision a real effort for the future, even here in the United States. Much of the rest of the world has already taken similar steps: Europe has taxed energy highly for years, and as a result, they already use half as much per capita as we do. Yet they've adopted strong national plans to trim that usage further still even though they're starting to cut into muscle instead of fat. Even in China, where the stark and immediate pressures of poverty make it harder to think very far into the future, officials are adopting innovative policies: Their automobile mileage standards, for instance, are higher than ours.

There's no question that reducing carbon emissions will be a difficult task, in both engineering and political terms. The vested interests tied to the status quo in this country are enormous, and the momentum of economic development in much of the rest of the world is daunting. But to dismiss the possibility out of hand because human nature doesn't allow it is as useless as it is wrong. We will see what human nature is made of in the next couple of decades—we'll see, in some sense, whether higher intelligence and consciousness turn out to be adaptive or destructive. It's very clear that foresight is not our collective strength, and so we've waited until the last possible moment to act has not been decided—not by our evolutionary heritage It's still an open and fascinating problem.

From: McKibben, Bill, "Thinking Past Ourselves," *Bulletin Of The Atomic Scientists* 63, no. 6 (2007): 28–31.

QUESTIONS:

1. What is the connection for McKibben between personal identity and climate change? How do capitalism and individualism shape identity in our culture?
2. What solutions does McKibben propose to address climate change? How do these solutions relate to his view of human nature?

26.3:   *World Development Indicators* (World Bank)

The World Bank is a capitalist international financial institution created by the Bretton Woods Conference in 1944. Its official goal is to reduce poverty, and so most of its lending goes to developing countries. The loans are primarily aimed at economic development connected with trade and foreign investment, but its lending gives it influence over many developing countries' financial policies. As part of its mission it tracks data about economic activity, environmental quality, and education around the world. The data presented here comes from the World Bank's World Development Indicators report for 2013.

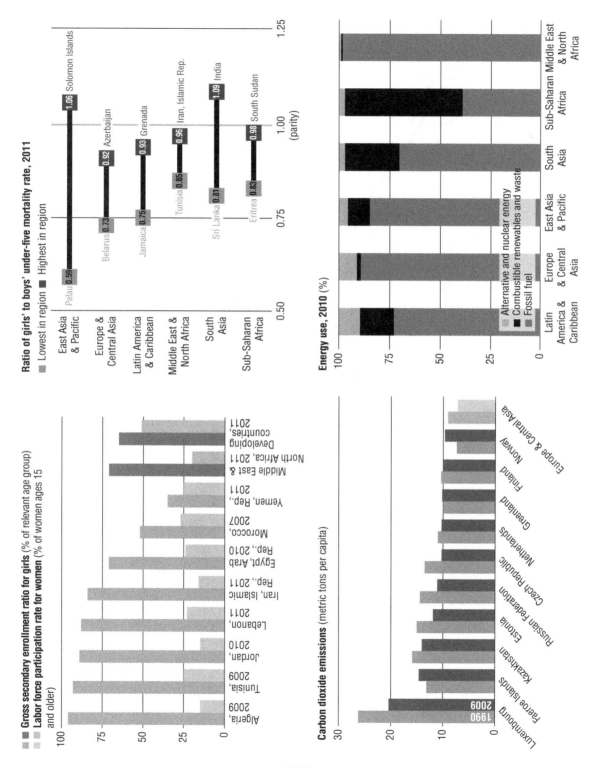

Gross secondary enrollment ratio for girls (% of relevant age group)
Labor force participation rate for women (% of women ages 15 and older)

Ratio of girls' to boys' under-five mortality rate, 2011

■ Lowest in region ■ Highest in region

East Asia & Pacific	Palau 0.59	Solomon Islands 1.06	
Europe & Central Asia	Belarus 0.73	Azerbaijan 0.92	
Latin America & Caribbean	Jamaica 0.75	Grenada 0.93	
Middle East & North Africa	Tunisia 0.85	Iran, Islamic Rep. 0.96	
South Asia	Sri Lanka 0.81	India 1.09	
Sub-Saharan Africa	Eritrea 0.83	South Sudan 0.98	

0.50   0.75   1.00 (parity)   1.25

Energy use, 2010 (%)

Alternative and nuclear energy
Combustible renewables and waste
Fossil fuel

Latin America & Caribbean   Europe & Central Asia   East Asia & Pacific   South Asia   Sub-Saharan Africa   Middle East & North Africa

Carbon dioxide emissions (metric tons per capita)

1990   2009

Luxembourg   Faeroe Islands   Kazakhstan   Estonia   Russian Federation   Czech Republic   Netherlands   Greenland   Finland   Norway   Europe & Central Asia

213

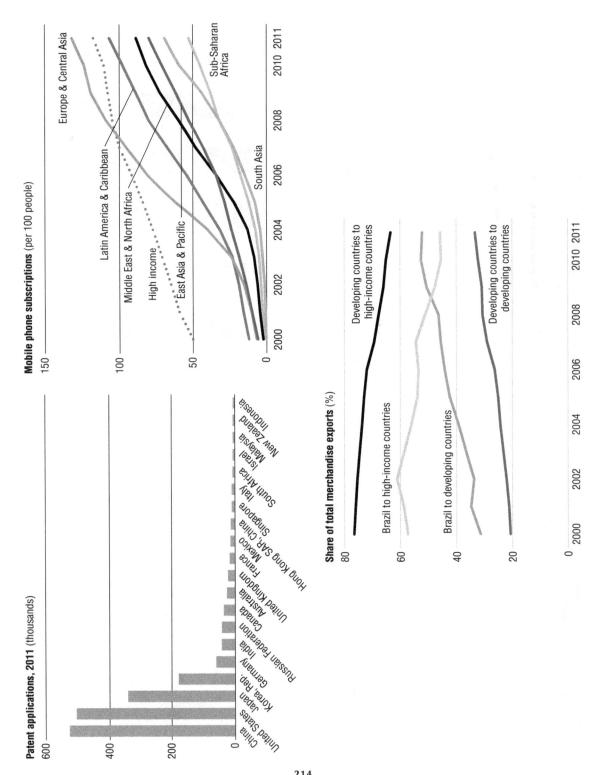

Mobile phone subscriptions (per 100 people)

Europe & Central Asia

Latin America & Caribbean

Middle East & North Africa

High income

East Asia & Pacific

Sub-Saharan Africa

South Asia

Patent applications, 2011 (thousands)

China
United States
Japan
Korea, Rep.
Germany
India
Russian Federation
Canada
Australia
United Kingdom
France
Mexico
Hong Kong SAR, China
Singapore
Italy
South Africa
Israel
Malaysia
New Zealand
Indonesia

Share of total merchandise exports (%)

Developing countries to
high-income countries

Brazil to high-income countries

Brazil to developing countries

Developing countries to
developing countries

214

QUESTIONS:

1. What do these charts tell us about the connections between economic development, education, and environmental quality?
2. What do these connections tell us about the operations of the modern global network?

26.4: *Jennifer Government* (Max Barry, 2003)

Max Barry (1973–) is an Australian author. His 2003 novel *Jennifer Government* is a funny satirical look at an unspecified near-future world in which the United States and the large part of the world it has taken over are controlled by private corporations, with public government functions reduced to a very bare minimum. The resulting sense that people live in and as part of a world of brand naming and advertising is heightened by the fact that in the novel's world, individual's last names are the names of their employers—or, in the case of children, of the corporations that sponsor the privatized schools they attend. The opening of the novel excerpted here gives you the flavor, but the whole book is well worth reading. Barry also created an online game, *NationStates,* based on the world of *Jennifer Government.*

1 NIKE

Hack first heard about Jennifer Government at the water-cooler. He was only there because the one on his floor was out; Legal was going to come down on Nature's Springs like a ton of shit, you could bet on that. Hack was a Merchandise Distribution Officer. This meant when Nike made up a bunch of posters, or caps, or beach towels, Hack had to send them to the right place. Also, if someone called up complaining about missing posters, or caps, or beach towels, Hack had to take the call. It wasn't as exciting as it used to be.

"It's a *calamity,*" a man at the watercooler said. "Four days away from launch and Jennifer Government's all over my ass."

"Jee-sus," his companion said. "That's gotta suck."

"It means we have to move fast." He looked at Hack, who was filling his cup. "Hi there."

Hack looked up. They were smiling at him as if he was an equal—but of course, Hack was on the wrong floor. They didn't know he was just a Merc Officer. "Hi."

"Haven't seen you around before," the *calamity* guy said. "You new?"

"No. I work in Merc."

"Oh." His nose wrinkled.

"Our cooler's out," Hack said. He turned away quickly.

"Hey, wait up," the suit said. "You ever do any marketing work?"

"Uh," he said, not sure if this was a joke. "No."

The suits looked at each other. The *calamity* guy shrugged. Then they stuck out their hands. "I'm John Nike, Guerrilla Marketing Operative, New Products."

"And I'm John Nike, Guerrilla Marketing Vice-President, New Products," the other suit said.

"Hack Nike," Hack said, shaking.

"Hack, I'm empowered to make midrange labor-contracting decisions," Vice-President John said. "You interested in some work?"

"Some . . ." He felt his throat thicken. "Marketing work?" "On a case-by-case basis, of course," the other John said. Hack started to cry.

"There," a John said, handing him a handkerchief. "You feel better?"

Hack nodded, shamed. "I'm sorry."

"Hey, don't worry about it," Vice-President John said. "Career change can be very stressful. I read that somewhere."

"Here's the paperwork." The other John handed him a pen and a sheaf of papers. The first page said CONTRACT TO PERFORM SERVICE, and the others were in type too small to read.

Hack hesitated. "You want me to sign this now?"

"It's nothing to worry about. Just the usual noncompetes and nondisclosure agreements."

"Yeah, but . . ." Companies were getting a lot tougher on labor contracts these days; Hack had heard stories. At Adidas, if you quit your job and your replacement wasn't as competent, they sued you for lost profits.

"Hack, we need someone who can make snap decisions. A fast mover."

"Someone who can get things done. With a minimum of fucking around."

"If that's not your style, well . . . let's forget we spoke. No harm done. You stick to Merchandising." Vice-President John reached for the contract.

"I can sign it now," Hack said, tightening his grip.

"It's totally up to you," the other John said. He took the chair beside Hack, crossed his legs, and rested his hands at the juncture, smiling. Both Johns had good smiles, Hack noticed. He guessed everyone in marketing did. They had pretty similar faces, too. Just at the bottom there."

Hack signed.

"Also there," the other John said. "And on the next page . . . and one there. And there."

"Glad to have you on board, Hack." Vice-President John took the contract, opened a drawer, and dropped it inside. "Now. What do you know about Nike Mercurys?"

Hack blinked. "They're our latest product. I haven't actually seen a pair, but . . . I heard they're great."

The Johns smiled. "We started selling Mercurys six months ago. You know how many pairs we've shifted since then?"

Hack shook his head. They cost thousands of dollars a pair, but that wouldn't stop people from buying them. They were the hottest sneakers in the world. "A million?"

"Two hundred."

"Two hundred million?"

"No. Two hundred pairs."

John here," the other John said, "pioneered the concept of marketing by refusing to sell any products. It drives the market *insane.*"

'And now it's time to cash in. On Friday we're gonna dump four hundred thousand pairs on the market at two and a half grand each."

"Which, since they cost us—what was it?"

"Eighty-five."

"Since they cost us eighty-five cents to manufacture, gives us a gross margin of around one billion dollars." He looked at Vice-President John. "It's a brilliant campaign."

"It's really just common sense," John said. "But here's the thing, Hack: if people realize every mall in the country's got Mercurys, we'll lose all that prestige we've worked so hard to build. Am I right?"

"Yeah." Hack hoped he sounded confident. He didn't really understand marketing.

"So you know what we're going to do?"

He shook his head.

"We're going to shoot them," Vice-President John said. "We're going to kill anyone who buys a pair."

Silence. "What?" Hack said.

The other John said, "Well, not everyone, obviously. We figure we only have to plug . . . what did we decide? Five?"

"Ten," Vice-President John said. "To be safe."

"Right. We take out ten customers, make it look like ghetto kids, and we've got street cred coming out our asses. I bet we shift our inventory within twenty-four hours."

"I remember when you could always rely on those little street kids to pop a few people for the latest Nikes," Vice-President John said. "Now people get mugged for Reeboks, for Adidas—for *generics*, for Christ's sake."

"The ghettos have no fashion sense anymore," the other John said. "I swear, they'll wear anything."

"It's a disgrace. Anyway, Hack, I think you get the point. This is a groundbreaking campaign."

"Talk about edgy," the other John said. "This *defines* edgy."

"Um . . ." Hack said. He swallowed. "Isn't this kind of . . . illegal?"

"He wants to know if it's illegal," the other John said, amused. "You're a funny guy, Hack. Yes, it's illegal, killing people without their consent, that's very illegal."

Vice-President John said, "But the question is: what does it cost? Even if we get found out, we burn a few million on legal fees, we get fined a few million more . . . bottom-line, we're still way out in front."

Hack had a question he very much didn't want to ask. "So . . . this contract . . . what does it say I'll do?"

The John beside him folded his hands. "Well, Hack, we've explained our business plan. What we want you to do is . . ."

"Execute it," Vice-President John said.

2   MCDONALD'S

Until she stood in front of them, Hayley didn't realize how many of her classmates were blond. It was like a beach out there. She'd missed the trend. Hayley would have to hotfoot it to a hairdresser after school.

"When you're ready," the teacher said.

She looked at her note cards and took a breath. "Why I Love America, by Hayley McDonald's. America is the greatest group of countries in the world because we have freedom. In countries like France, where the Government isn't privatized, they still have to pay tax and do whatever the Government says, which would really suck. In USA countries, we respect individual rights and let people do whatever they want."

The teacher jotted something in his folder. McDonald's sponsored schools were cheap like that: at Pepsi schools, everyone had notebook computers. Also their uniforms were much better. It was so hard to be cool with the Golden Arches on your back.

"Before USA countries abolished tax, if you didn't have a job, the Government took money from working people and gave it to you. So, like, the more useless you were, the more money you got." No response from her classmates. Even the teacher didn't smile. Hayley was surprised: she'd thought that one was a crack-up.

"But now America has all the best companies and all the money because everyone works and the Government can't spend money on stupid things like advertising and elections and making new laws. They just stop people stealing or hurting each other and everything else is taken care of by the private sector, which everyone knows is more efficient." She looked at her notes: yep, that was it. "Finally I would like to say that America is the greatest group of countries in the world and I am proud to live in the Australian Territories of the USA!"

A smattering of applause. It was the eighth talk this period: she guessed it was getting harder to work up enthusiasm for capitalizm. Hayley headed for her seat.

"Hold it," the teacher said. "I have questions."

"Oh," Hayley said.

'Are there any positive aspects to tax?"

She relaxed: a gimme question. "Some people say tax is good because it gives money to people who don't have any. But those people must be lazy or stupid, so why should they get other people's money? Obviously the answer is no."

The teacher blinked. He made a note. That must have been an impressive answer, Hayley thought. "What about social justice?"

"What?"

"Is it fair that some people should be rich while others have nothing?"

She shifted from one foot to the other. She was just remembering: this teacher had a thing about poor people. He was always bringing them up. "Urn, yeah, it's fair. Because if I study really hard for a test and get an A and Emily doesn't and fails"—renewed interest from the class; Emily raised blond eyebrows—"then it's not fair to take some of my marks and give them to her, is it?"

The teacher frowned. Hayley felt a flash of panic. "Another thing, in non-USA countries they want everyone to be the same, so if your sister is born blind, then they blind you, too, to make it even. But how unfair is that? I would much rather be an American than a European Union . . . person." She gave the class a big smile. They clapped, much more enthusiastically than before. She added hopefully, "Is that all?"

"Yes. Thank you."

Relief! She started walking. A cute boy in the third row winked at her.

The teacher said, "Although, Hayley, they don't really blind people in non-USA countries."

Hayley stopped. "Well, that's kind of hypocritical, isn't it?"

The class cheered. The teacher opened his mouth, then shut it. Hayley took her seat. *Kick ass,* she thought. She had aced this test.

3 THE POLICE

Hack sat in traffic, biting his nails. This had not been a good day. He was beginning to think that visiting the marketing floor for a cup of water was the worst mistake he'd ever made.

He turned into a side street and parked his Toyota. It rattled angrily and let loose a puff of black smoke. Hack really needed a new car. Maybe if this job paid off, he could move out of St. Kilda.

He could get an apartment with some space, maybe some natural light—

He shook his head angrily. What was he thinking? He wasn't going to *shoot* anyone. Not even for a better apartment.

He climbed the stairs to the second floor and let himself in. Violet was sitting cross-legged on the living-room floor with her notebook computer in her lap. Violet was his girlfriend. She was the only unemployed person he had ever met, not counting homeless people who asked him for money. She was an entrepreneur. Violet was probably going to be rich one day: she was smart and determined. Sometimes Hack wasn't sure why they were together.

He dropped his briefcase and shrugged off his jacket. The table was littered with bills. Hack hadn't bargained very well in his last performance evaluation and it was really biting him now "Violet?"

"Mmm?"

"Can we talk?"

"Is it important?"

"Yes."

She frowned. Hack waited. Violet didn't like being disturbed during her work. She didn't like being disturbed at all. She was short and thin and had long brown hair, which made her look much more fragile than she was. "What's up?"

He sat on the sofa. "I did something stupid."

"Oh, Hack, not again."

Hack had missed a couple of turnoffs on the way home lately: last Tuesday he'd gotten himself onto a premium road and eaten through eleven dollars in tolls before he found an exit. "No, something really stupid."

"What happened?"

"Well, I got offered some work . . . some marketing work—" "That's great! We could really use the extra money." "—and I signed a contract without reading it."

Pause. "Oh," Violet said. "Well, it might be okay—"

"It says I have to kill people. It's some kind of promotional campaign. I have to, urn, kill ten people."

For a moment she said nothing. He hoped she wasn't going to shout at him. "I'd better look at that contract."

He dropped his head.

"You don't have a copy?"

"No."

"Oh, *Hack.*"

"I'm sorry"

Violet chewed her lip. "Well, you can't go through with it. The Government's not as pussy as people think. They'd get you for sure. But then, you don't know what the penalties in that contract are . . . I think you should go to the Police."

"Really?"

"There's a station on Chapel Street. When are you meant to . . . do it?"

"Friday."

"You should go. Right now"

"Okay. You're right." He picked up his jacket. "Thanks, Violet."

"Why does this kind of thing always happen to you, Hack?" "I don't know," he said. He felt emotional. He shut the door carefully behind him.

• • •

The station was only a few blocks away, and as it came into view he began to feel hopeful. The building was lit up in blue neon, with THE POLICE in enormous letters and a swirling light above that. If anyone could help him out of this situation, it would be someone who worked in a place like this.

The doors slid open and he walked up to the reception desk. A woman in uniform—either a real cop or a receptionist dressed in theme, Hack didn't know which—smiled. Playing over the PA system was the song from their TV ads, "Every Breath You Take."

"Good evening, how can I help you?

"I have a matter I'd like to discuss with an officer, please." "May I ask the nature of your problem?"

"Urn," he said. "I've been contracted to kill someone. Some people, actually."

The receptionist's eyebrows rose a fraction, then settled. Hack felt relieved. He didn't want to be chastised by the receptionist. "Take a seat, sir. An officer will be right with you."

Hack dropped into a soft blue chair and waited. A few minutes later, a cop came out and stopped in front of him. Hack rose.

"I'm Senior Sergeant Pearson Police," the man said. He shook Hack's hand firmly. He had a small, trim mustache but otherwise looked pretty capable. "Please accompany me."

Hack followed him down a plushly carpeted hallway to a small, professional-looking meeting room. On the wall were pictures of cops escorting trims out of buildings, in front of courthouses, and busting protestor heads outside some corporate building. As Pearson took a seat, Hack caught a glimpse of handcuffs and a pistol.

"So what's your problem?" He flipped open a notebook.

Hack told him the whole story. When he was done, Pearson was silent for a long time. Finally Hack couldn't take it anymore. "What do you think?"

Pearson pressed his fingers together. "Well, I appreciate you coming forward with this. You did the right thing. Now let me take you through your options." He closed the notebook and put it to one side. "First, you can go ahead with this Nike contract. Shoot some people. In that case, what we'd do, if we were retained by the Government or one of the victims' representatives, is attempt to apprehend you."

"Yes."

"And we *would* apprehend you, Hack. We have an eighty-six percent success rate. With someone like you, inexperienced, no backing, we'd have you within hours. So I strongly recommend you do not carry out this contract."

"I know," Hack said. "I should have it read it, but—"

"Second, you can refuse to go through with it. That would expose you to whatever penalties are in that contract. And I'm sure I don't need to tell you they could be harsh. Very harsh indeed.

" Hack nodded. He hoped Pearson wasn't finished.

"Here's your alternative." Pearson leaned forward. "You subcontract the slayings to us. We fulfill your contract, at a very competitive rate. As you probably know from our advertisements, your identity is totally protected. If the Government comes after us, it's not your problem."

Hack said, "That's my only alternative?"

"Well, if you had a copy of the contract, I'd tell you to go talk to our Legal branch. But you don't, do you?"

"Um, no." He hesitated. "How much would it be to..."

Pearson blew out his cheeks. "Depends. You don't need specific individuals done, right? Just people who buy these Mercury shoes."

"Yes."

"Well, that's cheaper. We can make sure we don't take out anyone with means. For, you know, retribution. And you need ten capped, so there's a bulk discount. We could do this for, say, one-fifty"

"One-fifty what?"

"Grand," Pearson said. "One-fifty grand, Hack, what do you think?"

He felt despair. "I'm a Merc Officer, I earn thirty-three a year—"

"Come on, now," Pearson said, looking pained. "Don't start that."

"I'm sorry." His vision blurred. Twice in one day! He was falling apart.

"Look, final offer: one-thirty. You can go talk to the NRA but you won't get better than that, I promise. Now do we have a deal?"

"Yes," Hack said. He wiped angrily at his face as Pearson began to draw up the contract.

From: Barry, Max, *Jennifer Government: a novel* (New York: Doubleday, 2003).

QUESTIONS:

1. What values does Max Barry attack in his satire of hyperprivatized culture? What values does he support (explicitly or implicitly)?
2. What does Barry's naming system imply about identity in hypercapitalist culture? Name some specific ways this culture affects how people in it think about and see the world.

26.5: *Citizens United v. Federal Elections Commission* (U.S. Supreme Court, 2010)

Some might say that the real life version of the world of *Jennifer Government* occurs when corporations donate large amounts of money to politicians' campaigns. Others, of course, might disagree. This debate showed up on the docket of the Supreme Court of the United States, which offered its majority and minority opinions in the 2010 decision in *Citizens United v. Federal Election Commission* (the majority ruling is followed by the minority dissent in the source). At issue were campaign finance laws that limited corporate contributions, laws that the plaintiffs challenged as unconstitutional limits on free speech. The fundamental questions are whether money is a form of speech and whether corporations are people with rights protected by the Constitution of the United States. *Citizens United* is thus a case at the intersection of states, social spheres, corporate spheres, and the global network.

SUPREME COURT OF THE UNITED STATES CITIZENS UNITED, APPELLANT v. FEDERAL ELECTION COMMISSION ON APPEAL FROM THE UNITED STATES DISTRICT COURT FOR THE DISTRICT OF COLUMBIA

[January 21, 2010]

JUSTICE KENNEDY delivered the opinion of the Court.

Federal law prohibits corporations and unions from using their general treasury funds to make independent expenditures for speech defined as an "electioneering communication" or for speech expressly advocating the election or defeat of a candidate. The holding of *McConnell* rested to a large extent on an earlier case, *Austin* v. *Michigan Chamber of Commerce* . . . (1990). *Austin* had held that political speech may be banned based on the speaker's corporate identity.

In this case we are asked to reconsider *Austin* and, in effect, *McConnell*. It has been noted that "*Austin* was a significant departure from ancient First Amendment principles," . . . We agree with that conclusion and hold that *stare decisis* does not compel the continued acceptance of *Austin*. The Government may regulate corporate political speech through disclaimer and disclosure requirements, but it may not suppress that speech altogether. We turn to the case now before us.

I

A

Citizens United is a nonprofit corporation. It brought this action in the United States District Court for the District of Columbia. A three-judge court later convened to hear the cause. The resulting judgment gives rise to this appeal.

Citizens United has an annual budget of about $12 million. Most of its funds are from donations by individuals; but, in addition, it accepts a small portion of its funds from for-profit corporations.

In January 2008, Citizens United released a film entitled *Hillary: The Movie*. We refer to the film as *Hillary*. . . . *Hillary* mentions Senator [Hilary] Clinton by name and depicts interviews with political commentators and other persons, most of them quite critical of Senator Clinton. *Hillary* was released in theaters and on DVD, but Citizens United wanted to increase distribution by making it available through video-on-demand.

. . . In December 2007, a cable company offered, for a payment of $1.2 million, to make *Hillary* available on a video-on-demand channel called "Elections '08." Some video-on-demand services require viewers to pay a small fee to view a selected program, but here the proposal was to make *Hillary* available to viewers free of charge.

To implement the proposal, Citizens United was prepared to pay for the video-on-demand; and to promote the film, it produced two 10-second ads and one 30-second ad for *Hillary*. . . .

III

The First Amendment provides that "Congress shall make no law . . . abridging the freedom of speech." Laws enacted to control or suppress speech may operate at different points in the speech process. . . .

The law before us is an outright ban, backed by criminal sanctions. Section 441b makes it a felony for all corporations—including nonprofit advocacy corporations—either to expressly advocate the election or defeat of candidates or to broadcast electioneering communications within 30 days of a primary election and 60 days of a general election. . . .

Section 441b is a ban on corporate speech notwithstanding the fact that a PAC created by a corporation can still speak. . . . PACs are burdensome alternatives; they are expensive to administer and subject to extensive regulations.

. . .

. . . [I]t is inherent in the nature of the political process that voters must be free to obtain information from diverse sources in order to determine how to cast their votes. At least before *Austin*, the Court had not allowed the exclusion of a class of speakers from the general public dialogue.

We find no basis for the proposition that, in the context of political speech, the Government may impose restrictions on certain disfavored speakers. Both history and logic lead us to this conclusion.

A

The Court has recognized that First Amendment protection extends to corporations. . . .

This protection has been extended by explicit holdings to the context of political speech.

. . .

The Court is thus confronted with conflicting lines of precedent: a pre-*Austin* line that forbids restrictions on political speech based on the speaker's corporate identity and a post-*Austin* line that permits them. No case before *Austin* had held that Congress could prohibit independent expenditures for political speech based on the speaker's corporate identity.

. . .

If the First Amendment has any force, it prohibits Congress from fining or jailing citizens, or associations of citizens, for simply engaging in political speech. If the antidistortion rationale [limiting corporate contributions to limit the potential for corruption] were to be accepted, however, it would permit Government to ban political speech simply because the speaker is an association that has taken on the corporate form. . . .

Political speech is "indispensable to decision making in a democracy, and this is no less true because the speech comes from a corporation rather than an individual." . . . *Austin* sought to defend the antidistortion rationale as a means to prevent corporations from obtaining "'an unfair advantage in the political marketplace'" by using "'resources amassed in the economic marketplace.'"

. . . All speakers, including individuals and the media, use money amassed from the economic marketplace to fund their speech. The First Amendment

protects the resulting speech, even if it was enabled by economic transactions with persons or entities who disagree with the speaker's ideas.

Austin's antidistortion rationale would produce the dangerous, and unacceptable, consequence that Congress could ban political speech of media corporations.

. . .

Austin interferes with the "open marketplace" of ideas protected by the First Amendment. . . . It permits the Government to ban the political speech of millions of associations of citizens. . . . Most of these are small corporations without large amounts of wealth. . . .

The censorship we now confront is vast in its reach. The Government has "muffle[d] the voices that best represent the most significant segments of the economy." . . . By suppressing the speech of manifold corporations, both for-profit and nonprofit, the Government prevents their voices and viewpoints from reaching the public and advising voters on which persons or entities are hostile to their interests. . . .

The purpose and effect of this law is to prevent corporations, including small and nonprofit corporations, from presenting both facts and opinions to the public. This makes *Austin*'s antidistortion rationale all the more an aberration.

. . .

The appearance of influence or access, furthermore, will not cause the electorate to lose faith in our democracy. By definition, an independent expenditure is political speech presented to the electorate that is not coordinated with a candidate. The fact that a corporation, or any other speaker, is willing to spend money to try to persuade voters presupposes that the people have the ultimate influence over elected officials. This is inconsistent with any suggestion that the electorate will refuse "'to take part in democratic governance'" because of additional political speech made by a corporation or any other speaker.

. . .

Austin is overruled, so it provides no basis for allowing the Government to limit corporate independent expenditures.

. . .

The judgment of the District Court is reversed with respect to the constitutionality of 2 U. S. C. §441b's restrictions on corporate independent expenditures. The judgment is affirmed with respect to BCRA's disclaimer and disclosure requirements. The case is remanded for further proceedings consistent with this opinion.

It is so ordered.

[From: *Opinion of the Court*, Pp. 1–57, *passim*.]

CITIZENS UNITED, APPELLANT v. FEDERAL ELECTION COMMISSION ON APPEAL FROM THE UNITED STATES DISTRICT COURT FOR THE DISTRICT OF COLUMBIA

[January 21, 2010]

JUSTICE STEVENS, with whom JUSTICE GINSBURG, JUSTICE BREYER, and JUSTICE SOTOMAYOR join, concurring in part and dissenting in part.

The real issue in this case concerns how, not if, the appellant may finance its electioneering. Citizens United is a wealthy nonprofit corporation that runs a political action committee (PAC) with millions of dollars in assets. Under the Bipartisan Campaign Reform Act of 2002 (BCRA), it could have used those assets to televise and promote *Hillary: The Movie* wherever and whenever it wanted to. It also could have spent unrestricted sums to broadcast *Hillary* at any time other than the 30 days before the last primary election. Neither Citizens United's nor any other corporation's speech has been "banned," [as the majority claim]. All that the parties dispute is whether Citizens United had a right to use the funds in its general treasury to pay for broadcasts during the 30 day period. The notion that the First Amendment dictates an affirmative answer to that question is, in my judgment, profoundly misguided. Even more

misguided is the notion that the Court must rewrite the law relating to campaign expenditures by for profit corporations and unions to decide this case.

. . .

The Court's ruling threatens to undermine the integrity of elected institutions across the Nation. The path it has taken to reach its outcome will, I fear, do damage to this institution.

. . .

1. Antidistortion

The fact that corporations are different from human beings might seem to need no elaboration, except that the majority opinion almost completely elides it. *Austin* set forth some of the basic differences. Unlike natural persons, corporations have "limited liability" for their owners and managers, "perpetual life," separation of ownership and control, "and favorable treatment of the accumulation and distribution of assets . . . that enhance their ability to attract capital and to deploy their resources in ways that maximize the return on their shareholders' investments." . . . Unlike voters in U. S. elections, corporations may be foreign controlled. Unlike other interest groups, business corporations have been "effectively delegated responsibility for ensuring society's economic welfare"; they inescapably structure the life of every citizen. "'[T]he resources in the treasury of a business corporation,'" furthermore, "'are not an indication of popular support for the corporation's political ideas.'" "'They reflect instead the economically motivated decisions of investors and customers. The availability of these resources may make a corporation a formidable political presence, even though the power of the corporation may be no reflection of the power of its ideas.'" . . .

It might also be added that corporations have no consciences, no beliefs, no feelings, no thoughts, no desires. Corporations help structure and facilitate the activities of human beings, to be sure, and their "personhood" often serves as a useful legal fiction. But they are not themselves members of "We the People" by whom and for whom our Constitution was established.

These basic points help explain why corporate electioneering is not only more likely to impair compelling governmental interests, but also why restrictions on that electioneering are less likely to encroach upon First Amendment freedoms. One fundamental concern of the First Amendment is to "protec[t] the individual's interest in self-expression." . . . Freedom of speech helps "make men free to develop their faculties." . . . Corporate speech, however, is derivative speech, speech by proxy. A regulation such as BCRA §203 may affect the way in which individuals disseminate certain messages through the corporate form, but it does not prevent anyone from speaking in his or her own voice. "Within the realm of [campaign spending] generally," corporate spending is "furthest from the core of political expression." . . .

It is an interesting question "who" is even speaking when a business corporation places an advertisement that endorses or attacks a particular candidate. Presumably it is not the customers or employees, who typically have no say in such matters. It cannot realistically be said to be the shareholders, who tend to be far removed from the day-to-day decisions of the firm and whose political preferences may be opaque to management. Perhaps the officers or directors of the corporation have the best claim to be the ones speaking, except their fiduciary duties generally prohibit them from using corporate funds for personal ends. Some individuals associated with the corporation must make the decision to place the ad, but the idea that these individuals are thereby fostering their self-expression or cultivating their critical faculties is fanciful. It is entirely possible that the corporation's electoral message will conflict with their personal convictions. Take away the ability to use general treasury funds for some of those ads, and no one's autonomy, dignity, or political equality has been impinged upon in the least.

[From: *Opinion of J. Stevens* Pp. 1–77, *passim.*]

From: http://www.supremecourt.gov/opinions/09pdf/08-205.pdf, excerpts from the "Opinion of the Court" and from the "Opinion of J. Stevens."

QUESTIONS:

1. Is money a form of speech? Why (not)? Are corporations people? Why (not)?
2. How do the different justices answer these questions, based on what kinds of evidence?

CHAPTER 27

Modern Hierarchies: States, Societies, and Conflicts Since 1970

INTRODUCTION

The pervasive global network of the modern world and the steady spread of industrialization has affected relationships among hierarchies, transforming domestic politics and the forms of conflict between states. The sources in this chapter explore some of the dynamics of states, societies, and war since 1970, as well as some of the responses to conflict, including the continued assertion of democratic ideals and human rights in the face of oppression.

27.1: *A Dirty War: A Russian Reporter in Chechnya* (Anna Politkovskaya, 2001)

Anna Politkovskaya (1958–2006) was an investigative journalist in Russia, much of whose work appeared in *Novaya Gazeta*, a newspaper known for its willingness to publish regime-critical reportage. Politkovskaya, the daughter of Ukrainian diplomats to the UN (she was born in New York), grew up and studied journalism during the Soviet era, when she wrote about accidents and emergencies. After the fall of the USSR, she began to write for *Novaya Gazeta* and eventually turned the focus of her journalism to the Chechen war. She published two books translated into English on the Chechen war. The excerpt here is from the first of those two books. She was a fiercely courageous journalist who took perpetrators of violence on both sides of the Chechen war to task. She also wrote critically about Vladimir Putin: the last book published during her life was *Putin's Russia* (2004). Politkovskaya was killed in the elevator of her apartment building on October 7, 2006 under circumstances that are still unsolved. She was the recipient, both during her life and posthumously, of countless journalism awards.

CRIMINAL MOTHERS

Hundreds Break the Law

On 30 September ground operations effectively began in Chechnya. On 1 October Putin declared that the only legal authority in the republic is the 1996 parliament "elected according to the laws of the Russian Federation. All other bodies formed in the Chechen Republic can be termed legitimate only with serious reservations." Such a statement by the Prime Minister amounts to no less than the renunciation of the Peace Treaty signed by Yeltsin and Chechen President Maskhadov on 12 May 1997. The authorities have taken yet another major step towards making this war irreversible.

VICTOR POPKOV
Novaya gazeta, 4 October 1999

"It's true, I tricked him into coming with me. I took away all his documents. I locked him in the apartment. I argued and insisted. And I'm sure I was right. We mothers, whose children are now serving in the army, have no choice. There's no 'voluntary principle'. Young lads who have come as mere conscripts are being forced to go and fight, without any explanation or preparation. I consider the State has put us in an impossible position."

Hundreds of mothers today, kidnappers against their will, would repeat her words. On 16 September Lydia Burmistrova, a Muscovite, took away her 19-year-old son Ivan, a private with the Taman division (Unit 73881), just before the next contingent was setting out and after more than 2,000 of the division's soldiers had already been sent to the Caucasus. This is her disturbing and moving tale:

"Ivan was very reluctant, but I broke his resistance. I brought my sons up by myself. The State gave me nothing, not a kopeck. . . .

Officially we are in "Tent School No 8". Almost goo children are taught by 21 volunteer teachers. Of course they are not being paid, though there have been a great many promises. The admirable young director, Minkail Ezhiev, is devoted to his profession and, until September, was Head of School 21 in Grozny. Today that school is nothing but ashes.

Class 3C. Russian Language. Composition. Jamila Djamilkhanova, the young teacher from Grozny, speaks a faultless literary Russian; she does not conceal her surprise and pride at the patriotism of her pupils.

There's nothing else to add. I did not select the best compositions. There were only twelve altogether because the classes in the school are small. The tents are not large and many children cannot attend regularly; they have nothing to wear. As a rule, one member of a family attends school today, and tomorrow a different child goes. No one complains if they miss their studies; no one calls in the parents for an explanation.

There is something else distinctive about these compositions. The girls are usually more lyrical, but the boys are severe, single-minded and uncompromising. It's frightening, isn't it?

The first important discovery: not one of the children said that the Russian Federation was their homeland. That's all finished! They have cut themselves off from us.

Second, and equally important: these texts are the work of small children and so they have made quite a few mistakes. Their teacher Jamila has given them all full marks, however, no matter what errors they made in spelling or grammar.

. . .

She handed me the twelve flimsy scraps of paper. Condensed emotion. Undeniable proof and material expression of their love. It does not get any more truthful than this.

. . .

Abdelazim Makhauri:

I have only one homeland. Grozny. It was the most beautiful city in all the world. But my beautiful city was destroyed by Russia and together with it, all Chechnya and the people living there. The people that Russia had not yet managed to destroy went to Ingushetia, as I did. But I miss my home. I so terribly want to go home although I know already that my house has been bombed to pieces. All the same, I want to go. . . Why do I want to live at home? So I can have the right to do what I want, and no one would tell me off.

LEAVE US ALONE, RUSSIA. WE'RE ALREADY FED UP WITH YOU. There were only a few Chechens before you started. GO HOME and put things in order there, not in our country . . .

Ali Makaev:

I always wanted to see my country Chechnya free from terrorism. Now here I am studying in a cold tent while Russian children can work on computers in warm schools. . . I do not know if Putin has a heart. But if he did he would not have started such a war. Putin thinks that human life is worth 50 kopecks. He is deeply mistaken. He is stealing these lives from people. I'd like Putin to know that we are also human beings. Until war came Chechnya was more beautiful than Moscow. I would like to go home and live there to the end of my life.

Bislan Dombaev:

My homeland is the most beautiful and richest country. I was born in Grozny. We lived in Chernoreche. Our village was very beautiful. But now when you look at our homeland you don't want to cry even, you no longer want to live. All has been bombed into the ground and destroyed. My kind, quite innocent little homeland.

Our country is being bombed. Its young people are tormented. Grown-ups and little children are being killed, one after another. What kind of lawlessness is this? What did our people ever do wrong? Why are we suffering?

Islam Mintsaev:

I very much miss my school, my friends and all that I know and love. We don't live badly here in Ingushetia. We go to school in a tent settlement. But Ingush children go to big schools, to a three-storey building like we had in Grozny.

At night I often wonder when this cursed war will come to an end and we can go home. Grown-ups say that the houses are no longer beautiful there: everything has been destroyed and each day young people and our furniture are carried away on APCs [armoured personnel carriers]. They take the young people to Mozdok and torture them there like in the worst films. When I hear the roar of aeroplanes I again feel terrified, just like when we were at home Again they are bombing my homeland. How many of our relatives have died? And how many are left homeless?

Shaikhan Sadulaev:

My homeland is Vedeno. When I was in the first class at school we moved to Grozny, to the Zavodskoi district. I went to School 21. During the first war I lost my father. The soldiers took him away and he has not been found to this day. I thought then that the war had ended but on 1 September it began again, when all children should be going to school. But they did not let us study. On 21 September Russian planes began to bomb our homes, schools, hospitals and all that we needed. They flew over us, and scared us night and day. So we had to leave our homeland.

The soldiers from Russia are killing children, our sisters and brothers. They say they are bandits. But they are not bandits, they are defending the homeland. Because we love our homeland.

Zaira Magomadova:

My homeland is the most beautiful city on earth, Grozny. I loved the city. During school holidays I went with my parents to the village of Chishki. It is a fine, richly green part of my homeland. Many children from different villages and towns used to go on holiday there. Everything was fine but then the war came. It destroyed my city and all our dreams. It carried off many lives. Who was the person who thought up this war? He also has children, hasn't he? Good people, stop the war!

. . .

Aminat Sedieva:

I was born and lived in the capital of the republic, Grozny. Our city used to be very beautiful. I went to School 14. Our teacher was called Tamara Usmanovna. I would like to study in our school, in our classroom. But now we go to school in cold tents. We came here to Ingushetia because they bombed our city and it was frightening there. Now we have neither city nor school. I don't know when we'll go home.

Koka Musostova:

Because of the military operations we moved to Ingushetia. Here the military helicopters and aeroplanes of Russia fly over us. They almost come as low as the roofs. I want to go back to Chechnya as quickly as possible, to live, study, play and make friends. I very much love my homeland. Help me to do that.

Marina Magomedkhadjieva:

My city Grozny always radiated beauty and goodness. But now all that is gone like a beautiful dream and only memories remain. The war is blind, it doesn't see the city, the school or the children. All this is the work of the armadas from Russia, and therefore not only our eyes are weeping but also our tiny hearts.

Now we have nowhere to go to school, to play and enjoy ourselves. Now we run back and forth and don't know what to do. But if they asked us we would say "That's enough bloodshed. If you do not stop this senseless war we shall never forgive you." Soldiers! Think of your children, of your own childhood! Remember the things you wanted in Childhood and what your children want, and you'll understand how sad and difficult it is for us. Leave us alone! We want to go home.

. . .

THE ORDINARY MAN DOES NOT NEED FREEDOM

Chechnya's New Leader

On 8 June 2000 Ahmad-Hadji Kadyrov was appointed by President Putin to head the provisional administration of the Chechen Republic. Born in Karaganda, Kazakhstan, in 1951 he studied at the agricultural college in Sernovodsk (Chechnya) and at the construction institute in Novosibirsk, but failed to graduate from either. In the 1980s he received a religious education in Central Asia, attending the *medresseh* (Koranic school) in Bukhara and the Tashkent Institute of Islam. Since 1991 he has lived in Chechnya, becoming the republic's deputy Mufti in 1993 and Mufti in 1995.

Q. **There have been many different leaders in Chechnya over the last ten years—someone, you might say, to suit everyone's taste: Dudayev, Zavgayev, Khadjiev, Maskhadov and Koshman. Now you. Every time a new leader arrived, the people heard enticing words about the happy future that was just round the corner. But it never came. Instead, they faced poverty and violent death. What are the main tasks of the new Kadyrov regime?**

A. My task is to save the Chechen nation from the path that it has repeatedly been deceived into following for the last 300–400 years.

And at first everything indeed seemed to end in victory for the Chechen people. In 1996 the federal forces withdrew, we held elections and President Maskhadov had all the power in his hands.

I did a great deal to ensure this happened and consider his election to be my personal achievement. Without me the elections would never have taken place. After that all Maskhadov had to do was preserve the reputation the Chechens had won after the first war; the Arab and Muslim world were then simply in raptures over us. But Maskhadov failed in this, as in so much else. Gradually people lost confidence. He allowed ordinary people to be robbed. He should have sent away all the mujahedin who had come from abroad, but he didn't.

Q. **How could he? If you fight in a war you always expect your share of the booty.**

A. It's very simple. He should have told them: "If, as you say, Allah led you to join us then we are very grateful. We owe you nothing, and you've already stored up enough wealth in paradise. Off you go." Instead we let them take enormous liberties, gave them oil wells and they brought criminals here from all over the world. Finally, the assault on Daghestan began and the federal troops entered Chechnya. Once again Maskhadov did nothing to stop the war, though he was given the chance: I appealed to him, and so did Moscow.

I personally witnessed the phone conversation between Voloshin, the Head of the Presidential Staff, and Alsultanov, then Chechnya's Deputy Premier, who was actually in Maskhadov's office. "If you make an announcement that you condemn terrorism," said Voloshin, "then a meeting with Yeltsin can take place." Maskhadov replied: "I won't say any such thing. Its only the Russians, only Moscow, who need me to say it." It is my conviction that Maskhadov abandoned the Chechen nation after the first war.

Hence my main goal today: the nation must no longer be left stranded half-way; no longer must it be deceived by this "independence" and "liberty" that no one has ever actually given us and never will. Freedom, in fact, is something the ordinary man—and I count myself one, I come from a very modest peasant family—does not need. He needs work and in return a wage and security.

Q. **That's just what no one here, apart from yourself, possesses at the moment. You have a job, you're paid a salary for doing it and your personal security is assured by your own bodyguards, supplemented by members of the Alfa group [elite FSB commandos, Tr.] disguised as Chechens. You're taken by helicopter to work in Gudermes from your home in Tsentoroi village and then flown back again. Meanwhile Grozny is stricken with hunger and infectious diseases; there is no water, gas or electricity but a great many mentally disturbed people. In the villages entire families are now suffering from tuberculosis.**

A. That's the price you pay for phony freedom.

Q **You're saying that as long as you're in power the idea of an independent Chechnya will never be discussed?**

A. There will be no discussions, no ideas of that kind. Today all that people want is an end to the shooting. Simply not to be robbed or killed. Of course, when everything settles down they'll want to get back to work. And they'll need jobs and wages. That will be freedom for Chechnya. I take Ingushetia and Daghestan as an example. They're also Muslims and they're in no hurry to go anywhere else; they don't let themselves be deceived. But we Chechens, I wouldn't say we're stupid, but we are more warlike than other nations and have allowed our warrior

instinct and ourselves to be exploited. Now I want to obtain a document from Moscow that guarantees that we'll be left alone for 40–50 years.

. . .

POSTSCRIPT

This interview left a strange feeling. On the one hand, it all made sense: Kadyrov is on the side of the truth and ordinary people. On the other, literally every word was tinged with petty untruths. This is clear to anyone who has spent a couple of days driving round Chechnya as it is today and talking to people. Ask anyone in any part of the country "Who is in charge round here?" and no matter whether you're in Chiri-Yurt, Argun, Shah, Grozny, Oktyabrsk or even Gudermes, the answer is the same: "No one is in charge." "But what about Kadyrov?" "If he were in charge we would at least have seen him."

Having taken Koshman's place in Gudermes, Kadyrov never leaves there. He is afraid to. He does not drive or walk anywhere. It is pointless to ask him anything about the economy. He cannot answer the most elementary question of that kind—for instance, how many enterprises there are in Chechnya and which of them are working today. Kadyrov is wholly engrossed in political feuding, in his hatred for Maskhadov and his urge to show that he has won and can draw the field commanders to his side. And he displays a fatal absence of ideas about how to ensure the most important thing of all, a peaceful existence for his republic.

Once you realise that, you can no longer accept his fine words about the "Chechen nation" and how it "must not be deceived any more."

From: Politkovskaya, Anna, *A dirty war: a Russian reporter in Chechnya* (London: Harvill, 2001), pp. 42, 45, 156–62 passim, 192–94, 200–1.

QUESTIONS:

1. What impact does a conflict such as the Chechen War have on civilians, including mothers and children? What moral commentary on the war do these effects offer? What is this reporter's role in shaping this commentary?
2. What contradictions between Kadyrov's words and his real-world context does Politkovskaya expose with her commentary at the end? How does this commentary affect your reading of his words?

27.2:   *The Arms Trade Is Big Business* (Anup Shah, 2013)

Anup Shah (1974–) is a citizen of the United Kingdom. He lived in the United States for four years from 1997 to 2001, where he became interested in global issues. His website, *Global Issues,* gathers information and presents his own views on issues including the global arms trade. That page is excerpted here.

THE ARMS TRADE IS BIG BUSINESS

World Military Spending Out Does Anything Else

[W]orld military spending has now reached one trillion dollars, close to Cold War levels.

As summarized from the *Military Balance, 2000/2001,* by the International Institute for Strategic Studies (October 2001), for the larger arms-purchasing nations each year:

- Arms procurement is normally 20–30% of their military budgets
- The main portion is usually on operations, maintenance and personnel
- Some 40 to 50 billion dollars are in actual deliveries, (that is, the delivery of sales, which can be many years after the initial contract is signed)
- Each year, around 30–35 billion dollars are made in actual sales (agreements, or signing of contracts).

In more recent years, annual sales of arms have risen to around $50-60 billion although the global financial crisis is slowly beginning to be felt in arms sales too.

. . .

As World Trade Globalizes, so Does the Trade in Arms

Control Arms is a campaign jointly run by Amnesty International, International Action Network on Small Arms (IANSA) and Oxfam. In a detailed report titled, Shattered Lives, they highlight that **arms are fueling poverty and suffering, and is also out of control**. In addition, The lack of arms controls allows some to profit from the misery of others.

- While international attention is focused on the need to control weapons of mass destruction, the trade in conventional weapons continues to operate in a legal and moral vacuum.
- More and more countries are starting to produce small arms, many with little ability or will to regulate their use.
- Permanent UN Security Council members—the USA, UK, France, Russia, and China—dominate the world trade in arms.
- Most national arms controls are riddled with loopholes or barely enforced.
- Key weaknesses are lax controls on the brokering, licensed production, and 'end use' of arms.
- Arms get into the wrong hands through weak controls on firearm ownership, weapons management, and misuse by authorised users of weapons.

— *The Arms Bazaar, Shattered Lives, Chapter 4, p. 54, Control Arms Campaign, October 2003*

The top five countries profiting from the arms trade are the five permanent members of the United Nations Security Council: the USA, UK, France, Russia, and China.

From 1998 to 2001, the USA, the UK, and France earned more income from arms sales to developing countries than they gave in aid.

The arms industry is unlike any other. It operates without regulation. It suffers from widespread corruption and bribes. And it makes its profits on the back of machines designed to kill and maim human beings.

So who profits most from this murderous trade? The five permanent members of the UN Security Council—the USA, UK, France, Russia, and China. Together, they are responsible for eighty

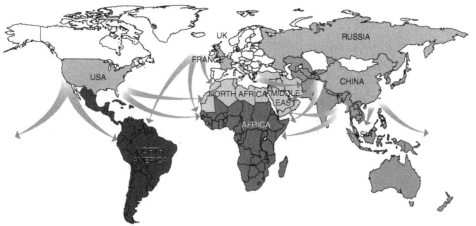

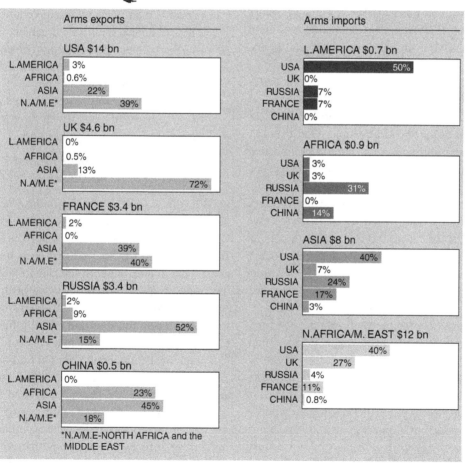

Arms exports

USA $14 bn
L.AMERICA	3%
AFRICA	0.6%
ASIA	22%
N.A/M.E*	39%

UK $4.6 bn
L.AMERICA	0%
AFRICA	0.5%
ASIA	13%
N.A/M.E*	72%

FRANCE $3.4 bn
L.AMERICA	2%
AFRICA	0%
ASIA	39%
N.A/M.E*	40%

RUSSIA $3.4 bn
L.AMERICA	2%
AFRICA	9%
ASIA	52%
N.A/M.E*	15%

CHINA $0.5 bn
L.AMERICA	0%
AFRICA	23%
ASIA	45%
N.A/M.E*	18%

*N.A/M.E-NORTH AFRICA and the MIDDLE EAST

Arms imports

L.AMERICA $0.7 bn
USA	50%
UK	0%
RUSSIA	7%
FRANCE	7%
CHINA	0%

AFRICA $0.9 bn
USA	3%
UK	3%
RUSSIA	31%
FRANCE	0%
CHINA	14%

ASIA $8 bn
USA	40%
UK	7%
RUSSIA	24%
FRANCE	17%
CHINA	3%

N.AFRICA/M. EAST $12 bn
USA	40%
UK	27%
RUSSIA	4%
FRANCE	11%
CHINA	0.8%

© Control Arms Campaign

eight per cent of reported conventional arms exports.

"We can't have it both ways. We can't be both the world's leading champion of peace and the world's leading supplier of arms." Former US President Jimmy Carter, presidential campaign, 1976.

— *The Arms Industry, Control Arms Campaign,*
October 2003

The third world is often the destination for arms sales as the Control Arms Campaign also highlights graphically:

In order to make up for a lack of sales from domestic and traditional markets for military equipment, newer markets are being created or sought after. This is vital for the arms corporations and contractors in order to stay afloat.

Respect for human rights is often overlooked as arms are sold to known human rights violators.

Heavy militarization of a region increases the risk of oppression on local people. Consequently reactions and uprisings from those oppressed may also be violent. The Middle East is a current example, while Latin America is an example from previous decades, where in both cases, democracies or popular regimes have (or had) been overthrown with foreign assistance, and replaced with corrupt dictators or monarchs. Oppression (often violent) and authoritarianism rule has resulted. Sometimes this also itself results in terrorist reactions that lash out at other innocent people.

A deeper cycle of violence results. The arms trade may not always be a root cause, because there are often various geopolitical interests etc. However, the sale of arms can be a significant contributor to problems because of the enormous impact of the weapons involved. Furthermore, some oppressive regimes are only too willing purchase more arms under the pretext of their own war against terrorism.

In quoting a major international body, six basic points harshly criticizing the practices and impacts of the arms industry are listed below, by J.W. Smith:

1. That the armament firms have been active in fomenting war scares and in persuading their countries to adopt warlike policies and to increase their armaments.

2. That armament firms have attempted to bribe government officials, both at home and abroad.

3. That armament firms have disseminated false reports concerning the military and naval programs of various countries, in order to stimulate armament expenditure.

4. That armament firms have sought to influence public opinion through the control of newspapers in their own and foreign countries.

5. That armament firms have organized international armament rings through which the armament race has been accentuated by playing off one country against another.

6. That armament firms have organized international armament trusts which have increased the price of armaments sold to governments.

— *J.W. Smith, The World's Wasted Wealth II,*
(Institute for Economic Democracy, 1994), p. 224

But, this was not of the arms industry of today. Smith was quoting the League of Nations after World War I, when "Stung by the horrors of World War I, world leaders realized that arms merchants had a hand in creating both the climate of fear and the resulting disaster itself." And unfortunately, it also summarizes some of the problems of today, too. Justification for arms and creating the market for arms expenditure is not a new concept. The call to war and fear-mongering is an old tradition.

This rush to globalize arms production and sales ignores the grave humanitarian and strategic consequences of global weapons proliferation. Already, profit motives in the military industry have resulted in arms export decisions that contravene such U.S. foreign policy goals as preserving stability and promoting human rights and democracy.

— *Globalized Weaponry, Foreign Policy in Focus,*
Volume 5, Number 16, June 2000

Hidden Corporate Welfare?

Industrialized countries negotiate free trade and investment agreements with other countries, but exempt military spending from the liberalizing demands of the agreement. Since only the wealthy countries can afford to devote billions on military spending, they will always be able to give their corporations hidden subsidies through defence contracts, and maintain a technologically advanced industrial capacity.

And so, in every international trade and investment agreement one will find a clause which exempts government programs and policies deemed vital for national security. Here is the loophole that allows the maintenance of corporate subsidies through virtually unlimited military spending.

— Stephen Staples, Confronting the Military-Corporate Complex, presented at the Hague Appeal for Peace, The Hague, May 12th 1999

Vast government subsidies are sought after in the pursuit of arms trading.

US and European corporations receive enormous tax breaks and even lend money to other countries to purchase weapons from them. Therefore tax payers from these countries end up often unknowingly subsidizing arms sales.

While there are countless examples, a recent one that made a few news headlines was how Lockheed managed to get US subsidies to help sell a lot of fighter planes to Poland at the end of 2002/beginning of 2003. This was described as the biggest deal ever in Europe at that time.

From: http://www.globalissues.org/article/74/the-arms-trade-is-big-business.

QUESTIONS:

1. Whose interests are served by the global arms trade? Whose are potentially harmed? Where might the balance lie?
2. What does the global arms trade tell us about the intersection between networks and hierarchies in the modern world?

27.3:   *Universal Declaration of Human Rights* (United Nations, 1948)

The United Nations Universal Declaration of Human Rights was adopted by the UN General Assembly in 1948 during a meeting in Paris. It was drawn up in the aftermath of World War II as the first world wide assertion of rights inherent to all human beings. Its provisions have been adopted and elaborated in various international treaties, and in 1966 the UN combined the Declaration along with a number of these treaties into The International Bill of Human Rights, which took effect as international law in 1976 after enough countries had ratified it.

PREAMBLE

Whereas recognition of the inherent dignity and of the equal and inalienable rights of all members of the human family is the foundation of freedom, justice and peace in the world,

Whereas disregard and contempt for human rights have resulted in barbarous acts which have

outraged the conscience of mankind, and the advent of a world in which human beings shall enjoy freedom of speech and belief and freedom from fear and want has been proclaimed as the highest aspiration of the common people,

Whereas it is essential, if man is not to be compelled to have recourse, as a last resort, to rebellion against tyranny and oppression, that human rights should be protected by the rule of law,

Whereas it is essential to promote the development of friendly relations between nations,

Whereas the peoples of the United Nations have in the Charter reaffirmed their faith in fundamental human rights, in the dignity and worth of the human person and in the equal rights of men and women and have determined to promote social progress and better standards of life in larger freedom,

Whereas Member States have pledged themselves to achieve, in co-operation with the United Nations, the promotion of universal respect for and observance of human rights and fundamental freedoms,

Whereas a common understanding of these rights and freedoms is of the greatest importance for the full realization of this pledge,

Now, Therefore THE GENERAL ASSEMBLY proclaims THIS UNIVERSAL DECLARATION OF HUMAN RIGHTS as a common standard of achievement for all peoples and all nations, to the end that every individual and every organ of society, keeping this Declaration constantly in mind, shall strive by teaching and education to promote respect for these rights and freedoms and by progressive measures, national and international, to secure their universal and effective recognition and observance, both among the peoples of Member States themselves and among the peoples of territories under their jurisdiction.

Article 1.

All human beings are born free and equal in dignity and rights. They are endowed with reason and conscience and should act towards one another in a spirit of brotherhood.

Article 2.

Everyone is entitled to all the rights and freedoms set forth in this Declaration, without distinction of any kind, such as race, colour, sex, language, religion, political or other opinion, national or social origin, property, birth or other status. Furthermore, no

distinction shall be made on the basis of the political, jurisdictional or international status of the country or territory to which a person belongs, whether it be independent, trust, non-self-governing or under any other limitation of sovereignty.

Article 3.

Everyone has the right to life, liberty and security of person.

Article 4.

No one shall be held in slavery or servitude; slavery and the slave trade shall be prohibited in all their forms.

Article 5.

No one shall be subjected to torture or to cruel, inhuman or degrading treatment or punishment.

Article 6.

Everyone has the right to recognition everywhere as a person before the law.

Article 7.

All are equal before the law and are entitled without any discrimination to equal protection of the law. All are entitled to equal protection against any discrimination in violation of this Declaration and against any incitement to such discrimination.

Article 8.

Everyone has the right to an effective remedy by the competent national tribunals for acts violating the fundamental rights granted him by the constitution or by law.

Article 9.

No one shall be subjected to arbitrary arrest, detention or exile.

Article 10.

Everyone is entitled in full equality to a fair and public hearing by an independent and impartial tribunal, in the determination of his rights and obligations and of any criminal charge against him.

Article 11.

(1) Everyone charged with a penal offence has the right to be presumed innocent until proved guilty according to law in a public trial at which he has had all the guarantees necessary for his defence.

(2) No one shall be held guilty of any penal offence on account of any act or omission which did not constitute a penal offence, under national or international law, at the time when it was committed. Nor shall a heavier penalty be imposed than the one that was applicable at the time the penal offence was committed.

Article 12.

No one shall be subjected to arbitrary interference with his privacy, family, home or correspondence, nor to attacks upon his honour and reputation. Everyone has the right to the protection of the law against such interference or attacks.

Article 13.

(1) Everyone has the right to freedom of movement and residence within the borders of each state.

(2) Everyone has the right to leave any country, including his own, and to return to his country.

Article 14.

(1) Everyone has the right to seek and to enjoy in other countries asylum from persecution.

(2) This right may not be invoked in the case of prosecutions genuinely arising from non-political crimes or from acts contrary to the purposes and principles of the United Nations.

Article 15.

(1) Everyone has the right to a nationality.

(2) No one shall be arbitrarily deprived of his nationality nor denied the right to change his nationality.

Article 16.

(1) Men and women of full age, without any limitation due to race, nationality or religion, have the right to marry and to found a family. They are entitled to equal rights as to marriage, during marriage and at its dissolution.

(2) Marriage shall be entered into only with the free and full consent of the intending spouses.

(3) The family is the natural and fundamental group unit of society and is entitled to protection by society and the State.

Article 17.

(1) Everyone has the right to own property alone as well as in association with others.

(2) No one shall be arbitrarily deprived of his property.

Article 18.

Everyone has the right to freedom of thought, conscience and religion; this right includes freedom to change his religion or belief, and freedom, either alone or in community with others and in public or private, to manifest his religion or belief in teaching, practice, worship and observance.

Article 19.

Everyone has the right to freedom of opinion and expression; this right includes freedom to hold opinions without interference and to seek, receive and impart information and ideas through any media and regardless of frontiers.

Article 20.

(1) Everyone has the right to freedom of peaceful assembly and association.

(2) No one may be compelled to belong to an association.

Article 21.

(1) Everyone has the right to take part in the government of his country, directly or through freely chosen representatives.

(2) Everyone has the right of equal access to public service in his country.

(3) The will of the people shall be the basis of the authority of government; this will shall be expressed in periodic and genuine elections which shall be by universal and equal suffrage and shall be held by secret vote or by equivalent free voting procedures.

Article 22.

Everyone, as a member of society, has the right to social security and is entitled to realization, through national effort and international cooperation and in accordance with the organization and resources of each State, of the economic, social and cultural rights indispensable for his dignity and the free development of his personality.

Article 23.

(1) Everyone has the right to work, to free choice of employment, to just and favourable conditions of work and to protection against unemployment.

(2) Everyone, without any discrimination, has the right to equal pay for equal work.

(3) Everyone who works has the right to just and favourable remuneration ensuring for himself and his family an existence worthy of human dignity, and supplemented, if necessary, by other means of social protection.

(4) Everyone has the right to form and to join trade unions for the protection of his interests.

Article 24.

Everyone has the right to rest and leisure, including reasonable limitation of working hours and periodic holidays with pay.

Article 25.

(1) Everyone has the right to a standard of living adequate for the health and well-being of himself and of his family, including food, clothing, housing and medical care and necessary social services, and the right to security in the event of unemployment, sickness, disability, widowhood, old age or other lack of livelihood in circumstances beyond his control.

(2) Motherhood and childhood are entitled to special care and assistance. All children, whether born in or out of wedlock, shall enjoy the same social protection.

Article 26.

(1) Everyone has the right to education. Education shall be free, at least in the elementary and fundamental stages. Elementary education shall be compulsory. Technical and professional education shall be made generally available and higher education shall be equally accessible to all on the basis of merit.

(2) Education shall be directed to the full development of the human personality and to the strengthening of respect for human rights and fundamental freedoms. It shall promote understanding, tolerance and friendship among all nations, racial or religious groups, and shall further the activities of the United Nations for the maintenance of peace.

(3) Parents have a prior right to choose the kind of education that shall be given to their children.

Article 27.

(1) Everyone has the right freely to participate in the cultural life of the community, to enjoy the arts and to share in scientific advancement and its benefits.

(2) Everyone has the right to the protection of the moral and material interests resulting from any scientific, literary or artistic production of which he is the author.

Article 28.

Everyone is entitled to a social and international order in which the rights and freedoms set forth in this Declaration can be fully realized.

Article 29.

(1) Everyone has duties to the community in which alone the free and full development of his personality is possible.

(2) In the exercise of his rights and freedoms, everyone shall be subject only to such limitations as are determined by law solely for the purpose of securing due recognition and respect for the rights and freedoms of others and of meeting the just requirements of morality, public order and the general welfare in a democratic society.

(3) These rights and freedoms may in no case be exercised contrary to the purposes and principles of the United Nations.

Article 30.

Nothing in this Declaration may be interpreted as implying for any State, group or person any right to engage in any activity or to perform any act aimed at the destruction of any of the rights and freedoms set forth herein.

QUESTIONS:

1. How does the Universal Declaration of Human Rights differ from the declarations in Chapter 18? What, specifically, has been added?
2. What historical events can you detect in the additions and wording of the twentieth-century document?

27.4:   *Jihad against Jews and Crusaders* (Osama bin Laden et al., 1998)

Osama bin Laden (1957–2011) founded Al-Qaeda, the terrorist organization responsible for flying hijacked commercial airliners into the Twin Towers in New York on September 11, 2001, as well as many other attacks around the world, leading to mass casualties. A member of a wealthy Saudi Arabian family, he joined Islamic resistance forces in Afghanistan in 1979, fighting against the Soviets and the Soviet-supported regime there. He formed Al-Qaeda in 1988. Exiled by the Saudi government in 1992, he moved first to Sudan and in 1996 to then back to Afghanistan, where he declared war against the United States, a declaration "explained" in this 1998 proclamation. United States special forces tracked Bin Laden to a private compound in Pakistan in 2011 and, on orders from President Barack Obama, executed a secret operation in which they killed Bin Laden.

JIHAD AGAINST JEWS AND CRUSADERS

World Islamic Front Statement

23 February 1998

Shaykh Usamah Bin-Muhammad Bin-Ladin

Ayman al-Zawahiri, amir of the Jihad Group in Egypt

Abu-Yasir Rifa'i Ahmad Taha, Egyptian Islamic Group

Shaykh Mir Hamzah, secretary of the Jamiat-ul-Ulema-e-Pakistan

Fazlur Rahman, amir of the Jihad Movement in Bangladesh

Praise be to Allah, who revealed the Book, controls the clouds, defeats factionalism, and says in His Book: "But when the forbidden months are past, then fight and slay the pagans wherever ye find them, seize them, beleaguer them, and lie in wait for them in every stratagem (of war)"; and peace be upon our Prophet, Muhammad Bin-' Abdallah, who said: I have been sent with the sword between my hands to ensure that no one but Allah is worshipped, Allah who put my livelihood under the shadow of my spear and who inflicts humiliation and scorn on those who disobey my orders.

The Arabian Peninsula has never—since Allah made it flat, created its desert, and encircled it with seas—been stormed by any forces like the crusader armies spreading in it like locusts, eating its riches and wiping out its plantations. All this is happening at a time in which nations are attacking Muslims like people fighting over a plate of food. In the light of the grave situation and the lack of support, we and you are obliged to discuss current events, and we should all agree on how to settle the matter.

No one argues today about three facts that are known to everyone; we will list them, in order to remind everyone:

First, for over seven years the United States has been occupying the lands of Islam in the holiest of places, the Arabian Peninsula, plundering its riches, dictating to its rulers, humiliating its people, terrorizing its neighbors, and turning its bases in the Peninsula into a spearhead through which to fight the neighboring Muslim peoples.

If some people have in the past argued about the fact of the occupation, all the people of the Peninsula have now acknowledged it. The best proof of this is the Americans' continuing aggression against the Iraqi people using the Peninsula as a staging post, even though all its rulers are against their territories being used to that end, but they are helpless.

Second, despite the great devastation inflicted on the Iraqi people by the crusader-Zionist alliance, and despite the huge number of those killed, which has exceeded 1 million. . . despite all this, the Americans are once against trying to repeat the horrific massacres, as though they are not content with the protracted blockade imposed after the ferocious war or the fragmentation and devastation.

So here they come to annihilate what is left of this people and to humiliate their Muslim neighbors.

Third, if the Americans' aims behind these wars are religious and economic, the aim is also to serve the Jews' petty state and divert attention from its occupation of Jerusalem and murder of Muslims there. The best proof of this is their eagerness to destroy Iraq, the strongest neighboring Arab state, and their endeavor to fragment all the states of the region such as Iraq, Saudi Arabia, Egypt, and Sudan into paper statelets and through their disunion and weakness to guarantee Israel's survival and the continuation of the brutal crusade occupation of the Peninsula.

All these crimes and sins committed by the Americans are a clear declaration of war on Allah, his messenger, and Muslims. And ulema have throughout Islamic history unanimously agreed that the jihad is an individual duty if the enemy destroys the Muslim countries. This was revealed by Imam Bin-Qadamah in "Al- Mughni," Imam al-Kisa'i in "Al-Bada'i," al-Qurtubi in his interpretation, and the shaykh of al-Islam in his books, where he said: "As for the fighting to repulse [an enemy], it is aimed at defending sanctity and religion, and it is a duty as agreed [by the ulema]. Nothing is more sacred than belief except repulsing an enemy who is attacking religion and life."

On that basis, and in compliance with Allah's order, we issue the following fatwa to all Muslims:

The ruling to kill the Americans and their allies—civilians and military—is an individual duty for every Muslim who can do it in any country in which it is possible to do it, in order to liberate the al-Aqsa Mosque and the holy mosque [Mecca] from their grip, and in order for their armies to move out of all the lands of Islam, defeated and unable to threaten any Muslim. This is in accordance with the words of Almighty Allah, "and fight the pagans all together as they fight you all together," and "fight them until there is no more tumult or oppression, and there prevail justice and faith in Allah."

This is in addition to the words of Almighty Allah: "And why should ye not fight in the cause of Allah and of those who, being weak, are ill-treated (and oppressed)?—women and children, whose cry is: 'Our Lord, rescue us from this town, whose people are oppressors; and raise for us from thee one who will help!'"

We—with Allah's help— call on every Muslim who believes in Allah and wishes to be rewarded to comply with Allah's order to kill the Americans and plunder their money wherever and whenever they find it. We also call on Muslim ulema, leaders, youths, and soldiers to launch the raid on Satan's U.S. troops and the devil's supporters allying with them, and to displace those who are behind them so that they may learn a lesson.

Almighty Allah said: "O ye who believe, give your response to Allah and His Apostle, when He calleth you to that which will give you life. And know that Allah cometh between a man and his heart, and that it is He to whom ye shall all be gathered."

Almighty Allah also says: "O ye who believe, what is the matter with you, that when ye are asked to go forth in the cause of Allah, ye cling so heavily to the earth! Do ye prefer the life of this world to the hereafter? But little is the comfort of this life,

as compared with the hereafter. Unless ye go forth, He will punish you with a grievous penalty, and put others in your place; but Him ye would not harm in the least. For Allah hath power over all things."

Almighty Allah also says: "So lose no heart, nor fall into despair. For ye must gain mastery if ye are true in faith."

From: http://www.fas.org/irp/world/para/docs/980223-fatwa.htm.

QUESTIONS:

1. What screen image of Islam and of America does Osama bin Laden project in this document? How might these images justify his program of terrorist attacks?
2. What ideologies other than his appeal to Islam inform bin Laden's statement?

27.5:   *Living with Violence: A National Report on Domestic Abuse in Afghanistan* (Global Rights, 2008)

Global Rights is, as their website states, "a human rights organization working in partnership with local activists in Africa, Asia, and Latin America to build grass roots movements that promote and protect the rights of populations marginalized because of gender, ethnicity, race, socio-economic status, gender identity or disability." The document excerpted below is a study they produced in 2008 of living conditions for Afghan women.

Global Rights' Living with Violence: A National Report on Domestic Abuse in Afghanistan (the Report) presents the findings of surveys on domestic violence conducted with women in 4,700 households in 16 provinces located across Afghanistan in 2006. The research is unique in many respects. It is the first to report on domestic violence throughout the country based on samples of women that are representative of the ethnic and geographic diversity of Afghanistan. It is also the first that gathers statistical data from surveys with women at the household level rather than relying on secondary sources such as records of reported violence at police stations or hospitals. Perhaps the most significant feature of the research, however, is that it reflects a collaborative effort between Global Rights

and Afghan civil society. Global Rights partnered with four Afghan women's organizations in conducting the research, and trained women leaders to conduct surveys with women in the communities in which they lived. An Afghan research institute was involved in analyzing the data, and workshops and consultations were held with women's rights advocates and service providers to draw on their experiences to provide a context for interpreting the research findings.

The findings of this research are alarming: an overwhelming majority of women, 87.2%, experienced at least one form of physical, sexual or psychological violence or forced marriage, and most, 62.0%, experienced multiple forms of violence. Overall, 17.2% of women reported sexual violence, with 11.2% experiencing rape. Furthermore, 52.4% of women reported physical violence, with 39.3% saying they had been hit by their husband in the last year. Women who experienced psychological abuse totaled 73.9%, while 58.8% of women were in forced marriages, as distinct from arranged marriages. There were broad variations between provinces with 100% of Kochi women living in Kabul reporting at least one form of physical, sexual or psychological violence; 42.6% of women in Kandahar experiencing sexual violence; and 91.6% of women in Khost experiencing forced marriages.

The research identified a number of risk factors for domestic violence, as well as factors that tended to protect against violence, under the circumstances. These factors, as well as other factors that influenced levels of violence are summarized in the following tables.

RISK FACTORS
• The experience of one form of violence as it increases the likelihood of women experiencing other forms of violence • Being in a forced marriage • Being single through divorce or widowhood violence • Being in a polygamous marriage • Being under 15 years of age and married • Having rigid perceptions of gender roles • Living in rural communities • Living in the southern and eastern border provinces

PROTECTIVE FACTORS
• Employment of both women and men (at least in impacting upon forced marriage and physical violence) • Consenting to marriage • Literacy of both women and men • Knowing a husband prior to marriage • Enjoying a higher household income (at least when measured by proxy indicators of income) • Perceiving satisfactory gender relations in the home in Afghan society and being satisfied with one's husband • Living in urban communities • Living in the northern and western provinces

OTHER FACTORS TO CONSIDER
• Husbands are not the sole abusers in families: mother-in-laws were identified as the main abuser by almost a quarter of the women surveyed. • Domestic violence is highly normalized in Afghan society: many women noted satisfactory marital relationships while simultaneously reporting experiences of violence in the home • Almost a quarter of women were dissatisfied with relationships between men and women in the home in Afghan society. These women represent a force for change that can lead efforts to end domestic violence in the country if mobilized. • Only 18% of women knew other women who had been beaten by their husbands, suggesting that most women are isolated in their experiences of violence. • The lower likelihood of women experiencing violence in urban settings and in certain provinces may be associated with a stronger government presence and rule of law compared to rural communities and other provinces. • The higher likelihood of women experiencing violence in provinces where there is greater Taliban control suggests that oppressive ideology towards women may contribute to increased domestic violence. • The regions where women have a greater likelihood of experiencing violence are those with greater levels of armed conflict, suggesting linkages between community violence and violence in the family. Further research is needed to substantiate this observation. • Domestic violence is a rights violation in itself but also prevents women from exercising their civil, political, social, economic and cultural rights.

IMPLICATIONS OF THE RESEARCH FINDINGS FOR DESIGNING INTERVENTIONS TO END DOMESTIC VIOLENCE

Based on the risk, protective, and other factors listed above, Global Rights urges civil society organizations particularly, but also government and international organizations, to develop the following types of interventions to contribute towards preventing domestic violence:

- Advocating for the State's realization of the Constitutional protections to the Right to Education, particularly Article 44, which commits the State to providing programs to eliminate illiteracy;
- Providing basic literacy training to both men and women as components of activities to reduce domestic violence in communities;
- Increasing employment opportunities for men and women through a diversity of vocational training programs or micro-credit schemes to enable men and women to better generate income;
- Providing opportunities for women to challenge rigid gender roles by learning how Islam, Afghan law and international human rights law safeguard gender equality and other women's rights;
- Targeting training and support services to divorced, widowed and other single women, with a focus on services to protect them from sexual violence;
- Raising awareness about the frequency with which women are perpetrators of domestic violence and highlighting to women as well as men that such behavior constitutes a crime under Afghan law and under Islam;

- Facilitating opportunities for women to talk about domestic violence so as to break the sense of many women that they are isolated in their experience of it;
- Sending strong messages through public service announcements that violence is a crime under Afghan law and under Islam so as to challenge the normalization of violence;
- Raising awareness about relationships between violence and a woman's lack of knowledge of her husband before marriage to encourage families to allow their daughters to become better acquainted with their husbands prior to marriage, even if such marriages are arranged;
- Advocating for an end to forced marriage, child marriage, and polygamy and the traditional practices that encourage them;
- Ensuring that efforts to address domestic violence are not limited to urban centers but extend to rural regions and to provinces in the south-eastern border zones where the likelihood of violence tends to be higher than in other provinces;
- Ensuring that any efforts to prevent, protect against, and punish violence against women involve women themselves in the design and implementation of activities so as to draw on their lived experiences and ensure effectiveness, but also to serve as a means of empowering women to take action to make positive changes in their lives; and
- Advocating for the expansion and enforcement of the rule of law throughout the country to increase provision of formal justice mechanisms, the monitoring of informal justice mechanisms, and the availability of health, education and other government services.

From: Global Rights, *Living with violence: a national report on domestic abuse in Afghanistan*, (Washington, DC and Kabul: Global Rights, 2008), pp. 1–3.

QUESTIONS:

1. Why do you suppose the Global Rights researchers chose not to rely on secondary reports of domestic violence such as hospital and police reports but instead collected data from in-home interviews?

2. What are the key findings of the causes of domestic abuse in Afghanistan? How practical do the proposed solutions seem to you, and what does this study imply about domestic abuse in Afghanistan as a product of a globally networked set of societies?

CHAPTER 28

Networked Frames and Screens: Culture Since 1970

INTRODUCTION

In this last chapter, we present sources that sample the rich cultural output of the world since 1970. The sources explore questions of cultural identity, commodification of culture, and the impact of the global network on patterns of cultural expression, as well as examining current understandings of human cognition, bringing these sources full circle to the Cognitive-Linguistic Revolution with which "modern" human history began some 70,000 years ago.

28.1: Images of Identity: Automobile Advertisements

You may be familiar with modern means of transportation that use internal combustion engines to . . . oh, never mind. These images need little introduction. Cars have been sold since they were invented, and have been advertised for as long as they have been sold. This selection of car ads is a window onto the projection of images of identity, images created by carmakers to appeal to their customers.

DISPENSE WITH A HORSE

and save the expense, care and anxiety of keeping it. To run a motor carriage costs about ½ cent a mile.

THE WINTON MOTOR CARRIAGE

is the best vehicle of its kind that is made. It is handsomely, strongly and yet lightly constructed and elegantly finished. Easily managed. Speed from 3 to 20 miles an hour. The hydrocarbon motor is simple and powerful. No odor, no vibration. Suspension Wire Wheels. Pneumatic Tires. Ball Bearings. ☞ *Send for Catalogue.*

Price $1,000.   No Agents.

THE WINTON MOTOR CARRIAGE CO., Cleveland, Ohio.

1898 Winton Motor Carriage ad. The Mitchell Archives.

1952 Dodge ad. Advertising Archives.

1969 Chevrolet Camaro ad. Advertising Archives.

2013 Aston Martin car ad. Advertising Archives.

QUESTIONS:

1. What do these car advertisements promise that car ownership will contribute to identity? Whose identity do the ads implicitly address?
2. How has that promise changed over the last century?

28.2:   *Preserving Endangered Languages* (Suzanne Romaine, 2007)

Suzanne Romaine (1951–) is professor of linguistics at Oxford University whose specialities are historical linguistics, sociolinguistics, and linguistic anthropology. In addition to a variety of academic appointments, she was a member of the UNESCO Expert Group that produced UNESCO's position paper on *Education in a Multilingual World* (Paris:UNESCO, 2003). In this article, she discusses why so many languages in the world today are endangered and why that matters.

1. Introduction

Over the last few decades an increasing number of books, scholarly articles and media reports have predicted an alarming decline in the number of languages. . . . Some linguists think that as many as 60 to 90% of the world's approximately 6900 languages may be at risk of extinction within the next 100 years. Nettle and Romaine (2000: 2) estimate that about half the known languages in the world have disappeared over the past 500 years. Crystal (2000: 19) suggests that an average of one language every 2 weeks may vanish over the next 100 years. Krauss (1992) believes that only the 600 or so languages with the largest numbers of speakers (i.e., more than 100,000) may survive. If this is true, few of the approximately 6000 remaining languages will have a secure future. No children are learning any of the nearly 100 native languages in what is now the state of California. Only a handful of the hundreds of Aboriginal Australian languages may survive into the next century. Similar dismal statistics and gloomy prognostications emerge from various parts of the globe.

The aim of this article is to offer a more sophisticated understanding of what works and what does not in efforts to preserve endangered languages. However, the first step in the solution to any problem is to acknowledge its existence and understand its origins. Only by understanding the historical and social circumstances that have created the current threat to the world's languages can we hope to reverse it. This article will provide a detailed overview of the scale and character of the problem of language endangerment, consider some of its causes and consequences, and outline some of the range of efforts currently underway worldwide to ameliorate the situation.

2. Current State of the World's Languages: Character and Scale of the Problem of Language Endangerment

. . .

Language shift is symptomatic of large scale processes and pressures of various types (social, cultural, economic, and military) on a community that have brought about the global village phenomenon, affecting people everywhere, even in the remotest regions of the Amazon. Language shift may be thought of as a loss of speakers and domains of use, both of which are critical to the survival of a language. The possibility of impending shift appears when a language once used throughout a community for everything becomes restricted in use as another language intrudes on its territory. Usage declines in domains where the language was once secure, e.g., in churches, the workplace, schools, and, most importantly, the home, as growing numbers of parents fail to transmit the language to their children. Fluency in the language is higher among older speakers, as younger generations prefer to speak another (usually the dominant societal) language.

. . .

Having examined some substantial disparities in the geographic spread and size of languages, we are in a better position to address the question of how much of the world's linguistic diversity is in danger. Estimates of the number of threatened languages vary a great deal from 50 to 90% depending on the criteria used to assess risk.

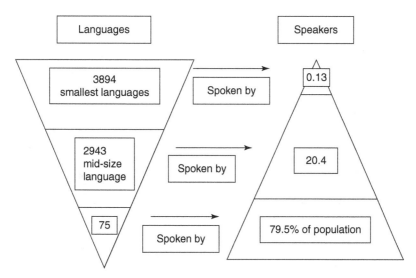

Inverse relation between number of languages and size of population.

UNESCO's *World Atlas of the World's Languages in Danger of Disappearing* (2001) estimates that 50% of languages may be in various degrees of endangerment. . . .

If we use size as a proxy for degree of endangerment, estimates of the scale of the problem will still vary, depending on how many speakers are thought to be needed for a language to be viable. Table 1 shows the percentage of indigenous languages in different continents with fewer than some number of speakers. The languages in Australia and the Pacific and the Americas are mostly very small; over 20% have fewer than 150 speakers, and nearly all have fewer than 100,000. Africa, Asia, and Europe, in contrast, have a fair number of medium-sized ones (100,000 to 1 million speakers), in addition to some giant languages. Such languages are probably safer in the short term at least. If Krauss (1992) is right in thinking that only languages with over 100,000 speakers are safe, then up to 90% of the world's languages may be at risk.

Size does not tell the whole story, but it may be the best surrogate at the moment for vulnerability to the kinds of pressures leading to language loss. A large language could be endangered if the external pressures on it were great (e.g., the South American language Quechua, with millions of speakers), while a very small language could be perfectly safe as long as the community was functional and the environment was stable (e.g., Icelandic, with fewer than 300,000). Small size has been a stable characteristic of languages in Australia and New Guinea for millennia, many of which were quite healthy until a couple of centuries, generations, or decades ago. However, small languages can disappear much faster than large ones, and forces have now been unleashed in the world that small communities find very difficult to resist, while larger groups may have the resources to do so. In present circumstances size may be quite critical in determining survival. All our estimates are guesses, but even if the viability threshold is set at the lower level of 10,000 speakers, 60% of all languages are already endangered. The situation is slightly better in Africa (33%), Asia (53%), and Europe (30%), but much worse in North and South America (78% and 77%) and Australia and the Pacific (93%).

Not only is the geographic spread of languages unequal, but so is their status. The functions a language is used for may also tell us something about its long-term viability. Fewer than 4% of the world's

TABLE 1 PERCENTAGES OF LANGUAGES ACCORDING TO CONTINENT OF ORIGIN HAVING FEWER THAN INDICATED NUMBER OF SPEAKERS (FROM NETTLE 1999: 114)

Continent/Region	< 150	< 1000	< 10,000	< 100,000	1 million
Africa	1.7	7.5	32.6	72.5	94.2
Asia	5.5	21.4	52.8	81.0	93.8
Europe	1.9	9.9	30.2	46.9	71.6
North America	22.6	41.6	77.8	96.3	100
Central America	6.1	12.1	36.4	89.4	100
South America	27.8	51.8	76.5	89.1	94.1
Australia/Pacific	22.9	60.4	93.8	99.5	100
World	11.5	30.1	59.4	83.8	95.2

languages have any kind of official status in the countries where they are spoken. A small minority of dominant languages prevail as languages of government and education. English is the dominant de facto or official language in over 70 countries; French has official or co-official status in 29 countries. The fact that most languages are unwritten, not recognized officially, restricted to local community and home functions, and spoken by very small groups of people reflects the balance of power in the global linguistic marketplace.

3. Language Preservation: What Is Being Done and What Can and Should Be Done

The prospect of the loss of linguistic diversity on such a large scale has prompted both communities and scholars to propose programs of intervention to preserve and revitalize languages . . . . Because much typically needs to be done quickly with too few resources, setting realistic priorities is paramount. There is no one-size-fits-all solution for revitalization and preservation. The immediate need is to identify and stabilize languages under threat so that they can be transmitted to the next generation in as many of their functions as possible. This means assessing which functions are crucial to intergenerational transmission and have a reasonable chance of successful revival and continuation. Every group must decide what can best be done realistically for a particular language at a particular time.

4. The Ecology of Language

The preservation of a language in its fullest sense ultimately entails the maintenance of the group who speaks it, and therefore the arguments in favour of doing something to reverse language death are ultimately about preserving cultures and habitats. Languages can only exist where there is a community to speak and transmit them. A community of people can exist only where there is a viable environment for them to live in and a means of making a living. Where communities cannot thrive, their languages are in danger. When languages lose their speakers, they die. Extinctions in general, whether of languages or species, are part of a more general pattern of human activities contributing to radical alterations in our ecosystem. In the past, these extinctions took place largely without human intervention. Now they are taking place on an unprecedented scale through our intervention, in particular, through our alteration of the environment. Nettle and Romaine (2000) see the extinction of languages as part of the larger picture of worldwide near total ecosystem collapse.

Not only do biodiversity and linguistic diversity share the same geographic locations, they also face common threats. For example, an increasing number of languages die each year, as the homelands of small indigenous communities are being destroyed, or the communities are assimilated into larger nation–states, some of which are actively seeking to exterminate them. Because the historical and current causes

TABLE 2 EXTINCTION PREDICTIONS FOR LANGUAGES
AND SPECIES (BASED ON DATA FROM SUTHERLAND 2003)

Fish	5%
Plants	8%
Birds	11%
Mammals	18%
Languages	32% (50–90%?)

of the threats facing the earth's languages, cultures, and biodiversity are the same, the solutions are also likely to come from the same place: empowering local people and communities. The measures most likely to preserve small languages are the very ones that will help increase their speakers' standard of living in a long-term, sustainable way.

Because language plays a crucial role in the acquisition, accumulation, maintenance, and transmission of human knowledge concerning the natural environment and ways of interacting with it, the problem of language endangerment raises critical issues about the survival of knowledge that may be of use in the conservation of the world's ecosystems. The 49 members of the Great Andamanese tribe, the last survivors of the pre-Neolithic population of Southeast Asia, face a serious threat of extinction, but all survived the huge tsunami unscathed after it hit the Indian Ocean and Bay of Bengal in December 2004 because they knew exactly which trees would not be swept away. . . . Folk traditions and other forms of knowledge passed down orally for generations are always only a generation away from extinction.

Furthermore, the issue of endangered languages cannot be separated from people, their identities, their cultural heritage and their rights. When we lose sight of people and the communities that sustain languages, it becomes easy to argue, as have a number of critics, that there is no reason to preserve languages for their own sake. However, maintaining cultural and linguistic diversity is a matter of social justice because distinctiveness in culture and language has formed the basis for defining human identities. We should think about languages in the same way as we do other natural resources which need careful planning to ensure their survival: they are vital parts of complex local ecologies that must be supported if global biodiversity, as well as human cultures and even humanity in general, are to be sustained.

From: Suzanne Romaine, "Preserving Endangered Languages," *Language and Linguistics Compass* 1/1–2 (2007): 115–32.

QUESTIONS:

1. Why does Romaine argue that it is important to protect endangered languages? How is this similar to preserving biological diversity according to Romaine?
2. How does the pattern of endangered languages reflect the impact of the global network on cultures worldwide?

28.3: *Open Letter to Kansas Board of Education* (Church of the Flying Spaghetti Monster, 2005)

In elections held in 2004, candidates espousing creationism and "Intelligent Design" won a 6–4 majority on the Kansas Board of Education. In 2005, this new board proposed changes to the state's science curriculum requirements that presented evolution as a widely challenged and flawed "theory" and that presented Intelligent Design as a viable—and indeed more scientific—alternative "theory." Scientific groups boycotted the hearings the Board held on the grounds that they did not wish to lend any legitimacy to the claims of creationists, and both Board and hearings were subject to widespread ridicule. Part of the reaction included the following letter from Bobby Henderson, a "concerned citizen" and representative of the Church of the Flying Spaghetti Monster (FSM) and its Pastafarian religion. Elections in 2006 removed the creationist majority and in 2007 the new Board passed science guidelines in line with accepted national standards.

OPEN LETTER TO KANSAS SCHOOL BOARD

I am writing you with much concern after having read of your hearing to decide whether the alternative theory of Intelligent Design should be taught along with the theory of Evolution. I think we can all agree that it is important for students to hear multiple viewpoints so they can choose for themselves the theory that makes the most sense to them. I am concerned, however, that students will only hear one theory of Intelligent Design.

Let us remember that there are multiple theories of Intelligent Design. I and many others around the world are of the strong belief that the universe was created by a Flying Spaghetti Monster. It was He who created all that we see and all that we feel. We feel strongly that the overwhelming scientific evidence pointing towards evolutionary processes is nothing but a coincidence, put in place by Him.

It is for this reason that I'm writing you today, to formally request that this alternative theory be taught in your schools, along with the other two theories. In fact, I will go so far as to say, if you do not agree to do this, we will be forced to proceed with legal action. I'm sure you see where we are coming from. If the Intelligent Design theory is not based on faith, but instead another scientific theory, as is claimed, then you must also allow our theory to be taught, as it is also based on science, not on faith.

Some find that hard to believe, so it may be helpful to tell you a little more about our beliefs. We have evidence that a Flying Spaghetti Monster created the universe. None of us, of course, were around to see it, but we have written accounts of it. We have several lengthy volumes explaining all details of His power. Also, you may be surprised to hear that there are over 10 million of us, and growing. We tend to be very secretive, as many people claim our beliefs are not substantiated by observable evidence.

What these people don't understand is that He built the world to make us think the earth is older than it really is. For example, a scientist may perform a carbon-dating process on an artifact. He finds that approximately 75% of the Carbon-14 has decayed by electron emission to Nitrogen-14, and infers that this artifact is approximately 10,000 years old, as the half-life of Carbon-14 appears to be 5,730 years. But what our scientist does not realize is that every time he makes a measurement, the Flying Spaghetti Monster is there changing the results with His Noodly Appendage. We have numerous texts that describe in detail how this can be possible and the reasons why He does this. He is of course invisible and can pass through normal matter with ease.

I'm sure you now realize how important it is that your students are taught this alternate theory. It is absolutely imperative that they realize that observable evidence is at the discretion of a Flying Spaghetti Monster. Furthermore, it is disrespectful to teach our beliefs without wearing His chosen outfit, which of course is full pirate regalia. I cannot stress the importance of this enough, and unfortunately cannot describe in detail why this must be done as I fear this letter is already becoming too long. The concise explanation is that He becomes angry if we don't.

You may be interested to know that global warming, earthquakes, hurricanes, and other natural disasters are a direct effect of the shrinking numbers of Pirates since the 1800s. For your interest, I have included a graph of the approximate number of pirates versus the average global temperature over the last 200 years. As you can see, there is a statistically significant inverse relationship between pirates and global temperature.

In conclusion, thank you for taking the time to hear our views and beliefs. I hope I was able to convey the importance of teaching this theory to your students. We will of course be able to train the teachers in this alternate theory. I am eagerly awaiting

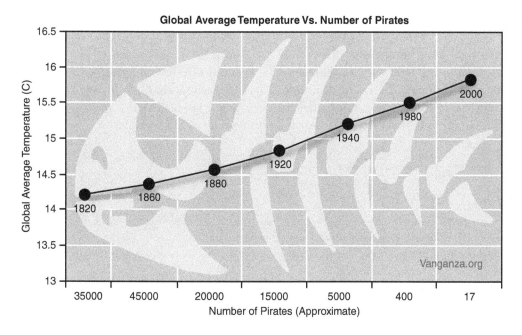

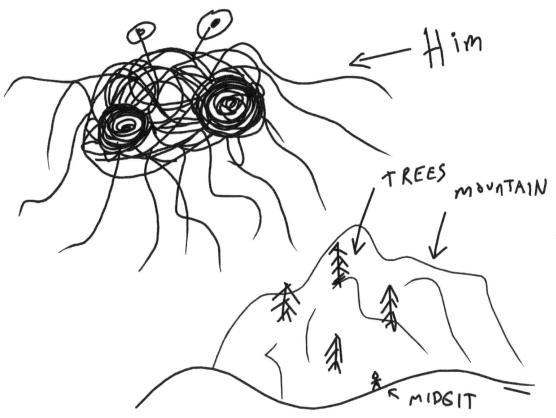

your response, and hope dearly that no legal action will need to be taken. I think we can all look forward to the time when these three theories are given equal time in our science classrooms across the country, and eventually the world; One third time for Intelligent Design, one third time for Flying Spaghetti Monsterism (Pastafarianism), and one third time for logical conjecture based on overwhelming observable evidence.

Sincerely Yours,

Bobby Henderson, concerned citizen.

P.S. I have included an artistic drawing of Him creating a mountain, trees, and a midget. Remember, we are all His creatures.

From: http://www.venganza.org/about/open-letter/.

QUESTIONS:

1. What relationship between science and religion does this letter make fun of? What more serious point is Henderson making about the relationship between church and state?
2. Does the humorous presentation of Henderson's argument make it more or less effective in your opinion?

EMBODIED COGNITION

The next two selections present a small slice of the fascinating science of human cognition—the modern understanding of the Cognitive-Linguistic Revolution.

28.4a: *Out of Our Heads* (Alva Noë, 2009)

Alva Noe (1964–) is a professor of philosophy at the University of California, Berkeley. His specialties include theories of perception and consciousness, cognitive science, and philosophy of mind. Much recent work in cognitive science has studied the idea that human thinking is not just a product of our brains, but of our brain's necessary relationship with our bodies as well. His 2009 book *Out of Our Heads* presents his explanation of consciousness in this context, and expands that context even further.

4   WIDE MINDS

In the previous chapter I offered evidence that the brain gives rise to consciousness by enabling an exchange between the person or animal and the world. What emerges from this discussion is a new conception of ourselves as expanded, extended, and dynamic. In this chapter I place this discovery in a larger context. Our bodies and our minds are active. By changing the shape of our activity, we can change our own shape, body, and mind. Language, tools, and collective practices make us what we are. Where do you stop, and where does the rest of the world begin? There is no reason to suppose that the critical boundary is found in our brains or our skin.

Where Do We Find Ourselves?

We now think of economies as globalized, corporations as internationalized, information networks as distributed. We ourselves are also dynamically distributed, boundary crossing, offloaded, and environmentally situated, by our very nature. What explains our inability until now to understand consciousness is that we've been searching for it in the wrong place.

I remember vividly one day in the 1970s— I must have been eleven or twelve—when my father addressed me sharply on the street in front of our building in New York: "Stop acting that way immediately. You're behaving like . . ." He paused to find the right word. "You're behaving like an

American!" I don't recall what I was doing. Perhaps I was singing aloud, or doing a little dance step, or in some other way carrying on in public. My father was an immigrant who'd arrived in New York at the end of 1949, having made it through the clutches of the Nazis and the Soviets; he was grateful to America—convinced he would not have survived but for their intervention in the war—and glad to enjoy the freedom and anonymity of New York City. But a part of him, at least sometimes—so I was startled to discover—was anything but at home here. America, for my father, was brash, unmannered, loud, superficial, and above all foreign. Although he loved me, at that moment, at least, he was revolted—I don't think that is too strong a word—by his very own son for being what he—that is, what I—could not help being: a native of this new place.

I've since learned that this is a very common bind for immigrants. It is usually hardship that forces them to seek a home in a strange land. But what struck me—and I think I appreciated this even as a child, in the face of my father s displeasure—was the thought that he was divided against himself. The revulsion he felt toward me and toward the place where he found himself showed just how displaced and indeed, in a way, disfigured he was.

This is a book about consciousness, about the human mind and the project of understanding it as belonging to our biological natures. It is not a memoir or a tale of my father's immigration. I mention this personal anecdote because it underscores an important idea—and also because my own preoccupation with this problem may have had its beginnings in this early experience. What my father's plight illustrates is that, at a very basic level, we are *involved*—that is to say tangled up—with the places we find ourselves. We are *of* them. A person is not a self-contained module or autonomous whole. We are not like the berry that can be easily plucked, but rather like the plant itself, rooted in the earth and enmeshed in the brambles. When we transplant ourselves as immigrants get transplanted,

when we move from one town to another or one country to another, we suffer injury, however subtly or grotesquely or even painlessly, and so we are altered. This should not come as a surprise. Our life is a flow of activity, and it depends on our possession of habits and skills and practical knowledge whose very actuality in turn implicates our particular niches. No matter how good you are at breathing, you can't breathe underwater, just as you can't swim where there is no water. And no matter how charming you may be, how wonderful a raconteur, if you find yourself in a strange land where a strange language is spoken, you can't tell a good story—that is, you can't be what you are. You yourself are changed.

Where do you stop, and where does the rest of the world begin? The blithe confidence of the neuroscientist that the brain is the seat of consciousness amounts to an unearned conviction that we can draw the boundary between ourselves and the rest of the world at the skull. For some purposes that may be a good way to go. If you want to know how many people are in attendance at the ball game, don't count the number of arms: count heads. But counting depends on settled ways of individuating that which we wish to count. It is a highly purpose-relative activity. Are the dandelions in the meadow one plant, joined as they are through a common root system, or many? Is the Macintosh OS one program, the operating system, or is it many: a mail program, a calendar program, etc.? Is Williams-Sonoma one company or many? How we draw these lines usually depends on what we are interested in. Are we programmers or potential investors? Do we work for the antitrust division of the Justice Department? It also depends on what we want to accomplish. One of the central claims of this book is that if we seek to understand human or animal consciousness, then we ought to focus not on the brain alone but on the brain in context—that is, on the brain in the natural setting of the active life of the person or animal. For what we bearers of consciousness are—as the example of my father serves to illustrate—depends on where we are and what we can do.

Magical Boundaries and the Rubber-Hand Illusion

Where do you stop, and where does the rest of the world begin? One extreme view would have it that you are your brain: you stop at its limits. The skull, roughly, is the boundary of yourself. You may think that the pain of stubbing your toe is in your toe and that the feeling of the glass is in your hand, but you are mistaken. The feeling itself is not in your hand or toe; it is *in your brain*. Granted, it is the action of the cup on the sensory fibers in your hand, or the activation of nerve endings in your toe, that causes the neural activation in your head in which your feeling consists. But you'd have the feeling even if there were no cup or no foot, just so long as the right pattern of activation was brought about. The real sensation is in your head, not in your body. Something vaguely like this idea may inform people who say that the brain is the most important erogenous zone.

This claim is yet another version of the prevalent neuroscientific dogma that you are your brain and that all the rest—the sense of our emplacement in a world that is meaningful and populated by others—is a myth promulgated for us by our brains. However intoxicating it might be to think that science has this to teach us—"we live behind a veil of illusion"—there is no reason to be convinced. The established facts are only these: sensation requires the action of the nervous system; there is no human or animal life without a nervous system. But from this it does not follow either that the nervous system is alone sufficient for sensation or that our selves are confined to our brains and nerve tissue.

The rubber-hand illusion, as it is sometimes called, provides a lovely piece of support for what I am claiming. This demonstration, first performed by Matthew Botvinick and Jonathan Cohen and reported in the journal *Nature* in 1998—in an article entitled "Rubber Hand Feels Touch That Eyes See"—is a stunning illustration of the fact that the sense of where we are is shaped dynamically by our interaction with the environment in multiple sensory modalities.

The demonstration went like this (I simplify only slightly): You are asked to sit at a table. Your right hand is on your lap and is concealed from your view by the table. Across the table rests a rubber hand, the sort of thing you might find in a shop selling scary toys for Halloween. You watch as a person gently taps and strokes the rubber hand with a delicate paintbrush. Tap tap, stroke stroke, tap stroke, stroke stroke stroke tap. In perfect synchrony, an experimenter is tapping your *actual* right hand out of view underneath the table. Now something remarkable happens. You have the very distinct feeling that you are being touched on the rubber hand: that the feeling of being touched that is, in fact, occurring on your own, connected right hand under the table is taking place on the rubber hand across the table! As the article's title suggests, you feel the touching of the rubber hand that the eyes see. If you are asked to point with your left hand, which is also under the table, to the place where you feel yourself being touched, you will point (roughly) in the direction of the rubber hand.

This is an example of a very striking and prevalent phenomenon: the power of what we see to influence our nonvisual sensory experience. This is known in psychology as visual capture. It is the phenomenon that underlies ventriloquism. What causes you to hear the words coming from the mouth of the dummy is the fact that you see the dummy's mouth opening and closing in sync with the words themselves. You hear what you see. This is a robust effect; we experience it when we go to the movies, where the actor imaged on the screen seems to be producing the sounds. In fact, the sounds emanate from speakers that are located elsewhere in the room. In one important study, speakers play two distinct unrelated streams of speech, creating a jumble of speech noise. You can't understand either stream until you are given visual cues in the form of video images of the faces doing the talking. The spatial distinctness of the visually apparent sources of the sounds enables you to discern the distinct streams of speech when you were unable to do this otherwise.

In fact, visual capture—the powerful influence of vision on other sensory modalities—is an important element in normal, true speech perception. We unconsciously read lips when we are engaged in conversation, and what we hear—what sounds we take in—depends critically on what we see. To different speech sounds there correspond distinct patterns of lip movement and mouth shaping. Part of what enables us to succeed in hearing the speech sounds correctly is that we see what sounds are being produced. It's important to realize that it is difficult to hear speech sounds. The acoustic stimulus is liable to be heard in different ways. We experience this when we try to spell an unfamiliar word or an unusual name on the telephone. If you want to be sure that the airline people get your name right, you had better spell it out using conventional ways of naming the letters (e.g., "Romeo" for *r*, "Alpha" for *a*, etc.). Otherwise, they just won't be able to understand you.

A demonstration of the robustness of the influence of seeing on hearing is the McGurk effect, named after the developmental psychologist Harry McGurk. You hear a recording of someone saying "ba," but you see a synchronized video image of someone saying "ga." What you experience is the video head producing the sound "da." Whatever the details of the explanation of this phenomenon, the basic idea would seem to be clear: we use information in the acoustic stimulus and information in what we see—how the mouth is moving—in order to achieve a perception of a speech sound itself. If these sources of information are not consistent with each other, our ability to perceive correctly what is said breaks down.

It is probable that our ability to hear words also depends, to some degree, on our knowledge of what is being talked about and our expectations of what will come next. The linguist Geoffrey Pullum once offered a nice example of this in conversation. You say to someone, "Here is a hat, here is a scarf, here is a dlove." Invariably he or she will actually hear that last word as "glove." "Hat" and "scarf" prime the listener for another article of winter clothing, such as a glove; moreover, the "dl" sound just doesn't occur in English.

Returning to the rubber-hand illusion: we might have thought that when it comes to feeling being touched, or feeling touched on your right hand, there's no need for disambiguation—that is, no need for contextual clues about where and how you are being touched. After all, don't feelings exhibit their intrinsic quality in their very occurrence? But in fact there is need for interpretation or comprehension. You may be touched on your hand, but you will feel yourself touched on the place where you seem to see yourself being touched. Now, in one sense this is clearly an illusion. After all, you really are being touched on your right hand under the table. But in another sense there's no illusion—or rather, the mechanisms at work in this illusion, if we want to call it that, are those of normal, successful perception. Granted, the rubber hand isn't a part of you. But what explains this is not the mere fact that it is a rubber hand, or that it is not connected to your body. The more fundamental fact is that you and the rubber hand have distinct fates. There is nothing more than a superficial and accidental coordination of your experience with the rubber hand. Your own hand, by contrast, is reliably implicated in your sensory and motor interactions with the world around you and with your other sensory experiences. If it were possible to incorporate the rubber hand into a dynamic of active engagement with the world and the body, then, to that degree, the rubber hand would become a part of you.

We have a very special relationship with our own bodies. Evolution itself is to thank for this, no doubt. But the rubber-hand demonstration causes us to rethink what the special relationship is. It does not consist merely of the fact that my hands and arms, say, channel nerve tissue into me, or rather, into my brain. Connectedness, attachment, contiguity—these are important, but mere connectedness or attachment yields only a superficial explanation of what the body is. What makes connection and contiguity important is that they themselves track coordination and common fate. This is the hand—my hand—whose movements I see when I look. Part of what makes it my hand is that I see it grasping the cup. Part of what makes it my hand is the fact that it is the one with which I grasp the cup. Indeed, there is no specific feeling or characteristic sensation that is or would be the feeling that this is my hand. I feel with it (e.g., the cup is too hot!) and in it (I am being tapped and stroked!). Its "mine"-ness consists in the way it is actively, dynamically, visually involved in my living.

Maurice Merleau-Ponty, the French philosopher, has made just these points. Our lives take place in a setting. This setting—the floor, the walls, the noise, the outside—is the background for whatever activity we are engaged with, such as driving, or walking, or baking a cake. The body, for Merleau-Ponty, shows up as mine (or yours) in just this way as the background condition of my carrying on as I do. These hands belong to me, for it is with them that I break the eggs and mix the batter. As Merleau-Ponty puts it: "The body is the vehicle of being in the world, and having a body is, for a living creature, to be intervolved in a definite environment, to identify oneself with certain projects and be continually committed to them."

From: Noë, Alva. *Out of our heads: why you are not your brain, and other lessons from the biology of consciousness* (New York: Hill and Wang, 2009), pp. 67–75.

QUESTIONS:

1. According to Noë where are our "minds"? Why is this book called *Out of Our Heads*?
2. Noë quotes Merleau-Ponty, who argues that living creatures are "intervolved in a definite environment". Describe an instance of how you are (and have been) ***intervolved*** with your world.

28.4b: from *Gut Feelings* (Gerd Gigerenzer, 2007)

Gerd Gegerenzer (1947–) is a German psychologist whose work focuses on how humans make decisions. As this selection from his 2007 book *Gut Feelings: the intelligence of the unconscious* argues, he sees decision making happening in many of the brain's subsystems, and happening below our conscious awareness. In other words, we often decide without even realizing that we have decided.

Imagine you are asked to participate in a psychological experiment. The experimenter gives you the following problem:

Linda is thirty-one years old, single, outspoken, and very bright. She majored in philosophy. As a student she was deeply concerned with issues of discrimination and social justice and participated in antinuclear demonstrations.

Which of the following two alternatives is more probable?

Linda is a bank teller

Linda is a bank teller and active in the feminist movement.

Which one did you choose? If your intuitions work like those of most people, you picked the second alternative. Amos Tversky and Nobel laureate Daniel Kahneman, however, argued that this is the false answer, because it violates logic. A conjunction of two events (Linda is a bank teller *and* active in the feminist movement) cannot be more probable than only one of them (Linda is a bank teller). In other words, a subset can never be larger than the set itself. "Like it or not, *A* cannot be less probable than *(A&B)*, and a belief to the contrary is fallacious." They labeled the intuition shared by most people the *conjunction fallacy*. The Linda problem has been used to argue that human beings are fundamentally illogical and has been invoked to explain various economic and human disasters, including U.S. security policy, John Q. Public's fear of nuclear reactor failures, and his imprudent spending on insurance. The evolutionary biologist Stephen Jay Gould wrote,

> I am particularly fond of [the Linda] example, because I know that the [conjunction] is least probable, yet a little homunculus in my head continues to jump up and down, shouting at me—"but she can't just be a bank teller: read the description." . . . Why do we consistently make this simple logical error? Tversky and Kahneman argue, correctly I think, that our minds are not built (for whatever reason) to work by the rules of probability.

Gould should have trusted the gut instinct of his homunculus, rather than his conscious reflections. Academics who agree with the conjunction fallacy believe that mathematical logic is the basis for determining whether judgments are rational or irrational. In the Linda problem, all that counts for the logical definition of rational reasoning are the English terms *and* and *probable*, which are assumed to have only one correct meaning: the logical AND (that we use, for example, in search machines) and mathematical probability (a comparison of the number of favorable outcomes to the number of possible outcomes). I call such logical norms *content-blind* because they ignore the content and the goals of thinking. Rigid logical norms overlook that intelligence has to operate in an uncertain world, not in the artificial uncertainty of a logical system, and needs to go beyond the information

given. One major source of uncertainty in the Linda problem is the meaning of the terms *probable* and *and*. Each of these terms has several meanings, as any good English dictionary or its equivalent in other languages will reveal. Consider the meanings of *probable*. A few, such as "what happens frequently," correspond to mathematical probability, but most do not, including "what is plausible," "what is believable," and "whether there is evidence." Perception solves this problem of ambiguity by using intelligent rules of thumb, and, I argue, so does higher-order cognition. One of these unconscious rules that our minds appear to use to understand the meaning of language is the conversational *maxim of relevance*.

> Assume that the speaker follows the principle "Be relevant."

The unconscious inference is thus: if the experimenter reads to me the description of Linda, it is most likely relevant for what he expects me to do. Yet the description would be totally irrelevant if one understood the term probable as mathematical probability. Therefore, the relevance rule suggests that probable must mean something that makes the description relevant, such as whether it is plausible. Read the description—Gould's homunculus understood this point.

Is most people's answer to the Linda problem based on a reasoning fallacy or on an intelligent conversational intuition? To decide between these alternatives, Ralph Hertwig and I asked people to paraphrase the Linda task for a person who is not a native speaker and does not know the meaning of *probable*. Most people used nonmathematical meanings such as whether it is possible, conceivable, plausible, reasonable, and typical. Only very few used "frequent" or other mathematical meanings. This suggests that conversational intuition rather than logical error is at issue, specifically the ability to infer the meaning of ambiguous statements by means of conversational rules. As a further test of this hypothesis, we changed the ambiguous phrase *probable* into a clear *how many?*

> There are a hundred persons who fit the description above
> (i.e. Linda's). How many of them are
> bank tellers?
> bank tellers and active in the feminist movement?

If people don't understand that a set cannot be smaller than a subset, and consistently make this logical blunder, then this new version should produce the same results as the old one. If on the other hand, there is no blunder but people make intelligent unconscious inferences about what meanings of *probable* make the description of Linda relevant, these meanings are now excluded and the so-called fallacy should largely disappear. And this is indeed what happened. The result is consistent with earlier research by the Swiss psychologists Bärbel Inhelder and Jean Piaget, who performed similar experiments with children ("Are there more flowers or more primulas?") and reported that by the age of eight, a majority gave responses consistent with class inclusion. Note that children were asked how many, not how probable. It would be very strange if later in life adults could no longer understand what eight-year-olds can. Logic is not a sensible norm for understanding the question "Which alternative is more probable?" in the Linda problem. Human intuition is much richer and can make reasonable guesses under uncertainty.

The Linda problem—and the hundreds of studies it has generated to find out what conditions make people reason more or less logically—illustrates how the fascination with logic leads researchers to pose the wrong questions and miss the interesting, psychological ones. The question is not whether people's intuitions follow the laws of logic but rather, what unconscious rules of thumb underlie intuitions about meaning. Let us take a closer look at natural language comprehension.

The Linda problem—and the hundreds of studies it has generated to find out what conditions make people reason more or less logically—illustrates how the fascination with logic leads researchers to pose the wrong questions and miss the interesting, psychological ones. The question is not whether people's intuitions follow the laws of logic but rather, what unconscious rules of thumb underlie intuitions about meaning. Let us take a closer look at natural language comprehension.

Peggy and Paul

In first-order logic, the particle AND is *commutative*, that is, *a AND b* is equivalent to *b AND a*. Yet again, this is not how we understand natural language. For instance, consider the following two sentences:

> Peggy and Paul married *and* Peggy became pregnant.
> Peggy became pregnant *and* Peggy and Paul married.

We know intuitively that the two sentences convey different messages. The first suggests that pregnancy follows marriage, whereas the second implies that pregnancy came first and was possibly the reason for marriage. If our intuition worked logically and treated the English term *and* as the logical AND, we wouldn't notice the difference. *And* can refer to a chronological or causal relationship, neither of which is commutative. Here are two more pairs:

> Mark got angry *and* Mary left.
> Mary left *and* Mark got angry.
>
> Verona is in Italy *and* Valencia is in Spain.
> Valencia is in Spain *and* Verona is in Italy.

We understand in a blink that the first pair of sentences conveys opposite causal messages, whereas the second pair is identical in meaning. Only in the last pair is the *and* used in the sense of the logical AND. Even more surprising, we also know without thinking when *and* should be interpreted as the logical OR, as in the sentence

We invited friends *and* colleagues.

This sentence refers to the joint set of friends and colleagues, not to their intersection. Not everyone is both a friend and a colleague; many are either or. Once again, intuitive understanding violates the conjunction rule, but this is not an error of judgment. Rather it is an indication that natural language is more sophisticated than logic.

How do our minds infer at one glance what *and* means in each context? These inferences have the three characteristics of intuitions: I know the meaning, I act on it, but I do not know how I know it. Since a single sentence is sufficient as context, the clues must come from the content of the sentence. To this day, linguists are still working on spelling out the rules of thumb that underlie this remarkably intelligent intuition. No computer program can decode the meaning of an *and* sentence as well as we can. These are the interesting unconscious processes that we only partly understand, but which our intuition masters in the blink of an eye.

FRAMING

Framing is defined as the expression of logically equivalent information (whether numerical or verbal) in different ways. For example, your mother has to decide whether she will have a difficult operation and is struggling with the decision. Her physician says that she as a 10 percent chance of dying from the operation. That same day another patient asks about the operation. He is told that he has a 90% chance of surviving.

Logic does not make a difference between either of these statements, and consequently, logically minded psychologists have argued that human intuition should be indifferent, too. They claim that one should ignore whether one's doctor describes the outcome of a possible operation as a 90 percent chance of survival (a positive frame) or a 10 percent chance of dying (a negative frame). But patients pay attention and try to read between the lines. By using a positive frame, the doctor might signal to the patient that the operation is the best choice. In fact, patients accept the treatment more often if doctors choose a positive frame. Kahneman and Tversky, however, interpret attention to framing to mean that people are incapable of retranslating the two versions of the doctors' answer into a common abstract form and are convinced that "in their stubborn appeal, framing effects resemble perceptual illusions more than computational errors."

I disagree. Framing can communicate information that is overlooked by mere logic. Consider the most famous of all framing examples:

The glass is half full.
The glass is half empty.

According to the logical norm, people's choices should not be affected by the two formulations. Is the description in fact irrelevant? In an experiment, a full glass of water and an empty glass are put on a table. The experimenter asks the participant to pour half the water into the other glass, and to place the half-empty glass at the edge of the table. Which one does the participant pick? Most people choose the previously full glass. When other participants were asked to move the half-full glass, most of them chose the previously empty one. This experiment reveals that the framing of a request helps people extract surplus information concerning the dynamics or history of the situation and helps them to guess what it means. Once again, intuition is richer than logic. Of course, one can mislead people by framing a choice accordingly. But that possibility does not mean that attending to framing is irrational. Any communication tool, from language to percentages, can be exploited.

The potential of framing is now being recognized in many disciplines. The renowned physicist Richard Feynman emphasized the importance of deriving different formulations for the same physical law, even if they are mathematically equivalent. "Psychologically they are different because they are completely unequivalent when you are trying to guess new laws." Playing with different representations of the same information helped Feynman to make new discoveries, and his famous diagrams embody the emphasis he placed on presentation. Yet psychologists themselves are in danger of discarding psychology for mere logic.

From: Gigerenzer, Gerd. *Gut feelings: the intelligence of the unconscious* (New York: Viking, 2007), pp. 16–19, 93–100.

QUESTIONS:

1. According to Gigerenzer, why are gut feelings reliable? What gives them their efficacy? How and why do they work?
2. Why can human cognition not be described by logical rules of rationality?

28.5: *Commodifying the Other (Tourism Advertisements)*

Like the car advertisements at the beginning of the chapter, the tourist advertisements collected here project images of commodified identity. They are a fitting finale to our selection of sources about the increasingly global world of today.

Greek National Tourism Organization, Archives.

The Advertising Archives.

Tunisian National Tourist Office.

Tourism Authority of Thailand.

QUESTIONS:

1. How does tourism marketing attempt to appeal to a global market using local identity? What do these advertisements emphasize; what do they omit?
2. Which of these advertisements appeals most strongly to you personally? Where would you like to go? Why?